Journeys in Caribbean Thought

Creolizing the Canon
Series Editors:
Jane Anna Gordon, Associate Professor of Political Science and Africana Studies, University of Connecticut
Neil Roberts, Associate Professor of Africana Studies and Faculty Affiliate in Political Science, Williams College

This series, published in partnership with the Caribbean Philosophical Association, revisits canonical theorists in the humanities and social sciences through the lens of creolization. It offers fresh readings of familiar figures and presents the case for the study of formerly excluded ones.

Titles in the Series

Journeys in Caribbean Thought

The Paget Henry Reader

Edited, with an introduction, by Jane Anna Gordon, Lewis R. Gordon, Aaron Kamugisha and Neil Roberts, with Paget Henry

ROWMAN & LITTLEFIELD

INTERNATIONAL

London • New York

Published by Rowman & Littlefield International, Ltd.
Unit A, Whitacre Mews, 26-34 Stannary Street, London SE11 4AB
www.rowmaninternational.com

Rowman & Littlefield International, Ltd. is an affiliate of Rowman & Littlefield
4501 Forbes Boulevard, Suite 200, Lanham, Maryland 20706, USA
With additional offices in Boulder, New York, Toronto (Canada), and London (UK)
www.rowman.com

British Library Cataloguing in Publication Information Available
A catalogue record for this book is available from the British Library

ISBN: HB 978-1-78348-935-0
ISBN: PB 978-1-78348-936-7

Library of Congress Cataloging-in-Publication Data

Names: Henry, Paget, author. | Gordon, Jane Anna, 1976– editor.
Title: Journeys in Caribbean thought : the Paget Henry reader / edited, with an introduction by Jane
    Anna Gordon, Lewis R. Gordon, Aaron Kamugisha and Neil Roberts, with Paget Henry.
Description: Lanham, Md. : Rowman & Littlefield International, 2016. | Series: Creolizing the canon
    | Includes bibliographical references and index.
Identifiers: LCCN 2016000805 (print) | LCCN 2016004986 (ebook) | ISBN 9781783489350 (cloth :
    alk. paper) | ISBN 9781783489367 (pbk. : alk. paper) | ISBN 9781783489374 (electronic)
Subjects: LCSH: Philosophy, Black—West Indies.
Classification: LCC B1028 .H47 2016 (print) | LCC B1028 (ebook) | DDC 199/.729—dc23
LC record available at http://lccn.loc.gov/2016000805

∞™ The paper used in this publication meets the minimum requirements of American
National Standard for Information Sciences Permanence of Paper for Printed Library
Materials, ANSI/NISO Z39.48-1992.

Printed in the United States of America

To the Caribbean

Contents

Acknowledgments

Journeys in Caribbean Thought is intended as both a celebration of Paget Henry's 70th birthday and an intellectual gift to the world. After all, in addition to Henry serving as a mentor to each of us at various stages in our respective lives, his work is foundational to the understanding of what historic and contemporary Caribbean thought mean. Through this assemblage of core Henry writings and a recent interview, we therefore wish to say *thank you* to the texts' author.

We would also like to express our appreciation for the Williams College Dean of Faculty's office, which graciously provided essential funding that facilitated the preparation of the book manuscript. Finally, we are grateful to the following presses and periodicals for permissions to reprint previously published materials by Paget Henry: *Antigua and Barbuda Review of Books*, *C. L. R. James Journal*, Ian Randle, Routledge, *Social and Economic Studies*, and Hansib.

Jane Anna Gordon
Lewis R. Gordon
Aaron Kamugisha
Neil Roberts

Acknowledgements

Introducing Paget Henry

"My original birth certificate is somewhere beneath the lava," Paget Henry once quipped. Though an Antiguan, he was actually born on the nearby volcanic island of Montserrat in 1946. His father, a police officer from Antigua, was briefly stationed there. As his family joined him, his pregnant wife gave birth, and they all returned to Antigua, where the young Paget spent his time on that area of the archipelago known as the Leeward Islands and also the "Lesser Antilles," until his family left for New York City when he was in his late teens.

It is perhaps fitting that a Caribbean scholar who has made his intellectual home in sociology, philosophy, and political economy would begin life born in one place but "belonging" to another. He achieved his doctorate in sociology from Cornell University in 1976, and despite the fine ethnographic and historical work he subsequently produced on the East Indian populations of Guyana and the Tallensi people of Ghana, the readers of this compilation have most likely come to its pages because of his reputation as a philosopher and social theorist.

If asked, however, Henry would no doubt insist he is a sociologist who became concerned about the racism of the philosophy profession with regard to the inclusion of Africana philosophy. As a scholar also interested in the sociology of knowledge and the formation of disciplines, he became "embedded," as it were, among the various philosophical clans as he observed the growth of African diasporic philosophy in the academy.

His sociological work included examining the latest developments in social thought, which in the period from the 1970s into the early 1990s meant research in dependency theory (especially through the thought of Samir Amin) and exploring the impact of poststructuralism (primarily through the thought of Michel Foucault, whom he met at Cornell through the efforts of his mentor Dominick LaCapra) and Marxist historicism (to which he came earlier through another of his mentors—namely, C. L. R. James). Marx, we should remember, is one of the great "fathers" of sociology. The other two, from the Eurocentric model developed from Talcott Parsons onward, included Max Weber and Émile Durkheim. Sociology, in other words, had (and continues to have) its own battle with Eurocentrism. There was, however, at least the legitimacy of sociological work on race and racism, social inequalities, and black inner-city life, and the demographic reality of the discipline was such that meeting fellow

African-descended sociologists wasn't unusual. Still thinking as a social theorist, Henry was able to consider the project of conjoining poststructuralism and Marxism (through which he addressed dependency theory) by way of ideas emerging from the region to which he most devoted his work: his beloved Caribbean. The correlates of Foucault and Marx became, in Henry's thought in the late 1980s until very early 1990s, the Guyanese novelist and poet Wilson Harris and the Jamaican literary theorist, novelist, and playwright Sylvia Wynter, on one hand, and the Trinidadian historian, sports writer, novelist, and playwright C. L. R. James and the Egyptian economist Samir Amin, on the other. These two poles are characterized in his writings as poeticist and historicist strains of thought, which he eventually labeled "poeticist/historicist."

The poeticist/historicist dichotomy was, for Henry, ultimately a battle between two conceptions of structure with different aims. The poeticists, for the most part committed to articulating how the imagination offers alternative portraits of the self and Caribbean life, saw the use of what Wynter, drawing upon Aimé Césaire, called the science of the word. The historicists, guided by Marxism, focused on social transformation through the change of material conditions of institutional capital or power. For Henry, there was, however, something missing. Though he could look to Wynter and James, the overwhelming legitimation practice offered Foucault and Marx as foundational. Even Harris's poeticism and Amin's historicism, though offering novel conceptions of consciousness, raised important foundational questions. Why, he asked, must what grounds *Caribbean* thinkers come from Europe instead of the places most operative in the lived reality of Caribbean peoples—namely, Africa, Asia, and ultimately the legacies of the Caribbean's first nations? His concern wasn't with acknowledging the European intellectual heritage. It was about its exaggeration or, worse, it functioning as a source of exclusion of those other contributory dimensions. Though all these elements were and still are there, it's without question that the Caribbean's *black* identity was simultaneously most repressed paradoxically despite, and perhaps because of, it being also most present.

There was, then, a missing element. He found that in 1992 in the form of Africana phenomenology. The missing element, as he saw it, especially given his commitment to what Frantz Fanon would call Caribbean "national consciousness," was that the lived reality of the Caribbean, that of which Caribbean peoples were conscious, was elided under what he subsequently called the linguistic turn of poststructuralism and the class-dominated model of Marxism. We should stress that Henry was and remains partial to the latter. His concern, however, was that the historicist approach, too, rendered questions of Caribbean existence irrelevant. This offered no solace for a theorist concerned with the theoretical and political absence of the world in which he grew up, one that nurtured him and offered a worldview from a position in no way marked by *the* center but functioning, nevertheless, as its own valued point of view. He needed a theory and a way of doing theory that respected and brought forth what his childhood neighbor, Jamaica Kincaid, just across the street in St. John's, later aptly described as a small place.

"Welcome to the rock!" Henry loves to say to guests visiting his island home of 14 by 11 miles. Passengers no doubt prayed for the pilots landing there right not only for purposes of safety but also for arriving on *terra firma* instead of in the embrace of the Caribbean Sea.

Henry's love for Antigua extends to several significant decisions in his professional life. He was among the scholars who introduced the German philosopher and sociologist Jürgen Habermas's thought to North American audiences in the 1970s. His colleagues at Stony Brook had encouraged him to build his reputation on the thought of the influential European thinker, especially given his original readings and critical insight into Habermas's thought. His response was that there was no shortage of academics studying European thinkers. His own country, by contrast, lacked sufficient study of its history and sociological conditions. His remedy took the forms of his first article and monograph, "Antigua: A Society in Transition" (1973) and *Peripheral Capitalism and Underdevelopment in Antigua* (1985a).

This was not the first time Henry chose an unexpected path. His intellectual curiosity while a youth was primarily occupied with physics, which he discussed at length with his relative Roy Henry while walking, many an hour, along the Antiguan beaches and swimming in their waters. Henry's family had hoped he would become a Methodist minister. The beautiful seashores called him there too often, even at the expense of Sunday school instruction, however. Exposed for such treachery by his elders, he sought redemption in deeper study in the local library. His efforts led him to philosophical work on epistemology, metaphysics, and science, the result of which was the slow evaporation of religious devotion. He became an atheist.

Henry was then determined to examine the laws of reality through physics and philosophical reflection. He sought to attend the University of the West Indies at Mona, Jamaica, but life circumstances took him to City College in New York City instead. Arriving in Harlem, he surveyed the structural misery of Afro- and Latin America and resolved to address their social conditions. That path moved from physics to sociology, with philosophy accompanying him, as he received the Philosophy Prize upon achieving his bachelor's degree in 1970. That path was full of extraordinary circumstances ranging from attending lectures at Union Theological Seminary by the finest intellectuals of the day to enjoying live reflections from Martin Buber and Eric Fromm under the auspices of the Philosophy Club at City College. He also took the time to attend lectures and courses taught by such intellectuals as Hannah Arendt and Herbert Marcuse. And then, of course, there was simply the Harlem of the 1960s, where he enjoyed the opportunity of listening to Malcolm X's speeches and the various soul, rhythm and blues, and rock bands of the day. Having spoken to him in detail over the years, we cannot think of a single artist or intellectual who passed through New York City in that decade whom Henry had not availed himself of seeing and learning from on his youthful life's way.

Arendt and Buber held much biographical significance. Henry had visited Arendt during her final year of teaching at the New School for Social Research at the recommendation of C. L. R. James. Explaining such to her led to his attending her important seminar on Kant and problems of judgment. Buber, however, is of extraordinary salience in the résumé of Henry's thought. On his way from classes to the World Fair in 1965, he passed a classroom in which sat a bearded old man at the center of a small circle of students. The scene struck him, so he joined it and then proceeded, with youthful atheistic vigor, to argue against the old man's devotion to what ultimately must not be named. After hours of his proverbial best shots, he concluded that the wise old man had insight into something he was failing to see. Buber's calm and committed attention to his words exemplified for Henry a level of connection that stood among the most moving spiritual encounters of his life. He changed his attitude toward the spiritually committed and subsequently included, among his areas of concentrated study, the philosophy and sociology of religion.

The sociologist Paget Henry thus had an experientially rich foundation for his social theory and subsequent philosophical work. At the institutional level, there are two marked examples of how his commitments came to the fore. The first was his taking on the task of editing the *C. L. R. James Journal* in the late 1980s, which subsequently became the official journal of the Caribbean Philosophical Association. The second is his foundation of the *Antigua and Barbuda Review of Books* in 2007. His goal with these two journals is to provide a context for intellectual work from the Caribbean to come to print and into circulation. The first journal offers philosophical ideas with the great C. L. R. James's name as a clarion call for the *production* of thought, and the second is for his country's artists and other intellectuals to have an outlet for their creative work—at times very big ideas—from proverbial small places.

This sociologist of knowledge is thus also committed to building homes from which ideas may flourish. This work, in terms of his research, writing, and institution building, amounts to an important conviction: We, humanity, should no longer pay the price of failing to address what people from the periphery offer for the benefit of humankind. Their knowledge, however, should not be divorced from their humanity, which means, then, raising a consideration, in stream with such luminaries as W. E. B. Du Bois, Frantz Fanon, and C. L. R. James—namely, the points of view of hitherto ignored reality. For Henry, this meant the intersubjective relations of consciousness, of relational consciousness, of intentionality, of, in other words, phenomenology. To achieve this task, he explored the dynamics of double consciousness and its potentiated variety. The former asks what it means to be a problem from the perspective of despised peoples. The second emerges from those peoples' realization of the contradictions and injustice of a world that makes them into problems. This, he concluded, was also a failing with Western philosophy. Africa and the Caribbean represented an occult zone, even among many of the peoples from that continent and region, when many sought the benefits of philosophical and other forms of theoretical insight. His meditations led to his now canonical work in Africana philosophy, Caribbean philosophy, and the sociology of philosophy: *Caliban's Reason: Introducing Afro-Caribbean Philosophy* (2000a).

We don't offer here an exhaustive portrait of Henry's life and thought. Our aim is simply to give the reader a taste of the mind behind this rich set of ideas. The premier winner of the Frantz Fanon Outstanding Book Award of the Caribbean Philosophical Association, *Caliban's Reason* is a treatise that challenges the disciplinary boundaries between philosophy and sociology, as it offers both a phenomenologically rich philosophical treatment of the problems of philosophy in the Caribbean context and a sociologically rich discussion of the philosophical groups through which such thought is developed. It is no overstatement to say that surveys of philosophy across the globe since 2000 would be shortchanged without discussions of Caribbean philosophy and that this circumstance should be attributed to Henry's *tour du force*, a classic work that proves, without reservation, that ideas of global magnitude continue to come from that archipelago of islands that gave birth to so many noteworthy intellectuals whose alumni include Frantz Fanon and C. L. R. James.

We have thus organized this reader working backward. The first section includes selections from Henry's philosophical writings. In addition to his reflections on Afro-Caribbean philosophy and phenomenology, we also offer his argument and plea for the study of Indo-Caribbean thought. That essay includes Henry's discussion of one of his great philosophical and spiritual influences: Sri Aurobindo. The second section turns to political economy, the main basis of Henry's historicism and to which he has devoted creative analyses of conditions of social transformation. And the third section brings us back to the beginning and the question of home in the form of his beloved country of Antigua-Barbuda.

Paget Henry is a great and, in our view, underappreciated thinker. His contributions are of global significance. It is our hope that this reader will whet the appetite of those who peruse its pages and encourage them to drink more from the very deep well we call the thought of Paget Henry.

Part I

The Distinctive Character
of Africana Philosophy

ONE

The General Character of Afro-Caribbean Philosophy

The power of philosophy floats through my head
Light like a feather, heavy as lead.

—Bob Marley

There are idealist views of philosophy that see it as an affirmation of the autonomy of a thinking subject. As the primary instrument of this absolute subject, philosophy shares in its autonomy and therefore is a discipline that rises above the determinations of history and everyday life. The distinguishing characteristics of Afro-Caribbean philosophy do not support this view. Here we find a tradition of philosophy so indelibly marked by the forces of an imperial history, and by its intertextual relations with neighboring discourses, that it is necessary to begin with a general characterization of philosophy that is more appropriate to its pattern of development.

From the Afro-Caribbean perspective, philosophy is an intertextually embedded discursive practice, and not an isolated or absolutely autonomous one. It is often implicitly referenced or engaged in the production of answers to everyday questions and problems that are being framed in nonphilosophical discourses. However, it is a distinct intellectual practice that raises certain kinds of questions and attempts to answer them by a variety of styles of argument that draw on formal logic, paradox, coherence, the meaningful logic of lived experiences, and the synthetic powers of totalizing systems.

From this intertextual perspective, philosophy appears as an open but diverse discursive field in which ontological, epistemological, logical, ethical, transcendental, historical, and other formations flow into one another. This rather fluid field is responsive to various strategies of organization either from within or without. In cases like the Caribbean, where philosophy functions as a minor or auxiliary discourse, organization usually comes from outside and is often less centralized than in cases in which philosophy is a major or more autonomous discourse. In the minor mode, philosophy's organization usually reflects the pushes and pulls of its interdiscursive connections. In the major mode, organization tends to be from within and reflects the importance currently attributed to particular subfields by philosophers.

The kinds of questions raised by philosophy tend to be those regarding the origins, ends, and truth value of our everyday activities. Consequently, philosophy's primary concerns tend to be foundational, ideological, and discursive in nature. Foundational concerns include the bases of all discursive practices we employ in grasping self and world, as well as questions such as the origin of life and creation. Teleological concerns include the ends of many of our social activities, the fate of the individual, and the ends of creation. Consequently, whenever we write or attempt to answer a significant problem we necessarily raise philosophical issues, which may or may not be addressed explicitly.

The analysis of these kinds of questions may be done by philosophers or nonphilosophers using one or more of the styles of philosophical production indicated above. Indeed, there is a strong tendency to draw lines in the sand around the use of particular styles or around particular subfields such as ontology, formal logic, or ethics. Thus the attempts to reduce philosophy to the making of arguments or to processes of world constitution are cases of unnecessary polarization between these different tendencies. Even the most cursory look at Afro-Caribbean philosophy indicates that it is both. Similarly, Kwame Gyekye is right in asserting that philosophy cannot be viewed as being primarily one of its subfields as Robin Horton and others have attempted to do with logic and epistemology (Gyekye 1995: 3–8). Such attempts at rigid closures represent little more than the egocentricity and academic politics of professors of philosophy.

Thus, in spite of its preoccupation with the absolute, philosophy is neither an absolute nor a pure discourse. It is an internally differentiated and discursively embedded practice, the boundaries of which will continue to change as work in other fields requires the taking up of new philosophical positions. In other words, there is a consistently significant philosophical substratum to be found in the works of physicists, sociologists, biologists, creative writers, and other knowledge producers. Conversely, there are quite significant literary, religious, sociological, and other discursive substrata in the works of philosophers. This is an interdiscursive embeddedness from which there can be no escape via argument. Like all other discourses, philosophy comes into being as a necessary part of a larger and more diversified discursive field that is a foundation of all human cultural production.

Looked at concretely, Afro-Caribbean philosophy is just such an internally differentiated and intertextually embedded discourse. Its formation and current structure reflect the imperial history of the cultural system that has housed the larger discursive field of Caribbean society. Consequently, many of the original features of our philosophical and other discursive practices have been shaped by the colonial problematics and contours of our cultural history. Within this imperial framework, the original contents of Caribbean philosophy emerged as a series of extended debates over projects of colonial domination between four major social groups: Euro-Caribbeans, Amerindians, Indo-Caribbeans, and Afro-Caribbeans. The discursive productions of the first group were contributions to the creating of hegemonic situations through the legitimating of colonial projects. The productions of the other three groups were attempts at destroying Euro-Caribbean hegemony through the delegitimating of their colonial projects. This was the imperial communicative framework within which Afro-Caribbean philosophy emerged, a framework that always embodied an unequal discursive compromise.

This colonial reframing within the dynamics of legitimacy needs produced a seismic shift in the orientation of Caribbean philosophy. This shift would take it in a very definite politico-ideological direction. In *Black Skin, White Masks*, Fanon argues that the colonial situation created an "existential deviation" in the psyche of the Afro-Caribbean. This deviation was the result of racially induced "aberrations of affect" that relocated the Afro-Caribbean in an antiblack world from which he or she must be extricated. The colonial reframing of Afro-Caribbean philosophy noted above, its reinscription in aberrations of legitimacy demands, produced a discursive deviation that paralleled Fanon's existential deviation.

This discursive deviation was the form that the broader seismic shift took in the case of Afro-Caribbean philosophy. It initiated the foregrounding of colonial, racial, and national struggles and the backgrounding of classical philosophical issues such as being, truth, spirit, and the nature of the self. Binaries such as colonizer/colonized, colony/nation, or black/white quickly eclipsed those of being/nonbeing, spirit/matter, good/evil, and so forth. Classical ontologies that provided comprehensive accounts of existence, discourses that plumbed the depths of the self, rapidly gave way to the strategic and ideological productions demanded by the aberrations of legitimacy affect. As a result, Afro-Caribbean philosophy was relocated to an antiblack, antiphilosophical world, from which it now has to be extricated.

From the point of view of the creative or world-constituting self, the culture of a people may be defined as the expression of a distinct consciousness of existence articulated in a variety of discourses. Philosophy is often the discourse in which we get the most general formulations of that consciousness of existence. Among Euro-Caribbeans, the consciousness that informed culture and philosophy was one that framed existence as a Faustian/imperial struggle to subdue all of nature and history. This was an insurrectionary rupture with the established cosmic order of things that inaugurated a new era in the relations between the European ego and the world. It globalized the European project of existence, weakened the powers of the gods, relocated Europeans at the center of this new world, and refigured the Caribbean into one of its subordinate peripheries. As a result, some of the earliest expressions of Euro-Caribbean philosophy are to be found in the writings of Hakluyt, Las Casas, Montaigne, Richard Ligon, Bryan Edwards, Immanuel Kant, Georg Hegel, Thomas Carlyle, and others who helped to shape the new images of Amerindians and Africans in Europe's imperial vision of itself. Together, but in very fragmentary forms, these writings constituted the Euro-Caribbean layer of the imperial framework that shaped the growth of Caribbean philosophy.

Among the most enduring accounts of the refiguring of Caribbean identities produced by this European/Euro-Caribbean tradition of writing has been the character Caliban, from Shakespeare's play *The Tempest*. This work was inspired by the colonizing voyages that Europeans were making to the Caribbean, particularly the highly publicized wrecks of Thomas Gates and George Summers off the coast of Bermuda. The play dramatized the new vision of existence as the global conquest of nature and history. To imperial Prospero, native Caliban (the Carib) was identical with nature—a cannibal, a child, a monster without language, and hence a potential slave to be subdued and domesticated along with nature and history. Much like the raw materials of nature, the labor of Caliban was there to be exploited for the purposes of imperial Prospero. In return for his labor, Prospero would give Caliban language and endow his "purposes with words that made them known" (Shakespeare 1954: 32–33). But even with this revelation of purpose, Caliban will only experience a small measure of humanization. That is, in spite of the gift of language, Caliban remains too heavily mired in nature for its uplifting powers of reason and civilization. So ran one of the most enduring narratives of Caribbean identity to emerge from European literature and philosophy.

With the arrival of slaves from Africa, Caliban became African. As George Lamming points out, "the slave whose skin suggests the savaged deformity of his nature becomes identical with the Carib Indian who feeds on human flesh. Carib Indian and African slave, both seen as the wild fruits of nature, share equally that spirit of revolt which Prospero by sword or language is determined to conquer" (Lamming 1984: 13).

Among Afro-Caribbeans, a corresponding view of our culture and philosophy could be formulated as a consciousness of existence as being the racialization and colonization of Africans and our way of life within the framework of Euro-Caribbean plantation societies. The works of Caliban's reason are Afro-Caribbean philosophy's contributions to the cultural articulation of the problems of this particular existence—and how to respond to them.

The development of this distinct philosophy can be divided into three broad phases: the idealism of traditional African religions, the Christian moralism that combined with or displaced African idealism, and the poeticism and historicism that have dominated both the late-colonial and postcolonial periods. The first phase (1630–1750) is rooted in traditional African thought because from the seventeenth to the late nineteenth century, Africans were forcefully brought to the region to work as slaves in the plantation economies being created as integral parts of European imperial projects. In this phase, Afro-Caribbean philosophy was primarily embedded in religious discourses and could not be separated from the latter's associated practices. These were the primary lenses through which the consciousness of a racialized and colonized existence was articulated. As such, they were at the same time antiracist, anticolonial, and hence delegitimating discourses. Thus, the seismic shift in orientation that marked the development of Afro-Caribbean philosophy was evident in the militant spiritualism of Shango, Vodou, and other religious discourses. Consequently, the idealist characterization of this phase should be taken as an indicator of the predominant role of spirit in this philosophical system. That is, this dominance should not be equated with exclusivity. As we will see in chapter 1, traditional African philosophy incorporates a number of competing themes into well-integrated totalities. [1] Thus in addition to its idealist themes, we also find strong existential, moral, cosmogonic, and empirical ones.

The second phase (1750–1860) is Afro-Christian because of the very asymmetrical processes of interculturation and creolization that were produced by the colonial cultural system. The period is marked by an incredible variety of mixings between African and European religions, as well as other cultural practices. Because the practice of philosophy remained primarily embedded in religion, these are the mixings of most importance for us. They produced the slave narratives such as those of Ottobah Cugoano and Mary Prince. Out of them, slaves and former slaves turned peasants and urban workers also formed popular religious discourses that were delegitimating. Examples of these would include Myalism, Zion, Revival Zion, Vodou, Cumfa, Santeria, and Rastafarianism. The major philosophical consequence of this development was the growth of an ascetic Christian moralism that often challenged the idealist tendencies of traditional African religion. Again it is important to note that this label is not an exclusive one. For example, strong historicist tendencies are to be found in this moral discourse. These are most visible among the Rastafarians. This intermediate phase will not be examined in great detail in this work.

The third phase (1860 to present) that straddles the late and postcolonial periods cannot be indicated by one major label. It is shared by two major schools within which there are important subdivisions. These are the poeticist and historicist schools. Major representatives of the first would include Claude McKay, Aimé Césaire, Wilson Harris, Édouard Glissant, Derek Walcott, and Sylvia Wynter. Major representatives of the second would include Edward Blyden, George Padmore, Marcus Garvey, C. L. R. James, and Frantz Fanon. Figures like McKay, Césaire, James, and Fanon bridged to some degree the tensions between these two traditions. This cleavage is one of the major dualities confronting Afro-Caribbean philosophical thought that it has not been able to incorporate into a larger totality and a wider self-understanding.

Rather than achieving this larger unity, the tendency has been toward particularization and fragmentation within these schools. As we will see in chapters 8 and 9, the historicist school tends to divide along Pan-Africanist and Marxist lines with further differentiating of positions within each.[2] For example, within the Pan-Africanist variant we find the racial historicism of Garvey and the providential historicism of Blyden and the Rastafarians. In the Marxist variant we can distinguish between democratic, Leninist, and insurrectionary approaches to a class-oriented historicism. In chapters 4 and 5, we will examine two distinct approaches within the poeticists school, those of Harris and Wynter.[3] In spite of these tendencies toward fragmentation, the texts of these individuals all include the working out of philosophical positions as prefaces to their incorporation in poetic, historical, political, or economic contributions to the debates over European colonialism. The result is the large number of subtextual philosophical positions I've tried to categorize with some difficulty.

In short, Afro-Caribbean philosophy is a complex, multilayered, subtextual discursive formation. Its subtextual, auxiliary status has made it a minor, rather than a major or dominant, discourse. As a minor discourse, Afro-Caribbean philosophy has remained an open, de-centered field that has been shaped by its diverse intertextual connections. Consequently, it has been without the internally centered forms of organization and the pattern of rapidly changing positions associated with philosophy as a major discourse. In its earliest layers, this minor philosophy was primarily spiritual. It was the intense spirituality of Africa that was the source of its creative responses to the plantation order of Caribbean society. In its intermediary layers, it was also primarily spiritual. However, the discursive order of the spirituality of this phase was an Afro-Christian one in which there was a shift from mythic to moral and historical discourses. In its more current layers, Afro-Caribbean philosophy has aestheticized and historicized its creative and oppositional responses to the neoplantation orders of Caribbean society. The result has been a more secular set of critiques and related philosophical positions.

From this brief portrait at least three general features are worthy of careful notice. First, Afro-Caribbean philosophy is a highly politicized formation whether we are speaking of its predominantly spiritual, moral, or secular phases. This politicization points clearly to its embeddedness in the social and political problems of Caribbean societies. Second, its productions such as racial historicism, Rastafarianism, magical realism, or socialism make it clear that both world constitution and the production of arguments are important features of Afro-Caribbean philosophy. In other words, both the nature of its arguments and of its totalizing strategies are important for its thorough understanding. Third, the formation as a whole has been the work of ministers, doctors, lawyers, historians, economists, political activists, creative writers, and philosophers all working together. This feature points to the intertextual embeddedness of Afro-Caribbean philosophy in the larger Caribbean intellectual tradition. Consequently, by no stretch of the imagination can this philosophy be considered an autonomous one. On the contrary, both its politicization and its production by nonphilosophers points to its origins in the teleological, foundational, and discursive aspects of life projects being undertaken by various groups in Caribbean society.

PHILOSOPHY AND THE CARIBBEAN INTELLECTUAL TRADITION

Because it is not an isolated discourse, the portrait of Afro-Caribbean philosophy that we have developed so far can be effectively supplemented by looking at it from the perspective of the larger intellectual tradition in which it is planted. From this perspective, we can compare the general features of Afro-Caribbean philosophy with those of Afro-Caribbean literature, dance, music, and other cultural forms. Viewed in this comparative way, four additional features stand out.

First, in spite of its importance, philosophy as a whole has been allocated a restricted role in the division of intellectual labor. It has prefatory and auxiliary roles to play but none of its own making. Hence it has carried on a rather subterranean existence with a comparatively low level of visibility within the larger intellectual tradition. However, within this low level of visibility, some traditions of philosophy are more visible than others. By far the most invisible has been the African, a fact that has created significant problems for Afro-Caribbean philosophy.

Second, compared to the other Afro-Caribbean cultural forms, such as dance or literature, Afro-Caribbean philosophy is the least creolized of these important media. That is, the African, European, and Indian elements in it are the least integrated. If we take Afro-Caribbean fiction, Calypso, and Reggae as examples of well-integrated creole forms, then Afro-Caribbean philosophy has a long way to go.

Third and closely related, Afro-Caribbean philosophy was unique among Afro-Caribbean art forms in the extent to which it overidentified with its European heritage and underidentified with its African inheritance. In short, it inherited many of the anti-African biases that have made African thought the most invisible discourse in the Caribbean intellectual tradition.

Fourth and finally, the communicative framework within which Afro-Caribbean philosophy had to make its delegitimating critiques was a particularly unequal one. Communicants were not viewed as equals, and arguments were not accepted on merit. As we will see, it was a racially distorted communicative situation that systematically undermined the arguments and value of Afro-Caribbean philosophy and thus inhibited its growth.

Although this larger intellectual tradition was necessary for the emergence of Afro-Caribbean philosophy, this tradition also hindered that growth in many ways and was the source of some of the most embarrassing paradoxes and contradictions that have been integral parts of the formation of this philosophy. The most glaring are, of course, the paradoxes of anti-African biases in an Afro-Caribbean philosophy, its patterns of creolization, and the overidentification with European philosophies in a tradition that is supposed to be critical of the European heritage. The invisibility of black philosophy in the Euro-American tradition has been given very careful logico-political and existential analyses by Charles Mills and Lewis Gordon (Mills 1998: 1–19). At the same time, Gordon has also analyzed the phenomenon of antiblack tendencies in Afro-Caribbean and other black philosophies (Gordon 1995a: 104–116). Here I would like to supplement the analyses of Mills and Gordon by briefly indicating some of the sociological factors that made it possible for our intellectual tradition to generate such internally contradictory and crisis-ridden discourses.

COLONIALISM AND THE CARIBBEAN
INTELLECTUAL TRADITION

From a sociological standpoint, the contradictory tendencies and patterns of communicative inequality that characterize our intellectual tradition derive from the colonial nature of the cultural system that institutionalized it. These colonial roots of the tradition emerge very clearly from its history. This history has been extensively explored by Gordon Lewis and Dennis Benn. In the work of both authors, the dialogical structure already noted in the case of philosophy emerges as a basic feature of the tradition as a whole. In both *The Growth of the Modern West Indies* and *Main Currents in Caribbean Thought,* Lewis describes and analyzes some of the main features and products of the tradition. One of the primary results of Lewis's analysis is the hegemonic position of European texts and discourses within the tradition. Although critical of this hegemony, Lewis is so caught up in its power that he has a very hard time seeing the intellectual contributions of Afro-Caribbeans. So much is he in the grip of the spell of invisibility cast over Afro-Caribbean thought, he is able to suggest that European colonization was capable of creating a "cultural tabula rasa" upon which it could rewrite Caribbean culture (Lewis 1968: 69). Thus the picture that emerges is one of radical discursive and communicative inequality between Euro- and Afro-Caribbeans. Although not as extreme, much the same pattern emerges from Benn's work (Benn 1987: 1–31). From both authors we can conclude that the colonial cultural system that framed our intellectual tradition established within the tradition a radical inequality between Afro- and Euro-Caribbeans that reflected the politico-economic order of the society.

However, to explain the patterns of creolization, the levels of politicization, the anti-African biases, and the contrasting patterns of visibility and invisibility affecting Euro- and Afro-Caribbean contributions, it is necessary to go beyond this fact of radical inequality. We need to go further and ask what is it about the dynamics of colonial cultural systems that result in the ongoing reproduction of these patterns. From the sociological standpoint, the peripheral dynamics of these cultural systems hold the keys to the explanation of these patterns of politicization, creolization, invisibility, and communicative inequality.

Colonial cultural systems can be subsumed under the broader category of peripheral cultural systems as they share many of the dynamics of the latter. Peripheral cultural systems are historically specific types of cultural formations. They exist only in relation to core or central cultural systems. Both types emerge within the context of imperial or transnational formations such as empires or world economies and disintegrate soon after the collapse of the latter. Between core and peripheral cultural systems there are very definite accumulative dynamics. Core cultural systems must accumulate authority at the expense of peripheral ones. The centralizing or peripheralizing of cultural systems begins with their incorporation into these systematically related patterns of cultural accumulation and disaccummulation. The imperatives of these processes of accumulation and disaccumulation often produce major changes in discursive practices, modes of cultural organization, output, and canonical standards.

Given this mode of formation, peripheral cultural systems are marked by at least five distinguishing characteristics. First, they are plural cultural systems whose integration is achieved by a colonial state with high "legitimacy deficits" (Habermas 1975: 47). Imperial conquest brings with it a new hegemonic culture to the society. Consequently the authority of local cultural elites is replaced by that of the colonial state and a group of foreign cultural elites. This hegemonic shift generates major legitimacy problems for the emerging colonial order, as both the colonial state and its cultural elites emerge as illegitimate formations in local political dis-

courses. Yet the future stability of this order requires that these illegitimate formations be made to appear legitimate. This is the contradictory
nature of the legitimacy demands that colonial societies make on peripheral cultural systems. From the point of view of this state, culture is not
the consciousness of a distinct existence, but rather a producer and sup-
plier of legitimating symbols and arguments.

Second, the supplying of these legitimacy demands will require differential rates of cultural accumulation in the local and imperial layers of
the system. Within the confines of the system, imperial texts, whether
religious, poetic, economic, or philosophical will have to accumulate authority at a faster rate, or produce corresponding decreases in the authority of local discourses. These differential rates of accumulating authority
or canonicity are important structural characteristics of peripheral cultural systems.

Third, closely associated with these patterns of differential accumulation, have been patterns of discursive competition in which European
discourses tend to replace African and Indian ones. In the words of Rex
Nettleford, within these systems there has been a "battle for space" between the discourses of their European layers and the corresponding
African and Indian ones (Nettleford 1993: 80). As these battles intensify,
spatial distributions become more unequal and of increasing significance
to the drive to accumulate authority and legitimacy.

As these spatial distributions become more unequal, they institutionalize what Clive Thomas has called a "dynamic divergence" between
local centers of cultural production and the primary sites of cultural demand (Thomas 1974: 59). For the purposes of this study these sites will be
the following: (1) ego-genetic processes such as identity formation; (2)
sociogenetic processes such as information based economic production;
and (3) hegemony-producing processes such as the legitimating of state
power. As colonization deepens, the cultural demands of these three reproductive sites are increasingly met by outputs from the imperial layer,
establishing a "dynamic convergence" between the two (Thomas 1974:
125). These shifting patterns of divergence and convergence result in significant decreases in the demand for African and Indian cultural production, setting the stages for their decline and underdevelopment.

Fourth, peripheral cultural systems are characterized by a polarized,
internal competition between imperial and indigenous sites of production over the supplying of the symbols and discourses that will define
and legitimate personal identities in their societies. Like political structures, human identities are in need of cultural legitimacy, and hence are
major sites of cultural demand as well as production. These legitimating
discourses may be ritualistic, religious, scientific, or philosophical in nature, as long as they provide the ego with the support it needs.

What is peculiar about ego genesis in peripheral cultural systems is
that discursive competition over ego-formative needs is not just between

qualitatively different discourses such as science and literature but also between local and imperial traditions of the same discourse. In the case of the Caribbean, this competition has been between European discourse such as religion, language, or science and their African and Indian counterparts. Thus here too in the domain of self-formation, Nettleford's battle for space rages on, as indigenous traditions are forced to yield their monopolies over the supplying of identity forming symbols and discourses.

Fifth and finally, peripheral cultural systems are characterized by the racializing of the identities of their different cultural groups. In the Caribbean, this process of racialization turned Africans into blacks, Indians into browns, and Europeans into whites. The process was most extreme between blacks and whites. In the origin narratives, stories of conquest, civilizing missions, and other legitimating discourses of European imperialism, the blackness of Africans became their primary defining feature. In these narratives, color eclipsed culture. The latter became more invisible as Africans were transformed into negroes and niggers in the minds of Europeans. This racial violence shattered the cultural foundations of the African self, causing the latter to implode. Race became the primary signifier of Europeans and Africans and of the differences between them. Consequently, the identities of these two groups were rigidly inscribed in a set of binary oppositions that linked the binary black/white to other binaries such as primitive/civilized, irrational/rational, body/mind, prelogical/logical, flesh/spirit. Similar sets of racialized binaries came to define white/brown interactions and also black/brown ones.

In particular, these perceptions of Afro-Caribbeans amounted to a radical dehumanization that reduced them to the biological level. This biological reduction was also a radical deculturization that shattered both self and world and also made the African's capacity to labor very visible to Europeans. However, this was no ordinary capital/labor relation. Faust, the capitalist developer, was here metamorphosed into Prospero, while his racialized worker was transformed into Caliban. This "Calibanization" of Africans could not but devour their rationality and hence their capacity for philosophical thinking. As a biological being, Caliban is not a philosopher. He or she does not think and in particular does not think rationally. In the European tradition, rationality was a white trait that, by their exclusionary racial logic, blacks could not possess. Hence the inability to see the African now reinvented as Caliban, in the role of sage, philosopher, or thinker. In short, this new racialized identity was also the death of Caliban's reason.

At least in the case of the Caribbean, it should be clear that the above peripheral dynamics profoundly shaped the internal organization of cultural systems, their hierarchical patterns, the nature of discursive output, and the standards and criteria by which this output was recognized and made a valuable part of the heritage. Both individually and collectively, these dynamics pushed Caribbean cultural systems in the direction of producing and reproducing black invisibility, anti-African, and anti-Indian biases.

In the case of the dynamic of differential rates of cultural accumulation, it contributed to the systemic need to devalue African and Indian cultures. Also, the hegemonic need to make an illegitimate state appear legitimate produced strong systemic interests in dogmatic positions and stereotypical misrepresentations of Africans and Indians. The strategic battles for space between imperial and local discourses point very clearly to strategies of control that required the displacing of African and Indian cultural authority. These twin motives of control and displacement are most evident in the struggles over whose cultural definitions of Indians and Africans would be institutionalized as normative. When the Calibanization of the African identity became an integral part of these peripheral dynamics, the Caribbean intellectual tradition was ready for the ongoing production and reproduction of the black invisibility, the patterns of creolization, and anti-African biases that Afro-Caribbean philosophy would inherit.[4]

In sum, to understand this particularly embarrassing set of problems that have plagued Afro-Caribbean philosophy, we have to work our way through these layers of Calibanization, racial othering, discursive competition, dynamic divergences and convergences, legitimacy deficits, and inverse patterns of cultural accumulation that the tradition cultivated in order to make its contributions to the production of colonial hegemony. Also, it was in the midst of the crossfires of these peripheral dynamics that Caliban's reason lost its visibility. These were important sociological conditions and factors in the broader cultural context that shaped the formation of Afro-Caribbean philosophy. Only when we take them into account can we understand the African and creole problems of Afro-Caribbean philosophy.

THE PROBLEMS OF AFRO-CARIBBEAN PHILOSOPHY

The extent of the negative impact of these dynamics makes it unmistakably clear that Afro-Caribbean philosophy has major problems with the contexts of its formation. These problems would certainly make a strong case for its autonomy. With contexts like these, who needs support! However, such an absolute break is not really an option. What is in fact available to Afro-Caribbean philosophy is the option of using its limited autonomy to transform this antiblack context into an epistemic order that is more supportive of its growth.

This option confronts Afro-Caribbean philosophy with the difficult task of trying to change a tradition on which it is dependent and whose antiphilosophical, antiblack, and other negative values it has internalized. Hence it is not going to be an easy undertaking. The dissolution of European colonialism has not produced the end of imperial or antiblack values and constraints. On the contrary, it has resulted in a shift from colonial incorporation into classic empires to peripheral insertion into an American-dominated world economy. Consequently, critiques of doctrines of manifest destiny, of the Caribbean being in America's backyard, and of equally, if not more virulent, antiblack practices, have been important elements in the delegitimating discourses of the region. However, there have been structural changes in the postcolonial period that should make this task easier. First, the shift from a colonial to a nationalist state has changed significantly the legitimacy pressures coming from the political arena. Second, important and stimulating developments have been occurring in African and Afro-American philosophy. These nationalist changes and the developments in Africana philosophy have opened up an effective space in which we can begin to deal constructively with the problems of Afro-Caribbean philosophy.

In addition to these anti-African, antiblack, and creole problems that Afro-Caribbean philosophy has inherited, there are a number of more internal ones for which the solutions may be more creative than reformist. These problems are related to the fragmented state of our philosophy. As a body of thought, it is marked by deep fissures, wide cleavages, and oppositional constructions of binaries or dualities such as spirit/matter, spirit/history, premodern/modern, poeticism/historicism, race/class. Consequently, it is a poorly integrated body of thought that is conscious of itself primarily in part and only rarely as a whole. Some of these divisions can be linked to the peripheral dynamics examined earlier, but they are also related to the existential dynamics of world constituting activities, that is, to conceptions of the ego, its self-creative experiences, and their legitimacy needs.

As noted earlier, Afro-Caribbean philosophy is not just about the making of arguments. It cannot be described as a logicist, analytical, or positivist tradition. The constructing of integrated worlds of meaning is too central a part of its activities for it to fit comfortably under any of these designations. These totalizing strategies have posed unique challenges for Caribbean philosophers and hence have a distinct history and pattern of development that has remained underthematized.

In spite of this uniqueness, the experience of European philosophy with totalizing strategies has been normative in the Caribbean academy. Hence it has shaped profoundly our understanding of these processes of discursive formation and change. Wole Soyinka has developed a wonderful metaphor for the European experience that is worth quoting in full:

> You must picture a steam engine which shunts itself between rather closely spaced suburban stations. At the first station it picks up a bal-

last of allegory, puffs into the next emitting a smokescreen on the eternal landscape of nature truths. At the next, it loads up with a different species of logs which we shall call naturalist timber, puffs into a halfway stop where it fills up with the synthetic fuel of surrealism, from which point yet another holistic world-view is glimpsed and asserted through psychedelic smoke. A new consignment of absurdist coke lures it into the next station from which it departs giving off no smoke at all, and no fire, until it derails briefly along constructivist tracks and is towed back to the starting point by a neo-classic engine. (Soyinka 1990: 37–38)

What Soyinka describes so artfully is the rhythm or logic behind the changing of worldviews in the West. It is one of periodically selecting an aspect of reality, an intuition, or a scientific fact and turning it into a separatist and sometimes absolute truth, that is supported and elaborated by proliferating sets of analogies and arguments. For Soyinka, this rhythm is motivated by a search for absolutes in the absence of a symbolic totality that gives a concrete sense of the absolute through integrating humans into the life of the cosmos. Further, such integrating totalities are capable of symbolically reconciling many of the smaller contradictions as well as the more elusive antinomies that accompany everyday human thought.

Given the minor status of philosophy in the Caribbean, our experience with worldviews has been quite different. There is no train puffing out ever-changing constructions of a world that continues to elude the grasp of these attempts. Rather, this forward, linear pattern of worldview development has been contained or counterbalanced by a series of lateral, syncretizing moves, that Édouard Glissant has labeled "transversal" (Glissant 1997: 58). As Wilson Harris has pointed out, the discursive raw material that the creative imagination confronts in the region consists of the damaged bodies of shattered selves and mutually imploded and imploding worldviews (Harris 1967: 31). The history of discursive violence in the region has produced high levels of mutual decentering and interculturation between the African and European worlds, the European and Indian worlds, and the Indian and African worlds. This violence has left parts of these systems fairly intact, other parts highly mixed, and others that are damaged beyond repair. This is the heritage upon which creative totalizations must build. These imploded foundations have led to superficial comparisons with postmodern thought that can be misleading. The latter is the latest set of smoke from the Western train now fueled by a technocratic objectification of self and world that is still quite alien to the Caribbean. We consume many of the products of this Western self-objectification, but we do not produce them.

Given this heritage of imploded worldviews, three clear tendencies have emerged in Afro-Caribbean art, religion, and philosophy: (1) reconstructive work within these traditions; (2) synthetic work between them;

and (3) transformative projects beyond them. Reconstructive work has taken the form of a search for lost origins that has involved reconstituting aspects of shattered Amerindian, Indian, and African worldviews. Synthetic work has entailed the search for ways to advance the mixed or hybrid parts of these imploded worldviews and the projecting of creole cultural formations as a basis for a new regional identity. Transformative work has centered around the projecting of new national communities that draw on these reconstructed and creolized traditions. In short, there are strong tendencies toward reconceptualizing the fragments of broken traditions, creolizing the differences between them, and projecting transformative alternatives. Both of these hybridizing and reconstructive tendencies are evident in the Afro-Christian and Afro-Hindu syntheses among the masses. These point to a possible creole solution to the problems of this history of cultural division and of the different identities they legitimate. However, these creolizing tendencies exist simultaneously with their opposites, that is, tendencies toward Christian, Hindu, African, or Indian purisms. These neotraditional tendencies are often the result of political manipulation, but they are also related ego-legitimacy needs.

In short, world-constituting activities among both the elite and masses are caught in the pure/creole binary. They oscillate back and forth, never really finding a point of reconciliation or resolution. As the Rastafarians make clear, the Caribbean masses have retained the ability to repair or refashion the integrating totalities of India and Africa, which are able to convey a sense of the absolute and of cosmic integration. This type of spiritual production has been and still is their first line of discursive creativity. Political vision and philosophical and cultural creativity often rest on the categorical foundations of this capacity for spiritual creativity. With this solution to the problem of the absolute, there has been no need among the Caribbean masses for the Soyinkan train.

Among the intelligentsia, the response to the heritage of mutually imploded worldviews has been quite different. This group has lost the ability to be creative in the language of spirit. That is, we have lost the ability to fashion deities and to create classic totalizations based on a spiritual analogy. Instead our first line of creativity has become a bipolar discursive space that is structured around art and history. The first has given rise to the well-established poeticist tradition and the second to an equally strong historicist tradition. The latter has emphasized popular and state-led transformations of colonial/plantation institutions with a view toward creating national and egalitarian communities and corresponding changes in consciousness. In the poeticist tradition, the emphasis has been on the aesthetic reworking of the elements of broken traditions, with a vision toward transforming the consciousness and identity of Caribbean people, whose changed behavior would in turn change their societies. This aesthetic work has kept our intellectual tradition quite

close to the traditional African and Indian totalities and their solutions to
the problem of the absolute.

However, the totalizations that have come out of this space, whether
poeticist or historicist, are qualitatively different from traditional totalizations. Among poeticists, there have been fictional attempts at recreating
these earlier totalizations. Such efforts must run into difficulties as they
are narrative attempts to create what has been realized only in the language of spirit. The shifts to the languages of art and history mark not
only the switch to new creative media but also the emergence of a new
phase in the development of primal subjectivity in the region. These
changes have brought with them a more assertive role for the Caribbean
ego in relation to its spiritual, natural, and sociohistorical environments.
While not the techno-instrumental mode of self-assertion of the Western
ego, the new Caribbean subject is capable of intervening creatively and
practically in its environments. It is ready to rename, revalorize, reima-
gine, or practically transform plantation geographies, identities, and societies. However, this new assertiveness did not result in projects of total
control over spiritual, natural, and social spaces. Rather, it is counterbalanced by strong relations that root the ego organically in an unconscious
or spiritual ground. Through these relations the ego is "grown" or constituted more than it creates itself. This rootedness together with the minor
status of philosophy have slowed considerably the train on which this
group of Caribbean worldviews are traveling.

This new discursive abode of the Caribbean imagination is a large
organically unified space, whose contours and strange unity we have not
fully explored. That is, the unity of this space precedes, rather than follows, any attempts to thematize or systematize it. Further, intertextually
embedded within it are a number of other positions that get formulated
in terms of analogies and arguments drawn from its poeticist and historicist poles. However, most of its occupants have been unable to see or
thematize this unity. Rather, we have only been able to work within its
subpositions, or one of the major polar positions. Thus my work has
moved primarily within the historical wing and is only now exploring its
organic connections with the poeticist tradition that once appeared to be
its opposite. This has revealed a unity that has been there all along and
that I did not see before. The major exceptions to being trapped in these
divisions and binaries have been figures such as Claude McKay, C. L. R.
James, Aimé Césaire, Frantz Fanon, Nicolás Guillén, Rex Nettleford, Tim
Hector, Orlando Patterson, and the calypsonians Short Shirt and David
Rudder, who have all straddled the major polarities of art and history, as
well as other oppositions internal to this space. In them we get good
glimpses of this underlying but underthematized unity.

As a group, these divisions and dualities constitute the major set of
internal theoretical problems of Afro-Caribbean philosophy. The latter's
current state of fragmentation reflects the ways in which it has resolved

or not resolved, recognized or not recognized, these problems. As we will see, there is still a marked tendency to ignore them, or to see them as not being important. Consequently, both the extent and the quality of the exchanges between the different positions within this space have not been very great. By contrast, much more effort has been expended by Afro-Caribbeans on debates in European philosophy that touch on the interests of particular positions. Our contributions to European debates on existentialism, Marxism, Liberalism, and poststructuralism all support this claim. The hidden unity of poeticism and historicism cries out for thematization. So also do the tensions between history and spirit and those between historicism and the African heritage.

Only by taking more seriously these problems that are unique to its own internal formation will Afro-Caribbean philosophy continue to grow and discover its rhythms and patterns of internal organization. These are the regions unknown to Caesar that Caliban must now enter. At the moment we can only guess at some of the answers to these questions. Given the limitations of the poeticist/historicist space we now occupy, even as a whole this must be viewed as a limited affirmation of what we are as a people. But we will not proceed to wider affirmations of ourselves until we have internalized the secret unity of these polarities. Consequently, in chapter 10 and the conclusion, I will return to some of these issues regarding oppositions and polarities.[5]

PROSPECTUS

The arguments of *Caliban's Reason* unfold in three basic parts. In the first, I examine a number of founding texts with the aim of establishing a number of basic themes and concerns. These include the nature of the African philosophical heritage and the primary claims of the poeticists and historicists. The second part consists of three intermediary reflections that take up some important issues in and around Afro-Caribbean philosophy: its relationships to poststructuralism, to Afro-American philosophy, and to Western concepts of rationality. In the third and final part, I focus in depth on the historicist school and the major problems confronting it.

NOTES

* First published in *Caliban's Reason: Introducing Afro-Caribbean Philosophy* (New York: Routledge, 2000), the introduction.

1. Henry is referring here to the first chapter of *Caliban's Reason*, "The African Philosophical Heritage," which is not included in this volume [editors].

2. Henry is here referring to "Pan-Africanism and Philosophy: Race, Class, and Development" and "Caribbean Marxism: After the Neoliberal and Linguistic Turns," chapters 8 and 9 of *Caliban's Reason* [editors].

3. Henry is referring here to "Wilson Harris and Caribbean Poeticism" and "Sylvia Wynter: Poststructuralism and Postcolonial Thought" in *Caliban's Reason* [editors].

4. For a more detailed treatment of these peripheral dynamics, see my "Towards a Theory of Peripheral Cultural Systems" (1986).

5. Chapter 10, "Caribbean Historicism: Toward Reconstruction," and the conclusion of *Caliban's Reason* are not included in this volume [editors].

TWO

Africana Phenomenology

Its Philosophical Implications

Given some of the exclusive claims on reason that the West has made, it has been difficult to see clearly the rationality of non-Western peoples. This eclipsing of the rationality of non-Western peoples, particularly people of African descent, has made problematic the status of theory in fields such as Africana Studies. Quite often, it is assumed that developments in this field will take the form of case studies that will help to confirm or disconfirm theories and methodologies produced by the West. In other words, nothing new of theoretical importance is expected to emerge from the growth of Africana Studies. Indeed, even some Africana scholars have associated theory and rational linear thought with white males. This is certainly not how I see Africana Studies. My disagreement with this view is confirmed with every new development in the growing field of Africana philosophy. Here the theoretical side of Africana Studies becomes particularly evident, given the nature of philosophical practices. In this paper, I examine the case of Africana phenomenology, an emerging subfield within the larger discursive terrain of Africana philosophy. Like the larger terrain of which it is a part, Africana phenomenology is not very well known because it too has been forced to exist in the nonrational and atheoretical shadow cast over it by Western philosophy in general, and Western phenomenology in particular. Thus our aim in this paper is twofold: the first is to bring the field of Africana phenomenology clearly into view by outlining its contours, problems and theorists. In particular, I will focus on the contributions of W. E. B. Du Bois, Frantz Fanon and Lewis Gordon. Second, I will explore the philosophical implications of the emergence of Africana phenomenology as a subfield of Africana philosophy. These I will argue point to a metaphysical distinctness that can only be adequately engaged by a more comparative approach to philosophy.

CULTURE AND PHENOMENOLOGY

By phenomenology, I mean the discursive practice through which self-reflective descriptions of the constituting activities of consciousness are produced after the "natural attitude" of everyday life has been bracketed by some ego-displacing technique. An Africana phenomenology would thus be the self-reflective descriptions of the constituting activities of the consciousness of Africana peoples, after the natural attitudes of Africana egos have been displaced by de-centering techniques practiced in these cultures. This thematizing of the specificity of Africana phenomenology raises two important theoretical questions: the relationship of phenomenology to specific cultures and disciplines. In relation to the first of these, the notion of a distinct Africana phenomenology very explicitly suggests a cultural dimension to this enterprise. This cultural approach to phenomenology is an unusual one as it culturally conditions the certainty of self-reflective knowledge and raises very explicitly the need to do phenomenology from a comparative cultural perspective. This I shall argue is one of the important theoretical consequences that have accompanied the emergence of Africana phenomenology from its history of invisibility.

With regard to our second theoretical question, the self-reflective core of phenomenology suggests that as an epistemic practice it is not peculiar to philosophy as a discipline. Rather, it is an activity that can be initiated from inside any knowledge-producing human discipline. It also supports their more routine practices. However, the distance to this ground varies between disciplines and is determined largely by qualitative differences in creative and knowledge-producing codes. But in spite of these differences, it is the existence of this shared ground that explains why phenomenological philosophy has been able to reach the transcendental spaces of other discourses, and in the West has been enriched by Edmund Husserl's reflections on the foundations of mathematics. In the case of Africana phenomenology, it is the reflections of creative writers and race theorists that have been particularly enriching.

This problem of culture and phenomenology has in part been concealed by the ways in which reason and culture have been brought together in the identity of European phenomenology. In its classic formulations by Descartes, Kant, Hegel and Husserl, European phenomenology was seen as the self-reflective practice that disclosed the latent movements of a universal reason, which was also the prime constituting force operating within the core of the European subject. Consequently, it was the phenomenology of this subject that would for the first time make manifest these latent activities of universal reason. The crucial significance of this reason as a constituting force was the perceived universality of its categories, positings, claims—in short, its self- and knowledge-producing capabilities. In its fully realized state, Husserl saw reason as "the form of a universal philosophy which grows through consistent apodictic insight and supplies its own norms through an apodictic method" (1970: 16).

However, this possibility of a universal reason was, quite paradoxically, limited to a very specific cultural particularity: the cultural particularity of Europe. This particularization of universal reason was at the same time the universalizing of the European subject as its science and phenomenology would give reason a fully realized vision of itself. In this peculiar configuration, Europe acquired a monopoly that made it co-extensive with the geography of reason. This geography is well known to us from the works of Hegel, Kant, Husserl, and Weber. For Husserl, the development of European phenomenology was tied to the question of whether or not "European humanity bears within itself an absolute idea, rather than being merely an empirical anthropological type like 'China' or 'India'" (1970: 16).

To grasp the reality and presence of Africana phenomenology, this imperial geography and its exclusive relationship between reason and European culture has to be pulled apart. Without such a clearing, it will be impossible to perceive or even imagine the reality of an Africana phenomenology. In preparing the ground for such new phenomenological possibilities, a number of additional factors will also have to be reconsidered. Here I will briefly mention three: (1) the occasion for self-reflection; (2) the path into the practice of self-reflection; and (3) the role played by knowledge produced in the natural attitude in our constructions and reconstructions of the transcendental domain.

In the history of Western philosophy, the occasion for phenomenological reflection has consistently been the problem of rationality and the consequences of rational/scientific knowledge production. Thus the dialectical logic of Hegel's phenomenology was an attempt to keep the creative and explanatory agency of Spirit as an integral part of the changing discursive spaces produced by the rise of the natural sciences (1967: 86–105). In Husserl, the occasion for self-reflection was the crisis produced by the positivistically reduced notions of rationality and humanity that accompanied the rise of mathematics and the natural sciences (1970: 3–16). Habermas has formulated this reduction as the colonization of the Western life-world by its systems of technical and instrumental rationality (1987: 322). It is only in its existential and grammatological variants that these problems of the rational cogito have been replaced by those of the desiring and the signifying subjects. In Sartre, the occasion for self-reflection is the bad faith that the European subject has consistently brought to the knowing situation and the capacity that bad faith has given it to mobilize reason in the service of unreason and untruth (1956:

47–67). In Derrida, the occasion for self-reflection has been Western philosophy's practice (including its phenomenology) of restricting the nature and scope of writing, in relation to speaking and thinking, to a fraction of what it really is (1976: 6–26). Derrida's grammatology has as its goal rescuing of writing from a metaphysically imposed obscurity, similar to Husserlian phenomenology's goal of rescuing a more fully realized concept of reason from its positivistically imposed obscurity.

These variations within the overall telos of rationality that has governed the self-image of European phenomenology are important for raising the question of other occasions for self-reflection that are outside of this rational horizon. These possibilities are important for us as I will argue that the governing telos of Africana phenomenology has been racial liberation and the problems of racial domination from which it springs. In our examinations of Du Bois, Fanon and Gordon, we will see how variations on the problem of racial liberation displace the problem of rationality as the source of occasions for self-reflection.

The second and closely related set of variations necessary for a clear seeing of Africana phenomenology are those variations that have occurred in the paths to self-reflection. In Descartes, it was the method of radical doubting (1960: 7–22). In Hegel, it was the practice of spiritual and theological meditation (1971). In Husserl, self-reflection was practiced through the phenomenological reduction (1975: 5–20). In Sartre, it was through existential analysis (1956: 557–75), and in Derrida it took the form of reflection on the creativity of the systems of writing in which the subject was embedded (1976: 75–93). What do these variations in methods of producing self-reflective knowledge mean for some of the universal claims made by European phenomenology? Are these the only methods of producing self-reflective knowledge? Here I will argue that these variations problematize these universal claims, and that Africana phenomenology further complicates the situation by adding yet another method: that of poetics.

The third and final point that I want to make in preparing the ground for an Africana phenomenology is the relation between the everyday ethical/practical projects of phenomenologies (rescuing reason, writing, or racial equality) and our constructions and ongoing reconstructions of the transcendental domain. These constructions and reconstructions seem to be profoundly influenced by the nature of these world-oriented projects. Thus Kant's logical reconstruction of this domain was clearly shaped by his interest in clarifying the foundations of the natural sciences. Hegel's spiritual reading was inseparable from his interests in clarifying the foundations and validity of the spiritual and theological discourses. Husserl's goal of making the transcendental domain the presuppositionless and rigorously formulated foundation of all discourses was clearly related to his interest in clarifying the status of the processes of idealization that constitute the foundations of mathematics. Finally,

Derrida's semiotic vision of the transcendental domain is also inseparable from his project of clarifying the foundations of writing. These examples point to a circle of mutual influencing between the world-oriented projects of phenomenologies and their corresponding views of what is foundational or transcendental for knowledge production. But such a pattern of influence points to a historicizing of the transcendental domain that would limit any absolute claims for Spirit, logic, pre-suppositionless idealization, or arche-writing. In all of these accounts of the transcendental domain there has been a clear tendency to extend their foundational reach beyond what this circle of mutual influence would suggest. In Africana phenomenology, this tendency has been distinctly weaker and could be related to the differences in the telos and nature of its ethical/practical project.

With these three points in place, our conception of phenomenology should now be a more open and flexible one. This flexibility extends to its relations with cultures, historical processes, disciplines, ethical/practical projects, occasions for self-reflection and methods of self-reflection. On the horizon of such a comparative conception of this subfield of philosophies around the world, the reality and possibility of an Africana phenomenology can be clearly seen.

AFRICANA PHENOMENOLOGY

In the tradition of Africana phenomenology, the occasion for self-reflection has not been the positivistic reduction of rationality and the mechanized caricature of the European subject that it threatens to produce. Rather, the occasion for reflection has been the racist negating of the humanity of Africans and the caricature of "the negro" that is has produced. Unlike European phenomenology, these Africana reflections have been interested in clarifying the systemic error producing foundations of the European humanities and social sciences that have had to legitimate and make appear as correct this racist reduction of African humanity. The positivistic reduction European humanity and the racist reduction of African humanity are opposite sides of the coin of modern Western capitalism. The mechanical caricature is a part of the upper and rational side of itself that Western capitalism likes to affirm. The racist caricature of "the Negro" is a creation of the "underside" of this mechanized capitalism, a part of its irrational shadow that it cannot affirm but must project onto others that it perceives as its opposite. The sociological setting for the production of the caricature of "the negro" was not the Habermasian internal colonization of a life-world by its own systems of technical and instrumental reason. Rather, this setting was the external colonization of one life-world (the African) by another (the European). This process of imperial domination by a society of a different race and a different culture shattered the traditional socio-cultural worlds of pre-colonial Africa. It racialized identities that were predominantly spiritual, physically captured, enslaved and exported millions of Africans for economic exploitation on plantations in the Western hemisphere. In short, it was in this context of colonial conquest that Africans became part of "the underside of modernity" (Dussel: 1996) or what Husserl earlier referred to as "the Europeanization of all other civilizations" (1970: 16).

The implosive impact of this Europeanization on the life-worlds of African societies can be quickly indicated by some of its classic representations in literature. In continental Africa, Chinua Achebe's novel, *Things Fall Apart*, has become one of the classic metaphors for the shattering impact of European colonization. In the Caribbean, a novel that holds a corresponding symbolic status is George Lamming's *In the Castle of My Skin*. Here the impact of racialization or what Fanon will call negrification is much greater than in Achebe's novel. The African has ceased to be a Yoruba or Akan and has become a "black," a "negro" or a "nigger." In Afro-America, Richard Wright's *Black Boy* or Ralph Ellison's *Invisible Man* would be corresponding works. In both of these novels, the process of racialization (niggerization) is even more extreme than in the case of Lamming. Thus the terrain of self-reflection in the Africana world has been a rather burned out, exploded and blackened one, very different from the technological dystopia of Aldous Huxley's *Brave New World* or George Orwell's *1984*.

In spite of this broken and blackened nature of the terrain of Africana self-reflection, it is still very much a human world with hope and genius. This hope has been one of its classic expressions by another Afro-Caribbean writer, Derek Walcott. He writes: "break a vase and the love that reassembles the fragments is stronger than the love which took its symmetry for granted when it was whole. The glue that fits the pieces is the sealing of its original shape. It is such a love that reassembles our African and Asiatic fragments, the cracked heirlooms whose restoration shows its white scars" (1993: 9). This blackened imploding of the pre-colonial African consciousness and its loving reconstruction are two important poles defining the world of Africana phenomenology.

DU BOIS AND AFRICANA PHENOMENOLOGY

Although the roots of Africana self-reflection are to be found in Africa, the pattern of development of the field is such that it is best to start with the reflections of the period of enslavement and its aftermath. These periods produced the writings of eighteenth- and nineteenth-century ex-slaves such as Olaudah Equiano, Ottobah Cugoano, Frederick Douglass, Harriet Jacobs, Mary Prince, and David Walker. In the twentieth century, self-reflective Africana writing continued in the works of Edward Blyden, Anténor Firmin, Marcus Garvey, Ida B. Wells, W. E. B. Du Bois, Alain Locke, Frantz Fanon, Wilson Harris, Sylvia Wynter, Lewis Gordon and many others. Of these writers, the first to outline a comprehensive phenomenology of Africana self-consciousness was Du Bois, whose life and work spanned the late nineteenth and the first half of the twentieth century.

In his work, *The Autobiography*, Du Bois tells us that he entered Harvard with the goal of pursuing a career in philosophy. The courses he took exposed him to the thought of the American pragmatists, particularly William James and Josiah Royce, and the engagements of the school with Hegel's philosophy (Zamir 1995: 113–33). This was the context in which the young Du Bois encountered Hegel's phenomenology. When we consider the latter's impact on C. L. R. James, René Ménil (founding member of *Légitime défense*), Frantz Fanon and Wilson Harris, it is probably the European phenomenology that has had the most influence on Africana phenomenology. Hegel's phenomenology is a classic example of what Habermas calls a general interpretation as opposed to a general theory (1971: 246–73). The former is a generalized narrative of self-development directed at a subject and must therefore have an "addressee." General theories are aimed at objects rather than subjects. The application of a general interpretation thus becomes a process of self-application— one must literally try on the theory and respond to the experienced sense of fit. In other words, general interpretations require the explicit thematizing of the responses of specific subjects to its discursive offerings. In the case of general theories, application takes the form of an externally imposed subsumption that requires experimental evaluation rather than confirmation from an addressee. As a general interpretation, the application of Hegel's phenomenology to the self-consciousness of the Africana subject can only be judged appropriate by the sense of fit this subject reports. The changes that Du Bois made in Hegel's phenomenology derived from the experience of an imperfect fit.

For the young Du Bois, the Africana subject was a culturally distinct, and hence non-European, site of original meanings, discourses and experiences. Consequently, to make himself the addressee of Hegel's phenomenology, Du Bois's engagements with it had to be different from those of European or Euro-American philosophers. As Hegel's primary addressees, the latter could very easily test it by putting themselves in the role of the self-consciousness that had reached the stage of the master. Further, they could identify with the earlier stages in this process of self-development as they were drawn directly from European history. Because the self-consciousness of Africana subject is not the primary addressee of Hegel's phenomenology, self-application cannot produce the same results. Further, Du Bois cannot identify with either the earlier or later stages in Hegel's general interpretation as they are not drawn from the history of the Africana subject. Thus what Du Bois will take from Hegel is how to view the racialized African subject and its possibilities for recovery from the standpoint of the self- and world-constituting activities of its consciousness. In short, it is the general phenomenological approach of grasping self and world from the perspective of a constituting consciousness that Du Bois takes from Hegel. However, unlike Hegel, Du Bois will not make an absolute onto-epistemic commitment to this perspective.

For Hegel, the self-development of the European subject was not a smooth, unitary process of growth. Rather, it was an upward movement that was marked by splits, doublings, and self/other binaries that resulted in premature exclusions and negations that would have to be overcome in subsequent stages. Thus in the paragraphs that open the section on "Lordship and Bondage" in *The Phenomenology of Mind*, Hegel writes extensively about the doubling or duplication that arises from the fact that self-consciousness exists not only for itself, but also for another self-consciousness. In other words, it is the fact that self-consciousness must be both for itself and for another that produces its "double meanings" (1967: 229). Here, too, we find another significant influence that Hegel had on Du Bois's phenomenology.

The first attempt of the young Du Bois to bring the Africana subject into an engagement with Hegel's phenomenology was his 1890 Harvard commencement address: "Jefferson Davis as Representative of Civilization." There, clearly in the role of the slave, Du Bois presents the Africana subject as "the Submissive Man" who is "at once the check and complement of the Teutonic Strong Man" (Levering-Lewis 1995: 19). With this different metaphor of Africana selfhood, the young Du Bois is here making a significant departure from Hegel on the basis of the different phenomenological history of the Africana subject. The "Submissive Man" is both check and complement to the European subject because not even to the latter's mind is it given to recognize the whole truth of human ontogenesis (Levering-Lewis 1995: 19). Such a vision of the totality can only emerge from conversations in which the contributions of all civilizations are acknowledged and their complementarity recognized. With this concept of a global complementarity between cultures, Du Bois breaks with the conflating of Europe and the universal that was such an integral part of Hegel's phenomenology. This break in turn sets the stage for the positions that Du Bois will take in his important essay, "The Conservation of Races," and for the way in which he will engage Hegel in *The Souls of Black Folk*.

DOUBLE CONSCIOUSNESS AND DU BOISIAN PHENOMENOLOGY

In the opening essay of *Souls*, "Of Our Spiritual Strivings," Du Bois outlines his theory of double consciousness, which constitutes the core of his phenomenology. The double consciousness of which he speaks in this essay is not just the result of the Africana subject having also to exist before another self-consciousness. Its life in Africa made existing for another self-consciousness an already familiar reality for this subject, and quite possibly the Hegelian form of double consciousness. Du Boisian double consciousness results from the Africana subject having to exist for a self-consciousness that racialized itself as white. In the dialectic of racial recognition that takes place between the two, it is not the humanity but the blackness of the Africana subject that confirms the whiteness of the Teutonic "Strong Man." As a result, the racialization of the African as black produced a very different form of doubling than in the case of Hegel's non-racialized master or slave.

For Du Bois, this racialization of identities and supporting institutional orders were not leftovers from the traditional past but integral parts of the modern world order of European capitalism. It was as integral as the processes of commodification, colonization, rationalization, and secularization that Marx, Weber and Durkheim thought were so central to the rise Western capitalism. The growth of processes of racialization throughout the formative and mature periods of Western capitalism is evident in its expanding discourses on the hierarchies of races and the increasingly global reach of its institutions of white supremacy.

In Du Bois's view, the impact of these processes of racialization on both the psyche and the transcendental consciousness of the Africana subject was the creating of new divisions within them—divisions that were different from Hegelian forms of doubling. With regard to the psyche, the new division was created by the shattering and contesting of the "We" or the collective identity of the Africana subject. It was shattered by the caricature image of "the negro" as the polar opposite of "the white" that existed and continues to exist in the mind of the European and the Euro-American. This stereotyped image of the African in the white mind was given some of its clearest expressions in the "blackface" that whites would put on when they played "negroes" on the vaudeville stage. It was the institutionalizing of this absolute racial distance between whites and blacks that shattered and contested the pre-colonial collective identities of the Akan, Hausa, Yoruba, Fon and other African ethnic groups. Du Boisian double consciousness is a phenomenological account of the self-consciousness of these African subjects whose "We" had been shattered and challenged by this process of negrification.

Du Bois represented the double life-world created by racialization through the metaphor of the veil. Thus he spoke of life within and outside of the veil. This concept/metaphor is another important descriptive term in Du Bois's phenomenology. In *Darkwater*, Du Bois gave us a hint as to how he had adjusted to life behind the veil. He retreated into a "tower above the loud complaining of the human sea" (1999: 17), from where he would attempt to grasp and engage the world intellectually.

This is one possible existential response to the involuntary presence of this racial veil. This response reminds us of George Lamming's retreat into *The Castle of My Skin*, taking with him only the tools of the creative writer. Tower and castle are here important symbols of the response of Africana subjects to the double life-world created by the veil. In *Souls*, Du Bois mentions the responses of other Africana subjects that were not so "fiercely sunny: their youth shrunk into tasteless sycophancy, or into silent hatred of the pale world about them and mocking distrust of everything white, or wasted itself in a bitter cry, why did God make me an outcast and a stranger in my own house" (1969: 16). It is these less sunny psyches that will be the focus of Fanon's phenomenology. Thus along with the images of tower and castle, sycophancy, waste, stranger, and outcast are also important descriptive terms of Africana self-consciousness before the veil of the racial other.

The specifics of this dilemma of the racial veil are such that it really has no counterpart in any of the stages of Hegel's phenomenology of European self-consciousness. Zamir's suggestion that Africana double consciousness can be seen as a case of Hegel's "unhappy consciousness" does not really work. The divided Hegelian subject moves between a desire for an "I" that is autonomous and self-constituting and the need for confirmation and recognition from the other. These are some of the existential dilemmas that the Africana subject would have experienced before its racialization. In the phase of the former's development that Hegel referred to as "the unhappy consciousness," this divided subject has moved beyond the terms of the master-slave relationship to explore stoic and skeptical responses to its inner divisions. What Hegel calls the "double-consciousness" (1967: 251) of this unhappy subject stems from an awareness of itself as "changeable" at the same time that it is also "consciousness of unchangeableness" (1967: 252). As the latter, it must seek to liberate itself from its changeable existence but is unable to reach the life of the unchangeable. This is the particular "dualizing of self-consciousness" that constitutes the dilemmas of the unhappy consciousness.

As a racialized subject, the Africana individual remains very much within the terms of the master-slave relationship. Consequently, the above dualizing is not the source of the two poles between which the Africana subject oscillates. This subject moves not between a changeable "I" and an unchangeable "Other" but between two "We's." Behind this particular experience of "twoness" is the earlier noted phenomenon of the external colonization of one life-world by another and the contempt and pity it produced. The self-reflections of the Du Boisian subject cannot avoid engagements with this specific type of twoness. He/she must encounter questions such as "what, after all, am I? Am I an American or am I a Negro? Can I be both? Or, is it my duty to cease to be a Negro as soon as possible and to be an American?" (Levering-Lewis 1995: 24). One feels here the clashing of two racialized and hence irreconcilable collective identities. This is not the dilemma of Hegel's unhappy consciousness.

In addition to the splitting of the Africana psyche, Du Boisian double consciousness also refers to a similar splitting of the transcendental consciousness of this racialized subject. The internalizing of the caricature of "the negro" also produced significant changes in the categoric structure of the transcendental domain of the Africana subject. This complex set of categoric changes Du Bois summed up under the label of "second sight" (1969: 16), which is a new or second way of seeing self and world. Second sight is the ability of the racialized Africana subject to see him/herself as a "negro," that is, through the eyes of the white other. It is new in the sense that it was not a capability that pre-colonial Africans had. This new half of the double vision of the Africana subject suggests that first sight is the ability to see one's self through one's own eyes. The categoric changes in the organization of the transcendental domain that are associated with double consciousness derive from the complex and changing dynamics that developed between first and second sight.

To the extent that second sight, the ability to see one's self as a "negro" replaced first sight, it constituted a major obstacle to any genuine Africana self-consciousness. Tied to the European or Euro-American life-worlds, second sight yielded the Africana subject "no true self-consciousness, but only lets him see himself through the revelation of the other world" (1969: 16). In other words, this exclusive form of second sight is in reality a categoric form of self-blindness, a deformation, a detour rather than a positive phase in the development of Africana self-consciousness. This "negro" detour will only take the Africana subject down a blind alley. It is a classic case of false consciousness that will only take this subject away from its self. This struggle to see through the darkness of second sight is the categoric dilemma of Africana self-consciousness as disclosed by Du Bois's phenomenology. This dilemma of second sight affected Africana knowledge production as profoundly as those of the tower, the outcast, or the stranger affected self production.

THE ETHICAL/PRACTICAL PROJECT OF DU BOIS'S PHENOMENOLOGY

As in the case of Hegel or Husserl, Du Bois's phenomenology was intricately linked to an ethical/practical project. This was a project of racial equality that included the deniggerization of Africana identities, the full recognition of the humanity of Africana peoples, and also of their cultural contributions to the shared problems of human ontogenesis. We saw glimpses of this project in the Jefferson Davis address. We will now develop it more fully by drawing primarily from *Souls*, the history of *The Suppression of the African Slave Trade*, and *The Philadelphia Negro*. This ethi-

cal dimension of Du Bois's phenomenology is quite distinct and constitutes another area of a clear break with Hegel. Du Bois's project of racial
equality displaces the Hegelian one of keeping the vision of Spirit a part
of the rational world of the European subject. I will develop this distinctness of the Du Boisian project around three crucial points: (1) Du Bois's
potentiated second sight; (2) his poeticist style of self-reflection; and (3)
his commitment to racial and cultural equality.

The categoric transformation represented by second sight was very
much a double-edged sword. On one side it guards against the achieving
of true self-consciousness by Africana subjects, and on the other it can
give the latter very special access and insight into the dehumanizing
"will to power" of the European imperial subject. This peculiar insight,
which I am calling potentiated second sight, is a crucial link between the
transcendental and the ethical dimensions of Du Bois's phenomenology.
The potentiating of second sight is always a latent possibility in the racialized and divided self-consciousness of the Africana subject. This possibility can be activated in two basic ways: first through the recovery of a
significant measure of first sight, that is, the ability to see one's self as an
African as opposed to "the negro" that the white mind was constantly
producing and projecting. This ability to see one's self as an African will
depend upon one's ability to creatively uproot the "blackface" stereotype
and reconstruct self and world within the creative codes of African discourses and symbols. To the extent that an individual or group is able to
do this, they will have an alternative space from which to see through
and critique the imposed "negro" stereotype. The Rastafarians are a good
example of this first way of potentiating second sight.

The second is clearly the finding of an independent point of self-
elevation such as Du Bois's tower or George Lamming's castle. From
such a point, there must be the cultivating of an informed and critical "I"
that is capable of distancing itself from the caricature of "the negro" so
that it is able to see clearly the latter's formation, its white psychosocial
significance, and also its dissolution. The cultivation of such an "I" would
then become either a new form of first sight or some form of third sight.
Whichever it is, in conjunction with the ability to see one's self as an
African, two very potent bases outside of the psychic terrain of "the
negro" identity will have been established. Together they are not only
able to see through and implode the imposed stereotype but also to provide great insight into the psyche of the creators and perpetrators of this
tragic farce. In the wide distances between the capabilities of the recovered African/tower identity and those of the "blackface" stereotype, the
Africana subject had a living and reflectively accessible measure of the
inhumanity of the Western imperial self. Lewis Gordon captures well the
ironic dimensions of potentiated second sight when he notes that it
emerges in the subject who has become aware of the lived contradiction
of this deception, and who like Fanon is therefore able to announce "the

absence of his interiority from the point of view of his interiority" (1995a: 33). It is from the reflective immediacy of the decaying carcass of "the negro" that the critiques of potentiated second sight derive their ethical/ moral power, pinpoint accuracy, and razor sharp quality.

In Du Bois, our first glimpses of such critiques are to be found in his early short story, "A Vacation Unique." In this story, Du Bois's hero, Cuffy, invites his Harvard classmate to disguise himself as a "negro" and to come and see the world from this point of view. Cuffy says to his classmate: "outside of mind you may study mind, and outside of matter by reason of the fourth dimension of color you may have a striking view of the intestines of the fourth great civilization" (Zamir 1995: 223). In other words, what the classmate will get is an intestinal view of American civilization, of the hunger that drives it to dominate and racialize. This intestinal view of the white imperial self is repeated in *Darkwater*, in another of Du Bois's classic statements of what I have called potentiated second sight. In the chapter, "The Souls of White Folks," he writes: "of them I am singularly clairvoyant. I see in and through them. I view them from unusual points of vantage. Not as foreigner do I come, for I am native, not foreign, bone of their thought and flesh of their language. . . . Rather I see these souls undressed and from the back and side. I see the workings of their entrails. I know their thoughts and they know that I know" (1999: 17). How did Du Bois know? By shining the light of his potentiated second sight on the creators of the "blackface" caricature that he has killed. To confirm that Du Bois is not the only Africana subject in possession of this special faculty of second sight, we need only think of Cugoano, Douglass, Garvey, Fanon, Malcolm X, or Angela Davis. But it was Du Bois who first gave it a systematic formulation, and as such it constitutes one of the distinguishing features of the ethical/ practical project of his phenomenology.

The second distinctive feature of this project is Du Bois's poeticist style of self-reflection. As noted earlier, all phenomenologies employ some technique of bracketing the natural attitude in order to reach the constituting movements of consciousness through what Husserl called "the self-evidence of original activity" (Derrida 1989: 163). The immediately evident self- and world-constituting activities of the Africana self were grasped by Du Bois poetically, and explored more fully through the writing of novels and short stories. Thus in his approaches to consciousness Du Bois used what we can call a poeticist reduction in contrast to the spiritual-theological and phenomenological reductions of Hegel and Husserl. Further, in *Souls*, Du Bois also made use of music to supplement his poeticist techniques of bracketing the everyday world. However, here again, Du Bois made no absolute onto-epistemic commitment to his poetics in spite of its vital role in gaining him access to the original or founding activity of the Africana self. He always used it in conjunction with other discourses, particularly history and sociology as both supplement and check. Du Bois's bracketing of the natural attitude and the everyday world was specific to his poetics. In his historical and sociological writings he returns quite easily to the everyday world. The dominance of intentional approaches that mark his poetics is reversed in these writings, where it takes second place to what we can call "extensional" approaches. As we will see, this shifting back and forth between intentional and extensional approaches is one important difference between the phenomenologies of Du Bois and Gordon. Thus the knowing subject in Du Bois changed identity and discipline as it wrote its many works. Earlier we noted that for Du Bois it was not given to any one culture to see the whole truth. Similarly, it was not given to any one discipline or mode of the knowing subject to see the whole truth. The partiality of vision that Du Bois saw as basic to all human cultures, he extended *a fortiori* to the disciplines and to the various modes that the knowing subject can adopt, including the poetic mode. Just as the "Submissive Man" must check and complement the "Strong Man," so must poetics check and complement sociology and history, as well as being itself checked and complemented by them. Although Du Bois never explicitly thematized the principles by which he was able to bring these different disciplines and modes of the subject together to produce that powerful discursive synthesis that I have called his socio-historical poetics, they are the primary keys to the metaphysical foundations of his thought. We will return to these foundations later. Here it must suffice to note that the poeticist element in this synthesis gave Du Bois his distinctive path to the process of self-reflection and thus access to the original activity of the Africana consciousness.

The third and final factor in this account of the ethical/practical dimension of Du Bois's phenomenology is its clear commitment to projects of cultural and racial equality. In this commitment we see the love that reassembles the broken fragments of the vase of which Derek Walcott spoke. The racial hierarchies, the class inequalities and the caricaturing of identities produced by the coming into being of Western capitalism have given rise to human tragedies of major proportions. In both social and political terms, Du Bois responded very thoughtfully and passionately to the devastating circumstances that these tragic outcomes created for Africana peoples. However, over the course of his long life these responses change a lot. In *The Philadelphia Negro*, Du Bois outlined a program of limited assimilation, led by a black elite, to deal specifically with the problem of racial as opposed to class inequality. In *Black Reconstruction*, Du Bois discovers and explores the potential of the self-organizing capabilities of the African American masses as a key part of the solution to the problem of racial inequality. In *Dusk of Dawn*, Du Bois explores an ethnic enclave strategy that calls for a period of separate economic and political organizing before integrating into the larger social mainstream. With his departure for Ghana toward the end of his life, it is possible to argue that Du Bois had given up on changing the racial order of America.

But in spite of these changes in his sociopolitical responses the racializing processes of Western capitalism, his ethical responses to the human crises that it produced never wavered.

This unwavering ethical stance is most elegantly stated in the "final word" that closes *The Philadelphia Negro*. There Du Bois links the problem of racial inequality directly to that question of questions: "after all who are men? Is every featherless biped to be counted a man and brother? Are all races and types to be joint heirs of the new earth that men have striven to raise in thirty centuries or more?" (1996: 385–6). Du Bois tells us that Western civilization has answered these questions in the negative on the basis of a widening but still very limited and exclusionary conception of humanity. After speaking about the conditional admittance of groups like the Celts and the Asians, Du Bois turns to the case of the Africans. He writes: "but with the Negroes of Africa we come to a full stop, and in its heart the civilized world with one accord denies that these come within the pale of nineteenth century humanity. This feeling, widespread and deep-seated, is, in America, the vastest of the Negro problems" (1996: 387). Here is Du Bois, the poet, closing with potentiated second sight a major sociological work.

This in brief outline is Du Bois's phenomenology of Africana self-consciousness. The Submissive Man, the tower, the veil, double consciousness, second sight, the love that puts the Submissive Man back together again are some of its distinguishing features. The double consciousness of which Du Bois speaks cannot be adequately view as one of the stages of Hegel's phenomenology. Rather, it is the theorizing of a period of imperial/racial domination in the self-consciousness of the Africana subject that is absent from the life of Hegel's European subject. Thus, when Zamir asks: "How is it then that Du Bois can read Hegel quite so critically, before he has begun to read Marx, without (as far as is known) a knowledge of Kierkegaard, well before Alexandre Kojève and Sartre's commentaries on the *Phenomenology*, and very much against the grain of the readings of Hegel common in nineteenth century America?" (1995: 117). I think that in addition to Du Bois's genius, the answer is to be found in the uniqueness of this period of black racialization that Du Bois's phenomenology had to theorize. Although by no means complete within itself, this phenomenology revealed in its inner structure the paradigmatic form that other Africana phenomenologies, such as those of Fanon and Gordon would take. They all share with Du Bois this distinguishing notion of double consciousness, different aspects of which they will thematize and develop.

FANON AND AFRICANA PHENOMENOLOGY

If Du Bois contributed the first important chapter to an explicitly thematized phenomenology of Africana self-consciousness, then the second was clearly written by the Martinican psychoanalyst and revolutionary, Frantz Fanon. His major contribution to this particular subfield of Africana philosophy is the more detailed and incisive psycho-existential analysis of this historical phase of double consciousness identified by Du Bois. In this effort, Fanon's achievements in *Black Skin, White Masks* remain unsurpassed. There is no finer or more detailed account of the state of racial double consciousness.

As self-consciousness, the human being was for Fanon "motion toward the world and toward his like. A movement of aggression, which leads to enslavement or to conquest; a movement of love, a gift of the self, the ultimate stage of what by common accord is called ethical orientation" (1967: 41). It is Fanon's view that every human consciousness has the capacity for these two kinds of movements. Further, it is the job of the phenomenologist and the psychologist to grasp in their originality and immediacy the specific meanings and the guiding telos of these two sets of creative movements that are inherent in human consciousness. This self-creative telos of individual human consciousness, Fanon comprehends as its "ontogeny" (1967: 13). Thus the primary goal of his phenomenology is an account of the crisis confronting the ontogenesis of the Africana subject as a result of the historical phase of double consciousness that it is going through. In short, like Du Bois, this crisis constitutes Fanon's occasion for self-reflection, the contradictory condition that motivates his journey inward.

However, again like Du Bois, Fanon makes no absolute epistemic commitments to this ontogenic approach as a whole or to its specific philosophical and psychoanalytic dimensions. Indeed, given the socio-historical origins of this phase of double consciousness, Fanon insisted that "ontology cannot explain the being of the black man" (1967: 110). Consequently, ontogeny must be supplemented by sociogeny. In other words, the self-constituting powers of the Africana consciousness must be dialectically supplemented and checked by the formative powers of socio-cultural orders.

Within this onto-/socio-genic approach, Fanon further refines his path to the practice of self-reflection by raising the ontogenic question of: how should "the psychic modality" of human consciousness be studied? Fanon identifies two distinct approaches to self-reflective knowledge within the overall framework of his ontogenic project. The first, which is on the "philosophical level" (1967: 23), aims at the immediate grasping of the human subject through intuitive accounts of its basic needs and its movements toward the world. These intuitive accounts will always be incomplete and provisional, but at the same time very necessary. Hence, this philosophical approach requires that one should "strive unremittingly for a concrete and ever new understanding of man" (1967: 22). In developing these intuitive accounts Fanon made use of both a poetic and a Sartrean inflected phenomenological reduction. As in the case of Du Bois, much of the power of Fanon's writing comes from his ability to incorporate poetic insights into his socio-historical and psychological writings. Indeed, Fanon's text is unimaginable without the self-reflective knowledge produced within the frameworks of these two epistemic reductions. Thus an important part of making Fanon's phenomenology more visible would be to make more explicit the ways in which he combined the use of these poetic and phenomenological reductions.

The second approach to self-reflection that Fanon identified was psychoanalytic. In contrast to the concrete orientation of the first or philosophical one, this approach first constructs what Habermas would call a general interpretation of the development of the human subject, and then attempts to grasp the concrete individual in terms of its deviations from this model. The use of this psychoanalytic model led to Fanon's engagements with Freud, Jung, Adler and Lacan. In other words, Fanon will supplement and check his more concrete and philosophical approach to self-reflection with this more abstract and psychoanalytic one. As in the case above with poetry and phenomenology, the links that Fanon establishes between the psychoanalytic and the philosophical are themselves original, creative movements of Fanon's consciousness toward the world that he did not explicitly thematize, but they hold the keys to the distinct metaphysical foundations upon which his thought rests. It is this complex and synthetic methodology that informs Fanon's phenomenology. Its psychoanalytic dimensions separate it from Du Bois's. However, both are interested in the "psychopathological and philosophical explanation of the state of being a Negro" (1967: 15).

DOUBLE CONSCIOUSNESS AND
FANONIAN PHENOMENOLOGY

What is the state of being a "negro"? It is a state of enforced negrification in which colonized Africana peoples lost their earlier cultural identities and became identified by the color of their skin. The outer form of this state is the substituting of an epidermal identity in the place of a cultural one. The inner content of this outer transformation is the socio-historical reality of being forced to live as the unconscious, liminal shadow, the repressed and undesirable side of the imperial European subject that had racialized its identity as white. The caricature of "the negro" is first and foremost for Fanon a dark projection that is basic to the cathartic and scapegoating mechanisms of the European psyche. This projective mechanism Fanon describes as follows: "in the degree to which I find in myself

something unheard-of, something reprehensible, only one solution remains for me: to get rid of it, to ascribe its origins to someone else" (1967:
190). The stereotype of "the negro" is a discursive crystallization of the
contents of an "inordinately black hollow" in the European psyche that it
must externalize and experience as belonging to someone else. Thus for
Fanon, in the West, "the Negro has one function: that of symbolizing the
lower emotions, the baser inclinations, the dark side of the soul"
(1967:190). This is the meaning of negrification, the state of being a "negro."

Because the African is not a "negro," negrification as a form of racialization produced what Fanon called a psycho-existential deviation, an
aberration of affect in the psyche of Africana peoples. Such a deviation
arises in the psyche of a people when "an inferiority complex has been
created by the death and burial of its local cultural originality" (1967: 18).
In the case of Africana peoples, this deviation is the opening up of that
racial fissure in their sense of a "We" that Du Bois described as double
consciousness. Fanon writes: "the back man has two dimensions. One
with his fellows, the other with the white man" (1967: 17). However,
these two sets of relations are not always of equal weight. As negrification takes hold, the second set begins to transform the first. In its being
for another Africana self-consciousness, the negrified African will be profoundly influenced by the relationship with the white other. Self-evalua-
tion will take the form: I am better of or worse than another "negro"
depending on whether I am whiter or more Europeanized. This detour-
ing of all intersubjective relations through white norms and evaluations
is a major disturbance in the interactive relations of the Africana subject
that follows from its "two dimensions."

For Fanon, this "self-division" and its consequences are the keys to the
state of being a "negro." His approach to this internal division is to examine carefully its distorting impact on the relations of "the negro" with
others, both black and white. Fanon begins his analysis of the disruptive
impact of this double consciousness with an examination of "the negro's"
attitude toward his own and the colonizer's languages. Here Fanon
shows that the distorting impact of double consciousness is the negrified
subjects desire to present him/herself as a master of the languages of
Europe. Before the white other, this display of linguistic mastery is a bid
for recognition and a demonstration of the degree to which he/she has
rejected the African past. Before the black other, the same display may be
an attempt to gain recognition for how far that individual has succeeded
in Europeanizing his/her existence. The underlying disturbance in self-
other relations that these attitudes to language reveal is the following:
that the racialized African "will be proportionately whiter—that is, he
will come closer to being a real human being—in direct ratio to his mastery of the French language" (1967: 18). In the midst of this disturbance
we can hear the Du Boisian questions: "What, after all, am I?" Am I a

French person or am I a "Negro"? Can I be both? Fanon could have made the same point using religion, music, philosophy, dance, or literature as the sociogenic reality behind these psycho-existential deviations.

However, this general account of the double consciousness of the negrified Africana subject was not the primary goal of Fanon's phenomenology. Rather, it was the exploration of two specific possibilities within this broader disturbance in Africana self-other relations. The first was the tragic possibility of "the negro" who deals with his/her negrification by attempting to conceal it behind "white masks." Fanon develops this possibility through examinations of cases of blacks who must have white lovers. In such cases, Fanon recognizes a self-negating desire in the black to be white, which for him represents the extreme point of self-alienation in "the state of being a Negro." Fanon also makes it clear that not all racialized Africana subjects are in such extreme states of alienation. But nonetheless, he wants to point out their existence and examine them in detail.

The second possibility within the broader disturbance in Africana self-other relations that Fanon takes up is indeed quite different. It is the agonizing possibility of an Africana subject working his/her way out of "the state of being a Negro." It is here that the awakening of potentiated second sight makes its appearance in Fanon. What is the lived experience of the racialized Africana subject who is awakening from the nightmare and false consciousness of his/her negrification? This is the question to which Fanon brought the combined powers of his distinct phenomenological methodology. It is here that we can see the breathtaking moments in which the poetic and phenomenological reductions are brought together produce self-reflective knowledge of the most profound nature.

The early awakenings of the negrified Africana subject are marked by the experience of not being able to affirm a self of one's own choosing in the presence the institutionally empowered stereotype of "the negro" that the white psyche must externalize and project onto another. Thus it is the experience of walking a tightrope located between the opposing but unequal egocentric pulls of these two sources of Africana selfhood. This is what Fanon meant when he said that "the black man has no ontological resistance in the eyes of the white man" (1967: 110). Normatively empowered by institutionalization, the image of the black in the white mind overpowers the self-image of the awakening Africana subject. This is the source of the power and weight of ordinary second sight. It is against this weight, and in spite of its ontological power that the awakening Africana subject must fight to regain first sight, potentiated second sight, explode the caricature of "the negro," and affirm an identity of his/her own choosing. Adding to the pain and terror of this struggle is the fact that below the tightrope on which the Africana subject is walking is "the zone of non-being." To fail is to experience a collapse of ones ego and a fall into nothingness. It is the stumbling and falling of this awakening subject on the edge of non-being, the experiences of going out of and coming back into ego-being that Fanon's phenomenology describes so powerfully.

This description begins with an archeological view of some of the organizing schemas that structure the consciousness of the Africana subject. At the most basic level we find an intentional schema that consists of the motions of this subject toward the world that Fanon earlier described as being basic to human beings. He then goes on to describe a corporeal or bodily schema that is also an integral part of the Africana self-image. On the third layer, Fanon identifies an epidermal or historico-racial schema that is yet another important part of the identity of the Africana subject. These are the key frameworks that ground and shape the identity of our awakening man or woman. In the mind of this subject, joy and recognition should accompany his/her motions toward the other and the world. His/her bodily schema is the basis of a "physiological self" that balances one in space, localizes sensations, and makes one physically attractive to the other. His/her historico-racial schema was African, African American, Afro-Caribbean or Afro-Latin American.

Fanon gives us several examples of the implosive ego collapse that the awakening Africana self has experienced before the institutionalized power of the white gaze. Echoing the youthful Du Bois's experience of racial stigmatization by a white playmate, Fanon uses the case of a young child to illustrate the power and content of the white gaze: "Mama, see the Negro! I am frightened." Behind this fright was a very different set of intentional, bodily, and historico-racial schemas that challenges those of the Africana subject in the early phases of denegrification. The resulting clash between these negrifying and denegrifying perspectives Fanon describes as follows: "Assailed at various points, the corporeal scheme crumbled, its place taken by the epidermal schema. In the train it was no longer a question of being aware of my body in the third person but in a triple person" (1967: 112). In other words, this encounter with the white other was experienced as "an amputation, an excision, a hemorrhage" (1967: 112).

If this awakening subject is to achieve denegrification and potentiated second sight, such amputations and falls into the zone of non-being must be endured and overcome. In the zone of non-being, "an authentic upheaval can be born," that is, new images of self, new projects for bringing one's self back into ego-being can be undertaken. This push for rebirth is strong, defiant, almost compulsive. Through this agency Fanon's awakening subject takes the broken pieces of his/her selfhood and refashions them into a new project of being in the world. One new project explored by Fanon is the possibility of asserting one's self "as a BLACK MAN" (emphasis in the original). However, like the earlier project, this one could also go down in defeat. In the event of such an outcome, one must return to the zone of non-being with faith in its self-creating powers. Out of it will come other possibilities such as asserting one's self as a rational or scholarly person, as in the case of Du Bois, or as an irrational seer, the very embodiment of unreason. These new projects of selfhood Fanon sees as dialectical possibilities that are open to the awakening black subject if he/she is "able to accomplish this descent into a real hell" (1967:10). In short, phenomenologically speaking, the zone of non-being is a valuable resource for the subject who is working his/her way out negrification and the double consciousness that it produces.

THE ETHICAL/PRACTICAL DIMENSIONS

Important as the above inner struggles against negrification are, they cannot by themselves overthrow the institutionalized power of white racism. As we've seen, this racism was for Fanon both onto- and socio-genic in nature. It was not the truth of negrification that defeated this struggling subject but the social power that came with its institutionaliza-tion. This sociological dimension had to be defeated through revolution-ary struggles of the type that Fanon described so powerfully in *The Wretched of the Earth*. Thus as in the case of Du Bois, Fanon's phenomenol-ogy is intricately linked to an ethical/practical project. This project has several distinguishing features such as its ethic of love or its commitment to national independence. For reasons of space, I will discuss only the ethic of love.

The ethical dimensions of Fanon's phenomenology have been given their most systematic treatment by Nelson Maldonado-Torres. The origi-nality of his treatment is the elucidating of the place of love in Fanon's ethics. Maldonado-Torres's key to locating the site of Fanonian love is a masterful "phenomenology of the cry" (2008) in Fanon's work. He shows that when examined in this way, the cry leads us to the loving responses of which Fanon's awakening subject is sometimes capable. These re-sponses echo very loudly the love that reassembles broken vases of which Walcott spoke.

For Maldonado-Torres, the cry is "a revelation of someone who has been forgotten or wronged" (2008: 111). It is the audible sigh that some-times follows a train of defeated attempts at self-affirmation. But as Mal-donado-Torres shows, the cry in Fanon is much more than this plea for self-preservation. It is also "a call for the Other" (2008: 114). It is this sociality in the cry of Fanon's awakening Africana subject that is the source of its moving ethical power. In other words, even though this subject will often find him/herself on the edge of non-being, it is still possible to rise above pure self-interest to cry for and reach out to others who are in similar or worse states of negrification. Thus it is no surprise that Fanon begins and ends *Black Skin, White Masks* with such strong affirmations of his belief in the possibilities of love. This in brief is Fanon's contribution to Africana phenomenology.

LEWIS GORDON AND AFRICANA PHENOMENOLOGY

If the first two chapters in an explicit Africana phenomenology were written by Du Bois and Fanon, then the third has been written by Lewis Gordon. His chapter makes several important contributions to this subfield of Africana philosophy that both engage and carry forward the work of Du Bois and Fanon. The way in which Gordon engages Fanon can be clearly seen in his *Fanon and the Crisis of European Man* and his engagements with Du Bois in his *Existentia Africana*. These engagements make it unmistakably clear that Gordon's occasion for self-reflection is also the racialization of Africana self-consciousness within the projective and exploitative structures of modern European capitalism. Here, for reasons of space, I will take up only two of the important contributions that Gordon has made to the subfield of Africana phenomenology. The first of these is the greater systematization that he has brought to this area of Africana thought. The second is his phenomenological analysis of "the state of being a Negro" in the postcolonial/postsegregation era. In other words, an era in which the institutional power of white projects of negrification have been significantly weakened as a result of the anticolonial and antiracist struggles of the 1960s. Let us begin with the first of these two important contributions.

Gordon makes clear very early the nature of his method of study. He refers to it as "descriptive ontology or what is sometimes called existential phenomenology" (1995a: 5). This is the methodology by which Gordon brackets the everyday world and enters on his own path to the practice of self-reflection. Gordon's path inward to the study of consciousness has been shaped by strong influences from Sartre and Husserl, as well as his own practice of creative writing. Gordon brings these three reflective streams together to forge a path to the study of consciousness that is original and distinct, and thus different from the paths used by Du Bois or Fanon. Gordon's distinctness stems from the stronger Husserlian influences on this area of his thought than is the case with Du Bois or Fanon. These influences account for the clear presence of reflections that are done within what Husserl called the phenomenological reduction, and the absence of the psychoanalytic strategies that are so strong in Fanon. Further distinguishing Gordon's self-reflective path is the fact that the influences of his poetics are not as strong as they are in the cases of Du Bois and Fanon. However, Gordon and Fanon share strong Sartrean influences on their strategies of self-reflection. In short, to understand how Gordon sees the world when puts on his phenomenological glasses, we need to understand these factors shaping the curve of their lenses.

Although Gordon and Fanon share strong Sartrean influences, they manifest themselves very differently in their reflective approaches to the study of Africana self-consciousness. Like Sartre, Gordon makes a sharper distinction between ego and consciousness than either Fanon or Du Bois. It is consciousness rather than the ego that is the primary focus of Gordon's analysis. This is an important difference with Fanon, who, as psychoanalyst, focused more on the ego. This accounts for the more philosophical as opposed to the psychological orientation of Gordon's work. It also accounts for why Gordon's contributions include the greater systematizing of the philosophical foundations of Africana phenomenology.

With his focus on consciousness, Gordon's definition of the human reality to be studied is different from Fanon's. Rather than motion toward the world, which would reflect the desires of the ego, as consciousness Gordon defines the core of human reality as freedom. As freedom, we are not determined by any law or necessity from within or without. We are free to choose our existence with nothing to legitimate or guarantee it other than our choice. Consequently, we are primarily responsible for who we are and what we will become.

However, according to Sartre and Gordon, phenomenological reflection reveals that the experiencing of ourselves as freedom produces disturbing feelings of anguish, of being nothing and hence an intense desire to be something definite. Thus we often evade this anguished freedom by fleeing into the facticity and determinateness of a closed ego. This ego could be structured around being a doctor, a lawyer, a philosopher or a parent. As any of these forms of ego-being, I now experience myself as something that is definite enough to negate the nothingness and anguish of my freedom. This "effort to hide from responsibility for ourselves as freedom" (1995a: 8) is what both Sartre and Gordon meant by bad faith. In bad faith, "I flee a displeasing truth for a pleasing falsehood. I must convince myself that a falsehood is in fact true" (1995a: 8). In short, to be in bad faith is to lie to ourselves and believe the lie.

As Fanon's ego produced a shadow, so too does Gordon's. However, although the projecting of these shadows is crucial to their accounts of "the state of being a Negro," it is important to note the significant differences in the origins of these shadows. Fanon's is psychological and engages the Freudian concept of an unconscious, while Gordon's is philosophical and has its roots in the dialectic between being and nothingness as its affects the formation human consciousness and freedom. It is the discursive use of the notion of bad faith to thematize this dialectic that enables Gordon to systematize the philosophical as opposed to the psychological foundations of Africana phenomenology.

In Gordon's case, it is the ontogenic tensions produced by the lie that separates the ego from its anguished shadow that produces the need for mechanisms of projective catharsis rather than the ego's need to repress its "lower emotions." But in both cases, self-reflection has produced portraits of the human subject as a site of agency that has to project a shadow while at the same time denying that it is doing so. And in both, this is directly linked to the production and persistence of what Gordon calls anti-black racism. This racism is for Gordon a bad faith attempt "to deny the blackness within" (anguished freedom) by projecting it onto the black skins of Africana peoples while asserting an ego that is structured around whiteness. This is the manner in which Gordon has more clearly systematized the links between phenomenological philosophy and the racialization of Africana self-consciousness.

In addition to thematizing and systematizing the dynamics of bad faith that remained implicit in Fanon, Gordon has also taken up the challenge of making more phenomenologically consistent the linking of ontogenic dynamics such as those of bad faith, with the sociogenic ones (e.g., institutions) that come together to produce oppressive social realities like anti-black racism. Consequently, like Alfred Schutz, Gordon needs a phenomenology of the social world in addition to that of individual self-consciousness. But the ethical/practical project of transformation to which Gordon's phenomenology is linked is not the one of rescuing rationality from its positivistic capture that Schutz shared with Husserl. Rather, with Du Bois and Fanon, Gordon's ethical/practical project is one of denegrification and racial equality. Consequently, he needs both a theory and a praxis that will allow him to link the strategic demands of dismantling racist social structures to the intentional activity of the transcendental domain as disclosed by phenomenology.

In effecting this synthesis, Gordon achieves greater phenomenological consistency than Du Bois or Fanon. The distinctness of Gordon's synthesis is that it grasps institutions in terms of bad faith rather than their historical materiality as established social structures. From the perspective of bad faith, Gordon sees institutions as social practices that limit freedom or encourage the evading of freedom. These limits are conceptualized by Gordon as a continuum of relations that range from choices to options. "Actional" choices that are institutionally recognized or supported are instances of the social affirmation of one's freedom. At the other end of the continuum are options. Options are "calcified" situations in which institutions are not only separated from the intentional streams of meaning out of which they arose but at the same time severely restrict the set of choices they make available to individuals (2006: 104). Thus it is in terms of options and choices that Gordon thematizes the problems of class and racial inequality. Three responses of individuals and groups to these differences in options and choices are of particular interest to Gordon. These are theodicean justifications by elites with actional choices, implosivity by groups who are without them, and revolution. The first two are for Gordon bad faith responses and are important for his intentional reading of institutions. Thus it is through the use of the notion of bad faith on both the ontogenic and sociogenic levels that Gordon is able to achieve a greater degree of phenomenological consistency.

As noted earlier, Gordon's second important contribution to Africana phenomenology is his analysis of the persistence of anti-black racism in the postcolonial/postsegregation era. In our examination of Fanon, we saw that negrification and anti-black racism, though having their roots in psycho-existential shadow of the white ego, derived a lot of their power and persistence from social processes of institutionalization. One of the primary marks of the postcolonial/postsegregation era has been the removal of many of the institutional supports that reinforced the stereotype of "the Negro." Indeed, it is possible to argue that in the present era, there remain three crucial areas of American society that continue to provide institutional support for anti-black racism: the practice of residential segregation, law enforcement, and the entertainment value of anti-black stereotype in mass media. This is a very different world from that of Fanon's or Du Bois's. Can anti-black racism persist within such a weakened institutional order? The significant contribution of Gordon's important book, *Bad Faith and Anti-Black Racism*, is its detailed answer to this question.

Gordon's answer is a definite yes. This answer in the affirmative is based primarily on the persistence of strong projective needs arising from the bad faith practices of white subjects that are still externalized onto black bodies. In other words, unless whites find new scapegoats or more good faith ways of facing the anguish of their freedom, they will continue to see Africana peoples through the eyes of that unacceptable anguish. This distorted seeing will persist in spite of the removal of its institutional props. This persistence means that Africana peoples are still being racialized and its accompanying processes of double consciousness still being reproduced. For Gordon the strongest indicator of this is the phenomenon of "black anti-blackness" which he analyzes as a manifestation of double consciousness. His analysis of black anti-blackness is a brilliant updating of C. L. R. James's classic summary statement of this peculiar phenomenon in *The Black Jacobins*: "'why do you ill-treat your mule in that?' asked a colonist of a carter. 'But when I do not work, I am beaten, when he does not work, I beat him—he is my Negro'" (1989: 15).

OTHER CONTRIBUTIONS

In addition to Du Bois, Fanon and Gordon, other important contributions to an Africana phenomenology have been made by Sylvia Wynter, Wilson Harris, René Ménil, Charles Long, Nelson Maldonado-Torres, James Bryant, and myself, which I can only mention briefly. My own contribution has been to open up the chapter on African existential thought before the start of colonization, slavery, negrification, and Europeanization

(2000a: 144–66). Bryant's contribution has been a careful phenomenological analysis of the transformation of pre-colonial African religious identities to Afro-Christian ones as a response to negrification. Long's contribution has been a phenomenology of the rituals and ceremonies of
African American religious life. As we've already seen, Maldonado-
Torres's contribution has been in the area of phenomenology and ethics.
Harris's contribution is a detailed exploration of the creative potential of
zone of non-being or what he calls "the void." René Ménil's contribution
has been a Hegelian inflected phenomenological account of the internalizing of the stereotype of "the Negro." Finally, Wynter's contribution has
been a historicizing and semioticizing of the transcendental domain that
can be usefully compared to the work of the German philosopher, Karl-
Otto Apel. Wynter introduces these changes through her important concepts of knowledge-constitutive goals and liminal categories. These contributions together with those of Du Bois, Fanon, and Gordon give us
fairly comprehensive picture of the phenomenological dimensions of
Africana thought.

PHILOSOPHICAL IMPLICATIONS OF
AFRICANA PHENOMENOLOGY

We began our analysis of Africana phenomenology with a clearing of the
cultural terrain needed to make this philosophy visible. In particular, this
clearing was directed at some of the exclusive claims that had been established between rationality and European phenomenology, as well as the
establishing of flexible variations in three crucial areas of phenomenological philosophy: the occasion for self-reflection, the path to self-reflection,
and the ethical/practical projects of phenomenologies. Now that we have
outlined Africana phenomenology in the space of this clearing it should
be evident that it is a discourse that has been conditioned by and draws
on a specific set of lived experiences and the cultural traditions of Africa
and Europe. In this sense, it is quite different from Western phenomenology.

What are we to make of the differences between these two philosophical discourses? Are they of a similar nature to the differences within each
of them? Are the rational and allegedly universal structures of Western
phenomenology such that they can incorporate Africana philosophy as a
particular case without significant philosophical remainders? From the
nature of the variations in cultural contexts, occasions for self-reflection,
paths to reflection and ethical/ practical projects, I think it should be clear
that neither of these phenomenologies could absorb the other as a case
without significant theoretical loss. The variations just referred to are not
quantitative but qualitative in nature. Thus in spite of important areas of
overlap and convergence, these qualitative differences have created sig-

nificant degrees of incommensurability between the creative and discursive codes of these two phenomenologies. The resulting divergences are such that they limit the universal claims of both, creating epistemic breaks that can only be engaged/resolved through conversation and comparative analysis.

From the philosophical standpoint, these incommensurate or inassimilable differences are primarily the result of metaphysical differences in the a priori foundations pre-supposed by the knowledge producing practices of these two phenomenologies. I am aware that Western philosophy is currently going through what Habermas and others have called a "post-metaphysical" phase. Does this mean that Africana philosophy is also going through a similar phase? I don't think so. The metaphysical foundations of Africana philosophy have never included the absolute claims for reason that have been at the center of the transcendental foundations of Western philosophy. In the Africana tradition, reason has always had to share the metaphysical stage with poetics and historical action. Indeed, in its post-metaphysical phase—a phase in which it is scaling down its claims for reason—Western philosophy may move closer to some of the fundamental metaphysical positions of Africana philosophy.

What is most striking about Habermas's post-metaphysical arguments is that, like Derrida's attempts to deconstruct Western metaphysics, they are profoundly metaphysical. Habermas uses the term *metaphysical* to designate the thinking of philosophical idealism from Plato through Plotinus to Kant, Fichte, Schelling and Hegel. On the other hand, he sees late medieval nominalism, modern empiricism, neo-pragmatism, and post-structuralism as anti-metaphysical philosophies (1992: 29). What I see both of these groups sharing is the necessity of going beyond "physics" the moment that they step out of specific exercises of knowledge production to assess the onto-epistemic significance of those exercises. Thus empiricists cannot on the basis of empirical practices rule out or establish their priority over intuitive or other non-empirical modes of knowing. To establish such as claim, the empiricist must move beyond his/her specific knowledge producing practice and by means of logic, rhetoric, future projections of knowledge accumulation, etc., make the argument for priority, or foundational status. It is these questions of discourse-constitutive priorities regarding explanatory factors (Spirit, matter, class, race), disciplines, methodologies, conceptions of the human being, and ethical/practical projects that constitute the ineliminable metaphysical elements in all discourses. They are shared by Habermas's metaphysical and anti-metaphysical groups of philosophers. These pre-theoretical or discourse-constitutive choices are inescapable, and their justification or non-justification takes us into the realm of metaphysics.

When we direct our focus at the discourse-constitutive foundations of Du Bois's thought, we can observe the presence of a familiar set of competing explanatory factors, disciplines, methodologies, conceptions of the human being as we find in Hegel or Husserl. What we do not find is a similar prioritizing or systematizing of these discourse-constitutive fundamentals in relation to reason or Spirit. Du Bois appears to enclose these fundamentals within a very different set of epistemic norms although he never really took the time to specify them. Consequently, there has been a lot of debate about this particular dimension of Du Bois's thought. Cornel West interprets this refusal to specify as a pragmatist evasion of epistemology (1989: 138–40). Robert Gooding Williams objects strongly to this reading of Du Bois's refusal (1991-92: 517–42).

Within this unspecified Du Boisian framework, reason and Spirit are two of the fundamentals rather than the supreme principle of prioritizing and systematizing. Earlier, we noted that Du Bois did not make as strong an onto-epistemic commitment to the paradigm of consciousness as either Hegel or Husserl. The same was true of his attitude toward the method of poetics as well as those of history and sociology. In his important essay, "Sociology Hesitant," Du Bois argues for the possibilities of doing sociology from the perspectives of both a free and an externally determined subject. At the same time he makes no arguments for continuity between the two positions or for a fixed, pre-theoretical hierarchical arrangement between them. One leaves this essay with the feeling that he is equally happy with both. I think that Du Bois's attitude to all of these discourse-constitutive fundamentals that he organizes and uses can be best compared to the attitude of a jazz musician to his/her improvisations. They are all real epistemic offerings, they possess creative potential, but they are partial and limited formations that could not only be done differently, but also need to be checked and complemented. Thus most, if not all, of Du Bois pre-theoretical orderings of selected fundamentals are provisional, variable, in need of complements, and therefore change significantly in his different texts. This is the metaphysical position that we confront in Du Bois's works. Thus, there appears to be an improvisational aesthetic norm guiding the metaphysical orderings that make Du Boisian knowledge production possible.

In the case of Fanon, we can observe a similarly relaxed and improvisational attitude toward the problems of prioritizing and systematizing discourse-constitutive fundamentals. This attitude is evident in his often-quoted remark: "I leave methods to the botanists and the mathematicians" (1967: 12). Without clear specification, Fanon employs poetics, existential philosophy and psychoanalysis to define his path to consciousness. In this strategy, we saw that Fanon embraced the concrete intuitive method of existential philosophy as well as the more abstract method of a general interpretation used by psychoanalysis. Further, we saw that this multi-layered ontogenic discourse was implicitly linked to a sociogenic base.

Methodologically speaking, this sociogenic base comes more fully into view in *The Wretched of the Earth*, where the focus of Fanon's phenomenological analyses is not so much individual as it is national consciousness. Thematized in primarily Marxist terms, the relationships between the sociogenic and the phenomenological factors constituting the national consciousness of the colonized in revolt are configured differently. These and other breaks in the composition and ordering of discourse-constitutive fundamentals between this work and *Black Skin, White Masks*, remind us of similar breaks between major works by Du Bois. The great metaphysical secret of *The Wretched of the Earth* is its almost seamless synthesis of existential phenomenology, transcendental phenomenology, psychoanalysis, Afro-Caribbean poetics, Marxist political economy, and Africana colonial history. How these different discourses were brought together, whence the "tidalectical" flows between them, or the occasions for shifting from one to the other? Of these creative and synthetic strategies Fanon does not really speak. He leaves us completely on our own and at the mercy of our own creative and synthetic capabilities.

Although not quite as improvisational as Du Bois, none of these priorities in factors of explanation, methods, and disciplines were made explicit, or the creative strategies by which they were synthesized carefully outlined. Thus the internal structure of Fanon's psychosocial poetics remains as much a mystery as Du Bois's socio-historical poetics. However, in spite of these outward signs of disorder, Fanon's discourses display remarkable coherence and unmatched explanatory power. To account for this, I suggest a set of improvisational metaphysical principles that are quite similar to those of Du Bois.

In the case of Gordon, where we find the greatest concern with the pre-theoretical systematization of discourse-constitutive fundamentals, the presence of this improvisational metaphysics is clearly evident. Indeed, in Gordon's case the connection to jazz is direct as it appears in his work and through the fact that he is a jazz drummer. As we've seen, Gordon has established a clear priority of consciousness over the ego, the intentional over the extensional, and the free over the externally determined subject. However, at the same time, there is no absolute commitment to the paradigm of consciousness that matches Husserl's or even the early Sartre. Rather, what we find is a similar improvisational attitude toward this particular piece of discursive systematization. The difference between Gordon and Du Bois or Fanon is not to be found in their attitudes toward specific systematic orderings, but in the fact that Du Bois and Fanon had more of these improvised orderings going at the same time. Gordon has fewer, has worked out the philosophical ones more systematically, but his attitude toward them is not final but improvisational. This distinct metaphysical position that we can observe in Gordon, Fanon and Du Bois was not evident in either the African or Afro-Christian phases of Africana philosophy. Rather, it emerged in the period that elsewhere I have called poeticist/historicist. This double designation was a way of representing the compound and synthetic nature of this phase of Africana thought. However, I did not really develop the provisional and improvisational nature of the creative codes that guided the formation of these compound syntheses.

If indeed this still to be thematized set of improvisational codes are the keys to the metaphysical foundations of this specific phase of Africana phenomenology, then it should be clear why it cannot be incorporated into Western phenomenology without significant philosophical loss. When more fully thematized, it is very likely to be an original metaphysics that reflects the experiences of Africana peoples and the distinct knowledge producing practices that were developed under the world shattering conditions of racialization and colonization. Its spirit is very different from that of Euro-American pragmatism or of mainstream of European philosophy. If I had to give this metaphysics a more conventional name it would be creative realism, as what it assumes to be ultimately real is the creative act in its spontaneous movements rather that any of its specific creations. This is the creative code, the compositional principle of Africana metaphysics that makes it impossible for its phenomenology to be absorbed by the rationalism of Western phenomenology. Within the context of this improvisational metaphysics, the process of de-centering reason that Western metaphysics is presently going through could hardly be viewed as a post-metaphysical event. Rather, it would very likely be seen as just one of many contrapuntal movements or complementary reversals that must take place among discursive formations. Such movements must take place as the capacity to disclose the whole truth is not given to any single discursive formation.

CONCLUSION

In the foregoing analyses, I have emphasized the differences between Africana and Western phenomenologies. These differences were both thematic, such as the issue of racialization, and metaphysical as indicated by the different rules guiding the prioritizing and systematizing of discourse-constitutive fundamentals. However, the broader comparative framework employed gave some indication of a number of areas of similarity.

The question that now arises from this clearer outlining of Africana phenomenology is the following: in what from the Africana perspective is a post-imperial as opposed to a post-metaphysical age, how are these two phenomenologies to relate to each other? Clearly the next phases in these phenomenologies are not going to be identical. The cultural and racial differences will in all probability continue to be important sources of difference. What will the post-"negro" phase of Africana phenomenology be like? What will it bring to the philosophical table in the place of double consciousness, second sight, white masks and an improvisational metaphysics? What will follow the "post-metaphysical" phase of Western phenomenology? What will it bring to the philosophical table in the place of its earlier claims for a universal reason? Is there a systematic relation between the post-imperial and the "post-metaphysical" phases of these two phenomenologies?

These important questions can be adequately answered only by developing new and more innovative modes of comparative philosophical analysis that do not attempt to subsume culturally distinct philosophies under the categories of another. Rather, these new modes of comparative analysis should seek to create bridges, partial points or areas of complementary convergence, meta-philosophical discourses and communicative groups between these culturally distinct philosophies. The need for such modes of comparative analysis is one of the important consequences that follow from this clearer recognition of Africana phenomenology.

NOTE

* First published as "Africana Phenomenology: Its Philosophical Implications," *C. L. R. James Journal* 11, no. 1: 79–112.

THREE

Between Naipaul and Aurobindo

Where Is Indo-Caribbean Philosophy?

In spite of Indo-Caribbeans being an integral part of Caribbean society for more than one hundred and fifty years, the external image of the region has remained primarily Euro- and Afro-Caribbean. This comparative invisibility of Indo-Caribbeans is also reflected in the intellectual traditions of the region and particularly in Caribbean philosophy, which has long been dominated by its European heritage. The Hindu or Islamic component of Caribbean philosophy that one would expect has been noticeably absent. Like Afro-Caribbean philosophy, Indo-Caribbean philosophy remains a discourse that has long been overlooked, negated and even abandoned. The degree to this neglect becomes clear when Indo-Caribbean philosophy is compared to Indo-Caribbean literature, history, music or dance. These are well-recognized discursive and artistic practices occupying their own distinctive spaces as the recent awarding of the Nobel Prize to V. S. Naipaul makes clear. In contrast to this spatial independence, Indo-Caribbean philosophy has been restricted to occasional appearances at crucial points or phases in the works of these disciplines and art forms. Thus Indo-Caribbean philosophy has shared a remarkably similar case of discursive invisibility with its Afro-Caribbean counterpart. This similarity in degree of invisibility is even more arresting when we consider the age of the Indian philosophical heritage, its many schools of thought and the classic texts that they have produced.

How are we to explain this neglect of both Indo- and Afro-Caribbean philosophies, along with their decline and absence from the Caribbean intellectual tradition? In *Caliban's Reason*, I focused on the excavating of the buried Afro-Caribbean heritage. In the course of this dicing, I repeatedly encountered many "artifacts" from the Indo-Caribbean heritage.

Hence my many calls for a more substantive dialogue between these two philosophical traditions.

In this paper, I want to open up this exchange by examining the nature of the Indian philosophical heritage and its relationships with both Indo- and Afro-Caribbean philosophy. I begin with the processes of colonial ethnogenesis that provide the broad sociological context for the invisibility and neglect of Indo-Caribbean philosophy, and the Eurocentric accounts of Indian philosophy that have helped to sustain this neglect. This imperial view is here examined in detail from the works of V. S. Naipaul. It is then contrasted with a more open and dynamic view of Indian philosophy as found in the works of Sri Aurobindo, India's greatest twentieth-century philosopher. In particular, I will contrast Aurobindo's innovative supramental phenomenology with Naipaul's characterization of the whole tradition as quietist. From this comparison, I suggest that we take the more dynamic view as the basis for philosophical dialogues between India and the Caribbean, as well as for the dialogues between Indo- and Afro-Caribbean philosophy.

PHILOSOPHY AND INDO-CARIBBEAN ETHNOGENESIS

To grasp clearly the decline and eclipse of Indo-Caribbean philosophy these trends must be sociologically situated within the larger processes of cultural contraction, fetishization and racialization through which European colonial states produced ethnic groups out of national and other autonomous cultural formations of peoples they either conquered or imported into the Caribbean region. These ethnogenic processes have been responsible for the culturally plural nature of Caribbean societies, which has been carefully studied by scholars such as M. G. Smith, Lloyd Braithwaite and Rex Nettleford. The latter have shown that prior to the period of Indo-Caribbean indenture, this cultural/ethnic pluralism was institutionalized around a Black African/White European binary with a small mulatto stratum between the dominant European and the subordinate African strata. As Euro-Caribbeans, mulattoes and Afro-Caribbeans became more culturally distinct from their parent European and African heritages, this whole system was often referred to as the "creole" order of Caribbean society.

In addition to important military, political and economic factors, European hegemony over this creole order rested upon extensive changes in the distribution of both institutional space and normative power between the specific discourses of the European and African cultural systems. For example, this hegemonic position required the substituting of European languages, religions and schools for African ones. This was "the battle for space" that Rex Nettleford has argued is so important for understanding colonial cultural formations (1993: 80).

As African philosophy was so closely tied to African religions, the former went into eclipse as the latter lost their battles for space with European Christianity. This was the colonial discursive order that systematically eliminated African rationality and philosophy. It would also be the crucible in which the Indian cultural heritage would be de-philosophized as an integral part of the experience of Indo-Caribbean ethnogenesis.

To grasp clearly the similarities in these two cases of philosophical disappearance, we need to follow a little more closely the Indian passage through this Caribbean race/ethnic ritual that transforms autonomous cultures into ethnic groups. I call this passage an ethnic ritual because it can be theorized as a process of liminalization in which it is "other" or anti-structure to the white supremacist order; one is stereotypically biologized, raced, dehumanized and put through a long period of social and cultural death. During this liminal period, it is only as biological being, and particularly as exploited laborers that members of the ethnicity-in-the-making are recognized. As the culturally dead, how could this ghostly group make claims tor a seat at the philosophical table? Certainly not before it had accepted the cultural surgery deemed necessary by the colonial state as a condition for socio-cultural rebirth as an ethnic group.

The period of Indian indenture that followed the end of African slavery brought approximately half a million men and women from India to Trinidad and Tobago, Guyana, Surinam, Jamaica, Guadeloupe, and Martinique, The majority of these indentured laborers went to Trinidad, Guyana, and Surinam, with smaller numbers going Jamaica, Guadeloupe and Martinique. In the first three territories, Indo-Caribbeans now constitute major ethnic groups, while in the latter three they constitute minor ones. Thus we can expect notable differences in the formative experiences of these Indo-Caribbean ethnic communities.

As post-slavery plantation workers, Indo-Caribbeans occupied the lowest tiers of the agricultural sector of Caribbean economies and were spatially confined to the rural areas of these societies. Initially, this segmentation kept them outside of the already established creole hierarchy. However, as increasing numbers completed the terms of their indenture and sought entry into new areas of Caribbean societies, they had to confront this white-mulatto-black hierarchy and its ethnogenic rituals of entry.

Like African slavery, Indian indenture profoundly racialized the identity of the Indo-Caribbean population. Their hair, skin and other biological features earned them the color brown from the white supremacists. This racial status was not as solidly fixed in stone as that of the Africans. However, their biological features were associated with specific capabilities and incapabilities. Europeans saw them as mild mannered, heathen, submissive, thrifty, miserly, hard working, and, of course, sources of cheap labor. These features together with their "brownnesss" produced the white supremacist stereotype of "the coolie." This coolietizing of Indo-Caribbean identity in the Euro-Caribbean mind established the bases for the processes of dehumanization and social death that start the movements through the ethnic ritual. Like the niggerization of Afro-Caribbean identities, coolietization was a process that biologized Indo-Caribbean identities and thus decultured them. It displaced their spiritual-religious self-understandings and replaced them with images of devalued plantation workers.

As in the case of Africans, Indians confronted colonial societies that understood themselves as white, Christian, and English, French, or Dutch speaking. Thus as the new immigrants attempted to move into new agricultural or urban areas of Caribbean societies, their "brown" skin, Hindu and Islamic religions as well as their Indo-Caribbean Creole, Gujarati, Bhojpouri and Hindi languages all encountered the censors and resistances of the ethnic ritual. These were all objectionable features of the coolie image that would require cultural surgery with the racist knife of the ethnogenic ritual. Coolies had to be creolized or molded into Europeanized Indo-Caribbeans if they were to gain access to the social mainstream.

Thus creolization came to mean speaking English, French, Dutch or Afro-Caribbean Creole, becoming Christian, attending colonial schools, adopting white supremacist stereotypes of other ethnic groups, and accepting the limited institutional space assigned to the fragments of Hindu and Islamic culture that survived the ritual surgery. This spatial compromise is the key signal that Hinduism or Islamicism would not as cultures be coterminous with the constitutional and territorial spaces of Caribbean society. Rather, they would now only valorize those sections of Caribbean societies assigned to them. This was the battle for cultural space that transformed Indians into Indo-Caribbeans.

As in the case of Africans, the fate of Indian philosophy in this ritual process was tied to that of Indian religion. The devaluations and exclusions experienced by the latter resulted in twice the obscurity for the former. Unlike the nigger, it was not that the coolie was seen by white supremacists as not having a philosophy. Rather, it was that this philosophy had been surpassed by that of the West, and hence had become a major hindrance to Indian and Indo-Caribbean acceptance in Western and Caribbean creolized societies. Hence the heavy demands on Indians and Indo-Caribbeans to abandon this philosophical heritage and go Western.

PHILOSOPHY AND THE INDO-CARIBBEAN
INTELLECTUAL TRADITION

The intellectual impact of this process of ethnogenesis can be seen not only in the calls to abandon Indian philosophy but also in the broader discontinuities that separate the Indian and Indo-Caribbean intellectual traditions. The latter has been constituted around Indo-Caribbean resistance to politico-economic exploitation, racist ethnicization and cultural colonization. Thus it shares anticolonial, Prospero/Caliban features with both the Indian and Afro-Caribbean heritages. However, these oppositional, anticolonial discourses constitute only a small part of the Indian heritage. As we will see, the latter has been able to mobilize the resources of a classical pre-colonial heritage to a degree that Indo- and Afro-Caribbeans have not been able to match.

Like these anticolonial intellectual traditions, the Indo-Caribbean heritage has been shaped by strong desires to regain independence, reconstruct the past, deracialize (de-coolietize) identities, recover selfhood, and overcome poverty. Thus it is not surprising that the Indo-Caribbean tradition, like the Afro-Caribbean heritage, also has strong historicist, poeticist, racial and economic traditions of writing. Indeed, these traditions of writing cannot be separated from their Afro-Caribbean counterparts, as they shared the institutional settings in which they were and are still being nurtured. Thus it is probably not accidental that both India and the Caribbean have won Nobel prizes for literature and economics. These two areas of scholarly practice along with racial and historical writing were areas of both the Indo- and Afro-Caribbean intellectual traditions that rose to prominence in the late and postcolonial periods. In the foundational assumptions and broader visions that informed these two traditions of writing, we can locate the central themes and positions of Afro- and Indo-Caribbean philosophy.

Because of the hegemonic goal of colonial ethnogenesis, it produced in the colonized very ambivalent feelings toward the ethnicized versions of their culture. On the one hand, it produced strong tendencies to reject this shattered and delimited heritage out of shame. On the other, it produced equally strong tendencies toward rigid attachments to the broken fragments that survived the ethnic ritual. As Fanon recognized in the case of Afro-Caribbeans, these attachments produced a freezing of the culture at a particular moment in time that made innovation, creativity, and further growth difficult. Thus in addition to the losses and feelings of shame produced by the ritual surgery, the Indo-Caribbean intellectual tradition has also been marked by notable rigidities and conservative attitudes toward the Indian elements that have persisted. This ambivalence is particularly clear in the case of Indo-Caribbean attitudes toward Indian philosophy.

The contradictory consequences of this ambivalence emerge very clearly in the work of V. S. Naipaul. In his first book on India, he described the subcontinent as "the background of my childhood . . . a country out in the void beyond the dot Trinidad . . . It was a country suspended in time" (1964: 29). Because these images were so remote and featureless, Naipaul referred to India as "an area of darkness." The surviving Indian rituals that helped to produce Naipaul's sense of being Indo-Trinidadian were fragmentary and disintegrated. He tells us that "more than in people, India lay about us in things" (1964: 31). It was there in the food, in string beds, straw mats, brass vessels, wooden printing blocks, books, drums, pictures of deities, unexplained prayers and rituals, fragments of Hindi, and vague caste influences. In spite of Naipaul's distaste for most of these fragments, his three books on India suggest that he cannot let go of many of them or of India. As we will see, this ambivalence very profoundly influenced his attitude toward Indian philosophy.

In Martinique and Guadeloupe, Moutoussamy describes a similar situation in which Indo-Caribbeans have been struggling to preserve fragments of a tradition "without the benefit of any original input" (1989: 31). This has resulted in a "fossilized Hinduism" (1989: 31) that is jealously guarded in spite of being increasingly influenced by the characteristics of these French Caribbean societies. However, the political dynamics of guarding these post-surgery heritages are quite different in the cases of Trinidad, Guyana and Surinam.

In the latter territories, the preserving of these ethnicized heritages has become the primary responsibility of political parties that compete with Afro-Caribbean parties. The latter are also ideologically mobilized around similar race/ethnic concerns. The resulting tendencies to close ideological and political ranks around these race/ethnic identities and interests have produced a lot of racial tensions and have given rise to distinct traditions of black and brown racial writing. Consequently, although the racial discourses of Afro-Caribbeans and Indo-Caribbeans share critiques of white supremacy, they have also clashed in their efforts to explain each other's racist practices. This attempt to theorize the racism of both Euro- and Afro-Caribbeans has been one very important intellectual response of Indo-Caribbeans to their ritualized prescriptions for entering the creole order of Caribbean societies. As such a response, it has been a very important site for the production of Indo-Caribbean philosophy.

Good examples of this distinctly Indo-Caribbean discourse on race can be found in the works of Ralph Premdas, Percy Hintzen, John La-Guerre, Patricia Mohammed, Ron Ramdin, Basdeo Panday and others. Philosophically speaking, this tradition of writing is part of a larger Caribbean tradition of racial historicism that also includes contributions from Afro- and Euro-Caribbeans. This is a tradition of writing that not only emphasizes the constitutive role of race and ethnicity in the shaping of the Caribbean past but also their political significance for the present and future. This is an important philosophical position of the Indo-Caribbean intellectual tradition.

Closely related to this Indo-Caribbean school of racial historicism is a tradition of Marxist historicism that places greater emphasis on the role of class domination in explaining the past, present and future of Indo-Caribbeans. As in the case of Afro-Caribbean Marxism, Indo-Caribbean Marxism has moved in three distinct directions: (1) the democratic socialism of both Krishna Deonarine (who changed his name to Adrian Rienzi) and later on Rudranath Capildeo in Trinidad; (2) the more orthodox Marxism of Cheddi Jagan and his People's Progressive Party in Guyana; and (3) the popular insurrectionary Marxism of Rupert Roopnaraine and others of the Working People's Alliance also in Guyana. Thus, within Jagan's class historicism, Indo-Caribbeans are seen primarily in terms of their resistance to exploitation as sugar workers, secondarily in terms of their racialization, and third in the terms of their cultural othering. This whole complex of domination and resistance is of course set within the larger framework of Western imperialism (1975). This standpoint of class historicism is another important philosophical position of the Indo-Caribbean intellectual tradition.

However, primarily because of the influence of Naipaul, the most widely known philosophical position informing the intellectual responses of Indo-Caribbeans to their indenture and ethnogenesis has been that of poeticism. Like Afro-Caribbean poeticism, Indo-Caribbean poeticism is a philosophy of the creative imagination. It affirms the enduring power of the creative acts of this imagination in spite of the tragedy, loss and oppression of indenture and ethnogenesis. This distinct power of creative representation is the unquestioned foundation of Indo-Caribbean poeticism. This philosophy of the creative imagination has been given it most articulate expression by Wilson Harris, a writer whose works are major bridges between the traditions of Afro- and Indo-Caribbean pietism. It can also be seen in the works of the novelists, poets and essayists who make up the tradition of Indo-Caribbean poeticism. As in the case of Indo-Caribbean historicism, this poeticist school cannot be separated from its Afro-Caribbean counterpart. They emerged under similar conditions and strongly influenced each other. Thus in *Finding the Center*, Naipaul shares with us the importance of the support of Andrew Salkey and Gordon Woodford in the early stages of his career.

Samuel Selvon and Harold Ladoo are among the earlier and more distinguished representatives of Indo-Caribbean poeticism, as are Ernest Moutousammy, Neil Bissoondath, Ismith Khan, Shiva Naipaul, Kenneth Ramchand, Sasenarine Persaud, David Dabydeen, and of course V. S. Naipaul. In the past two decades, this compliment of male writers has been joined by a growing number of female ones. These include Ramabai Espinet, Jan Shinebourne, Michelle Mohabeer, Kamala Kempadoo, Mahadai Das, Lakshmi Persaud and Rosanne Kanhai. Together, this latter group has extended the philosophical base of the Indo-Caribbean intellectual tradition by giving it a feminist dimension (Henry 2002–2003b, 2007d; Mehta 2000).

In short, these are the three primary sites to which we can go for the traces, footprints and other fleeting appearances that Indo-Caribbean philosophy has made within its own or the larger regional intellectual tradition. That is, we can find Indo-Caribbean philosophy in the discursive spaces in which these traditions of poeticist and historicist writing are practiced, as well as those in which the Indian philosophical heritage is interrogated. For the remainder of this paper, it is the last of these three spaces, the highly contested terrain of the Indian philosophical heritage that we shall be exploring.

NAIPAUL, INDIAN AND INDO-CARIBBEAN PHILOSOPHY

European colonization of India and Indian indenture in the Caribbean produced major problems of evaluation, recognition and hence visibility for Indian philosophy. Unlike the case of Africa, these experiences did not produce European declarations of the non-existence of Indian philosophy, but narrow typifications and radical devaluations that produced consistent calls for the abandoning or surpassing of the entire heritage. For Hegel, the Indian philosophical tradition was a dreaming idealism, an idealism that had not yet awakened to the sunlight, and precision of conceptual thinking. It was an idealism because it recognized "the interest of spirit." However, in this recognition we find only "the character of spirit in a state of Dream" (1956). For Arthur Schopenhauer, Max Weber and Albert Schweitzer, Indian philosophy was primarily a world- and life-rejecting discourse. Schopenhauer embraced these aspects of Indian thought in support of his pessimism of the will, but also found great solace in the Upanishads. For both Weber and Schweitzer these attitudes of world negation were seen as major obstacles to India's modernity and hence would have to be abandoned. Schweitzer suggested that "for Indian thought the task is to give up world and life negation and adjust itself to world and life affirmation" as the West has done (1957: 252). This suggestion prompted the well-known response of Sarvepalli Radhakrishnan regarding the yoga work and action as discussed in the Bhagavad Gita, and the strong world-rejecting tendencies of Christianity (1969: 64–80). However, such responses have been to little or no avail. Consequently, India has been stuck with the charge of an exhausted or outmoded philosophical tradition that it must jettison.

Naipaul's approach to Indian philosophy follows closely this well-established Western pattern. As a writer, Naipaul sees India as a part of the East and very much within the framework of that Western discourse that Edward Said has labeled Orientalism (1979). At the core of Indian philosophy, Naipaul sees a particular set of attitudes toward existence that he calls quietism. Although he acknowledges his own "metaphysical incapacity," Naipaul is interested in this philosophy because he thinks it is at root of the problems that Indians and Indo-Caribbeans have experienced in adjusting to the modern world: Naipaul also tells us that he "was born an unbeliever" and took no pleasure in religious ceremonies. Thus he concluded that "one whole side of India was closed to me" (1946: 44). Yet as a brilliant artist who creates through the lens of despair, it is this metaphysical side of India that Naipaul will explore.

The primary problem with Indian quietism for Naipaul is that it legitimates "the perfection of non-doing" (1979: 22). In other words, it justifies the attitude that individuals or groups do not have to take action to preserve or improve their lives and societies. Human self-assertion or intervention through action is either unnecessary or will only make matters worse. The creative action of the cosmos is all that is really necessary. The scandalous crime of Indian quietism is that it counsels the acceptance of past defeats and continues to philosophically prepare Indians for the acceptance of future defeats, rather than for successful action. For Naipaul, this is an absurd attitude toward existence that masks an underlying despair. It encourages and legitimates arbitrary or absurd choices of self by individuals as normal ways of dealing with despair. Like Weber, Naipaul links this quietism to the doctrines of karma and rebirth. Together they constitute a system of moral regulation and cosmic balancing that extends across the divide between life and death, and thus encompasses many lives. In such a system, where one's excesses in a past life are balanced in a future one, it is easy for an individual to resign him or herself to this play karmic forces.

In addition to seeing these quietistic attitudes in the Indian masses, Naipaul focuses quite intensely on the novels of the Indian writer R. K. Narayan and on Mahatma Gandhi's autobiography as further evidence of this quietism. In Narayan's 1949 novel, *Mr. Sampath*, Naipaul sees a near perfect comic fictionalization of this "almost hermetic philosophical system" of Hindu quietism (1979: 27). The main character, Srinivas, is the perfect embodiment of the attitude that "India will go on" without any effort on his part. It is an absurd choice of self which, when realized over time, makes his agency in the world progressively less necessary. Thus Srinivas's quietistic philosophy can be described as one of non-action or the irrelevance of willed ego-centered action, and the all-encompassing relevance and power of the higher karmic forces.

Naipaul is fascinated but puzzled by the way in which Narayan, a writer he admires, inhabits this world and is able to make such wonderful art out of it. Thus, it is not until *The Vendor of the Streets*, in which Narayan's "fictional world cracked open . . . and its Hindu equilibrium . . . collapses into something like despair," that Naipaul feels that he has really understood Narayan (1979: 38). In other words, it is only when Narayan shares or appears to share Naipaul's disbelief in Hindu quietism that there is a feeling of adequate understanding.

This deep skepticism about the modern value of the Indian philosophical heritage informs Naipaul's reading of Gandhi's autobiography. Naipaul is unable to get over just how inwardly oriented is Gandhi's personality. On the latter's account of his first voyage to England, Naipaul notes: "not a word of anything seen or heard did not directly affect the physical or mental well-being of the writer. The inward concentration is fierce, the self-absorption complete" (1979: 98). Naipaul continues even more emphatically: "no London building is described, no street, no room, no crowd, no public conveyance" (1979: 98).

In Naipaul's view, this kind of self-absorption brings with it "a kind of blindness." It is unable to see the everyday world objectively, people and things "are never described and never become individuals" (1979: 101). This "need to constantly explore and fortify the self gets in the way" (1979: 20). Naipaul links both this need and the Indian ability to de-center the self in meditation to the "underdeveloped nature of the Indian ego" (1979: 102). As such, the latter has a "childlike perception of reality" and a relatively tenuous grasp of the external world (1979: 103). That is, relative to the non-absurd, Western-style, mature personality that is individualistic and assertive (1979: 104). Finally, Naipaul tells us that the insights that Gandhi produced from his self-explorations "were not of universal application." Rather, they "only answered his own needs as a Hindu" (1979: 100).

These are strong claims that take us to the core of Naipaul's evaluations of Indian philosophy. I am particularly struck by the fact that Naipaul did not take up the works of writers with views different from Narayan's. Rabindranath Tagore, India's 1913 Nobel Laureate in literature, comes immediately to mind. Like Aurobindo, Tagore represents the active side of Brahmanic spiritualism. Tagore's springtime poetics fills his works with those amazing images of active, abundant energy and of creative overflowing that are gifts from the experience of union with Brahman. His poetics are anything but quietistic. It is also surprising that Naipaul did not address the well-known counter-claims of Indian philosophy regarding the blindness produced by his strong attachments to things, buildings, streets, rooms and the narrative empiricism by which he legitimates those attachments. These counter-claims can be seen in the already mentioned response of Radhakrishnan to Schweitzer and in Aurobindo's *The Foundations of Indian Culture*. I will not take these up in greater detail here, but let Aurobindo respond later. For now, this is Naipaul's account of the defective philosophical vision of India that led to his rejection of "the recurring crooked comedy of its holy men" (1979: 104).

This philosophical heritage of an absurd, comic quietism that masks an inability to be in the world informs just as strongly Naipaul's portrayals of the Indo-Caribbean situation. These themes emerge very clearly from his classic novel, *A House for Mr. Biswas*. Biswas's existence is a series of arbitrary and absurd choices through which he attempts to establish himself in the everyday world. As a character, Biswas's most striking feature is his lack of all capacity for self-determination, and hence mastery over his life. His repeated attempts at self-definition and at projects for realizing his being in the world all end in failure. This inability to be points to the existential crisis in which he is caught. Whether or not this crisis stems from the difficulties of a coolie trying to enter the creole world of Trinidadian society it is not possible to say. But whatever is its cause, Biswas turns to texts of both Indian and Roman quietism to mask his inabilities. Thus after his failure as a shopkeeper, "he turns to religion and philosophy. He reads the Hindus and the Marcus Aurelius and Epictetus which Mrs. Wier had given him" (1980: 182). However, Biswas's despair over his crisis is always breaking through these quietistic masks, which he must then quickly repair. As a result, Biswas too is constantly self-absorbed.

The absurd nature of the choices by which Biswas defines himself is made clear by the fact that they are consistently initiated by others. His boyhood friend Alec is someone Biswas doesn't really know. It is a friendship that happens to him. One of the earliest of Biswas's many socio-economic identities was that of the reader of a syndicated column to his uncle-in-law. He falls into this role through the initiative of his aunt Tara. His next major attempt at self-definition also stems from the initiative of this aunt, on whom Biswas remains very dependent. She wanted him to become a pundit, and so he trained for eight months to become one. This is the manner in which the remainder of Biswas's life proceeds. He falls into his marriage into the Tulsi family and into the positions of sign painter, shopkeeper, estate sub-overseer, journalist and community welfare officer. In all of this Biswas reminds us of Narayan's character Srinivas. The only signs of genuine initiative are Biswas's attempts to build a house of his own away from the Tulsi mansion. Symbolic of his attempts to establish his selfhood, they all end in failure.

Together, these episodes are part of a very subtle, complex and masterful exercise in character development. Biswas has got to be one of the most carefully detailed portrayals of a man in the all-consuming grip of an existential crisis. He is easily the Roquentin (anti-hero of Sartre's *Nausea*) of Indo-Caribbean existentialism. As such he reveals the bad faith of both Indian and Indo-Caribbean quietism. Biswas stands in sharp contrast to another well-known character of Indo-Caribbean literature, Samuel Selvon's Tiger. Biswas has none of the agency, the ingenuity and rebelliousness of Tiger. In Tiger, we see the activism of Caliban striking out, speaking back, and coming to terms with the ethnic/creole reality of

Trinidad. He is not hindered in these endeavors by a philosophic quietism (2000). Consequently, Selvon does not share Naipaul's vision of the
Indian or the Indo-Caribbean philosophic heritage.

Even when Indians and Indo-Caribbeans make "the right" move and
adopt Western attitudes and technologies, the old philosophical heritage
still gets in the way. Rather than a creative synthesis with or a complete
mastery over the Western mode, the result is often unimaginative mimic-
ry. These are themes that Naipaul takes up in both *The Mimic Men* and
India: A Wounded Civilization. These instances of hybridity do not result in
the creative in-betweenness of Homi Bhabha, but in paralyzing clashes
between the two cultural traditions that inhibit creativity and modern
self-assertion. Hence for Naipaul "the only hope lies in the further swift
decay" of this ancient philosophical heritage (1979: 28).

INDIAN PHILOSOPHY: ITS DEVELOPMENTAL TRAJECTORY

In spite of Naipaul's misgivings about Indian self-absorption, Indian philosophers have quite confidently made the self a very privileged site of
inquiry. Unlike physical objects, it is intuitively open to self-reflective
analysis. That is, vital knowledge of it can be gained through such practices as meditative or phenomenological self-reflection. Within this self-
reflective framework, the distinctive concern of Indian philosophers has
been the conditions under which the human self can achieve a union with
ultimate reality or Brahman and so ground its life in the spiritual as
opposed to the everyday world. In other words, it is a distinctive concern
that views the self not from the perspective of its possibilities for a technocratic, rational, aesthetic or moral life but for a full-blown spiritual one
right here on earth.

An interest in the possibility for a spiritual life is not peculiar to India.
It is also basic to Christian and other religious-philosophical heritages.
What is unique about the Indian religious-philosophical heritage is the
degree to which it has been prepared to displace or devalue the actually
existing human world in order to achieve union with the spiritual world,
and from that union create a more spiritualized everyday world. Thus
from very early in its formation, this tension between the everyday and
spiritual worlds emerged as one of the central binaries of Indian philosophical thought. In the opening chapters of his major work, *The Life
Divine*, Aurobindo refers to this central concern as "the two negations."
One he labels the "materialist denial" and the other the "refusal of the
Ascetic" (1987: 17).

However these evaluations and displacements of the everyday world
have not been as static as Naipaul's quietistic portrayal suggests. Beginning with a tendency to see the everyday world as insignificant in relation to these experiences of union with Brahman, the developmental tra-

jectory of Indian philosophy has been one of progressive change toward a more balanced position in these evaluations without abandoning or decreasing the absolute priority given to experiences of union. No finer barometer of these changing relations in the twentieth century can be found than the work of Aurobindo. His supramental phenomenology marked a radical break with the Shankaran formulation of Indian philosophy upon which Naipaul's quietistic portrait is based. We will examine Aurobindo's philosophy after a quick survey of some of the earlier phases and formulations of this great philosophical heritage.

The first great schools of Indian philosophy emerged out of or in opposition to the beliefs and practices of Brahmanic spiritualism. The roots of this religious philosophy are found in the hymns of the Rig Veda, some of which have been dated as early as 2000 BCE. In these hymns that accompanied ritual sacrifices to deities such as Indra and Agni, we find descriptions of the mystical experiences of Rishis or religious leaders that will become the foundation of Brahmanic spiritualism. These are descriptions of experiences in which the everyday world is displaced and contact made with the vast, all encompassing, creative, spiritual world of Brahman that was inaccessible while the everyday world was in operation. The discovery of this spiritual world became the great secret and treasure of Brahmanic spiritualism. Dwelling on this plane and getting to know it became much more important than life in the everyday world. The latter was displaced by a variety of ego decentering techniques, as it was the ego that established the apparent dominance of the everyday world. Some Rishis drank intoxicating soma while others used ascetic practices. Whatever the technique, the goal was to reach the shores of the spiritual world that were concealed by the life activities of the ego-mediated everyday world.

It was in this context that the question of the value and significance of the ego and the everyday world arose as well as their relationships to the spiritual world. How should we relate to the everyday world now that we are aware of the infinitely brighter world of Brahman? Do we try to reform it or leave it behind? The dilemma is not unlike that of the modern scientist who must relate to the space-time-matter framework of the everyday world after spending some hours in the subatomic, quantum world of particle physics. The Rishis and later the Brahmins of the Vedic period (2000–500 BCE) gave priority to individual experiences of union with Brahman that were accompanied by corresponding renunciations of the everyday world. It was the attempts to justify these claims and evaluations regarding both the spiritual and everyday worlds that produced the first systematizations of Indian philosophy. In particular, it was the discursive challenge of justifying their position on how radically the everyday world could and should be displaced that marks the distinctive creativity of the Indian philosophical heritage.

From the Brahmanic spiritualism of the Vedas or in opposition to it, there developed the many schools or darsanas of Indian philosophy. Among these were the Samkhya (900 BCE), the Charvakan materialist, the Buddhist (300 BCE), the Jainist (300 BCE), the Mimamsa (200 BCE), the Vedanta (200 BCE), Vaisesika (200 BCE), and the Nyaya (250 CE) schools. Each of these schools was marked by the production of sutras or aphoristic accounts of its position that could be easily committed to memory and commented on later in detail. These sutras became the bases for the extensive written commentaries by individual philosophers that came to be known as shastras. Consequently sutras and shastras were the two major forms of Indian philosophical production.

In the case of the Mimamsa School, philosophical production crystallized around the exegesis of the ritual practices contained in the Rig Veda. Its founding text, the Mimamsa Sutra, is attributed to Jaimini. In contrast to the Mimansa School, the Vedanta Dasarna focused on the more difficult Vedic discussions of the nature of ultimate reality. Hence it was a school that drew on the Upanishads, texts that constituted the final sections of the Vedas. Thus the primary text of this school, the Brahma Sutra (or Vedanta Sutra), is an attempt to systematize the doctrines of the Upanishads that has been attributed to Badarayana (King 1999; Mohanty 2000).

With the rise of these schools, Brahmanic spiritualism found itself confronted with a number of philosophical and politico-ideological challenges that would change it profoundly. First, there were the dualistic arguments regarding consciousness and matter coming from the Samkhya School. Second, there was the epistemicism of inferential reasoning emphasized by the Nyaya School. Third, there were arguments based on competing experiences of the process of union with Brahman, and different readings of the reality and significance of the everyday world. For example there were those who experienced Brahman as a more personal reality rather than the formless source of all creation celebrated by Brahmanic spiritualism. These alternatives gave rise to the great Bhakti traditions of religious love and devotion, which were directed at the more familiar deities of the Hindu pantheon such as Vishnu and Shiva.

Closely related to these more personal but competing experiences of Brahman were differences concerning just how difficult a process it was to displace the ego and achieve union. Some individuals, like Biswas, hide a misguided will to live behind smokescreens of world rejection. Others defiantly assert this empty will to live in opposition to life and world. Individuals thus exist at widely varying egocentric distances from union and enlightenment. Particularly among the Buddhists, individuals caught in such ego-centric difficulties were seen as needing many life times to achieve the strength and positivity that would make ego-transcendence possible. Thus the depths of the problem of human suffering opened up by the Buddhists challenged the blissful accounts of union and enlightenment that had been the centerpiece of Brahmanic spiritualism. These competing accounts of the ego and the conditions for its transcendence grounded many of the opposing arguments that arose between Buddhists and Brahmanic spiritualists.

Finally, the most extreme differences with Brahmanic spiritualism were voiced by groups of skeptics and materialists, who doubted the existence of Brahman and affirmed the everyday world as the only reality. These were the Charvakas, a school of philosophers who recognized sense perception as the only valid means to knowledge and rejected the truth claims of the Vedas and the validity of inferential reasoning. As a result of all of these challenges, there arose the "protestant or anti-Vedic systems of Samkhya, Buddhism, Jainism and Carvakan materialism between 500 BCE and 700 ACE." Each of these posed major challenges to Brahmanic spiritualism.

In addition to these philosophical challenges, Brahmanic spiritualism also experienced important challenges of a political nature. The rise of patrimonial and imperial kingdoms such as the Mauryas around 322 BCE changed significantly the relations between religious and political authority. The latter now required new and more complex legitimating arguments, broader theories of political rule and more detailed practical advice for rulers. These state-based discursive demands produced corresponding changes in Indian political thought that were reflected in shifts from the Brahmanic orientation of the ancient Manu tradition to the more realist and strategic orientations of Vyasa, Kautilya (345–300 BCE) and Sukra. Although he wrote before Machiavelli, Kautilya's work has often been described as Machiavellian. Further, as Randall Collins has shown, these political dynamics profoundly affected the competition with Buddhism (1998: 177–186).

Not surprisingly, the medieval period of Brahmanic spiritualism was a scholastic one in which it attempted to re-systematize itself in response to these challenges from the materialists, the political realists, the Buddhists, the Jains and the Samkhyists. This period was dominated by two philosophers: Shankara (780–820) and Ramanuja (1016–1100). And later, to lesser degrees by Madhva (1238–1317), Ramananda (1400) and Kabir (1440–1518). Kabir was Islamic, but the breath of his spirituality was such that he had a profound influence on many Brahmanic thinkers, including Rabindranath Tagore. Schweitzer refers to Shankara as "the Saint Thomas Aquinas of Brahmanism" (1957: 159). Shankara is best known for his commentaries on the Vedanta Sutra, the Upanishads, and the Bhagavad Gita in which he defended the monism of Brahmanic spiritualism against the dualism of the Samkhya School. In the course of these commentaries, he also re-systematized Brahmanic spiritualism by incorporating much from the Samkhya and other schools through the notion of levels of truth that can be "sublated" by higher ones. It was during this period of Skankaran restoration that the doctrines of karma and rebirth became centerpieces of Brahmanic spiritualism, the features that figure so prominently in Naipaul's quietistic portrait.

To grasp Aurobindo's place in this developmental trajectory, we must see him as the Shankara of the twentieth century, who will re-systematize Brahmanic spiritualism in a more worldly direction. This century, like earlier ones, made its unique demands for the re-systematizing of Brahmanic spiritualism. Arising in the context of modern anticolonialism and industrialization. Aurobindo's reformulation came as a part of a major nationalist challenge to British rule in India. This movement had its roots in the reformist Brahmo Samaj movement started by Ram Mohan Roy in the early nineteenth century. From the late nineteenth to the first half of the twentieth century, this movement included outstanding Indian poets, philosophers and religious leaders such as Keshab Sen (founder of the Arya Samaj), Sri Ramakrishna, Swami Vivekananda, Rabindranath Tagore, Balwantrao Tilak, Krishna Gokhale, Mahatma Gandhi, Jiddu Krishnamurti, Sarvepalli Radhakrishnan and of course Aurobindo. This movement for the most part affected a major break with the Shankaran synthesis that is so foundational for Naipaul's position.

In the second half of the twentieth century, some of the better known Indian scholars such as Amartya Sen, Gayatri Spivak, Ranajit Guha, Partha Chatterjee, Vijay Prashad, Ashis Nandy and others have kept alive the secular side of Indian thought. They have moved away from the Brahmanic heritage to pursue work in development economics, poststructuralism, Marxism and psychoanalysis. Also the natural sciences have grown tremendously with India's scientific establishment being the third largest in the world, contributing to the model minority image of Indian Americans discussed by Prashad (2000). All of these developments have greatly diversified the contemporary Indian philosophical environment moving it even further beyond its Shankaran phase. At the same time, these new trends have given rise to additional challenges from rationalistic materialism that Aurobindo's reformulation did not address. Is this then the end of the line for Brahmanic spiritualism? Is a new systematization possible? Is Aurobindo India's last great Brahmanic systematizer? Clearly he is not. Work within and on the tradition continues in the writings of philosophers such as J. N. Mohanty, Roy Bhaskar and Jonardon Ganeri.

This quick survey of the developmental trajectory of Indian philosophy makes clear the complexity of this heritage, some of the distinct phases it has gone through, and how it has repeatedly redefined itself in response to new and distinct problems. This is in sharp contrast to the monothetic portrait of quietism masking despair painted by Naipaul. This divergence becomes even sharper when we examine in detail the case of Aurobindo's reworking of the heritage.

AUROBINDO'S SUPRAMENTAL PHENOMENOLOGY

Sri Aurobindo (Aurobindo Ghose) was born in Calcutta in 1872 and sent by his highly anglicized father to study in England at the tender age of six. As a young man at Cambridge University, Aurobindo was a poet and a radical nationalist. He returned to India in 1892 at the age of twenty, after an absence of fourteen years, with a deep concern for "the proletariat among us" (Satprem 1993: II). He joined the radical wing of the struggle for independence and for thirteen years wrote for newspapers and engaged in underground activities that he hoped would lead to an armed insurrection. After his arrest in 1908 on charges of treason, Aurobindo's radical nationalism turned sharply in a spiritual and cultural direction. In jail for a year awaiting trial, Aurobindo used his time to study the Bhagavad Gita and the Upanishads, and also to further his still elementary acquaintance with yoga. This spiritual turn began before the arrest with Aurobindo reporting a number of spontaneous experiences of spiritual union in the years following his return to India. His famous 1909 speech at Uttarpara in which he first spoke publicly about these experiences was a crucial turning point. In 1910 after his continued harassment by the colonial government, Aurobindo withdrew from politics to pursue the path of a yogi undisturbed.

As he progressed on his path, Aurobindo's experiences of union with Brahman both widened and deepened. The time he spent in that state lengthened dramatically, and made possible his exploration of the dimension of Brahman that he would call supermind. In his writings, he would compare these experiences with those of the Rishis and draw from the comparisons mutual confirmation for claims made about the nature of Brahman. It is precisely these roots of Aurobindo's philosophy in original experiences of this type that distinguishes him from Radhakrishnan. This is the "inward concentration" that Naipaul dreads because it blocks an objective seeing of the everyday world. In both of these roles of activist and yogi, Aurobindo functioned as a powerful anticolonial voice. The essays collected in his *Foundations of Indian Culture* are classic installments in the exchanges between Prospero and Caliban.

To get into Aurobindo's massive corpus, I will begin with the comparatively late (1939) but very central text, *The Life Divine*. This is a work about consciousness, its vast range, its many levels, the interpenetration of these levels, their differing capacities to possess truth as self knowledge, and to resolve the sharpening social contradictions, the growing ecological imbalances and other recalcitrant impasses that had brought terrestrial existence to its then current state of planetary crisis. It argues that ego consciousness is only a tiny fraction of a vaster formation and that it must be surrendered for the higher levels of the larger totality if our crisis is to be resolved.

To anchor Aurobindo's unusual and expansive view of consciousness in my own ego-centered mind, I've often compared it to the phenomena of dark matter and dark energy that physicists now believe make up 95 percent of the stuff of the universe. Unlike the matter of the earth, other planets and stars, dark matter is invisible and is known to physicists only through its effects on "normal" matter. Thus our everyday conception of matter is a very misleading one as it is based upon a 5 percent sample. In Aurobindo's world, ego consciousness is the counterpart to our privileging of normal matter. It constitutes a tiny percent of a vaster totality most of which is as unknown to us as dark matter. The foundations for this exclusive focus on consciousness were already laid in works such as *The Human Cycle* and *The Ideal of Human Unity* where political, economic and scientific approaches to the above terrestrial crisis were critiqued and shown to be of only limited value. It is in the spaces left by the limited agency of these factors that Aurobindo locates the agency of consciousness and in particular its supramental plane.

One of the distinguishing features of Aurobindo's philosophy is its use of yoga to facilitate constant movements out of and back into ego consciousness. This becomes necessary as the latter is seen as not being capable of resolving the crucial impasses confronting humanity. The opposition between rationalistic materialism and ascetic idealism is the example of one such impasse that Aurobindo uses throughout this book. Within ego consciousness, we find it necessary to affirm one or deny the other. Hence we get the materialistic denial of spirit, which is very strong in the West, and the ascetic denial of everyday matter and life, which is very strong in India. How do we find a way out? Aurobindo's solution is to shift out of ego consciousness and to seek the creative input of a higher plane, the supramental consciousness. This centrality of yoga is taken up in another major work, *Integral Yoga*, that can only be compared to the Yoga Sutra of Patanjali (third century CE).

When Aurobindo makes his yoga-mediated exits out of ego consciousness, the new terrain on which he first lands is a new center of subjective activity that Aurobindo calls "the soul" or "the psychic being." The soul is marked by a qualitatively different mode of subjectivity than that of the ego. It is a "larger and purer" entity than the ego, and for Aurobindo constitutes the real self. It is our real self because, unlike the ego, it is not cut off by thick protective walls from the higher planes of the larger totality that is consciousness. In other words, it is a mode subjectivity in which our "individuality is in constant relation with our universality" (1987: 225). For Aurobindo, the soul is "the flame of the Godhead always alight within us . . . the Daemon of Socrates, the inner light or inner voice of the mystic" (1987: 225). As such it opens the way to the higher planes or the "dark matter" of consciousness that the walls of our egos make inaccessible.

Within the spiritual and expansive world of Brahman made accessible by the psychic being, Aurobindo distinguishes several levels of consciousness. Consciousness for him is always consciousness-force—a combination of knowledge, self-knowledge and a corresponding ability to create and make things real. Planes of consciousness can differ along all three dimensions, and are thus marked by different values or "quanta" of force, knowledge and self-awareness, hence their different creative and knowing capabilities. Among the most important planes of consciousness recognized by Aurobindo are the following: Brahman (the highest level), supermind, over mind, mind, life, and matter.

Supermind is a truth consciousness, which is in full possession of the truth of the unity of all things and can create on the basis of that knowledge. Overmind shares the unitary and comprehensive vision of supermind, but its force component is such that it cannot create on the basis of that unity. It is thus in effect a divisive consciousness that creates through the separation and combination of the various aspects of the supramental unity. It is "a screen of dissimilar similarity" through which supermind can act indirectly on mind and other lower plane (1987: 278).

Mind is Brahmanic consciousness in a state of ignorance. Thus it is a truth seeking as opposed to a truth possessing consciousness. Mind reaches for the truth but can only come up with "mental constructions and representations of it in word and idea" (1987: 272).

By life Aurobindo is referring to the vital or emotional mode of being. It too is a form or mask of Brahmanic consciousness the epistemic and force components of which are different from but also weaker than those of mind.

Finally, matter is Brahmanic consciousness in its most othered and "inconscient" state. In the material mode of being, the force component has completely suppressed the other side of the unity, consciousness-force. Thus matter is the great night of Brahmanic consciousness in which it cannot recognize itself as such. Thus all of creation is a manifestation of Brahman, and hence is a unity even though this unity can only be clearly seen from the overmental level and above.

Aurobindo describes each of these planes in great detail as forms of consciousness and the Brahmanic unity that embraces them. In this descriptive endeavor, we see an important difference with Krishnamurti, who insists on the indescribability of his experiences of the higher reaches of consciousness. Beginning with phenomenological descriptions of the capabilities and incapabilities of ego consciousness and its normal restriction to the planes of matter, life and mind, *The Life Divine* boldly goes beyond these restrictions by moving up and down this whole hierarchy of being, focusing on the agency of the supramental plane and its capacity for moving terrestrial existence beyond its deepening crisis. This is the higher but hidden world disclosed by Aurobindo's phenomenology and with whose supramental creativity he hoped to transform the everyday world. Aurobindo writes about this world in ways that remind us of Husserl's explorations of the transcendental consciousness. Thus before examining the supramental plane in more detail, it might be useful to briefly compare the phenomenologies of these two men.

AUROBINDO AND HUSSERL

Like Aurobindo, Husserl's point of departure is the displacing of the everyday world. Husserlian phenomenology "suspends" or "puts into brackets" the "natural attitude" upon which belief in the reality of the everyday world rests. However, these suspensions are not affected through the practice of yoga, but rather the phenomenological reduction. With the everyday world in suspension a new one opens up: the transcendental world. In other words, suspension discloses the knowledge- and world-constituting activities of a different consciousness, which is veiled or eclipsed by the epistemic activities of everyday life.

Husserl viewed his transcendental phenomenology as the science of this new field of transcendental subjectivity. This phenomenology was the science of the pure possibilities of transcendental activity just as mathematics was the discourse of the pure possibilities of nature. Phenomenology would then ground the human sciences in the way that mathematics grounded and informed the natural sciences.

What is the identity of the consciousness responsible for all of this activity? As noted earlier, this field of pure or transcendental subjectivity cannot be reached within the framework of everyday epistemic practices or even those of the natural sciences. Thus it is not the ego or cogito of any of these activities. Rather, this field can only be reached by silencing or suspending them. When this is done, the self-reflecting individual discovers that he/she possesses within "an essential individuality, self-contained and holding well together in itself . . . [and] through whose agency the objective world is there for me with all its empirically confirmed facts" (1975: 11). This "phenomenologically self-contained" but world-constituting subjectivity that we discover when we exit the everyday ego is the "transcendental Ego." Within the phenomenological reduction, it is not the world that is experienced as given as in the case of the everyday or natural attitude. Rather, it is this immaterial transcendental Ego that is experienced as immediately given, and whose agency constructs and validates the meaningful aspects of the world. The shift to the transcendental standpoint of this meaning-constituting activity radically reverses the ontological positions of both consciousness and the everyday world. The creative power and agency of the former expand dramatically while that of the latter contracts. Within the reduction "only transcendental subjectivity has ontologically the meaning of absolute Being" (1975: 14). The transcendental Ego and its field of activity calls to mind the psychic being of Aurobindo. They are both more expansive modes of subjectivity that are concealed by the activities of the everyday ego. Thus, the exiting of everyday ego consciousness produced similar results in both Husserl and Aurobindo.

Even though it could be argued that the psychic being and the transcendental Ego are different names for regions of consciousness that border on the everyday ego, it should be clear that after arriving there Aurobindo and Husserl move out in very different directions. Hence the differences in their accounts of the higher reaches of consciousness. In Husserl's language, "the modifications" in the transcendental Ego introduced by their different reflective standpoints took them in different directions. Husserl's modifications grasped the meaning-constituting aspects of the transcendental Ego. In other words, he transformed it into the informing consciousness of the transcendental inquirer who wants to create a science of pure consciousness. As a result, Husserl had only brief glimpses of the absolute or Brahmanic shores reached by Aurobindo.

On the other hand Aurobindo's modifications of the psychic being moved in a different direction. They resulted in not just a search for the meaning-constituting foundations of the everyday world, but also for the cosmos-constituting consciousness that sustains all existence. He is not as concerned as Husserl with the more restricted rational cogito, its epistemic practices, and the knowledge-constitutive activities they conceal. Rather, Aurobindo's focus is the entire compliment of ego activities and the ways in which they obscure the many planes of consciousness, and the supramental in particular.

In spite of these differences, both Husserl and Aurobindo saw philosophy as a practice that was rooted in self-reflective experiences. These experiences profoundly transformed (transcendentalized or supramentalized) the "I" of the reflecting subject. Both saw the everyday ego as inextricably mired in dualistic splits and cleavages. Thus Husserl's position on the conflicts between idealism and materialism or logicism versus historicism mirrors Aurobindo's positions on the conflict between ascetic idealism and rationalistic materialism. For both philosophers the whole point of going beyond ego consciousness is to bring a higher creativity to the resolution of these and other problems. Indeed, Aurobindo has often been compared to Hegel because of the major evolutionary dimensions to their thought. Thus Spivak sees in Aurobindo a reworking of "the Hegelian graph of spirit's journey" (1999:63). This I think is a mistake that obscures the originality of Aurobindo's supramental vision of our future. This vision does not force the graph of spirit in a national or Indocentric direction in the way that Hegel's steers it along a Eurocentric path. I think Aurobindo's originality emerges much more clearly from a comparison with Husserl, particularly when we compare the supramental and transcendental planes.

THE SUPRAMENTAL PLANE

The first description that Aurobindo gives of approaching the supramental plane is of a union with or entry into "that cosmic consciousness embracing the universe and appearing as an immanent intelligence in all its works" (1987: 21). This consciousness is "not organized mind, but that which, calm and eternal, broods equally in the living earth and the living human body and to which mind and senses are dispensable instruments" (1987: 21). It is "the witness of cosmic existence and its lord" (1987: 21). From the perspective of this consciousness, our dualities and their impasses look very different.

Although this cosmic consciousness encompasses all of creation, it is more than the universe and hence is not exhausted by it. Aurobindo sees this cosmic supramental consciousness as Brahman in its world-creating mode. It is an aspect of Brahman, the ultimate reality that is the source of all, and thus possesses knowledge of the unity of all things. As Brahman, the cosmic consciousness is also a self-existent reality that "lives independently in its own inexpressible infinity as well as in the cosmic harmonies" (1987: 22). In its independence, it exists in modes that are free from all material, vital, mental, and other codes of cosmic existence. This freedom of the cosmic consciousness from all positive terms of manifested existence is what Aurobindo means by non-being. This is an important aspect of the life of Brahman, which can be reached through this cosmic consciousness. In a state union, it is possible for the quieted ego to experience this non-being and to "enter into this world-transcending consciousness and become superior to cosmic existence" (1987: 22). This experience Aurobindo associates with the silence, stillness, and non-activity from whence the impulses of ascetic idealism spring. These have nothing to do with despair and everything with the peace of Brahman. Aurobindo insists that this "silence does not reject the world; it sustains it" (1987: 27). Thus from the perspective of the silent side of the cosmic consciousness, the world rejecting attitude of ascetic idealism turns out to be a binary "rendering of our supramental experiences in the sense of those intolerant distinctions" (1987: 27–8). Here we see one of the ways in which Aurobindo's supramental turn constitutes a radical break with earlier forms of ascetic idealism or quietism.

In addition to the above aspects, it is the supramental dimension of this cosmic consciousness that Aurobindo develops in greatest detail. As we've seen, this consciousness is the active cosmos-constituting side of Brahman, pouring itself into the infinite variety of forms that make the universe possible. Supermind is the all-comprehending aspect of this consciousness that is already in possession of the knowledge needed for world creation. It "is an initial coming out, in creative self-knowledge, of that which lay concentrated in uncreative self-awareness" (1987: 29). Thus, supermind does not proceed by thinking things out the way we do.

Rather, it works on them with the certainty of self-knowledge. Hence Aurobindo refers to it as a "truth consciousness."

Being one with Brahman, supermind has within it knowledge of the unity of all things. It "sees the universe and its contents as itself in a single indivisible act of knowledge, an act which is its life, which is the very movement of its self existence" (1987: 138). It is in this all-encompassing vision of supermind that the dualities and impasses that our ego-minds routinely produce can find resolution. It is in this vision of the universe being real because it exists in the world-constituting powers of the Brahmanic supermind that the duality between matter and spirit dissolves, and also that between rationalistic materialism and ascetic idealism. Outside of this unitary vision of supermind or unaided by it, the world must appear irreconcilably divided and contradictory to other forms of consciousness. Aurobindo often thinks of supermind (from our standpoint) as being "located" somewhere between the unitary self-existence of Brahman and the dualistic, ego-based, knowledge-seeking activity that is characteristic of our plane of mentality.

Supermind not only contains all the multiple cosmic forms it creates but "pervades them as an indwelling Presence and a self-revealing light. It is present even though concealed in every form and force of the universe" (1987: 135). It actively supports the life of all it creates without in any way compromising its own unity. These and its earlier-noted characteristics make supermind an omnipresent and omniscient cosmos-constituting consciousness that exists in at least three distinct "poises." In the first, supermind participates in the original Brahmanic unity of all things. In the second, it modifies that unity in order to make possible "the manifestation of the many in the one" (1987: 145). Finally, in the third poise, a further modification allows it to be active in both the life and the evolution of the life of many. Thus, it is more of a cosmic, universe creating consciousness than Husserl's knowledge or meaning-constituting transcendental consciousness.

This is supermind. This is the truth consciousness to which Aurobindo consistently turns to resolve the problems and dualities that stump our ego-minds. He uses the distinct creative capabilities of this consciousness in ways that parallel Husserl's use of the transcendental consciousness. However, his goal is not to create a science of this consciousness or its pure possibilities but to let it transform that very impulse toward scientific rationality. Aurobindo recognizes the transcendental plane and will often, after a vision of supramental reconciliation, take up its appearance of that reconciled opposition on the transcendental plane. Thus after the reconciliation of matter and spirit in the vision of the cosmic consciousness, Aurobindo takes up the issue of how it appears "in the transcendental consciousness" (1987: 30). There the vision of unity is lost and the supramental reconciliation takes on the form that all antinomies, including that between matter and spirit, must assume—opposed self-expressions of the one Brahmanic reality: "All affirmations are denied only to lead to a wider affirmation of the same reality. All antinomies confront each other in order to recognize one Truth in their opposed aspects and embrace by way of conflict their mutual unity" (1987: 33). This is a transcendental rendering of supramental reconciliation. It is the power of this supramental consciousness that Aurobindo wants to introduce more directly into our everyday lives. He wants to transform and restructure the latter by the light of this consciousness rather than by the light of reason. This is what he means by the spiritualization as opposed to the rationalization of everyday existence.

The spiritual transformation of our everyday life is a complex and difficult process for Aurobindo. Movement toward such a goal he sees as occurring on two different but related levels. The first is the evolutionary; the second is that of the ego. The evolutionary significance of supermind derives from the fact that its creative outpourings of itself can be viewed as a descent of the Divine into overmind, mind, life and matter, which Aurobindo calls its involution. This descent is one of two very important legs upon which cosmic existence rests. The other is the ascent of the involved spirit from matter through life, mind and overmind back to the Divine, which Aurobindo calls evolution. From this perspective, "the whole of creation may be said to be a movement between two involutions, spirit in which all is involved and out of which all evolves downward to the other pole of Matter, Matter in which also all is involved and out of which all evolves upward to the other pole of spirit" (1987: 29). Thus far, the upward evolutionary leg has produced life and mind out of matter and must create in the future a spiritual (overmental and supramental) plane here on earth as its next great achievement

We can aid this forthcoming evolutionary project of supermind by living in ways that would heighten spiritual awareness in our present state of mind-dominated existence. These must include the ego-displacing practices of yoga. For Aurobindo, the primary enemy of this spiritual revolution is human egoism, the egoism of the individual, the egoism of class and nation. It is when the creative activity of supermind is reflected upon our stilled and de-centered egos that we can advance this evolutionary project of spiritualization by letting this supramental creativity work more freely through us. Thus the blocking of the interpenetration of planes and other resistant effects of our egoisms must be quieted if we want to work for the spiritual transformation of our everyday world.

This in brief is Aurobindo's modern reworking of the Brahmanic heritage. This reformulation was very much a twentieth-century creation, and thus very different in spirit and outlook from those of Shankara, Ramanuja, Madhva and others who shaped the medieval phase of Brahmanic spiritualism. It marked a new and distinct phase in the history of this philosophical tradition, demonstrating its capabilities for self-renewal and constructive responses to the new challenges of Western political and intellectual colonization. This is not the place for a critique of this reformulation as my purpose in undertaking its brief exposition is to set it in contrast to Naipaul's rather static vision of Indian philosophy. Clearly the crucial questions for Aurobindo will arise about the possibilities for spiritualizing the everyday world. Can the latter take it and still be human? The competing European project of rationalization has come up against some rather revealing limits. The resulting crisis Habermas has aptly described as the colonization of the everyday world by systems of instrumental and industrial rationality. Could the project of spiritualization result in a similar crisis of colonization? The further development of this critique we must leave for another paper.

Here we must suffice with the making of three points regarding the implications of this view of Indian philosophy for Naipaul's arguments. First, our quick survey of the history of Indian philosophy showed that it has a complex developmental trajectory that Naipaul overlooked. This trajectory has been sustained by processes of argumentation between various schools, and by responses to real-world demands which have forced this tradition to renew itself.

Second, it should be clear that Aurobindo's contributions have advanced this trajectory by taking postcolonial Indian philosophy onto new planes and into new relations with the everyday world. In grounding Indian philosophy between the supramental plane and that of the transformation of our everyday world, Aurobindo has taken the Brahmanic heritage in a phenomenological direction that we can recognize as a modern philosophical defense of the agency of consciousness in the face of the instrumental colonization of the everyday world, whether of a capitalist or socialist nature.

Third and finally, the overall developmental trajectory of Indian philosophy does not support Naipaul's claim that this philosophy is one of quietism masking an underlying despair. As we've seen many times, it is the "Bliss" of Brahman rather than Biswasian despair that is the source of Brahmanic asceticism and its tendencies to devalue the world. Existential attitudes of world and life rejection based on experiences of suffering were positions against which Brahmanic spiritualism defined itself. Particularly in the case of Aurobindo, there is nothing to suggest that the quietistic aspects of his life and philosophy either negate action or mask despair. On the contrary they are models of how a meditative spirituality can be an active force in the world.

Given these points, Indo-Caribbean scholars have at least two competing views of the Indian philosophical heritage that they must consider: the quietistic and the spiritually transformative. I think the latter is the more accurate. This claim is well supported by the orientation of Aurobindo's supramental phenomenology, which is a more recent version of many Indian attempts to deploy spirituality in one of the grandest visions of social transformation ever imagined.

INDIAN, INDO- AND AFRO-CARIBBEAN PHILOSOPHY

If indeed we take this spiritually transformative vision of the Indian philosophical heritage as our basis for dialogues between the Afro- and Indo-Caribbean traditions, then what is such a move likely to produce? Clearly it would add a very novel perspective to the discussions about the nature of consciousness, spirituality and phenomenology already taking place in the region. It would reinforce and amplify some voices on these issues and pose major challenges to others.

For example, it would expand and amplify many of the concepts of spirituality found in the African heritage. The Bantu concept of spirit as force is echoed and amplified within Aurobindo's notion of Spirit as consciousness-force. In a similar way, the Akan notion of the Okra will find resonance in Aurobindo's concept of the psychic being. Finally, African notions of ego transcendence will find recognition and amplification in Aurobindo's approach to yoga (Henry 2000a: 1–46). Working out the similarities and differences between these and other African concepts of spirituality would be the foundations for important bridges between the Afro- and Indo-Caribbean traditions.

The building of such bridges goes beyond the African heritage itself to include the works of Afro-Caribbean thinkers such as Frantz Fanon, Wilson Harris, Lewis Gordon or Sylvia Wynter. In *Black Skin, White Masks*, Fanon describes for us several experiences of ego collapse and the worlds that open up during these cracks in the life and time of the ego. These can be usefully compared to Aurobindo's experiences of the psychic being or Husserl's experiences of the transcendental ego. What is striking about Fanon's account when compared to Husserl's or Aurobindo's is the brevity of the descriptions as Fanon is eager to recover his ego and return to the everyday world. These regions of consciousness that border on the ego do not become objects of intense curiosity the way they do in Aurobindo and Husserl. Rather, they are given fleeting descriptions that become bases for better understanding the ego, its psycho-existential dynamics, and its relations to the everyday world. But in spite of their brevity they still constitute important ego-transcending points of overlap between these three traditions.

Fanon's more existential and ego-oriented views of consciousness can also be found in Lewis Gordon. In Gordon's work, it is the often hidden but diverse ways in which egos exist in bad faith that is the focus of attention (1995). These bad faith modes of being are made possible by the self-evading capabilities of the ego through which humans are able to deceive themselves and live in worlds of false consciousness. With his primary focus on how these self-evading practices aid the formation of racist identities, Gordon too has not paid much attention to the worlds that border on egos in bad faith. However, there is a shared theoretical interest in the agency and nature of consciousness that links Gordon to Husserl and Aurobindo.

This dialogue would engage even the concerns of someone like Sylvia Wynter, who takes a very different approach to consciousness. Wynter's primary concern is the relationship between our ability to produce new models of the human subject and the transformation of our present social order (1984). Wynter is struck by the fact that we constantly disown our authorship of these subjectivities, and is determined to interrupt these mechanisms of disowning and expose us as the self- or auto-instituting beings that we are. To achieve these two goals, Wynter makes a transcendental turn. However, the resulting transcendentalism is not ego-based as in the case of Husserl, but semio-linguistically grounded. The creative, constituting agency uncovered by Wynter's turn is not an ego or a psychic being but, as in poststructuralism, a semio-linguistically organized set of signs whose binary nature gives the ego its dualistic structure. It is the transformation of the bourgeois version of these semio-linguistically produced models of human subjects that is the focus of Wynter's transcendental turn. There is a lot to be learned from comparing this project with Aurobindo's. Both share the assumption of vital worlds of creative activity that are normally hidden, but must be recovered by self-reflective thinking within a transcendental or supramental turn. Wynter's transcendental turn reveals very clearly the hidden continuity between poststructuralism and phenomenology. The former is a linguistic variant of the latter.

However, the Caribbean thinker who comes the closest to Aurobindo's conception of consciousness is clearly Wilson Harris, a figure who represents both the Afro- and Indo-Caribbean traditions. Harris's interest in the world of the ego is limited. He is equally fascinated, if not more so, by what is going on in the larger world of consciousness that surrounds the ego, but from which it is separated by its need for ontic closure. The view of consciousness that we find in Harris is indeed an expansive one. It is only in Aurobindo's supramental vision that it is surpassed.

The above examples make it clear that there are many different conceptions of consciousness operating in the region. To those discussed, we could add the non-transcendental ones that have emerged from the region's historicist and scientific traditions of writing. Thus Marxist conceptions of consciousness tend to see it as a social formation without these transcendentally or supramentally expanded dimensions celebrated by Harris, Husserl and Aurobindo. Within scientific traditions of writing, more empirical and positivistic conceptions of consciousness hold sway. Consciousness is restricted to the form it takes in the production of technical and scientific knowledge. Hence skepticism is expressed toward transcendental and supramental turns and the knowledges produced within them. Consequently, engaging the Indian philosophical heritage will necessarily mean much more lively and wide-ranging debates over the nature of consciousness, its phenomenological study and its role in transforming everyday life. Can we really read Aurobindo and not compare the epistemic consequences of thinking inside of or outside of transcendental or supramental turns? I don't think we can.

CONCLUSION

We began with the ethnogenic eclipse of Indo-Caribbean philosophy and then examined the Eurocentric accounts of Indian philosophy that reinforced this eclipse. To nurture the impulses for a philosophical rebirth that are now stirring in the region, a dialogue between the subjugated Indo- and Afro-Caribbean traditions is a must. These two heritages must be brought closer together through dialogue. Only a mutually embracing dialogue of this nature can give birth to a truly Caribbean philosophy. To achieve this dialogue, the institutional and discursive practices that have produced and maintained the invisibility of these traditions must be undone and bridges built where there were only stereotypical ethnic walls.

I have only begun to dispel the cloud of invisibility that has hung over the Indo-Caribbean heritage. Much more work needs to be done before this cloud will lift and let this heritage emerge in full view. Much more of the Indian heritage than Aurobindo needs to be reclaimed if those connections are to be strong and vibrant. In addition to these bridges with the Indian heritage, new and stronger ones must be built between the poeticist and historicist schools of both the Indo- and Afro-Caribbean traditions. When these are up and functioning, we just might be able to produce creolized philosophical formations that are comparable to those being produced in literature and music.

NOTE

* First published as "Between Naipaul and Aurobindo: Where Is Indo-Caribbean Philosophy?" *C. L. R. James Journal* 9, no. 1 (Winter): 3–36.

FOUR

Wynter and the Transcendental Spaces of Caribbean Thought

The thought of Sylvia Wynter must be approached with a firm grasp on the future of all of humanity, and not just that of Africana people. Anything less will fail to give it the justice that it so richly deserves. Rising from the particular crises of the racialized poor of the Caribbean, Wynter's thought moves out on powerful wings of poetic analogy to embrace the universal conditions of human self-formation and the global patterns of human domination of other human beings. Wynter brings these universal conditions and global patterns together in a powerful discourse of epistemic historicism to explain why so many in the Caribbean and other parts of the world are impoverished, racialized and condemned as lost or expendable. Like C. L. R. James and Frantz Fanon, it is the ongoing global production of this group, "the condemned of the earth," that remains the persistent focus of Wynter's thought. No matter how far above or below, how far to the left or to the right her thought goes it is always in the service of clarifying some aspect of the conditions that are responsible for the condemned being a necessary part of our world. This paradox of the persistence of the condemned of the earth in spite of our ideals of freedom, justice, equality, and brotherhood/sisterhood is the knot that Wynter will attempt to untie. In the course of this undertaking, she has challenged the global scholarly community as profoundly as it has ever been.

For us in the Caribbean, Wynter has insisted that we enter regions of ourselves and our social world that we have neglected or overlooked in our search for a way out of the crisis of the condemned in the postcolonial order that we have been attempting to create. This order was supposed to have been a new beginning, a radical break with its colonial past, but instead has been derailed by that past which has now left it with only neocolonial options. More than any other Caribbean thinker, Wynter has insisted that we turn our attention to the epistemic foundations of our discourses and social orders. This is not an area to which the Caribbean intellectual tradition has given a great deal of attention. Consequently, Wynter's insistence on exploring the transcendental spaces of Caribbean thought is the source of the originality of her contributions to the crisis of the condemned in our neo-/postcolonial order.

This transcendental turn has brought into clearer focus the hidden foundations of the discourses that we routinely use. It exposes and thematizes these epistemic depths that we take for granted when engaged in a particular exercise of knowledge production. Wynter's interest in the transcendental ground of knowledge production was not motivated by a desire to account for the success of the natural sciences as in the case of Kant. Rather, it was the repeated failures and ongoing production of systemic errors in the humanities and social sciences that motivated her transcendental turn. Particularly important were the systemic misrepresentations of subordinated, oppressed and condemned groups in these disciplines. As crises of technification in the European natural sciences drove Husserl to explore their transcendental foundations, in a similar way, the crises of misrepresenting the condemned of the earth forced Wynter to explore the transcendental grounds of the European humanities and social sciences. However, Wynter does not bring her crisis of the humanities and social sciences into a critical engagement with Husserl's crisis of the natural sciences. The primary reason for this is Wynter's claim that the European natural sciences have achieved a cognitive autonomy that still eludes the social sciences and humanities.

The primary purpose of this essay is an examination of Wynter's epistemic historicism and the ways in which it has opened up the transcendental spaces of Caribbean thought. I will show that her examination of these spaces has produced three important results. First, it has identified and outlined some of the major contours of the field of Caribbean transcendentalism. Second, she has used these contours to radicalize the transcendental discourses of Kant, Husserl, Habermas and Foucault. Third, Wynter's transcendental focus has enabled her to rework the Caribbean Marxist tradition in a very innovative way. Of these three results, our primary concern will be with the last. Consequently, this essay will be organized around four basic sections: First, the autopoetic foundations of Wynter's historicism; second, her theory of epistemes and epistemic change; third, her epistemic reading of James; and fourth, the consequences of that reading for Marxist discourses.

THE AUTOPOETIC FOUNDATIONS

Wynter is in the best sense of the term a radical thinker. She goes to the roots of things in her search for the levers and mechanisms of change. Yet the question with which she always begins is one that has been at the center of conservative sociological and political thought: the question of social order. How are social orders established? What are the mechanisms, the glue, or the centripetal forces that integrate societies and hold them together? In radical traditions of thought, the answer has consistently been force, power, authority or some combination of the three with culture playing a legitimating role. In conservative traditions, the answer has consistently been myth, religion, norms, mores, values or some combination of these cultural factors, with force, power and authority playing secondary roles. Wynter's approach shares the cultural focus of the conservative tradition but does not move at the level of already established cultural and discursive practices such as norms, mores or religious beliefs. Rather, it moves below such specific cultural practices and links the problem of social order to a more general set of a priori conditions that make cultural and discursive practices possible. These always presupposed conditions carry within them the order-producing codes and patterns that inform and frame the self-organizing capabilities of individuals and groups. In turn, these self-organizing capabilities make what could be called "self-speciation" possible (Wynter 2003: 278–79, 315). However, this ability of life forms, both human and non-human, to establish and realize their particular mode *of* being is one that comes with inherited codes and inherited coding processes. Thus in the animal kingdom, these codes *of* self-speciation are genetic in nature. In the human world, they are autopoetic in nature. Thus in our self-speciating or society creating activities, genetic codes have been significantly replaced by autopoetic ones. Following Fanon, Wynter refers to this shift as the move from phylogeny to sociogeny (Wynter 2003: 268).

Autopoeisis is thus Wynter's answer to the problem *of* social order and not the particular norms, values or discourses that it may subsequently make possible. It is responsible for the distinct species life *of* humans and also for the different social orders that we find in human societies. Consequently, autopoeisis is the process by which human self-organization has been able to establish and maintain internally coded social orders while at the same time adapting to changes in the surrounding environment. At its core, autopoeisis is a set *of* encoded creative possibilities that can be discursively mobilized and deployed in the service *of* human self-formation. In more deterministic language, it is the encoded manner in which human self-organization is bio-evolutionarily pre-programmed with the shift from phylogeny to sociogeny (Wynter 2003: 273).

This pre-programmed aspect of the autopoeisis of human social orders is important for two reasons. First, it points to the hidden status of the basic codes of social orders. They dwell in opaque spaces of constitutive otherness, and thus are beyond our immediate grasp. As we intervene in physical nature with the aid of scientific discourses, we can, with the aid of poetic discourses, intervene in these constitutive spaces of order-producing codes to lessen opaqueness, to adjust them to our needs, and to increase our levels of autonomy in relation to them. However, in spite of these interventions, we will never really transcend this mode of coded inscription or gain full control over it. The second importance of this autopoetic pre-programming by inaccessible, and as we shall see, epistemologically compromised codes, is that it constitutes a foundational layer of Wynter's philosophical anthropology. Here we see the beginnings of Wynter's view of the human as a being whose formation is embedded in codes from which it must be partially extricated. In short, autopoeisis is ontological writing. Through its coded possibilities it allows humans to write different versions of themselves into being.

In creating social orders, autopoeisis must write into being three dimensions of human speciation that are largely absent in the genetically coded speciations of the animal kingdom. First, human autopoeisis requires symbolic representations of the individual self or "I." Through these representations, the individual should be able to say to self and other who he/she is in reasonably definite terms. Second, human autopoeisis must include symbolic representations of the collective self or "we" of the social group. Again, through such representations, the group must be able to consciously affirm itself to itself and to others. Third and finally, human autopoeisis must include symbolic representations of the surrounding environment. These three sets of representations, linked together by narratives of origin and end, will frame the basic vision of existence that is the cultural heritage of the group. Such visions of existence and the human capacity to produce them is the crucial difference that separates autopoetic from genetically coded social orders.

However, this striking advantage of human autopoeisis brings with it some major epistemological responsibilities. Our visions of existence must accurately and truthfully represent self and world. If they do not, this advantage will quickly turn into a major disadvantage. Wynter thinks it is right here that the first major problems of human autopoeisis emerge. Throughout the evolutionary history of order-producing codes, their knowledge-producing processes have always been intensively and extensively shaped by the conditions necessary for securing the self-organization of the group. Consequently, all earthly organisms must necessarily know themselves and their environments in the terms needed to ensure the conservation and replication of its order-producing codes. Wynter argues that this is true for us as well as the organisms of the animal world. Thus, we too know reality in species-specific terms which may not coincide with the way things are outside of our particular viewpoint. Echoing Kant, Wynter concludes from this that the cognition made possible by our "governing" or order-producing codes involves cognition of things for us rather than of things in and for themselves (Wynter 2003: 271). This "for us" knowledge, Wynter refers to as adaptive truths or ethnoknowledges as they are subject to and conditioned by the self-replicating needs of our autopoetic governing codes. In short, the shift to sociogeny and its autopoetic codes, has not freed our knowledge-producing practices from species-specific constraints that they continue to share with the genetic codes of phylogeny.

For Wynter, the primary reason for these epistemological problems of human autopoeisis is the binary oppositional manner in which it produces its representations of self, other and world. Thus, in representing the "I," sociogenic autopoeisis cannot directly grasp the self but only indirectly through some type of trope that is semiotically linked to its opposite. These tropes and their abductive extensions become tape measures of being and non-being, of desired and undesired modes of the subject. These patterns of indirect representation through systems of binary oppositional tropes draw on prior classificatory systems of sameness and difference which serve as basic templates for processes of autopoetic production. For Wynter, different cultures rest on different semiotic organizations of these templates of sameness and difference. Thus it is the different scripts that can be semiotically extracted from these templates that make possible the systems of oppositional tropes by which specific modes of the "I" or the "We" are ontologized or written into being. However, it is this binary mode of inscription that raises Wynter's doubts about the truth-producing capabilities of autopoetically conditioned knowledge. The full implications of all this will emerge much more clearly when we take up the nature and limitations of epistemes. Here we need only to note that these are the autopoetic foundations that for Wynter shape both social and epistemic orders.

AUTOPOEISIS AND EPISTEMES

Although primarily linked to the problem of social order, the autopoetic templates of human sociogeny also serve as a transcendental or discourse-constitutive underside of human knowledge production. It is this underside of everyday discursive activity that Wynter theorizes in terms of epistemes and their transformation. Epistemes are pretheoretical, self-organizing, discourse-constitutive formations that make routine knowledge production possible. They ground such knowledge-constitutive practices as induction, deduction, abduction, the troping of self and other. Epistemes are coherently organized sets of analogies, categories, images, concepts, and rules of statement formation that rest upon the classificatory schemes of autopoetic codes and templates. Hence they are able to draw on the semiotic creativity and auto-instituting powers of the latter. As in the autopoeisis of social orders, the autopoeisis of epistemes rests on the semiotic manipulation of the signifiers of sameness and difference contained in the governing template. In the case of epistemic orders, these templates must be re-centered around binaries such as truth/error, founding/unfounding concepts, inside the order/outside the order. With such signifiers to be semiotically manipulated, abductively extended and deployed in a self-organizing manner, epistemes can be established.

Given this mode of formation, epistemes, like other autopoetic creations, also have very clear binary patterns of internal organization. Thus, very often it is quite clear what is inside an epistemic order and what must be kept on the outside. However, for Wynter the most important binary pattern of an episteme is the polarization between its founding category and its semiotic opposite. She refers to the latter as the "liminal" or "chaos" category of the episteme. For example, in the Christian episteme of medieval Europe, spirit constituted the founding category, while its semiotic opposite, the flesh, constituted the liminal category of this episteme (Wynter 1984).

In addition to these founding/liminal dynamics, the knowledge-constitutive creativity of epistemes is also profoundly shaped by what Wynter calls knowledge-constitutive goals. These are ordinary everyday goals that quite often are related to the social order that has been established. Thus salvation through the church, or fulfillment through political action are examples that Wynter has given of knowledge-constitutive goals. These goals help to orient the more formal aspects of epistemes to particular domains of reality, and thus aid in the production of specific kinds of knowledge whether spiritual, social or natural. Consequently, the organization of an episteme is never just a matter of the formal relations between categories, conceptual schemes and arguments, as in Kant's portrayal of the transcendental domain of the natural sciences. Rather, this organization must include definite socio-historical elements such as those goals that are definitely needed for epistemic closure. However, it is important to note that once epistemically selected this ordinary social goal is elevated and transcendentalized by the autopoetic powers of the episteme and thus becomes knowledge-constitutive in nature. Wynter's goals function a lot like Habermas's knowledge-constitutive interests (Habermas 1971). The latter also historicize Kant's formalism by opening two-way connections between the transcendental and social realms.

With this account of epistemes, Wynter then raises the question of their truth-producing capabilities. Although very necessary for human knowledge production, Wynter argues that epistemes are prone to systemic error from three basic sources. First, the dynamics between founding and liminal categories create significant truth-producing problems for epistemes. In Wynter's view, founding categories tend to inflate or "over-represent" the people, events and things assigned to them. In other words, whatever figure, claim or principle that is selected to serve as the center or ground of the episteme must at least have the appearance of an indefinite capacity to explain, and sufficient generality to subsume the contributions of other discourses. In securing these inflations, founding categories often make use of the "absolutization strategies" of epistemes. These include abductive moves such as mapping the contents of founding categories onto the cosmos itself or its eternal cycles and laws. In this way the significance of these contents are semiotically increased. These a priori or autopoetically prescribed features of epistemic centers are imposed on quite ordinary concepts and claims after they have been selected for this crucial role. Consequently, the built-in errors of founding categories are those of magnification and inflation in representational practices.

In contrast, liminal categories are marked by problems of systemic devaluation and minimalization in representation. This category and its contents are semiotically mapped onto negatives such as death, decay, evil and impermanence. Given such inscriptions, the question becomes how truthful or how adaptive will be the representations of this category? Will it be able to represent without being unduly influenced by the reproductive needs of its founding category? Wynter's answer is a clear no. Liminal categories distort and misrepresent their contents to the extent that they are semiotically read as threats to the autopoetic installing of the founding category. In short, they deflate and under-represent the objects, events and people assigned to them. Together, these dynamics between founding and liminal categories constitute the first major source of the tendencies of epistemes to systemic error (Wynter 1984: 39–41).

The second source derives from the incorporating of transcendentalized social goals into the semiotic logics of episteme formation. Like founding categories, knowledge-constitutive goals are inflated and over-represented because of their necessity to the internal order of the episteme. Very often they are absolutized to the degree that they are figuratively connected to the self-organization of the episteme. Correspondingly, whoever or whatever represents the opposite of these goals is deflated and under-represented. They cannot be read semiotically in an objective or positive light. They must be stigmatized, devalued and negated in the interest of the order of the episteme. So once again we have a necessary element in the constitution of epistemes that is prone to the systematic generation of error (Wynter 1992: 27).

The third and final source of systemic error in epistemes is the conditioning and orienting of their self-organizing activities by the larger auto-poetics of social orders. Earlier we examined the epistemological problems of these poetics. There we saw that they could only generate knowledge of an adaptive or "for us" nature. Wynter thinks that this basic pattern is reproduced on several levels of episteme formation and related discourse-constitutive activities. In short, because of this autopoetic inheritance epistemes are also unable to represent self, other and world without being unduly influenced by the self-organizing imperatives of the social orders in which they arise.

This error-prone view of epistemes could easily lead to a position of skepticism that could take us back to Hume or to some version of post-modern relativism. However, this is not the outcome that emerges from Wynter's historicizing of epistemes and the larger transcendental domain. Indeed, Wynter's autopoetic reading of Kant's transcendental a priorism makes some very distinctive contributions here. In this regard, Wynter's semiotic inscription of the transcendental domain can also be usefully compared to those of Charles Sanders Peirce and Karl Otto Apel (Peirce 1931: 227). Both have brought a semiotic dimension to the reading of transcendental activity that was largely absent in Kant and Husserl, and to a large degree also in Habermas. However, the socio-historical dimensions that are so evident in Habermas's transcendental analyses are much weaker in the cases of Pierce, Husserl and Apel. Consequently, the distinctness of Wynter's transcendentalism is the unprecedented degree to which it has both semioticized and historicized this knowledge-constitutive domain, and the ways in which it links the latter to the production of the condemned of the earth. Given this originality, it follows that Wynter's transcendentalism should lead to outcomes that are quite different from those of the above philosophers. The most important of these is of course Wynter's epistemic historicism.

EPISTEMIC HISTORICISM

Epistemic historicism is an approach to history as a medium of human self-formation (and not just as a discipline) that rests on the dynamic relationships that Wynter sees between epistemic change and the transformation of social orders. It is a view of history from the perspective of the epistemologically compromised autopoetic process of instituting and de-instituting social orders. In other words, it approaches history from the standpoint of the sociologically creative and founding activities of governing codes and templates. However, it is the representational instabilities of this epistemologically compromised sociological creativity that produces what I will call the epistemic motions that, for Wynter, drive the historical process. From this perspective, liminal and other epistemic crises do not lead to skepticism but to a revolutionary concept of historical possibilities that both challenges and engages those of Marxism.

Epistemic change is the complex process by which an individual or a group substantially transforms or moves beyond the episteme of its day by changing the binary oppositional orderings of its governing template and thus is able to think new thoughts in new discourses. For Wynter, the key to this process of change is the magnitude of errors generated by an episteme representation or misrepresentation of the people, objects, and events that are outside of its boundaries of inclusion. These errors will increase in magnitude as we approach the objects and subjects that the episteme semiotically reads as directly antithetical to its founding categories. This systemic mobilizing of error and mis-representation creates the most vulnerable area in the internal order of an episteme that may eventually lead to its decline. These representational instabilities of epistemes are part of the larger category of epistemic motions referred to earlier that constitute the wheels of history.

In cases of major errors of misrepresentation, the contrary signals or claims coming from the object or subject may force a shift in the organization of the episteme or its eventual overthrow and replacement by another episteme. The latter produces epochal changes while the former results in less dramatic changes in the existing social and epistemic orders. Thus the vulnerability introduced into the structure of an episteme by liminal strategies of representation arises out of the resistance of the liminalized to its portrayal and evaluation. The liminal other will persistently say, do, or achieve things that challenge and contradict its representation within the episteme. Such challenges create crises of credibility for the episteme and confront it with the need for change.

The nature and depth of these challenges will determine the extent to which the foundations of the episteme are shaken, or just some discursive formations on its upper surfaces. Clearly to achieve the former a challenge must be to have the semiotic power expose and reorder the binaries of the governing template on which the episteme was auto-instituted. In other words, the challenge must be to have the autopoetic power reorganize the episteme or write a new one into being. It must be able to get to the depths of the governing template, identify the sources of misrepresentation, propose and execute its rewriting. Only such a process will bring about revolutionary epistemic change and thus dramatic shifts in the representation of the condemned. Such shifts in the representation of this group could be the basis for major changes in the social order. This is the autopoetic link between epistemic and social orders that is at the heart of Wynter's epistemic historicism.

For Wynter, the paradigmatic example of a revolutionary epistemic shift remains the rise of the modern bourgeois episteme out of the spiritual episteme of medieval Christianity. Indeed, this epochal shift serves as one of the key founding analogies of Wynter's discourse of epistemic historicism. On the abductive wings of this analogy her thought expands to reach other themes such as race, gender, cinema, female circumcision, and specific authors such as Lamming, Glissant and James. Wynter has examined this shift in breathtaking detail, showing the ways in which challenges from lay humanists uprooted the founding flesh/spirit binary of the Christian episteme (Wynter 1984: 28–29). This is followed by equally detailed analyses of their reworking of the oppositions of its template that produced the bourgeois episteme. The latter was now re-centered around oppositions such as reason/lack of reason and property/lack of property. This was the secular episteme out of which the worlds of capitalism and socialism arose. As imperial extensions of the former, our colonial and post/neocolonial societies have been profoundly shaped by the governing template and codes of this episteme. In the anticolonial and antiracist discourses of Africana people, Wynter sees the possibility of an epistemic shift of epochal proportions. These discourses have exposed the systemic errors of the modern bourgeois episteme and hence have created crises of credibility for it.

Because of these *counter*impulses Wynter has called these Africana discourses "post-Western" (Wynter 1991: 88). However, Wynter remains deeply concerned about the fate of this Africana challenge as it does not appear to be decoding and rewriting the fundamental oppositions that have auto-instituted the Western bourgeois episteme. The Africana challenge has been unable to get to those depths because the discourses in which its alternatives are framed remain rooted in the bourgeois episteme and its governing template. As we will see, this is the context in which Wynter locates the current postcolonial/neocolonial impasse of Caribbean societies.

Looking at Caribbean societies from the perspective of Wynter's epistemic historicism, three broad epistemic periods emerge. First, a period governed by the pre-colonial episteme of African religions; second, a period governed by the spiritually hybrid Afro-Christian episteme; and third, the current period of our postcolonial episteme. In the first it was the codes, templates, and autopoetics of African sociogeny that informed the sociological creativity of Africans in the Caribbean. The second was the result of the replacing of some of these African codes and binary oppositions by Christian ones. Such changes in the governing codes and templates help to explain the rise of a distinct Afro-Caribbean subject. Finally, since the late nineteenth century there have been growing secular shifts culminating in our current postcolonial episteme. These have recentered the latter around binaries such as colonized/colonizer, black/white, freedom/domination, and developed/underdeveloped. These binaries in turn have made possible the articulating of important counter discourses that have guided major postcolonial transformations. However, these alternatives drew heavily on Western discourses such as Marxism, liberalism, positivism, and developmentalism, which indicated the extent to which our postcolonial alternatives were still rooted in the bourgeois episteme. Wynter's concern here is that with our currently mixed governing codes and templates, sociological creativity may be such that we are unable to write into being a genuinely post-Western social order in which the need for the condemned will be eliminated.

This in brief is Wynter's epistemic historicism. For the region it offers a new approach to the problems of historical action. Because of its theories of the auto-instituting of epistemic and social orders, it is an approach that demands of us a well-developed poetics, and, in particular, an interventionist poetics that is capable of rewriting the governing codes and templates that inscribe the a priori condition of epistemic and social orders. As intellectuals, we must become the rewriters of codes and so be able to change the current directions and velocities of epistemic motion in the interest of reclaiming the humanity of the condemned. As such, this poetics opens up revolutionary possibilities for social change at the same time that it challenges us to explore more deeply the repairing of liminal and other tendencies to systemic error that still continue to plague our sociological and epistemic creativity. We will return to these themes in our discussion of Wynter and James. But first, a brief phenomenological detour in which we examine more carefully the nature of the discontinuities that exist between the transcendental and everyday levels of discursive activity. This will also be important for our examination of the Marxian model of dialectical synthesis from the perspective of Wynter's epistemic historicism.

EPISTEMIC HISTORICISM, PHENOMENOLOGY AND POETICS

Throughout our exposition of Wynter's epistemic historicism we have made several references to the hidden foundations of discourses. We have referred to that domain of otherness in which governing codes, templates and epistemes work to establish the a priori conditions that make routine knowledge production possible. We've also suggested that this sub-textual level of activity was not available or accessible to us in the same way that the results of more conscious efforts at textual or discursive production are. What we have not made clear is the nature of this sub-textual hiddenness, the discontinuities it creates between episteme and discourse, and how Wynter and other transcendentalists have been able to get around these difficulties in moving between the textual and sub-textual levels.

In examining this problem of sub-textual unavailability, the key observation that must be kept in mind is that we are often unaware of the epistemic foundations upon which our discursive practices rest and thus are unable to articulate them. This suggests two important features of the relationships between episteme and discourse. First, epistemes are not established in the same symbolic registers as the discourses we routinely manipulate or produce. Epistemes are produced in autopoetic registers that are unconscious, semio-linguistically organized systems of symbolic creativity. The discourses that we normally produce on the a priori foundations established by epistemes are constructed within the creative registers of self-conscious subjects. These are two very different sets of creative codes and between them there is often little that is immediately or automatically translatable. Think of the cases of the language of physics or sociology on the one hand and that of the transcendental or epistemic on the other. There are significant problems of commensurability here. Hence Wynter's insistence that we "silence" or step out of our everyday discursive practices and learn the autopoetic language of epistemic and social orders.

Second, our inability to directly reach the epistemic from routine discursive locations suggests the possibility of a mutually displacing relationship between the two. If epistemes were always present, they would get in the way of normal knowledge production as we only make conscious use of small portions of them. To create knowledge with them, we must be able to lose sight of them, to let them go. The more we consciously focus on them the less we are able to engage in routine knowledge production. Indeed, the relationship between episteme and live acts of knowledge production is a lot like Heisenberg's uncertainty principle. We cannot have both at the same time. The more we have of one, the less available becomes the other. Another way of thinking about this mutually displacing aspect of the relationship between episteme and discourse is to view it as one in which the contributions of both must be written simultaneously in their different registers on opposite sides of the same sheet of paper. Thus, when we are writing, we are unable to access the epistemic inscriptions that are being made on the other side of the sheet. Indeed, we must forget them if we are to produce commonly desired forms of knowledge. This discursive forgetting of the epistemic is an integral part of most of our modes of knowledge production. To gain access to the epistemic from one of our normal discursive locations we usually have to interrupt our knowledge-producing activities, turn the sheet over and shift to the register of autopoetics. In other words, one has to be silenced or suspended for the other to emerge and be heard. In Wynter's language, it is in "the great silence" of the epistemic that live discursive production is born; and conversely, it is in the great silence of live discursive production that the epistemic is reborn or remembered.

These two factors, the need for silence and translation between episteme and discourse, points to the qualitatively different nature of the relations between these two as compared to relations between one discourse and another. Epistemes are absent presences, while discourses are present presences. There are imperatives that come with the former type of presences that are absent in the case of the latter. Modes of discursive silencing must be cultivated as well as practices of translation if absent presences are to be recovered. This recovery of the epistemic domain through the silencing or suspending of everyday practices brings us very close to the world of phenomenological self-reflection. Phenomenology, particularly as practiced by Husserl, can be viewed as a form of discursive remembering that is an antidote to the necessary forgetting of the epistemic foundations that human knowledge production requires. Thus phenomenological self-reflection is one way in which we can navigate the discontinuous transcendental terrain between discourse and episteme.

However, this phenomenological recovery of the transcendental domain can take place with the aid of different discursive searchlights. The subject who is returning to the transcendental ground will do so from some point inside of the discourse in which he/she is currently inscribed. Thus it is through the prism of that discourse that the transcendental domain will be perceived and not necessarily that of philosophical logic as in the cases of Kant and Husserl. As we have already seen it is through the prism of poetics that Wynter approaches the transcendental domain. This is why she is able to return from her explorations of this domain with epistemic gifts that are quite different from those of Kant and Husserl. The primary gifts with which Wynter returns are those of transcendental codes and templates and not that of the transcendental subject.

As novelist, playwright and critic, Wynter's roots are in the Caribbean poeticist tradition along with George Lamming, Wilson Harris, Derek Walcott, Jamaica Kincaid and others.[1] However, what is distinctive about Wynter's intellectual development is the extent to which she has been able to suspend normal processes of poetic composition and reach the epistemic ground of her own poetic creativity. Consequently, Wynter's approach to the transcendental has been through effective suspensions of the conditions of producing poetic knowledge rather than those of producing scientific, logical, moral or mathematical knowledge. It is out of this self-reflection of the poet, this turning over of the sheet upon which her poetic compositions were written, that Wynter's distinctive poetics arises and at the same time acquires its phenomenological dimensions. It is the extensive and intensive development of this poetic phenomenology that has given Wynter the ability to overcome the discursive discontinuities and inaccessibilities that normally keep the transcendental realm hidden. Thus if we too are going to be able to overcome these difficulties, then we are going to have to develop phenomenological practices that are appropriate for suspending the normal routines of discourses in which we are inscribed.

Out of her poetic phenomenology, Wynter has produced the important concept of ceremonies. Wynter's ceremonies address the autopoetic dimensions of the discontinuities between episteme and discourse. To engage these aporias or discourse resistant gaps, semiotic ways must be found to recode and de-institutionalize this very opposition and abductively related ones, so that processes of suspension, translation and loosening of auto-instituted epistemic boundaries can begin. Semiotic recodings such as these are at the core of Wynter's ceremonies. They are the reality behind the title of Wynter's classic essay, "The Ceremony Must Be Found: After Humanism." Ceremonies or appropriate semiotic recodings of binaries and their abductive extensions must be found and performed at the sites of autopoetically instituted divides, absolutizations, closures and liminal categorizations. This is the only way in which these discourse-constitutive formations can be undone or de-instituted. Everyday discursive critiques may shake but not change the epistemic foundations on which these discourse-constitutive elements are reproduced on an ongoing basis. Perhaps the divide between the creativity of transcendental subjects and that of transcendental templates persists because the appropriate ceremonies have not yet been found to de-institute the autopoetic inscriptions that keep it in place. For the more scientifically inscribed, Wynter's call for a science of signs to unlock autopoetically established divides may be more appealing. For the still more technically inscribed, I suggest thinking of these ceremonies as epistemic engineering. This is important as we should be able to reach these epistemic foundations from the various discourses in which we are inscribed. As we will see, this call for ceremonies will be extremely important for Wynter's reading of Marxism.

WYNTER, JAMES AND MARXISM

Working at these subtextual depths, there is the real danger that Wynter could become so entangled in an autopoetic textualism that she would lose sight of the pressing social concerns of the Caribbean and beyond. This was the concern that Brian Meeks raised so forcefully at the end of the presentation of this paper at the conference, "After Man, Towards the Human." Because of the poetic coherence and the comprehensive scope of her work, there is no such forgetting or losing sight of the social on Wynter's part. The social occupies two ineliminable places in Wynter's poetics. First the creation of social orders is the primary function of autopoetic processes. Second, Wynter's subtextual explorations have been consistently motivated by the misrepresentations of the condemned in the European social sciences and humanities. It is the latter social concern that has brought Wynter's epistemic historicism into its critical engagement with Marxism. This engagement has been a mutually influencing one, with each leaving definite marks on the other.

As a discourse of the European social sciences, Wynter approaches Marxism with an awareness of the compromised and error-prone epistemic foundations upon which it rests. But at the same time Marxism is openly critical of much of European social scientific knowledge. Much of this opposition was directed at the way in which the condemned working classes of Europe were represented in that tradition. Not only do these two philosophies converge here, but there are also important overlaps between their historical frameworks. Thus the crucial points of divergence will be over the roles of epistemicism and materialism in explaining the status of the condemned.

In Wynter's view, Marx made the mode of economic production the governing template and hence the foundation upon which his discourse rested. This materialism with the economic as its founding category was discursive produced by setting it in liminal opposition to the idealistic domains of spirit, art, ideology and so on. As such, it was a very distinctive move within the secular episteme of European modernity that definitely made possible new ways of economic seeing. This episteme had already de-transcendentalized spirit as a knowledge-constitutive and self-troping category, and replaced it with bio-economic ones. Consequently, both knowledge production and self-constitution could be done in these terms. Marx's transcendentalizing of the mode of production deepened and extended this bio-economic restructuring of the spiritual episteme of medieval Europe. Indeed, it was upon these foundations that Marx erected his labor theoretic concept of the human as worker/direct producer. The critical power of Marxism, its ability to recognize the exploited status of the European working classes, has a lot to do with its distinct location within the modern episteme of European social science. Given this distinct location, the key question for Wynter is whether or not this oppositional discourse within the Western episteme could adequately represent the condemned of the colonies who had also been racialized. Her doubts about Marxism in this regard were raised by two crucial factors: the needs that motivated James's repeated reworking of classical Marxism; and second, Wynter's concern that the dynamics of founding and liminal categories that had already compromised the modern Western episteme, were continuing to affect Marxism in spite of its distinct location and oppositional stances.

Wynter's entry into James's corpus is through what she calls his "poeisis." By this she means the discursive strategies through which James was able to reach the foundations of both Marxism and liberalism in order to restructure them. At this sub-textual level, Wynter sees the aim of James's poeisis as a "constant and sustained attempt to shift the 'system of abduction' first of colonial liberalism, later of Stalinist and Trotskyist Marxism, and overall, of the bourgeois cultural model and its underlying head/body, reason/instinct metaphorics" (Wynter 1992). In short, what interests Wynter in James's poeisis is the series of displacements and re-incorporations, or de-instituting and re-instituting activities around the labor theoretic foundations of Marxism in which he was constantly engaged.

In Wynter's view, these subtextual transformations of epistemic foundations made James's Marxism pluri-conceptual rather than mono-conceptual. In addition to the transcendentalizing of the mode of economic production and its labor theoretic concept of the human, James found it necessary to find epistemic spaces for categories of race and gender. Indeed, the biological elements in the modern European concept of the human had already transcendentalized racial and gender categories, making possible the unprecedented production of racial discourses. To generate the necessary counter discourses to this massive racial misrepresentation, James had to make subtextual adjustments in his Marxism.

Wynter suggests that James felt the need to make these adjustments because he had been racialized as a "negro." As such this identity was an integral part of a larger template that shaped an intricate permutation of color, levels of education, levels of wealth, and levels of "culture" (Wynter 1992: 68). This permutation of values derived from "the a priori categories" of an ego-constitutive template that included head/body, reason/instinct analogies (Wynter 1992: 68). Because of their fluidity and plurality, these permutations gave rise to multiple identities that carried different ratios of value and associated measures of misrepresentation and domination. Consequently, a "system of color value existed side by side with capital value, education value, merit value, and labor" (Wynter 1992: 69). Each of these had their own variations on the underlying themes of modes of coercion and domination. As a result, the factory model of domination was only one of many that were generated by this governing template of identity formation. Hence it could not be singled out and epistemically centered in the exclusive way that it had been in classical Marxism. For Wynter, "the quest for a frame to contain them all came to constitute the Jamesian poeisis" (Wynter 1992: 69).

This pluri-conceptual framework produced by James's poeisis, Wynter refers to as the pieza conceptual framework. The pieza was "the name given by the Portuguese, during the slave trade, to the African who functioned as the standard measure, the general equivalent of physical value against which all others could be measured" (Wynter 1992: 81). He was a man of about 25 years who was also in good health. In the Jamesian poeisis, "the pieza becomes an even more general category of value, establishing equivalences between a wider variety of oppressed labor power" (Wynter 1992: 81). With this pieza conceptual framework in place, the epistemic foundations of James's Marxism now had not one but a number of founding categories that were engaged in relations of mutual displacement and reincorporation. Consequently, the labor theoretic concept no longer had an exclusive hold on the a priori role of founding category. This now had to be shared with race theoretic and gender theoretic concepts that could displace and reincorporate labor theoretic concepts in a changed epistemic architecture. This was the pieza complexity that distinguished James's Marxism.

In addition to changing the conditions and possibilities of knowledge production, the pieza conceptual framework also changed the conditions and possibilities of self-troping. Within the pieza framework, as opposed to that of classical Marxism, it was not just the human as worker/direct producer that was in need of liberation. There were also other registers and social practices in which humans were condemned. Among these are the racialized and the jobless. For the latter, "the identity of labor is not the norm" (Wynter 1992: 75). Indeed, the jobless can become the liminal category of labor theoretic discourses. Thus in the pieza conceptual framework, the category of human beings to be liberated is a greatly expanded one that takes in the lumpen proletariat, peasants, the racialized, and women. In this context, there can be no one revolutionary subject or no single correct line. Rather, there must be multiple revolutionary subjects and multiple lines. This de-centering and reincorporating of the revolutionary potential of the proletariat into a larger whole is for Wynter "the great heresy of the Jamesian poeisis" (Wynter 1992: 75). This was the move on James's part that convinced Wynter that Marx's transcendentalizing of the mode of economic production was not radical enough of an epistemic change to make possible the adequate representation of the condemned in the colonies.

As noted earlier, Wynter's second concern about Marxism was its location within the error-prone Western episteme in spite of its reorganization of the latter. What this reorganization did not engage were the liminal dynamics that Marxism had inherited from this episteme. Hence the likelihood that these dynamics were still compromising Marxist processes of knowledge production. Again, it was James's reading first of Stalinism and later of Trotskyism that convinced Wynter of the relevance of these liminal dynamics to the crisis that had overtaken Marxism.

The liminal dynamics of Marxism can be seen on several levels of its discursive structure. As we saw earlier, the auto-instituting of the mode of production as founding category was in part achieved through the semiotic manipulation of binaries such as materialism/idealism as well as their abductive extensions and absolutizations. Linked to the material by relations of sameness, the economic can be epistemically centered by semiotically privileging materialism and its extensions over idealism and its extensions. In conjunction with a similar pattern of privileging between other relevant binaries, it was possible to establish the economic as a founding category. However, this necessarily entails the liminalization of the ideal and its figurative extensions that are linked to the economic as founding category by relations of difference. Hence, Wynter is not surprised by Marxism's difficulties in adequately representing the role of culture in social life.

This epistemically restricted view of the role of culture is an important factor motivating Wynter's reordering of relations between modes of economic production and modes of social speciation. This inversion is not between the economic and any specific cultural practice of everyday life, but between the former and the autopoetic instituting of the a priori conditions upon which such practices rest. This is the level at which Marxism's liminal reading of idealism runs into trouble. In other words, the cultural practice that Wynter demands of Marx is that of the explicit thematizing of those semiotic manoeuvres by which he was able to secure the centering of the economic. Only from such an examination of its own foundations will Marxism take control of its liminal dynamics, and come to a better knowledge of the founding powers of culture.

Much more significant are the liminal dynamics associated with the representation of both the social goal of Marxism and its opposite. The former is of course the liberation of the proletariat. Thus we should look for liminal dynamics in relation to whoever is semiotically represented as binary opposites of the proletariat. The most obvious of such relations of difference are those with the capitalist. But there are others. Wynter's entry into these liminal dynamics of Marxism is through James's category of the "millions in the forced labor camps" (Wynter 1991: 61).

Wynter is disturbed but not floored by the emergence of this Stalinist category. Her response is to locate its roots in the semiotic economy of Marxism. In doing this, she follows James in trying to identify what he called "the laws of thought" that could make necessary the use of such a category (Wynter 1991: 67). For Wynter, the laws of thought are autopoetically established. Hence it is to the founding template that provided the initial categories for self-troping that she turns. These categories are inscribed in the chain of signifiers and origin narratives that made possible the discursive production of the proletarian genre of the human as the desired mode of the subject. Wynter explains the rise of this discursive possibility by linking it to the foundations laid by liberal bourgeois notions of the human that were "encoded in the metaphysics of the privatized ownership of mobile property" (Wynter 1991: 67). The proletarian concept of the human was a variant of the liberal one, and was encoded in "the metaphysics of nationalized property" (Wynter 1991: 67). Remaining within the Western episteme and unable to thematize its own liminal dynamics, the proletarian concept of the human could only become a desired mode of the subject by creating and deploying undesired modes of the subject. Wynter suggests that into the latter category was placed all those who were read as representing the danger of a historical regression and a slide back into the dictatorship of private ownership of property. In addition to the capitalist, the Zek, still inscribed in the private/peasant mode of being, was also put into this category. Semiotically, the latter was seen as "a capitalist roader who sought to hold back the emancipation of the proletariat" (Wynter 1991: 80). Consequently, he could be condemned and interned as expendable and discardable forced labor.

This role of the Zek, Wynter links to the status of other liminalized groups who make up the condemned of the earth. She makes them semiotic equivalents of the workers and "negroes" of the liberal discourses based on private property. Wynter writes:

> we can therefore generalize the systemic role of James's "millions in the labor camps" to that of all such parallel group categories, to whom the generic name of les damnes, as defined by Fanon and translated by James as the condemned, can now be given. We can also, in the wake of both James and Fanon, generalize the definition of the systemic function played by their proscribed and interned status as . . . that of verifying the specific mode of over-representation by which the interests of

the ruling group are made equitable with projected interest of the "common good" of their system-specific collectivity. (Wynter 1991: 68)

Along with these cases of the former Soviet Union and Eastern Europe, Wynter has pointed to similar dynamics in the Grenadian Revolution of 1979. In short, it is these liminal dynamics that Wynter thinks are responsible for the crises and contradictory outcomes that have overtaken Marxism both in the Caribbean and abroad. Without a more radical and explicit thematizing of its own autopoetics, Marxism will not be able to avoid these liminal disasters that have their roots in the larger Western episteme in which it is embedded.

WYNTER'S CEREMONIES AND POST-MARXIAN SYNTHESES

The revolutionary project that Wynter's epistemic historicism holds up before us is a multi-dimensional one. It requires us to engage multiple logics of domination and coercion, to recognize multiple revolutionary subjects, and also to be deeply involved in the explicit thematizing of the autopoetics of the governing codes and templates by which the above logics are instituted as the a priori foundations of both discursive and social practices. More specifically, it means recognizing the distinct liminal logics that operate to condemn the humanity of women, blacks, workers, the jobless, Zeks, Jews and others so that particular elites can auto-institute and stably replicate their social projects and their own "ethno-class" concept of the human. Consequently, the intellectual challenge here is to find a pluri-conceptual or pieza framework that is even more inclusive than James's. This we can attempt by making its concept of the human none of the local genres listed above, but a more genuinely universal one in which they could all participate: a concept of the human that takes explicit account of the autopoetic processes by which all of these local or ethno-class concepts are discursively established. This transcendental concept of the human as a self-constituting agent, but one whose constituting activities are mediated by epistemologically problematic governing codes, templates and epistemes is the most comprehensive view that we get of Wynter's philosophical anthropology. In Wynter's view, such a concept of the human and its related episteme could be the basis for the first social order without a liminal other and hence truly human. This new episteme could also be one in which the representational problems of the humanities and social sciences would be solved. Such a freeing of these disciplines from current levels of subjugation to the adaptive needs of our autopoetic reproduction would put them on par with the natural sciences, which achieved their liberation with the emergence of the modern Western episteme. This liberating of the social sciences and the humanities would be the real basis for what Wynter has called the "post-Western" discourses or "the rewriting of knowledge"

(Wynter 1984: 43). In short, these are the dimensions of the powerful vision of the future to which Wynter's epistemic historicism calls us.

For Caribbean Marxists in particular, it means advancing the project begun by the Jamesian poeisis as well as that of Fanon's. For feminists, it means developing the ability to displace gender as an exclusive founding category of knowledge production and self-troping, and to reincorporate it into a more inclusive epistemic formation. However, this expansion must be secured by making its process of auto-instituting the feminine an integral part of its concept of the human. In this way it could become pluri-conceptual and at the same time establish control over its discourse-constitutive need to create and deploy a category of the conceptual other. For Pan Africanists, black nationalists, and other race theoretic discourses, Wynter's epistemic historicism means the de-centering of racial categories and their reorganization in an expanded epistemic framework in which their founding status would be shared with class and gender. Again, an epistemic change of this type could only be achieved by drawing on a concept of the human as a being that is capable of auto-instituting these and many other genres of the human. In short, we all have transcendental work to do, for which we are going to need a poeisis or a poetics that will empower us and supply us with the ceremonies by which our current local concepts of the human and their liminal others can be de-instituted and reincorporated in new and more inclusive epistemes.

However, it is precisely at this point that we encounter some of the major intellectual obstacles in the way of Wynter's project of rewriting epistemes and changing social orders. These difficulties arise because the ceremony "that will wed Desdemona to the huge Moor," the feminist to the womanist, or the proletarian to his jobless brother have not yet been found (Wynter 1984: 19). The absence of these ceremonies are evident in the splits that continue to divide these groups, and leave them open to the co-opting strategies of an increasingly plutocratic capitalism. Establishing genuine discursive syntheses and bonds of human solidarity, or co-speciation across these divides is indeed the crucial cultural and intellectual challenge before us. Overcoming them will require finding new ways and new ceremonies by which currently separated analytic discourses can be wed to constitute new discursive totalities or syntheses. On this point, a further examination of Marxism in the mirror of Wynter's epistemic historicism will be very rewarding.

In Marxism, the dialectical synthesis created around the political as a modality of the economic holds a very central and privileged position. This synthesis is perceived as a paradigm for other dialectical totalizations. In this case, the coming together of these two analytic domains clearly reinforces the explanatory power of the economic, making the advantages of the synthesis very clear. The crucial question that arises here is whether or not this classic Marxian synthesis can be a model for the ones that a pluri-conceptual and autopoetically self-conscious epistemic framework would require. Given all that has been said about the discontinuities between episteme and discourse, this question must be answered in the negative. To see this more clearly, let us take a closer look at the relation between economic discourse and the epistemic in Marxism.

The most likely response of Marxism to Wynter's epistemicism would be to include it as a partial cultural formation within its economically centered dialectal totalization. In other words, it would see the epistemic as another cultural modality in which the economic can be lived. Wynter's concept of knowledge-constitutive goals, by opening up episteme to historical influences lends some truth to such a reading. However, if at the same time epistemes are the autopoetically established a priori foundations of economic knowledge production, this status places severe limitations on the above reading for two basic reasons.

First, as a priori foundations, epistemes are not available for economic knowledge production in the same way that political and everyday cultural practices are. The latter are also written on the upper side of the page as the economic, just in different scripts. To reach them from inside an economic discourse it may not be necessary to turn over the page as in the case of reaching epistemes. Here a shifting of the gaze and some translating between knowledge-producing codes may be all that is necessary. Consequently, there is a sharper break separating the economic from the epistemic as compared to the economic and the political.

Second, there is greater incommensurability between the knowledge-producing codes of transcendental and economic discourses than between the latter and political discourses. Economic and political discourses share strategic and instrumental orientations as well as institutional concerns largely absent in the case of transcendental discourses. Between economic and political discourses the working out of what Charles Mills has called "intertheoretical inconsistencies" have been much easier to achieve because of this greater similarity in discursive codes (Mills 2001: 206). In short, because we do not have to turn over the economic page to find the political and the high level of commensurability between their creative codes, a classic dialectical synthesis is possible. However, between the economic and the epistemic/transcendental these ideal conditions do not hold. Consequently, a dialectical synthesis of similar discursive quality cannot be forged between the two. The result would of necessity be a synthesis that was more formal, abstract and with less explanatory power.

This difference in the discursive quality of epistemic/economic syntheses as compared to political/economic ones, raises questions about dialectical constructions of race/economic, gender/economic, gender/race and other syntheses that would have to emerge from Wynter's pluri-conceptual framework. Is it likely that they would have the discursive quality and explanatory power as the politico-economic one that stands at the heart of Marxism? I do not think so. I take this position because, as in the case of the epistemic, the discourse-constitutive conditions for such a synthesis will not be met in most of these cases. For example, mutual recodings of texts between the economic and the political have been much easier than those between economic and religious texts, or between semiotic and political texts. In other words, because of differences like these, more radical displacements of the centered discourse will be necessary for a seeing of the other than in the case of political economy.

These are the dynamics that Jean-Paul Sartre's *Search for a Method* (Sartre 1968) gestured toward but did not really find. In my view, these are also the dynamics that make Hardt and Negri's *Empire* a very problematic work (Hardt and Negri 2000). Its conceptual framework is a dialectical synthesis of the political and the semiotic. In this regard, it has attempted to shift the epistemic ground of Marxism by forging a new synthesis of the type that should emerge from Wynter's pluri-conceptual framework. However, as a synthesis it definitely does not cohere as well as the politico-economic one, and hence does not have its explanatory power. The intertheoretical inconsistencies that result from different creative codes are not well worked out. This attempt at a synthesis between the political and the semiotic is not as successful as Cornelius Castoriadis's *The Imaginary Institution of Society* (2000) or Jean Baudrillard's *The Mirror of Production* (1975). One feels throughout Hardt and Negri's text the unresolved tensions between political and semiotic codes. Further, the loss in explanatory power is evident in the fact that Marxian political economy allows for a better thematizing of the semiotic than this political/semiotic synthesis allows for a thematizing of the economic. Indeed, the economic becomes almost invisible and unthematizable within the framework of this synthesis. This stands in sharp contrast to Negri's solo work, *Time for Revolution* (2003), which rests on a synthesis of political economy and phenomenology. The failure of *Empire* raises the question of the appropriateness of a dialectical model of synthesis for bringing together these two distinct analytical registers.

Given these wide variations in the discursive quality of non-politico-economic dialectical syntheses, it is very likely that the problem resides in the dialectical framework that these totalizing attempts have inherited from classical Marxism. This model needs to be seen as being unique to the marrying of the political and the economic, and not paradigmatic for other discursive marriages. Marxism did indeed find the ceremonies by which its two key analytic discourses could be wed. It did not find the ceremonies by which others could be similarly joined. Consequently, the discovery of these ceremonies is the challenge before us.

To find these ceremonies, we will need a new or post-dialectical model of synthesis. Borrowing a term from the Caribbean poet, Kamau Brathwaite,[2] I will call this new model of synthesis tidalectical. The major difference between a dialectical and a *tidalectical* synthesis is that the latter will not be epistemically grounded in a single fixed center, but in multiple centers that are mutually displacing and reincorporating of each other. These fluid, back and forth currents are the epistemic motions that will distinguish tidalectical syntheses from dialectical ones. In the case of classical Marxian political economy, the epistemic center is primarily occupied by the economic with the political being its most important masked modality. The reverse is not really possible in this epistemic framework. Consequently, there can be no major back and forth tidalectical currents as in the case of James's race/economic synthesis. The suggestion that I am making is that in the cases of political/semiotic, gender/race and other syntheses, a tidalectical model may be more appropriate than the classical dialectical one. This more fluid framework is necessary as the comparative case with which the political can exist as a modality of the economic is not repeated in the cases of these syntheses. It is thus more difficult to reach one of these discourses from within the knowledge-producing field of the other. A result of this difficulty is that there has to be a greater displacing or silencing of one for the contributions of the other to be seen than in the case of political economy. Further, when one is reworked in the codes of the other, the quality of the reproductions are a lot poorer. Thus the only solution in these cases is a more fluid or tidalectical model of synthesis in which analytic discourses mutually displace and reincorporate one another.

If indeed the tidalectical model of synthesis is the more paradigmatic, then we must recognize that the autopoetic and epistemic ceremonies by which such syntheses can be established have not yet been found. These we must now work to uncover. For Caribbean Marxists, it will mean advancing the pluri-conceptual (race/political economy) tendencies found in James, Padmore, Fanon, and Du Bois in particular. In our search for these ceremonies, we will have to pay close attention to at least four sets of factors. First, we must note carefully the distinctive strategies of discursive forgetting by which the epistemic is silenced, and the corresponding patterns of phenomenological remembering by which it can be recovered within the categories of that discourse. As the work of Habermas and Wynter clearly suggest, these patterns of forgetting and remembering vary widely between discourses. Thus to the extent that these patterns are autopoetically prescribed, ceremonies will have to be found for their de-instituting, the flipping over of the page on which both episteme and discourse have been inscribed, and their re-instituting.

Second, as already noted, we will have to pay close attention to differences in incommensurability in the epistemic and discursive codes that figure prominently in the production of knowledge in the fields that are being synthesized. These will determine the magnitude of the intertheoretical inconsistencies that must be worked out for the totalization to be mutually beneficial. At the discursive level, the solution to recoding problems may be readily available and hence may not require any special ceremonies. However, in the case of codes that are epistemically pre-scribed, such ceremonies will be necessary. Thus the discursive crossing of categorical breaks or aporias that are epistemically inscribed, becomes a prohibition that is very difficult to remove from within the framework of any of the discourses being synthesized. We will have to become skilled at recognizing such aporias and other discourse-constitutive patterns that have been established a priori.

Third, finding these Wynterian ceremonies will require discursive techniques for reaching and engaging the governing templates that provide the classificatory systems of sameness and difference around which epistemes are auto-instituted. These techniques will in turn require the cultivating of a poetics or a science of signs that will be more inclusive than James's poeisis, and better able to control founding and liminal dynamics.

Fourth and finally, we will have to think more carefully about the relationships between the epistemic and the organizational structures of societies studied by sociologists. For Wynter, the governing categories of epistemes, through both knowledge-producing and cultural practices, are encoded in the organizational structures of societies. These "structural encodings of cultural conceptions are made possible by the fact that the structure serves as the abduction system for the thought systems and vice-versa" (Wynter 1992: 67). Thus the cultural and epistemic aspects of social organizations such as the state are as original as its structural aspects. In other words, each can serve as a code for the other's development. This "equiprimordiality" of structure and cultural concept points to three relatively autonomous levels of institutionalization in Wynter: the epistemic, the discursive and the sociological. The epistemic reaches the sociological or organizational level by making its codes and patterns of binary opposition constitutive analogies within the instrumental and functional logics of social organizations. Consequently, the social institutions that make up human societies are triply established by autopoetic/epistemic codes, discursive legitimation and social organizing. This suggests that institutions cannot be fully grasped at just the sociological and discursive levels as we often attempt to do. Their autopoetic and epistemic roots must also be recognized. Thus to unlock the autopoetic or epistemic connections that may be helping to keep an institution in place, new ceremonies will have to be found. In other words, to really change an institution we must "call into question both the structure of social reality and the structure of its analogical epistemology" (Wynter 1992: 67).

Without the discovery of ceremonies that are capable of undoing and redoing autopoetic and epistemic inscriptions we will not be able to produce the new tidalectical syntheses required by Wynter's pluri-conceptual framework. Without these syntheses the new discourses and new bonds of co-speciation needed for concerted mass action in the present period will continue to elude us.

CONCLUSION

The above ceremonial challenges are important consequences of the pluri-conceptual and tidalectical directions in which Wynter's epistemic historicism takes us. It lays bare the transcendental foundations of our discourses and the epistemic restructuring that we must carry out if we are to get going again with our postcolonial project of liberating the condemned through the establishing of a new social order. Although Wynter's historicism emphasizes the importance of the epistemic wheels of history, she is well aware that epistemic motion alone will not be enough to produce the overthrow of the bourgeoisie and its bio-economic concept of the human. Both have also been triply instituted. Consequently, uprooting its founding codes and destroying its discursive legitimation will often leave its sociological levels of institutionalization as viable bases from which to fight back. It is here that Wynter's epistemic historicism must seek sociological supplements from Marxism. Epistemic motion must be supplemented by social motion if real historical change is to be effected. Both are needed for the realization of a post-bourgeois social order. Marxism needs epistemic supplements if it is to uproot autopoetic codes and aporias. As Baudrillard has pointed out, "you cannot defend against the code with political economy or 'revolution'" (Poster 1988: 122). The ceremonies must be found that will link these two—code and political economy—if we are to move beyond our present bourgeois order. Wynter's epistemic historicism is a crucial step in the making of these important discoveries.

NOTES

* First published as "Sylvia Wynter and the Transcendental Spaces of Caribbean Thought," in B. Anthony Bogues (ed.), *After Man, Towards the Human: Critical Essays on the Thought of Sylvia Wynter* (Kingston, Jamaica: Ian Randle), 258–89.

1. For an analysis of this tradition, see my *Caliban's Reason* (Henry 2000a: 91–114).
2. See Elizabeth DeLoughery (1998).

Part II

Caribbean Political Economy and Cultural Development

FIVE

Grenada and the Theory of Peripheral Transformation

In their attempts to overcome the problems of national subjugation and underdevelopment, many peripheral countries have resorted to social strategies. These socialist projections have taken a variety of forms and have produced widely varying outcomes. The Caribbean has certainly not been an exception: for example, Cuba, Jamaica, Guyana and Grenada. Although Grenada's experiment came to a tragic and premature end, its history will continue to have great importance for both the practical and theoretical questions surrounding the possibilities for radical change in peripheral societies. From the standpoint of political theory, Grenada's experiment has demonstrated the extent to which concrete political practice had moved ahead of regional academic theorizing. In its political form, the latter has remained largely within the liberal framework.[1] To the extent that theorizing has moved beyond the rigid boundaries set up by the East–West conflict, it has occurred primarily in economics with the rise of dependency theory. As articulated in the works of theorists such as Beckford (1971), Girvan (1971) and Thomas (1974), it has provided some carefully formulated critiques of dependent capitalist models of development and suggested alternative proposals. Although significant, they have included only very limited accounts of alternatives to the liberal state and equally limited analyses of the problems that would accompany their establishment. This restricting of political theorizing to the liberal tradition was because the Guyanese and Jamaican experiments with socialism took place in a political context that left the basic elements of the liberal state very much in place. However, this was not the case in Grenada. Here the experiment brought with it new forms of political organization that moved beyond the liberal tradition. Consequently, the assimilation of this experience requires that regional political theory ex-

115

pand its conceptual infrastructure to include the political aspects of transition processes and the analysis of socialist political formations.

This paper represents a step toward the reformulation of regional
political theory to include the Grenadian experience. In particular, I examine the nature of the socialist state as it emerged in Grenada and the
problem of its legitimization in the English-speaking Caribbean, given
the social conditions and the political culture. I begin with an analysis of
the political, economic and cultural aspects of the transformation actually
achieved. Then I present a general outline of the most mature socialist
state that the regional political culture has been able to support, and
examine some conditions for its legitimation.

REGIONAL THEORIES OF THE STATE

Although the problems of the transition to socialism have been more
explicitly addressed in the economic literature, a review of the political
literature indicates that it, too, has been moving in this direction. As
major developments in the region have been consistently reflected in this
literature, it is possible to organize regional political theory around five
major issues: (1) the processes of political decolonization and (2) regional
integration, (3) the problems of race and (4) electoral politics, and (5) the
current struggles for economic independence. The importance of decolonization is clearly reflected in the works of theorists such as Munroe
(1972), Stone (in Henry and Stone 1983a: 37–61), Danns (in Henry and
Stone 1983a: 63–93), and Henry (1985a). Some of the problems and possibilities of regional integration have been analyzed in the works of Lewis
and Singham (in Munroe and Lewis 1971: 171–78). The issues of race and
politics have been central to the writings of Greene (1974), Ryan (1972),
Danns (1981) and Edmondson (in Ince 1979: 33–35). Detailed studies of
electoral behavior in the region have been made by Stone (1974), Greene
(1974) and Emmanuel (1979). Finally, the problems of economic independence are reflected in the works of authors such as Parris (in Ince 1979:
242–59), Stone (1980), Danns (1981), Ashley (in Henry and Stone 1983a:
159–76) and Maingot (in Fagen 1979: 254–301). More than any of the
previous sets of issues, the attempts to deal with the last of these problems led inevitably to the consideration of alternatives to existing dependent arrangements. This movement toward the problems and possibilities of radical transformation is very clear in the works on Jamaica and
Guyana, as they had been attempting to introduce some form of socialism although our theorists were not optimistic. At the end of the analysis
of Jamaica, Guyana and Trinidad, Maingot comes to the following conclusion:

> Short of full-scale social and political revolution, which appears no-
> where in the offing, these West Indian societies will not be able to break

out of the present pattern of structural dependence. The trend that a wide spectrum of the dominant elites of these nations prefer is a state directed populism with an assigned role for the private sector and an active but non-aligned Third World foreign policy. The evidence seems to be that this is in fact as much as the existing West Indian political cultures are willing to bear. (in Fagen 1979: 301)

Clearly, the frameworks of such analyses must be modified if we are to grasp the significance of Grenada's experiment. In particular, they need to be expanded so that it is possible to assume the existence of more radical socialist states, conceptualize their structure, and analyze the problems that they would face in the region.

With regard to Grenada, a significant step in this direction was first taken by Emmanuel (1983). This work deals with some of the issues raised by Grenada's experiment for both socialist theory and regional political theory. Emmanuel's focus is on the specifics of regional processes of political and class formation that do not square easily with established socialist theory. Also, there is a strong emphasis on the contradictions and difficulties of the non-capitalist theory of the transition period. Thus, the basic thrust of Emmanuel's argument is that the application of socialist theory could result in the obscuring of Caribbean realities, if its users do not carefully separate its uniquely European and Russian aspects from those that are of more general significance. And despite its resurgence in the region, Emmanuel suggests that "there is an indispensable dimension of Marxian political sociology which urgently needs to be developed if Marxian analysis and public policy are not to encounter several pitfalls" (1983: 9).

However, despite this healthy warning, there are at least three problems that remain unresolved or unaddressed in Emmanuel's analysis. First, the *dimensions* of the obstacles to transition that are derived from the specifics of Caribbean political and class formation are not clear. For example, Emmanuel stresses the fact that the Caribbean peasantry "was born out of proletarian conditions, and not the other way around" as was the case in the advanced countries (1982: 12). As a result of this difference, Emmanuel sees the development of "a peasantist state of mind" that is unresponsive to socialist strategies of collectivization. But exactly how unique or major a problem this would be is not indicated, only that it would be insurmountable.

Second, in his attempts to assimilate both the Grenadian experience and Marxian political sociology, Emmanuel, like many of the theorists mentioned above, overlooked the valuable contributions of C. L. R. James to the latter problem. James's Marxism is international in its focus and inclusive of the Caribbean. This global orientation is largely responsible for its two major poles: the first is its opposition to Stalinism, vanguardism, and the exemplary role of the Russian experience, and the second is its understanding of itself as a theoretical vehicle for the revolutionary self-organization of African, Afro-American, Caribbean, East European and other workers. The decentralization of Russian Marxism and its replacement by a more internationally contextualized Marxism are contributions that have been recognized for their non-dogmatic, worker-oriented and genuinely dialectical qualities. These achievements have made James the region's most important socialist theoretician. The understanding of Grenada's socialist experiment should be the event that gives him a more central place in regional political theory. Third, Emmanuel's analysis does not deal adequately with the nature of the socialist state and the problems of its legitimation within the context of Caribbean political culture. This issue needs to be re-examined in the light of Grenada's experience.

SOCIALISM AND THE TRANSFORMATION IN GRENADA

Given the uniqueness of peripheral conditions, it should come as no surprise that regional experiments with socialism were not the result of the fettering of a new but dormant mode of production. Similarly, it should not surprise us that they did not arise from the excessive exploitation of the peasantry by an obsolete aristocracy. On the contrary, these experiments had their roots in the exhaustion of the neocolonial strategies for encouraging growth within the framework of the center-periphery relationship. When functional, these strategies encourage the growth of a local political elite, the addition of new fractions to the foreign capitalist class, a more active role for the local bourgeoisie, and expansions into new areas of production. On the other hand, when they collapse, as they have since the late 1960s, images of future growth and harmony with the center begin to disappear. With these gone, the center-periphery contradiction re-emerges in all its starkness, exposing the order of the society — its patterns of class domination, the modes of surplus extraction, and the distribution of power — bringing with it new political struggles with socialist potential. Thus, factors such as class exploitation that are shared with the European and Russian cases are here recast within the framework of the center-periphery relationship. As this relationship is currently defined by a set of neocolonial arrangements, the latter becomes the broad context for interpreting the poverty, the inequality, and the crises of production and accumulation that have pushed the region in the direction of socialism.

If the above analysis is correct, then an understanding of the intensity of the socialist thrust in Grenada must be derived from the responses of various elites, classes and groups to the exhaustion of the growth potential of the neocolonial strategies that linked the country to the capitalist world economy.[2] In particular, attention must be paid to the role of the political elites who became a part of the local power structure in the pre-

and post-independence periods which were characterized by contradictory tendencies that defined their neocolonial character. For example, on the one hand, the growth of a local political elite was encouraged through the acceptance of their demands for control of state power. On the other, there has been increased entrepreneurial, financial and technological dependence. One of the important characteristics of the political elites that have emerged from these arrangements has been the tendency to use their control of state power to build power bases. Once established, they use them either to compete or cooperate with older or new power structures that are rooted in the ownership of productive forces by local and foreign capitalists. Also, they use these to distribute patronage to mass supporters and to victimize and repress mass opponents. However, there is wide variation in the region of this type of political behavior. Consequently, the particular brand of neocolonialism that emerges in a country is largely determined by the degree of autonomy of the local political elites, how they use their power base, their ideological orientation, and the kinds of class alliances that they are able to forge.

In the case of the Gairy regime that ruled Grenada for most of the pre- and post-independence periods, a relatively high degree of autonomy, an extremely conservative ideology, excessive use of its power base against opponents, and alliances with various class fractions produced a form of neocolonialism which made it possible to respond with repression, corruption and cynicism to the exhaustion of development strategies. This pattern of response polarized the local political struggles to a degree that was probably only surpassed in the region by Guyana.

Until the late sixties, Gairy's power was based largely upon his control of the state apparatus, his ability to reach compromises with elements of the planter class, while at the same time maintaining his image as a champion of the working class and of Grenadian nationalism. Thus, through his union and its party he was able at times to get the support of the majority of the agricultural and urban workers, elements of the middle class, and also sections of the dominant planter class. This support rested largely upon the initial dynamism of a neocolonial strategy that combined the mobilization of the people through a system of parliamentary democracy and union representation, with the diversification of export agriculture and the expansion of a largely foreign-controlled tourist sector. However, as this strategy ceased to be dynamic around the mid-1960s, the growth of opposition, repression and corruption very rapidly weakened the coalition of groups and class fractions that constituted much of Gairy's power. Initially, this opposition came from two sources: elements of the middle class and the foreign bourgeoisie (Committee of 22) and radical intellectuals (the groups that later became the New Jewel Movement). The former were opposed to Gairy's corruption, repression and mismanagement. The latter, in addition to being opposed to Gairy, were also opposed to neocolonialism. Hence "genuine independence," "self-reliance" and "anti-imperialism" were prominent features of their 1973 manifesto. This manifesto also included a broad program of economic nationalization, working-class hegemony and agrarian reform.

It was after years of struggle in conjunction with the other groups that the New Jewel Movement (NJM) decided to singly seize power on the morning of 13 March 1979. This solo seizure of power by the NJM created a new socio-historical possibility for Grenadian society—working-class hegemony. However, working-class rule was characterized by limitations and difficulties of its own. Among others, three factors made the achieving of working-class hegemony extremely difficult: (1) the underdevelopment of the Grenadian working class, and the dependence on petit bourgeois leadership that this created; (2) the dependence of this class and the Grenadian economy as a whole on the entrepreneurial skills of both foreign and local bourgeois elements; and (3) imperial opposition to working-class rule. Thus, although a desirable democratic goal, the building of working-class hegemony at this point involved the contradiction of establishing the dominance of a class that was not ready to rule, and whose hegemony was the source of considerable opposition both inside and outside of the society. It was these contradictions and limitations surrounding the project of working-class hegemony that produced the contradictory pattern of class alliances upon which Grenada's experiment was based.

So although the NJM acted alone in the seizure of power, it was with the support of their own mass following and their former allies that the takeover was consolidated. Consequently, it was a coalition of workers, peasants and elements of the middle and bourgeois classes that constituted the political base of the attempted transition to socialism. As in the case of other peripheral countries such as Cuba, Algeria or Tanzania, this process was not oriented toward the making of a qualitative change of the type that Marx had described for Europe. Rather, its focus was on increasing the degree of popular control, genuine independence, and transforming the process of local accumulation so that basic material needs could be met. In the words of Maurice Bishop, "our Revolution was for justice, for food, for health, for housing, for clothing, for pipeborne water, for education, for people's control of our resources, for people's participation" (Jules and Rojas 1982: 137). These differences in the goals of Grenadian socialism suggest that there are also important differences in the actual process of transformation: the political, economic and cultural aspects.

POLITICAL ASPECTS OF THE TRANSFORMATION

Once in power, the NJM very quickly replaced the exhausted development strategies of the Gairy regime with one that combined the mobilization of the people through a system of popular democracy with plans for building a nationally oriented economy. The political aspects of this strategy were of vital importance as they provided the attempt at transformation with much of the legitimacy and support that it needed. In particular, it was these political changes that enabled the NJM to make a sharp break with the past, and to make real the feelings and situations of a new beginning. This sense of a new beginning was clearly evident in the revitalized national pride, the enthusiasm, and the openness to the future that emerged from talking to Grenadians. Thus, despite their incompleteness, these reforms are crucial for any model of a socialist state in the region.

The major changes in the organization of the state may be summarized as follows: first, the creation of a People's Revolutionary Government (PRG). As a revolutionary government, it claimed supreme command and, therefore, proceeded to suspend portions of the Grenadian constitution to facilitate its revolutionary structure. The new revolutionary government was representative of the broader coalition of classes and groups that were a part of the anti-Gairy struggle. This was reflected in the composition of the cabinet of ministers, which constituted the core of the government. This cabinet included members of the business class and members of the opposition Grenada National Party. However, in this coalition that constituted the PRG, the NJM was by far the dominant faction.

The second important set of changes introduced was the creation of a People's Revolutionary Army. This was a regular army of full-time soldiers, whose primary function was to defend the revolution. The army was supported in this task by the People's Militia, which people joined on a voluntary part-time basis. They received training and could be called upon in the event of an emergency. The decision really to develop the militia was a response to a number of counterattacks such as the Queens Park bombings of 1980.

Finally, there was the introduction of the system of popular democracy. This was probably the most important set of political changes that was made. This change represented the first concrete alternative to the dissatisfactions with bourgeois democracy that had been increasing in the region since the mid-1960s. Building on the notions of people's assemblies and popular participation that had been gaining currency in the region, the PRG in 1981 undertook the setting up of a national system of popular democracy. It subdivided the country's six parishes into a number of zones and made each zone the locus of a council. These parish or zonal councils became the basic organs of the new system of popular democracy. They met once a month and were open to all members of a particular zone. These councils were the places where the masses met to discuss issues of public importance and to make recommendations, which were then passed on to the ministry of national mobilization.

Through the principle of accountability, they had the power to request the presence of public officials responsible for acting on their recommendations or other zonal projects.

In addition, the PRG also attempted to convert other organizations with restricted membership into mass organizations similar in structure to the councils. Thus it opened up its National Women's Organization (NWO) and its National Youth Organization (NYO) to the public, and created special councils for farmers. As these organizations were all similar in structure to the zonal councils, they also had zonal branches and institutionalized links with the appropriate ministry of government.

Also, for greater popular participation, the PRG devoted a lot of effort to the redefining of the role and structure of trade unions in Grenada. First, they repealed repressive pieces of legislation such as the Public Order Act and the Essential Services Act, and replaced them by more supportive legislation such as People's Law 29 of 1979. This law made it compulsory for employers to recognize their workers' trade union, chosen by the vote of the majority of the workers. Second, they encouraged the internal democratization of unions and their participation in the larger process of democratizing the society. Third, the PRG sought the cooperation of the unions in its attempts to increase worker productivity. These attempts centered around the creation of production, emulation, disciplinary, and grievance committees at the workplace. These committees were operative in several state enterprises. The PRG wanted the unions to create them in the private sector with the cooperation of management (Fedon 1982a: 12–13).

It was through this array of new and revamped organizations that the masses of Grenadians were able to participate more fully in the day-to-day affairs of their society. Good examples of how this greater involvement worked were the steps taken that preceded important government decisions. These included the decisions to establish a public transportation system, to take over the Grenada Electric Company, to improve substantially the supply and distribution of water, and the passage of the 1982 budget (Fedon 1982b).

These in essence were the political changes introduced by the PRG. Although the set was not complete, the reorganization achieved was substantial. It represented a rather comprehensive mobilizing of the society's political resources through their withdrawal from the control of the political elites and their allies in the local power structure, monopolizing them for a while, and then re-distributing a portion of them through the system of popular democracy. Of course, many problems were still to be resolved, such as the amount of power and resources that the PRG would continue to monopolize, the process of changing the leadership, etc., once the revolutionary period had passed. But, despite this incompleteness, these changes represented a mobilizing and reallocating of Grenada's political resources that was vital to the process of socialist transformation. This re-allocation was vital because it moved the political system beyond the framework of bourgeois democracy and began to make real the concept of proletarian democracy. More than the experiment in Jamaica, it challenged the universality of the former and brought home the reality of the latter. Also, by invoking all of the symbolism of a revolutionary government, the PRG claimed the right to a framework, and created such a framework, for making changes that moved beyond the neocolonial interpretation of the center-periphery relationship. In other words, through the creating of this genuine revolutionary situation, the PRG was able to generate the legitimacy required for its monopolization and subsequent redistribution of power.

ECONOMIC ASPECTS OF THE TRANSFORMATION

Compared to the political changes described above, the economic changes introduced by the PRG represented the mobilization of a much smaller proportion of the economic resources of the society. In other words, they were based upon a much more limited withdrawal of economic resources from established power structures and their re-allocation on a much less comprehensive scale. Thus, in the economic arena, the regime was less successful both in the amount of resources it was able to monopolize and in the scope of its attempts at reorganization. As a result, there were no equally clear outlines of a new economy based on a socialist mode of production that paralleled the clear outlines of the revolutionary state that had emerged. These limitations on the capacity for economic mobilization were no doubt related to the strength of bourgeois interests, external ownership, and the state's limited capacity for comprehensive economic planning.

Because the changes in the economy were not of the order of a comprehensively planned set of alternatives, we should not conclude that they were not important. To take such a position would be to sacrifice the specifics of the Grenadian situation to principles that have been derived from elsewhere. Also, as these limitations on the capacity for economic mobilization are not peculiar to Grenada but are to be found in most peripheral countries, theories of socialist transformation in the periphery must conceptualize these as normal conditions and not as abnormal or exceptional ones. That is, these theories cannot be constructed on the ideal assumptions that these mobilizing and planning capabilities will be present. Rather, they must be constructed to include the less comprehensive strategies of regimes whose political conditions and planning capacities make comprehensive re-allocation impossible.

In the case of Grenada, just such a scaling down of more orthodox socialist economic programs to a point that reflected its own capabilities can be observed. Thus, instead of an attempt at comprehensive restructuring, the PRG focused on a shifting of the balance of power and control between the national economy and the sector controlled by the capitalist world economy. By the national economy, I am referring to those sectors that are more oriented to local needs and are characterized by greater local ownership. Throughout the colonial period, this economy was largely a residual one, existing in the shadow of the externally controlled sector. The real content of the PRG's economic program was an attempt to shift the distribution of power and resources between these two economies so that the national economy would become the primary source of growth and accumulation. Consequently, it is in this light that the significance of these changes must be viewed, and not from the point of view of an attempt at comprehensive reorganization.

From the available evidence, it is clear that the early impact of the revolutionary process on the economy was a positive and expansionary one. In 1979, real growth in the Grenadian economy was 2 percent. In 1980 and 1981, it was 3.1 percent and 2 percent, respectively. This expansionary trend occurred despite the recession in the major capitalist countries, which had produced a steady decline in the number of stopover tourists. In 1979, this number was 32,300. By 1981, it had fallen to 25,000. Two broad categories can be used to assess the policies and changes that were responsible for this growth. In the first category are the changes of a more long-term nature, which were directed at the overall structure of the economy and the addition of new units of production. In the second are the more short-term reforms, which had been directed at increasing the output of existing economic units. The basic problem of the first was the changing of relations between the Grenadian portion of the capitalist world economy and the national economy. Toward this end, the regime had set for itself the goal of creating an economy with three distinct sectors: private, state and cooperative. It was through the expansion of the state and cooperative sectors that the PRG had hoped to change the relations between the national economy and the externally controlled sector. The regime's investment code indicated some of the ways (Fedon 1982c: 65). Within this mixed economic framework, some enterprises were singled out for special development: agriculture, agro-industries, fishing, tourism and forestry. Also, to facilitate production in these areas, the PRG had estimated and had already begun the expenditure of over EC$600 million on infrastructural development.

The development of these specific industries was guided by the vision of a national economy that was more productive and more sensitive to local needs. In the case of tourism, the regime distinguished between the old and the new tourism. The latter was now to be an instrument for the better understanding of different cultures, a source of linkages with agriculture, agro-industries, the construction and handicraft sectors, and an area of regional cooperation (Jules and Rojas 1982: 71). Similarly, the long-term plans for agriculture were to deepen its roots in the local market, and to make it more responsive to local needs and decision making. Existing plans called for expansions in both the areas of food and cash crop production, and for the making of agriculture into an engine of accumulation to help finance industrial projects. In the areas of forestry and fishing, development was proceeding under the guidance of two national companies: the Forestry Development Corporation and the National Fisheries Corporation. Both of these, however, were off to a slow start despite assistance to the latter by the Cubans.

Together, these constituted the broad framework within which the PRG had attempted to transform the Grenadian economy and to make changes in the relations between the export and national sectors. As such, it moved beyond existing neocolonial relations but fell short of both breaking the center-periphery relationship and being socialist.

However, these long-term changes rested upon a number of more short-term initiatives, which were directed more at expanding the output of existing units than at structural change. The most important of these were the attempts to increase worker productivity in enterprises controlled by the state and to bring idle capacity back into production.

With regard to low productivity, the PRG had worked out a very reasonable plan to deal with the problems: an attempt at eliminating the negative effects of mismanagement by the managerial strata. The PRG introduced the separation of the finances of state-owned enterprises from those of the central government. The goal here was to make these enterprises self-sufficient, eliminate corruption, and put an end to the "civil service" mentality that saw government largely as a collective father figure. By introducing these measures along with stricter accounting procedures, the regime had hoped to replace the old attitudes to work with new ones that were more sensitive to the relationship between income and productivity.

The other part of the plan was aimed at increasing productivity among the workers who were engaged in direct production. Here, the regime introduced a system of moral and material incentives, which centered around the greater participation of these workers in the production process. Operating on the assumption that workers would be more motivated to implement decisions that they had helped to make, the PRG introduced its production, education, disciplinary and emulation committees to facilitate this greater involvement.

To bring idle capacity back into production was largely the responsibility of the National Cooperative Development Agency (NACDA). On lands that the PRG had acquired under the Land Utilization Law of 1981 NACDA was to encourage the development of cooperatives in fishing, agriculture and handicrafts. However, similar to the initiatives in fishing and forestry, these too got off to a rather slow start.

Evaluating the effectiveness of this program of economic reform is clearly beyond the scope of this paper. However, given the goal of expanding the national economy, the continuing importance of foreign investments and the dependence on tourism does raise a number of difficult questions. These questions become all the more important when we examine the impact of the above factors on economies such as those of Antigua and Barbados. In these countries, the consequences of dependence on tourism and external investments in light manufacturing have included the decline of the power of the state in relation to the international bourgeoisie, the erosion of the power of the working classes, and the bursting of the nationalist framework of economic planning to meet conditions of accumulation in these areas. That is, they resulted in a worsening of the relations that the PRG was attempting to improve. Thus it would have been important to see whether or not this program, backed by a revolutionary state, would have been able to subject these forces to a logic of national accumulation and so maintain the fight for the hegemony of the national economy.

CULTURAL ASPECTS OF THE TRANSFORMATION

Because meaning cannot be administratively produced, cultural systems are peculiarly resistant to rational or administrative control. Cultural traditions remain alive and can emerge in a spontaneous manner.[3] Because of this quality, it is impossible to mobilize and re-allocate the cultural resources of a society in the way that is possible with its economic and political resources. Thus, it is not surprising that in Grenada there was no comprehensive restructuring of the cultural system that paralleled the restructuring of the political system. But, despite these peculiarities of cultural systems, there are aspects and products of these systems that are employed by elites in a strategic or instrumental manner. Because they are used in this manner, one may refer to them as the cultural resources of a society. From the standpoint of political theory, the most important of these are the expressive symbols and rational arguments that can be used to legitimate the social order, and to induce a general readiness to cooperate, or conversely, to do the opposite. Thus, poems, calypsoes, plays, and religious and philosophical beliefs can be used to legitimate or delegitimate the existing social order. In particular, the distribution of power and privileges, the division of labor, and the use of state power are characteristics of an order that must be justified to its members. This legitimation is usually derived, in part, from the adaptation of metaphysical and expressive creations for political purposes. For example, metaphysical thinking is important to the production of ideologies as it tends to smooth out contradictions and eliminate dissonances in its search for the comprehensive picture or the ultimate meaning.

Prior to the revolution, the Grenadian cultural system was very similar in structure and orientation to those of the other Caribbean territories.

In its linguistic sector there were two languages, Grenadian Creole and English. The use of these languages was governed by a very specific social code, which made clear the situations in which they would be appropriate. In the religious sub-sector of this system, the dominant beliefs were Catholicism and other versions of Christianity. Subordinate to these were the Shango and the practice of Obeah, the primary survivals of the African religious heritage. In the ideological sub-sector, there were, of course, the rival ideologies of neocolonialism and anti-imperialism. The educational sub-sector was characterized by little or no capacity for the generation of new technical knowledge; and what it was capable of storing and transmitting, it made available to only a few. Finally, the arts sector was characterized by productions in traditional media such as the calypso, the steel band, the play, the poem, and in a number of mass media, particularly newspapers and radio.

In addition to meeting the needs of Grenadians for meaning and answers to life's existential questions, the activities and products of the various sub-sectors of this system were also being used to legitimate the existing social order. In particular, they were linked to the premature harmonizing of the center-periphery contradiction, the capital-labor contradiction, and the support of Gairy's particular version of neocolonialism. Thus, patterns of language use and the existing school system helped to reinforce the classism of the bourgeois and middle classes. The dominant secular ideologies of the system justified and explained away the penetration of the capitalist world economy, and the compromised nationalism that it necessarily produces. The justification of the hegemony of the above two classes was, therefore, an important function of the system. This function, in turn, involved the cultural system in the contradictions of the neocolonial order. The internalizing of these contradictions manifests itself in the alienation of the system from its Afro-Caribbean base, and its strong Western orientation. The structural and identity crises that have resulted are old problems and are well known. However, this alienation could not be maintained if the manipulative aspects (the cultural resources) of the system were not monopolized to a high degree by the elites that were responsible for the management of Grenada's neocolonial order.

Consistent with its socialist strategy, the PRG made an effort to withdraw these cultural resources from the control of elites in the old power structure and to secure them in its own hands. In particular it attempted to gain firm control of the ideological and educational sub-sectors and of the mass media. With these resources under its control, the important cultural changes introduced by the regime were concentrated in the above two sub-sectors. Given the goal of changing the compromise upon which center-periphery and capital-labor relationships rested, the ideological resources clearly had to be withdrawn from the production of neocolonial arguments. Further production of such arguments would only have hindered these undertakings, which required a lessening of the involvement of the cultural system in the contradictions of the neocolonial order. Consequently, these resources were redeployed in the production of arguments that justified the above changes. These arguments were drawn from the history of socialist thought—particularly the theory of non-capitalist development—and from the experiences of the local struggles against Gairy's neocolonialism. For these aspects of the regime, and the theory of non-capitalist development see Jacobs and Jacobs (1982) and Ulyanovsky (1974).

However, although the above theory was the official ideological position of the regime, it is important to note at least two significant ways in which its actual practice differed from this theory. The first was the hegemonic role of the NJM in the PRG and the extent to which the former was able to make the latter into a vanguard party of the workers. This possibility developed to a much greater degree than the theory suggests and in turn produced a more radical degree of political transformation. The second important difference was the participatory nature of the regime, which revealed the influences of the Cuban model. As a result, worker participation developed to a much greater degree than would be expected from non-capitalist theory. But, despite these differences, it remained the official ideology of the regime.

In the area of education, a similar attempt at reorientation was undertaken. First, the new educational system was aimed at all of the people and not just a few. Second, the content of the education was to provide Grenadians with the technical, academic and organizational skills that were needed to develop the Grenadian economy. Third, this new education aimed at reorienting the secular world views of the masses, so that they would be more nationally conscious, and thus reduce the degree of alienation normally produced by this sub-sector and the cultural system as a whole (Fedon 1982c: 51–52).

To concretize some of these educational goals, we can begin with the PRG's attempts at mass education for all adults. In keeping with their often-repeated maxim, "democracy and illiteracy are irreconcilable," the regime undertook a mass literacy campaign, which was administered by the Centre for Popular Education (CPE). This campaign represented a first step in the implementing of the concept of "freedom schools" that were outlined in the 1973 manifesto of the NJM. These schools were to be run by volunteer teachers and were to provide the basic skills and information that people needed for their everyday lives. The literacy campaign used volunteers and was able to reach many that the previous system had discarded without reading and writing skills. To extend this program of mass adult education, a system of night school with 48 centers was set up. On completing this program of night study, the individual was given a certificate of merit. In short, the CPE represented a new layer of the Grenadian educational system that was designed to catch those who were left behind by the formal system. In addition to this program, a significant process of political education was also taking place in the mass organizations such as the NYO and the NWO.

With regard to the existing school system, the PRG sought to improve both its size and its quality: the regime instituted a mass teacher-training program, the National In-Service Teacher Education Program (NISTEP) which was designed to deal with the fact that the majority of the 500 primary school teachers were untrained. The program made it mandatory for them to attend training classes one day a week and for several weeks during vacations for three years.

At the secondary level of the system, three important changes were made: the elimination of fees, the building of an additional school, and the adoption of plans for a similar training program for teachers. For the graduates of these schools, the number of university scholarships was substantially increased, permitting Grenadians to study in a much wider variety of countries.

Again, it is very difficult to evaluate precisely the impact of this cultural mobilization on popular identity and outlook, and on the overall functioning of the cultural system. On the surface, there can be no doubt about the ideological changes. The prevalence of socialist ideas and a much more self-confident nationalism were very much in evidence. However, the more important question is the depth of the impact on individual consciousness and identity. Any such evaluation would have to include the impact of the collapse, and the continuities with the past that derived from the openness of the system, and the lack of change in the areas that were beyond the reach of the PRG's mobilizing capacities.

Despite their incompleteness, these changes amount to a remarkable record for four and one-half years. They represent the most systematic attempt at socialist reconstruction in the English-speaking Caribbean. As such, they had taken this process further than the experiments in Jamaica or Guyana, hence the greater difficulty in assimilating them into theoretical categories.

THE COLLAPSE OF THE REGIME

From this account of the attempt at transformation, there is little to suggest the possibility of a sudden collapse. This was the way it appeared in the middle of 1983, when the research for this study was being conducted. The economic contradictions that were identified, while they may have matured, had certainly not mushroomed into a full-blown crisis. Yet the sad fact remains that this fascinating experiment in socialist transformation collapsed rather suddenly, and came to an abrupt and tragic end. Basically, three explanations have been given for this collapse. The first is a power struggle between Prime Minister Maurice Bishop and his deputy, Bernard Coard. The second is that it was brought on by a factional fight, the Coard faction being more doctrinaire in its Leninism than the Bishop faction. The third is the suggestion that the process of transformation had come to a halt, and that the differences were over the appropriate course to take. A fourth position could be a combination of two or all of the above.

Up to this point, the available evidence on the events leading up to the collapse has come from the minutes of the NJM's Central Committee and the statements of various party members to the press. Although this body of evidence is by no means complete, it does point rather clearly to a power struggle of some sort. Thus, the issue no longer is whether or not there was a power struggle, but whether or not it was simply that. The struggle for power in the region has always been an intense one. Factional fights have checkered the history of regional parties, and the electoral contests between these parties have become escalating battles. The Odlum–Louisy split in St. Lucia, the Bird–Walter split in Antigua, and the high loss of life in the Jamaican elections of 1980 are cases in point. In these instances, additional issues were linked to the struggle for power. So it is quite possible that the case of Grenada might be another instance of this pattern with the additional factor that it occurred within a revolutionary party. But until more evidence becomes available, we will not know for sure.

Whatever this additional evidence may reveal about the conditions that led to the collapse of this socialist experiment its achievements will continue to raise important questions about existing institutions and possibilities for alternatives. The experiment has shown that the region's political culture can bear a revolutionary socialist state. This fact, in turn, leads to questions such as the conditions under which such a state will emerge, its structure and the conditions for its legitimation.

SOCIALISM AND REGIONAL POLITICAL CULTURE

In my analysis of the origins of Grenadian socialism, I connected them to the crisis tendencies of the neocolonial economy and the particularly repressive responses of the Gairy regime to the political consequences of these tendencies. Thus, the political color that a regime adds to the neocolonial situation becomes important for the turn to socialism in the periphery. As it is reasonable to assume the persistence of both neocolonialism and particularly repressive regimes in the region, it is rather unlikely that Grenada's will be the last experiment with socialism.

At the same time, it is important to note that the repressive regime may be strong enough, as in the case of Guyana, to maintain itself and contain the push for alternatives. When this occurs, the state develops more mature fascist features despite its liberal or socialist facades. Thus, the variety of political formations that have been emerging in response to the crisis tendencies of the region's neocolonial economies forces us to move beyond the liberal interpretation of the Caribbean state. To this interpretation must be added the systemic possibilities for both the fascist and the socialist alternatives.

Looking at all of the socialist experiments in the region, it is clear that they have produced political systems that vary widely in their degree of radicalism. This degree of radicalism, although extremely important, cannot be determined in advance, and any such determination must include the strength of the revolutionary vanguard party in the class coalitions behind the movement. Thus, it is quite possible for a regime more radical than the PRG to emerge in the region. However, the analyses in the remainder of this paper assume the existence of socialist states with degrees of radicalism similar to that of the PRG. These analyses will focus on the structure of these states and the legitimacy problems that they are likely to experience in the region.

Earlier, I argued that the process of the transition to socialism in the periphery must differ in a number of important ways from the experiences of either Europe or the Soviet Union. Being both an instrument and an integral part of the transformation process, the socialist state in the periphery, while sharing a number of basic features, will also be different as it must reflect and deal with local peripheral conditions. In its original Marxian formulation, the socialist state during the transition period was described as "the dictatorship of the proletariat." It was a state controlled by a self-organized working class. Its purpose was to consolidate the proletarian revolution and to guide the construction of a socialist society in which the state itself would no longer be necessary. Marx did not go into great detail about the nature of this state, consequently various additions have been made to fill this gap and to account for the transition experiences of other countries. Thus Lenin's theory of the socialist state was not a state based on the self-organization of the workers, but a state organized by a vanguard party on behalf of the workers (Lenin 1970: 30).

In the Caribbean context, the specific form that a socialist state is likely to take will also be reflective of local conditions. That is, even if in the most general sense it could be described as a "dictatorship of the proletariat," the actual shape that this form of working-class rule will take will be determined largely by local conditions. Given the political culture and the social conditions of the English-speaking Caribbean, I would argue that viable socialist states must fall somewhere between the above two models. First, the absence of a well-developed productive system and a politically organized working class necessitates modifications in Marx's model. Similarly, the importance of democracy in the regional political culture and the need to cooperate with the bourgeoisie will require modifications in Lenin's model. Also, the condition of being a periphery introduces additional factors that were not a part of the experiences of Europe or Russia. On this point, the experiences of Cuba and China become more relevant. But if, indeed, Grenada has provided the English-speaking Caribbean with its most radically socialist state, then it is from that experience that we must take our cues.

Given this account of the post-revolutionary state in Grenada, it should be clear that viable socialist states in the region will have all of the institutional structures of modern political systems. That is, they will contain such sub-systems as a judiciary, legislature, police, military, a vanguard party and representative institutions. However, the overall organization and functioning of these sub-systems will be based on socialist principles. In particular, this change in the orientation of these sub-systems will be related to two important sets of changes: in the balance of power that defines the center-periphery compromise, and changes in the balance of power that define the capital-labor compromise. It is the attempt to establish and legitimate this new distribution of power, functions and privileges that will set socialist states in the region apart from their colonial and neocolonial predecessors. The latter consistently routinized and legitimated compromises that gave undisputed hegemony to the center and to capital.

However, it is important to note that the dimensions of the changes that a particular state will be able to make in these compromises cannot be automatically or mechanically determined by its ideology. That is, we cannot make the classical assumption that power will be "shared with none" (Lenin 1970: 30), and that there will be a complete doing away with these compromises. On the contrary, because power will in all likelihood be shared, it must be assumed that the dimensions of the changes in these compromises will be affected by the conditions of that sharing. Thus, it is important to recognize that the actual degree of change in these crucial relations upon which socialist states are founded will vary with the conditions under which they come to power.

Given this commitment to significant change in center-periphery and capital-labor relations, there must be a reorganization of the state by the new regime, which aims both at the consolidation of power and at institutionalizing the structural consequences of the changes in these relations. The following is an examination of the major features of this process of reorganization. One of the first steps is the reorganization of the ideological sub-system. Clearly there must be changes in the output of this sub-system so that the new identity and commitments of the state can be recognized and understood by the public. In addition to declaring the state a workers' state, the Grenadian experience clearly demonstrates the advantages of also declaring the state to be a revolutionary one. The invoking of the powers, symbolism and imagery of a revolutionary state provides a more supportive framework for the kinds of changes that will take place in the transition period. Thus, the ability of the ideological sub-system to project clear images of both the revolutionary and socialist nature of the state is important in the process of political reorganization.

Given support for a state of this type, its consolidation will bring about changes in the party system. As the Caribbean working class is far from being a self-organized group, a working-class state could only be led by a vanguard party acting on behalf of this class. However, it cannot be assumed that the role of this party will be the same as it was in the Soviet Union or China. Rather, as in the case of the changes in the crucial compromises, this role will be modified by the conditions of power sharing. Thus, to the extent that it is in control, the vanguard party will take the lead in the process of socialist reconstruction.

The role of vanguard parties in the history of socialism is, of course, a controversial one. They have consistently led to the question of whether or not the party elite are ruling on behalf of the workers or on their own behalf. This contradiction is most clearly developed in the case of the Soviet Union. The Grenadian experience suggests that this contradiction cannot be allowed to develop in the region without severe losses of legitimacy.

Given the importance of this problem, James, Lee, and Chaulieu's critique of vanguardism in *Facing Reality* (1974 [1958]) becomes a very relevant contribution. Also important is the alternative they suggest of the small revolutionary group that realizes that the content of socialism is the self-organizing initiatives of the working class, and not its own ideological pronouncements. Such a model of the politics of transformation rests upon worker control and genuine dialogue from the start. This, in turn, reduces the tendencies to resist subsequent transfers of power from the vanguard elite to worker—the primary danger of vanguardism. Consequently, socialist states in the region will have to demonstrate their seriousness about working-class control by beginning very early the process of transferring substantial amounts of the power of the vanguard party to the workers. Thus, in my view, it was the introduction of the system of popular democracy in Grenada that compensated for the high-legitimacy costs of vanguard parties in the regional political culture. By themselves, they would not work.

With the establishment of both a vanguard party and organs of popular democracy, the distribution of power and the division of labor between them must be clearly defined and satisfactorily justified to all concerned. The situation that developed in Grenada, where the authority derived from the central committee of the NJM clashed with the authority derived from the popular base, must be avoided at all costs. Every effort must be made to define these relations clearly, and to encourage continuous transfers of power from the former to the latter as early as possible. Within the political culture of the region, the Jamesian principles regarding the form and content of socialism must be given precedence over the principles of vanguardism. This conflict between the power of the central committee and that of the organs of popular democracy is an important dimension along which socialist states differ. These differences are important indicators of the extent to which the workers are really in power. The way in which Cuba has dealt with this problem should be of great significance for constructing socialist states in the region (Seligson and Boot 1978: 114–28).

Also important to the creation of a revolutionary socialist state is the reorganization of the military and paramilitary forces, which should be made into the defensive arm of the party and the revolution. This is necessary if the revolutionary government is to have a believable command structure. Also, the opposition and the attempts at destabilization that this experiment is likely to generate will require an increased capability for self-defense. Usually, this reorganization of the military is not an easy task as they were the defenders of the old order and subscribed to its ideologies. In the Caribbean context, this task should be somewhat easier given the comparatively weak military traditions. In the smaller islands, these institutions are virtually non-existent. However, all this may change with the militarization of U.S. policy in the region following its invasion of Grenada.

Although this militarization is necessary, the dangers and risks that accompany it should not be overlooked. The take-over by General Austin in Grenada, the military regime in Suriname and the militarization of the Guyanese state all indicate how rapidly regimes can lose legitimacy and support through the abuse of military power. Consequently, this problem should not be taken lightly. Militarization should be avoided if at all possible. If it becomes necessary, every effort should be made to ensure that its power is unfavorably balanced vis-a-vis that of the party system. Grenada's experience also suggests that the need for the early introduction of checks and balances is greater in revolutionary situations as the possibilities for the abuse of power are greater. Containing the growth of military power is thus extremely important for the preservation of popular power. However, such take-overs and abuses are not inevitable as the case of Cuba makes clear (Holmes 1981: 81–102).

Even though this process of political reorganization would extend to other sub-systems of the state such as the police, the legal and electoral systems, the last example of such restructuring that I examine here is the reorganization of the regulative sub-system, particularly in relation to the economy. The economic activities of the peripheral capitalist state have always been at odds with the liberal elements in its ideology. Given the underdeveloped state of the local bourgeoisie, the entrepreneurial and other economic activities that this state has been forced to undertake have been far greater than this ideology stipulates. On the other hand, a vastly expanded role for the state in the economy is one of the major characteristics of socialist states. In the classic Marxist literature, the transition period is characterized by state ownership of the economy, which is then collectivized and centrally planned.

From this description of the economic transformation of Grenada, it should be clear that the increases in state regulation were relatively small. So, similar to the peripheral capitalist state, the socialist state in the periphery is also at odds with elements in its ideology. However, in this case the gap stems from an inability to meet expected or required levels of economic regulation. Consequently, although we would expect substantial changes in overall economic organization and regulation, it is not exactly clear when or how these will amount to a clear shift to a socialist mode of production. Thus, one of the most ambiguous areas of this process of political reorganization is the path by which the peripheral state acquires the capacities to meet its regulatory expectations. Specific mention of this rather vague aspect of socialist political reorganization is necessary for the upcoming analysis of the legitimation problems of socialist states.

LEGITIMATING SOCIALIST STATES

In the case of pre-revolutionary Grenada, a substantial portion of the mobilizable cultural resources was allocated to the legitimating of the neocolonial aspects of the social order. This pattern of resource use, together with high levels of structural dependence, was largely responsible for the major characteristics and contradictions of this cultural system: external dependence and commitment of resources to the reproduction of old justifications for the division of labor, the distribution of power, privileges, etc., that are characteristic of a social order based upon the penetration of the capitalist world economy.

Given these aspects of cultural formation in the region, it should not be surprising that the political aspects of life have been and continue to be interpreted through ideas and conventions drawn largely from the Western liberal tradition. Thus, at the core of the region's political culture is a series of local adaptations of European parliamentary democracy that define the political universe, on the one hand, by such features as political parties, voting, regular elections, civil liberties, separation of powers, etc., and, on the other, by the use of the state and the party as instruments of political accumulation. As in the case of Gairy, the latter often leads to Bonapartist tendencies, which rest on clientelistic relations with supporters and repressive relations with opponents. This particular mix of democracy and authoritarianism has been basic to the political culture of the region. Despite the difficulties experienced with this system, movements for political reform have remained largely within this cultural framework. Primarily, they have been aimed at lessening the clientelistic and repressive patterns that have accompanied local attempts at political accumulation, or at the introduction of greater opportunities for popular participation. But, in concrete terms, they have not been successful in substantially changing either the clientelistic or the liberal routines that constitute the core of this political culture.

Thus, it is reasonable to assume that the current attachment to this culture will be strong enough to generate substantial resistance to the type of socialist state outlined earlier. Its national assertiveness, its vanguard party, its command structure, its anti-imperialism, its proletarian democracy, etc., must appear strange to those who have been socialized into the above political culture. Consequently, a routine interpretation of this state, in terms of the norms of this culture, is sure to lead to its delegitimation. Hence, an effort must be made to convert what is likely to be a shortage into a surplus of legitimacy.

In dealing with the more resilient aspects of this culture, socialists have two basic options. First, building on the cultural detachments produced by the pre-revolutionary period, they can challenge the explanations and interpretations offered by this culture. That is, they can attempt a careful, but appealing, deconstruction of the ideological constructions that the culture uses prematurely to harmonize or explain away the contradictions of regional societies. In making use of this option, there are, of course, several aspects of established regional ideologies that are vulnerable. Their explanations for the existing international division of labor, for the mode of surplus distribution, for the condition of the working classes, and for the universalistic claims of bourgeois democracy are all possible areas of challenge. By challenging such generally accepted positions and explanations of the political culture, it is possible to change people's perception of the social order and their place in it. Such a change in public perception is a vital precondition for the establishing of the type of socialist state outlined above. However, it is important to note that the effectiveness of these critiques will be determined more by the general level of popular disaffection produced by oppression and revolutionary struggle.

As such changes in the political culture are difficult to make, legitimating of this state will require the use of the second option. This involves the adjusting of aspects of the process of transformation to resilient cultural traditions without excessively compromising basic goals. Here again there are several aspects of the transformation process that are inconsistent with, and could therefore be delegitimated by the principles and norms of this culture. For example, the suspension of traditional democratic practices, the institutional reorganization, the secular nature of Marxism and the attempts to change people's thinking that this process involves are sure to generate opposition. In the region this tension would probably be most acute in relation to the church and to the need to dislodge or contain the power of the bourgeoisie.

Any such undertaking, even if it represents only a slight shift in the distribution of power and privileges, will generate opposition. How the revolutionary state deals with this opposition is crucial for the maintaining of its legitimacy. In dismantling the structures of bourgeois rule and containing the opposition that it will generate, the revolutionary state must act in accord with basic humanist principles. These must be recognized as a set of legitimate limits on its command structure, and on the privileges of its revolutionary situation. Their abandonment in the name of the imperatives of the transition process will inevitably be costly, as they will be seen as abuses of revolutionary power. Thus to assume or attempt the level of class suppression suggested by Lenin would be a mistake. Consequently, this is one area in which adjustments will have to be made if legitimacy is to be maintained.

Although the actions described above would be crucial for the type of state outlined, such linkages with important cultural norms would not, by themselves, be enough. Given the economic responsibilities of this state, performance in this area will also be crucial. However, as we have noted before, socialist states in the periphery are characterized by a basic contradiction between their economic claims and their capacities for planning and managing a socialist economy. Closing this gap will be crucial for the legitimating of socialist states in the region. This gap stems from a number of sources. However, the primary one is the lack of adequate theories of economic transformation. This lack, in turn, creates the problem of a general scepticism regarding the economic viability of a socialist transformation. The problem is further compounded by the excesses of the Soviet experience and the difficulties of the reform models of the East European and some third world countries. This scepticism must be addressed if socialist states in the region are to overcome their legitimacy problems.

The basic problem with existing theories of socialist transformation is that they have not been sufficiently reworked so that their assumptions reflect local conditions. As a result socialist states in the periphery have had to work with models of change whose economic, political, cultural and technological assumptions do not reflect their domestic conditions. This situation has made good performance on a difficult path even more difficult. For peripheral states embarking upon the socialist path, there is very little theoretical literature to provide clear guidance for the process of economic transformation. Essentially, there are three sets of works: the theory of non-capitalist development, the works of Baran and those of Thomas. James, Lee, and Chaulieu's model, although very strong on the political conditions for transformation, is weak on the economic foundations of the process (James, Lee, and Chaulieu 1974 [1958]: 7–16).

The central feature of the non-capitalist theory is that it recognizes the need for a distinct preparatory stage for peripheral countries making the transition to socialism. However, this stage is very poorly defined. It is characterized in terms of the coalition of progressive forces that should constitute the government, the need to prevent the consolidation of local bourgeois power, and the need for closer cooperation with the socialist countries (Ulyanovsky 1974: 60–63). Because the theory is formed largely in terms of what is to be avoided, there is no clear picture of what the economy and relations of production should be like during this period, or what particular characteristics should be the major achievements of the period. Thus it is never really clear why an economy at the end of some period should be ready for an economic transformation of the Soviet type.

In the theories of Baran and Thomas, there is no corresponding period of preparation that is unique to peripheral countries. In both theorists, there is the assumption of an immediate turn to the comprehensive reorganization and planning of the economy following the revolution. In Baran's model, the process can be summarized in four steps: the mobilizing of the potential surplus through expropriation, nationalization, etc., the collectivization of agriculture, the investing of surplus in both agriculture and industry in a way that favors not just industry as a whole, but producer goods in particular. Finally, Baran (1968: 249–300) includes the judicious use of aid from both the capitalist and socialist blocks.

Thomas's (1974) model fills in many of the details left out by Baran. Like Baran, Thomas assumes the existence of a revolutionary state, which is in complete control of the economy, and is, therefore, capable of mobilizing the surplus. With the surplus mobilized and the economy under the control of the state, Thomas proceeds to outline his strategy. Conceptualizing the problem of economic underdevelopment as a dynamic divergence between resource use, domestic demand and local needs, Thomas's strategy for overcoming this condition must include strategies for the dynamic converging of these relations. These attempts at convergence must be achieved in the two key areas of agriculture and industry. The first step in the transformation of agriculture is the abandonment of over-specialized primary production for the export market. With the withdrawal of resources from this area, Thomas suggests their commitment to three other areas. The first of these is dairy products because of their nutritional value, and also because among agricultural products they have the highest income elasticities of demand (Thomas 1974: 146). The second area in which agricultural resources are to be put is that of mass consumption foods such as cereals, sugar, cocoa, coffee, etc. These are important because they represent the basic need of the population even if existing patterns of demand may not indicate it. Finally, resources must be committed to agricultural commodities that are required as basic inputs for industry, primarily textiles (Thomas 1974: 148–49).

Similarly, in the area of industry the achievement of a dynamic convergence would require an equally comprehensive attempt at reorganization. The key element in this reorganization is the creation of what Thomas calls a basic materials sector, which would include steel and textiles. In addition to this sector, Thomas also suggests the putting of resources into machinery and machine tools industries, agricultural industries and infrastructural development (Thomas 1974: 195–220).

Although this is not a complete summary, it is enough to give a sense of the comprehensive nature of the planning upon which Thomas's strategy rests. Such an undertaking would require that the revolutionary state possesses at least the following characteristics and capabilities: support drawn exclusively from an alliance of the working class and radical intellectuals, extensive or complete control of the economy, the ability to establish state or cooperative farming and industrial units as the basic centers of production, a highly developed capability in the area of central planning, and the ability for rapid and effective technological training.

However, when we compare the economic reforms of the PRG with those suggested by both of these models the gap between existing theories and concrete practice becomes clear. How are the gaps between the three-sector model of the regime with its mix of capitalist, participatory and cooperative relations of production and the comprehensive models of Baran and Thomas to be interpreted? Should the assumption be made that Grenada had not met the conditions for transformation? Or that its achievements were those of a preparatory phase?[4]

If Baran and Thomas are taken as formulated, then indeed the first assumption would have to be made, as it is clear that the PRG did not have the characteristics and capabilities listed above. It did not have complete control of the economy, it did not have the required planning capabilities, nor did it have the ability for rapid technological training. Consequently, the problems to which the regime was seeking answers were not those of the task of comprehensive economic reorganization. Rather, they were those of how to proceed with economic transformation under conditions of partial mobilization and control of the surplus, a multi-class political base, limited planning capabilities, etc. Thus, one of the central dilemmas facing the PRG was whether or not its reorganized state apparatus would have been able to contain the capitalist forces within the socialist framework that it was trying to construct, and subject them to a logic of national accumulation. Consequently, for these models to be useful, they will have to be further adjusted so that they can include attempts at transition in cases where the assumptions that they currently make are only partially met.

If, on the other hand, it was, indeed, a preparatory phase, the theory of non-capitalist development does not provide an adequate interpretation or guide to the achievements of this period. It does not provide us with criteria for evaluating the readiness of the PRG for the shift to comprehensive economic reorganization. Were the changes achieved by the regime sufficient preparation? As currently formulated, there is really no way of knowing.

Thus, my major point is that there is a sizeable gap between the theoretical guides to economic transformation and the practical situations faced by socialist regimes in the periphery. This gap derives from two basic sources: the first is that the initial phase of the process has not been clearly articulated in the theoretical literature. Compared to the later phases of comprehensive planning, this phase remains shrouded in ambiguity. This ambiguity affects the theoretical status of this phase, its practical significance and its basic goals. In other words, however explicit or implicit one wants to make this phase, a clearer set of guidelines is needed for this early phase of transformation in the periphery. The second set of factors contributing to this gap stems from the fact that some of the political assumptions upon which existing models of transformation have been formulated do not reflect peripheral conditions. On the contrary, they tend to reflect or universalize the conditions of non-peripheral countries that have attempted or have made the transition to socialism. Thus, the conditions that these theories are supposed to reflect and explain often become anomalies or exceptions. As a result, there tends to be an inadequate thematizing of conditions that are unique to peripheral countries.

Along with these broader issues, a number of more specific ones will also have to be reworked so that they, too, reflect more fully the special conditions of peripheral societies. Given the class compromise that is likely to be at the foundation of socialist states in the region, a continuing important role for the private sector is evident. This will necessitate the careful working out of relations between the market and the plan in the context of such a mixed economy. Grenada's three-sector economy and the importance of this issue in the East European countries suggest that it cannot be taken lightly.

Second, once this has been decided upon, a closely related set of decisions must be made regarding the nature of the planning that will be undertaken, and how the demand for the appropriate planners and statisticians will be met. Also, whatever notions about the content and nature of planning these planners may bring will have to be reworked so that plans are rooted in and reflect local conditions. The importance of this reworking of the planning process is made clear by both the Cuban and Chilean experiences.

Third, because a complete break with the advanced countries cannot be assumed, more realistic strategies will have to be worked out for dealing with the problems created by the external dependence of regional economies. The Grenadian case suggests that such strategies must be based on at least two sets of factors: (1) modifications in center-periphery relations that are reflective of the strength of the class forces represented by the revolutionary government, and (2) alternative arrangements with socialist and other third-world countries that will allow the regime not only to pursue stated goals, but also to absorb possible counter moves by the central capitalist countries. Jamaica's relations with the IMF between 1977 and 1980 make clear the importance of a realistic approach to the problems created by external dependence.

Fourth, if the financial instability of the present period becomes a permanent feature of the international economy, then special attention will have to be given to the problems of financial planning and management. On this point, the experiences of Jamaica and Guyana are very instructive. They suggest the need for a strategy that would avoid both excessive reliance on institutions such as the IMF, and degrees of state regulation that deviate excessively from market forces. In the former case, the state loses control of the economy to external forces, and in the latter to a local underground or parallel economy.

In short, socialist states in the periphery are in need of models of economic transformation whose contents are the socio-economic conditions and processes within their own societies. In particular, they need models that recognize the limitations of working-class hegemony, the concrete historical forces in these societies, the limited nature of their planning capabilities, and the realities of external dependence. Without models of economic transformation that have been constructed around these conditions and problems, the gap between socialist theory and practice in the periphery will remain a wide one.

The significance of this gap for the larger discussion is, of course, its implications for the economic performance of socialist states that might appear in the region, and hence for the levels of legitimacy that these states will be able to maintain. Our analysis of this gap suggests that these states are likely to be without theories of economic transformation that have been adequately adjusted to their political dimensions and capabilities. Until this problem is addressed these states will have a difficult time delivering their economic promises and maintaining high levels of legitimacy.

CONCLUSION

In this paper, I have attempted to show that the assimilation of Grenada's experiment with socialism will necessitate some changes in regional political theory. The need for this change stems from the fact that, except for the work of James, Lee, and Chaulieu, regional political theory has remained largely within a liberal framework, despite the Caribbean's experiments with socialism. This situation has been possible largely because the experiments in Jamaica and Guyana left old political structures in place. However, this was not the case in Grenada. In this case, the experiment with socialism brought with it new forms of political organization that move beyond the liberal framework. It demonstrated that under certain conditions the political culture is capable of supporting radical changes in the mode of political organization. Hence, regional political theory must expand and transform its conceptual base so that it can include this experience, and inform this type of political practice.

With regard to socialist writings in the region on the state, these have largely been implicit in works that are more directly focused on processes of economic transformation. Here, I have tried to show that there is still too wide a gap between the political assumptions upon which these models rest and the characteristics and capabilities of socialist states that are likely to emerge in the region.

NOTES

* First published as "Grenada and the Theory of Peripheral Transformation," *Social and Economic Studies* 39, no. 2 (June): 151–92.

1. The major exception here would, of course, be Cuba. For good accounts of recent political developments in Cuba, see Casal and Perez-Stable in Holmes (1981) and Leogrande in Seligson and Booth (1978).
2. For more details on events in Grenada, see Ambursely in Craig (1981); Ambursely in Ambursely and Cohen (1983); the EPICA Task Force (1983); Jacobs and Jacobs (1982); and Fedon Publishers (1982c).
3. Of course, this may all change with the growth of the mass media and the possibilities for the commercialization of cultural production that they make possible. However, in the case of Grenada and most peripheral countries, cultural production still occurs primarily outside of the sphere of commodity production. For a more detailed development of this type of cultural analysis, see my work on Antigua (1985a).
4. For a more economically focused critique of Thomas's model, see Farrell (1976).

SIX

Political Accumulation and Authoritarianism in the Caribbean

The Case of Antigua

This paper is an examination of the factors responsible for the authoritarian tendencies within the political systems of the English-speaking Caribbean countries. Unlike most other Third World political systems, these tendencies in the postcolonial period have for the most part manifested themselves within formal frameworks of liberal democracies.

Existing patterns of military development, class and elite formation have for the most part made more standard routes to authoritarian rule quite unlikely. Both the local military and religious elites along with the major classes have been weak relative to the power that mass parties in the region have been able to mobilize. As a result, the political elites generated by these parties have been successful in containing the claims of other possible contenders for state power. It is this dominance of political elites generated by mass parties over other contenders for state power that is the primary sociological foundation of Caribbean democracy.

However, despite the above fact, it is the primary argument of this paper that the accumulative behavior of the political elites produced by these parties is a primary source of the authoritarianism that has taken up residence in these democracies. I will substantiate this argument in three basic steps. First, I will provide a brief analysis of the concept of political accumulation. This will be followed by a detailed analysis of the accumulative strategies of Antiguan political elites and their relationship to the authoritarian tendencies of the Antiguan state. In the conclusion, I offer some thoughts on the regional significance of this case. To facilitate this undertaking and to keep its contributions in perspectives, I begin with a short review of three attempts to theorize the authoritarian tendencies of Caribbean state systems.

THEORIES OF CARIBBEAN POLITICAL SYSTEMS

The first of these to thematize explicitly the authoritarian problem was that of George Danns. In Danns's view, Caribbean political systems are essentially authoritarian. "The nature," he writes, "of governmental rule in the colonial and postcolonial Caribbean society can be immediately seen as authoritarian" (Henry and Stone 1983a: 66). Although Danns makes a very convincing case for Guyana, the major problem with his argument is the degree to which it can be extended to other territories of the region. It seems highly unlikely that countries such as Barbados, Antigua, Jamaica or St. Kitts-Nevis could be adequately understood with this model. Thus, it is reasonable to suggest that there are a number of important factors in the model that are peculiar to Guyana and not general to the remainder of the region. The most obvious of these is the level of militarization that clearly sets Guyana apart.

Another important attempt to conceptualize the authoritarian tendencies within Caribbean democracies can be found in the work of Carl Stone. Stone makes use of the theoretical literature on clientelism, corruption and machine politics to explicate "the syndrome of factors associated with the ordering of power" in Third World political systems of the parliamentary type (Stone 1980: 91). One important conclusion that Stone draws from his analysis of clientelism in Jamaica is that, "the formal organizational structure of the parties notwithstanding, the political parties are held together by an informal pattern of personalized loyalties to maximum leaders, past or present" (Stone 1980: 99). In the more extreme case of Guyana, the formal democratic power structure of either the party or state itself has become to a large degree an instrument of this informal power structure. But in both cases, the generative factor is the practice of clientelism.

This interpretation of the authoritarian tendencies of Caribbean political systems is significant because it captures the structural ambiguity that currently characterizes these systems. Because it recognizes both sides of this ambiguity, it is, in my view, closer to the realities of a larger number of Caribbean states than Danns's model. However, at the same time that it has this advantage, there are some problems with the model.

The major difficulty is the one recognized by Stone himself. The concept of clientelism cannot adequately cover the phenomenon that Stone is attempting to describe. It cannot, because it is only the strategic aspect of what Stone is trying to explain—the building of informal power structures. In Stone's model, the more limited concept of clientelism is used to explain the more general one of building power structures. The result is that significant portions of Stone's account of Jamaica remains outside of the clientelistic framework and is formulated on a more descriptive level. A more appropriate theory would be one that focused explicitly on the building of power structures that at the same time included clientelism as a major strategy.

The last of the new theories is that of Clive Y. Thomas. Thomas's theory falls within the Marxist literature on the postcolonial peripheral state. For my purposes, the unique contribution of Thomas to this literature is his introduction of the problem of class creation. The importance of this phenomenon is related to the fact that the class most associated with the growth of the postcolonial peripheral state is the petit bourgeoisie and not the dominant expatriate bourgeois fractions. A crucial consequence of this pattern of state-class relations is that it produces a "reversal of the classic relation of economic to political power" (Thomas 1984: 62). Thomas refers to the experience of the developed capitalist societies in which the bourgeoisie achieved control of the state after it had gained control of the economy. The reversal of this relationship in the periphery opens up the possibility of the use of the state by the petit bourgeoisie for purposes of establishing its control over the economy. It is in this context of class creation that Thomas situates the processes of corruption, clientelism, militarization, silencing the opposition, etc., that have accompanied the rise of authoritarianism in the region. Thus, in Thomas's view, behind the democratic practices that accompany the exercise of power, there is another process taking place—that of class creation. Hence, the structural ambiguity of regional political systems.

The advantage of Thomas's model is that it identifies and labels the activities of political elites that are oriented toward the building power structures—class creation. This is an important step in conceptualizing the problem. However, there are at least two problems. First, like Danns's model, Thomas follows too closely the Guyanese case. As a result, it overemphasizes the authoritarian aspects and so undermines its applicability to countries such as Antigua, St. Kitts-Nevis, Barbados or Jamaica where balance between authoritarianism and democracy is quite different.

Second, Thomas formulates the concept of class creation too economically. As a result, the impression is left that the political elites will, themselves, come to constitute the bourgeois fraction after gaining control of the economy. To avoid this erroneous impression, it is important to recognize that class fractions differ in the type of "capital" that serves as a basis for class creation. Thus, Bourdieu distinguishes between social capital (contacts, social networks), cultural capital (educational credentials, linguistic competence) and economic capital (economic wealth) (Bourdieu 1984: ch. 2). To these, I would add political capital. The variety of accumulative strategies that follow from these different types of capital will in turn diversify the nature of the processes that constitute class creation.

In sum, my primary criticism of Thomas is his failure to introduce a political model of class creation along side the economic one. Given the focus on the attempts of party-based elites to become members of dominant classes in the making, the political nature of their capital holdings places limits on an economic model of class creation. What is needed is a model of how political capital can be accumulated, converted into other forms of capital and reconverted into political capital. In short, a theory of political accumulation that explains the creating of a dominant class fraction and its continued reproduction as a political elite.

POLITICAL ACCUMULATION

The theories reviewed above all suggest the existence of patterns of elite behavior that give rise to informal power structures. I suggest that at the most general level we begin by viewing the creation of these informal structures as processes of political accumulation. I use this concept to refer to the systematic efforts of political elites to transform power from a resource that is delegated in relatively fixed, role-specific amounts into one in which these initial amounts become the basic capital for acquiring larger amounts. In this context, political power ceases to be a resource that is primarily in service of the needs, values and goals of the members of a political community. On the contrary, it becomes a form of private social capital that can be accumulated, converted into other forms of capital, reconverted into political capital and even transmitted to friends and relatives. As private capital, the use of power follows a different logic from that of its use in the reproduction or realization of the basic values and needs of a political community. The difference between these two types of political behavior parallels the Marxian distinction between exchange value and use value (Marx 1967: ch. 1). Consequently, the concept of political accumulation can be further explicated with the aid of this distinction.

In the case of use-value production, the output of useful goods is directly related to satisfying human needs. These needs, their social definition and the norms arising from the communications surrounding their satisfaction constitute a basic set of rules and imperatives governing use-value production. Consequently, production is not a self-legitimating or self-governing activity. Rather, it is one that is shaped and regulated by the consumptive and cultural needs of a community.

In the production of exchange value, output is more indirectly related to human needs. Between output and needs, there is the inserting of an accumulative dynamic. This dynamic introduces a new set of strategic relations between need and production which compete with the normative patterns that regulate use-value production. The central point is that the inserting of this accumulative dynamic subjects the production of goods to the additional constraint of generating a surplus or a profit. Generating increasing amounts of this surplus is the primary goal of exchange value production and not the satisfying of specific needs.

In a similar way, we can distinguish between communicative and accumulative forms of politics. Communicative politics is the consensus politics of small groups and communities. Accumulative politics inserts an additional set of conditions between the articulation of community needs and the executing of appropriate political decision. Desired decisions cannot be expected simply because political elites have legitimate authority and needs exist among the masses. Rather, decisions and needs come together if the executing of the former yields some form of additional value that can be converted into political or social capital. In other words, a state in which political accumulation has been institutionalized is one in which the output of desired decisions is also subject to widely generalized conditions of yielding "profits" or "tributes" to political elites. The more this dynamic characterizes the system, the less effective will be communicatively based politics and the less direct the relations between human needs and political actions.

The concept of political accumulation should be clearly distinguished from that of political mobilization. The latter usually refers to processes of organization and change in outlook, whose goals are more collective or organizational in nature (Nettl 1967: 32). Also, it should be clear that the goal of political accumulation is not the informal support that leaders need for effective decision making. For example, Neustadt has suggested that "a president's persuasiveness with other men in government depends on something more than his advantages for bargaining. Them he would persuade must be convinced in their own minds that he has skill and will enough to use his advantages" (Neustadt 1980: 44). Generating this type of informal support can be usefully viewed as a mobilizing of personal resources on the leader's part. Political accumulation differs from this type of mobilizing by its more extractive interests and the extent to which the expansion and defense of these interests ignores or manipulates constitutional constraints. It is precisely the extent to which this tendency for accumulative behavior often goes beyond normative and constitutional constraints that sets Caribbean democracies apart from those of Western Europe and North America.

POLITICAL ACCUMULATION IN PARTIES

Given the hegemonic position that is claimed for the party in regional political systems, the next task must be a general account of how the process of accumulation manifests itself in political parties, particularly those that are set within a competitive framework. In this regard, the work of Michels is extremely important as it contains a theory of political accumulation within the working-class parties of Europe.

"In theory," Michels wrote, "the principal aim of socialist and democratic parties is the struggle against oligarchy in all forms. The question, therefore, arises how are we to explain the development in such parties of the very tendencies against which they have declared war" (Michels 1968: 50). This concern of Michels has certainly become a concern of theorists of Caribbean political parties. To explain this contradictory phenomenon of oligarchic democracy, Michels developed a number of dynamic principles regarding the exercise of power within organizations in general and parties in particular. In developing this theory of power in organizations, Michels's point of departure is the necessity of organizing. The latter is a necessary step in the realizing of any complex task or goal that requires the cooperation of a large number of people. However, at the same time that organization is necessary, it also brings with it certain tendencies that will undermine the very goals that it is supposed to realize.

The peculiar characteristic of organizing that produces this contradiction is its principle of delegating functions. For our purposes, the most significant of the functions delegated by organizing are those of leadership. However, necessary as this step may be, it is at the same time the key structural factor that makes political accumulation in organizations possible. The delegating of leadership functions takes political power away from the group and places it in the hands of a small number of individuals. This transfer opens up the possibility that this power may be used in the private interest of the leaders. If this interest in private accumulation becomes dominant, the power and sovereignty of the group will be "devoured" by the leaders.

Within political parties, Michels explains the devouring of the sovereignty of the masses by identifying a number of basic strategies of accumulation, which we can put into four groups. In the first group are the strategies that "multiply the ramparts which defend their (the elite's) position" (Michels 1968: 206). In other words, these are self-entrenching strategies. They begin with a change of attitude that transforms a delegated office into a "customary right." Leadership positions become unchallenged and re-elections are expected to be matters of formality. The goal is to convert an elected office into a "life incumbency." If resisted, the leader responds with a series of moves—character assassinations, counter-mobilization, party disruption, sudden resignations, etc.—all in an effort at self-entrenchment.

In the second group are strategies that enable leaders to withdraw themselves from the control of the masses. In particular, Michels points to the exploiting of contacts outside the party and the accumulating of functions within the party. An example of the former is a leader's attempt to use the autonomy gained from winning a national election to disregard or unduly influence party policy or decision making. Michels refers to this phenomenon as "parliamentarism" and analyzes its strategic use by leaders of the German Socialist Party. Similar withdrawal strategies could be pursued through exploiting alliances or contacts with economic or other elites. As examples of the accumulating of functions, Michels discusses the cases of party leaders who attempt to add executive positions in parties or unions to their parliamentary functions.

In the third group are the strategies of factional competition and expulsion as leaders fight to control party resources. These competing factions often crystallize around such factors as the class origins of leaders, the objective needs of different branches of the party, personal jealousies and conflicts between different strata of the organization.

In the fourth group are strategies for converting political capital into social capital. These Michels discusses under the general theme of the embourgeoisement of the leaders. However, in contrast to Thomas, it is important to note that this embourgeoisement does not always lead to the creation of a bourgeois class that controls the economy, but the expanded self-reproduction of a political elite.

These strategies of accumulation, though largely a phenomenon of organization, require some additional factors to produce an adequate explanation of the oligarchic democracy of European working-class parties. The first is the adversary nature of working-class parties. These are fighting parties and the internal organization must reflect the imperatives of tactical and strategic mobilization. However, "democracy," says Michels, "is utterly incompatible with strategic promptness" (Michels 1968: 79). Consequently, this need to make the party a "hammer" in the hand of the leadership contributes to the growth of oligarchy.

The second factor which reinforces the oligarchic tendencies of parties is what Michels calls "the need for leadership felt by the mass" (Michels 1968: 85). This need derives from the inability of the mass to deal with the complexities of political leadership. Closely related to this is the gratitude they feel toward those who take on these complexities. This gratitude along with the need from which it arises are important factors that empower leaders and sustain political accumulation. In sum, although the latter was made possible by the needs for organization, administrative structures and elite strategizing, it must be supplemented by these political and psychological factors. We will see that many of the above strategies have been employed by the leaders of the Caribbean parties.

POLITICAL ACCUMULATION AT THE STATE LEVEL

Although important on its own terms, party power reaches its fulfilment in the administration of state power. This achievement gives party leaders control over bureaucratic positions, whose authority to regulate, legislate, command, judge, sentence and punish are national in scope. The power of these positions is, therefore, much greater than those that make up the party bureaucracy. Consequently, within an accumulative framework, the former represent vastly expanded resources of potential political capital.

Because of this ability of state power to greatly expand the actions that party power made possible, the response of Caribbean leaders to state power has been very similar to their response to party power. Although not explicitly thematized by Michels, many of the same strategies can be used to conceptualize the process of accumulation at the state level. The immediate manifestation of these strategies is the extracting of surpluses or tributes from the exercise of state power, or defensive moves to protect the accumulation process. However, these actions also point in the direction of class creation, while producing authoritarian consequences on the way.

The process of accumulation at the state level builds on and continues the practice at the party level. Thus, by the time a party has become a serious contender for state power, many of the strategies described above are already routinized features of its internal life. On these foundations, party leaders are able to advance toward the control of state power. Once in control, the strategies of accumulation that brought success at the party level are set in motion at the state level. After relatively short periods of time, self-entrenching strategies begin to emerge. The results of these strategies are the already familiar attempts at converting public offices into private long-term holdings. These tendencies are important sources of the informal structures that contradict the formal ones.

Also observable are strategies that allow leaders to reduce or withdraw themselves from the control of the electorate. We have already seen that being in power and responsible to a larger constituency is often used to escape the control of party rank and file. Similarly at the national level, technical complexity, national security, the imperatives of economic development, industrial courts and labor codes are strategies that have been used to lessen the power of mass control. Thus, the tendency for the autonomy of elected regimes to increase is a marked tendency of regional political systems.

However, the most disturbing consequence of accumulation at the state level is the imposing of the strategy of factional competition on the relationship between party and opposition. More than any of the above, the conflicts generated by party competition feed directly the authoritarian tendencies found in Caribbean democracies. As noted before, they have resulted in the rigging or manipulating of election results, attempts to silence opposition parties, clientelism and victimization. This competition for state power has resulted in an escalating war between the parties that has been labeled "political tribalism." It is this latter phenomenon more than any other that has been responsible for changes in the positions of regional societies in democratic rating systems such as those put out by Freedom House.

Finally, the converting of political capital into economic and social capital increases many times over at the state level. The strategies for this range from simple forms of corruption such as money for political favors or influence, to major deals with foreign capitalists. The result has been the generating of substantial wealth by party elites who gain control of state power.

This concludes our theoretical development of the concept of political accumulation. Our next task will be the examination of the accumulative behavior of Antiguan party elites.

ANTIGUAN POLITICAL PARTIES

To facilitate this analysis of Antiguan political parties, we can divide the development of these organizations into three major periods: the period of one-party dominance (1946–70); the period of two-party dominance (1970–80); and the post-two-party period (1980–90). During the first of these periods, five parties were created: the Antigua Labour Party (ALP); the Antiguan Democractic Labour Party (ADLP); the Antiguan National Party (ANP); the Barbuda Democractic Movement (BDM); and the Antigua and Barbuda Democratic Movement (ABDM). By far the most important was the ALP, which slowly emerged out of a trade union that was formed in 1939.

In the period of two-party dominance, two new parties emerged: the Progressive Labour Movement (PLM) and the Antigua People's Party (APP). Of the two, the PLM was the more important and the major rival of the ALP. The APP eventually merged with the ALP. The rise to prominence of the ALP and the PLM was accompanied by either the disappearance or absorption of all the other parties. Hence, the two-party nature of the period.[1]

In the post-two-party period, four new parties emerged: the Antigua Caribbean Liberation Movement (ACLM); the United People's Movement (UPM); the National Democratic Party (NDP); and the United National Democratic Party (UNDP). The ACLM, formed in 1980, is a small but very vocal revolutionary socialist party. The UPM is a centrist labor party that was formed from a faction of the PLM in 1983. The NDP is a small, liberal, middle-class-based party that was formed in 1985. The UNDP was the result of a 1986 merger between the UPM and the NDP.

THE PERIOD OF ONE-PARTY DOMINANCE

As indicated before, the dominant party throughout this period was the ALP. Empirical indicators of this dominance are provided by the election results of the period. These elections were for the gradually increasing number of elective seats in the legislature that decolonization was making possible. Throughout this period (1946–70), there were four elections. In each of these the ALP won all of the seats and a large percentage of the popular vote. For example, in the 1951 elections, the party won 87.4 percent of the popular vote and 86.7 percent in the 1956 elections. Because of this overwhelming dominance of the ALP, I will focus my examination of political accumulation on this party.

THE ANTIGUA LABOUR PARTY

The Antigua Labour Party began its career as the political committee of the island's first trade union, the Antigua Trades and Labour Union (ATLU). This committee played its first major electoral role in the 1946 elections; hence that year can be used to mark the birth of modern party politics in Antigua. Because of its role within the ATLU, the ALP was dependent on the union for both its sociopolitical orientation and its organizational structure. Ideologically, the party drew a lot of its inspiration from the democratic socialism of the British labor movement and was assisted by the left wing of the British Labour Party. However, with the passage of time and the ascension to power, this position shifted to a more conservative laborism.

The organized structure of the union and hence of the ALP was that of a centralized democracy. They shared an administrative structure that consisted of a president, a general secretary, a treasurer, and an eight-member executive. In theory, the team that filled these positions was elected at the union's annual convention. Immediately below these executive positions were the section leaders of both union and party. These leaders were responsible for reporting the demands and concerns of the members to the executive. Consequently, the annual convention and the section meetings were the basic institutional structures for popular input.

Although making popular input possible, these structures did not provide adequate institutional space for a legitimate opposition that would allow teams to compete for the leadership. Consequently, resolving differences of opinion and strategy within the organization have been rather difficult, leading to a number of purges.

STRATEGIES OF ENTRENCHMENT

Like Michels, by strategies of entrenchment, I am, of course, referring to two distinct sets of processes: the first is the various ways in which party leaders "multiply the ramparts" that defend their positions; the second is the various ways in which leaders withdraw themselves from the control of the masses. Both of these processes rest on a possessive, exploitative attitude toward the privileges of positions of leadership that result in their instrumental manipulation as political capital.

With regard to the first of these processes, the primary self-entrenching strategy employed by the leaders of the ALP was the formation of personal networks within the party. These networks were largely the result of two factors: the charisma of some of the leaders and the exchange of the power of their positions for support. In this exchange of the power and influence of leadership positions for personal loyalty, we can recognize an early clientelistic form of political surplus extraction. However, unlike the later forms, this operated largely within the ALP because of its overwhelming dominance at the time. In addition to this practice of intra-party clientelism, the personal charisma of leaders was also a factor in the formation of these networks. Thus, not all leaders had significant personal followings. These followings tended to crystallize around the more powerful and charismatic ones such as Vere Bird, Samuel James and Douglas Roberts. These personal networks reinforced the formal power of these leaders, enabling them to increase their hold on the initial allocations of party power.

At the same time that the leaders of the ALP were entrenching themselves through the formation of personal networks, they were also engaged in similar activities through the adoption of strategies that lessened the degree of control that the masses had over them. The primary strategy in this group was the attempt to gain and maintain control of the candidate selection process. Such control was, of course, unconstitutional in that all positions of leadership should be open to contestation at the annual convention.

This pulling away of leaders from mass control begins with the cultivating of heroic and unchallengable images first within personal networks and later with the party at large. These images are forged out of a mixture of actions, some of which are genuinely courageous while others are highly egocentric and self-serving. The value of these images is the reputation for being tough that they maintain. Being tough deters others from challenging the positions or crucial decisions of leaders. Thus, the image functions as a protective veil and is an attempt to put leaders beyond routine challenges. This self-entrenching strategy was used with varying degrees of success by leaders within the ALP: the two most successful were clearly Vere Bird and Douglas Roberts. The former, in particular, very early sought and achieved this status.

As pointed out before, one of the major consequences of this type of leadership behavior has been manipulation and control of the candidate selection process—which, in turn, has weakened the power of the party's annual convention. At these conventions, all expired positions should be open for competitive reappointment.

But such open contestation often did not occur. Rather, the pattern was the following: the higher the position of leadership and the more charismatic the occupant, the less likely that position is to be openly challenged. Although such a challenge is a constitutional right, it is seen as an affront to the leader and often results in sanctions. Such cases are particularly good examples of the clash between informal and formal power structures that has come to characterize Caribbean political parties.

Along with this refusal to challenge a powerful leader goes the tendency of not challenging the people that the leader has selected to work with him or her as a team. Thus, through the pressure of personal or informal influence, the selection of candidates for elections had often been the decision of a powerful leader. This situation increased the power of the leaders at the same time that it decreased the power over these individuals that the masses exercised at the annual convention. It was primarily through these strategies that early leaders of the ALP increased their independence of party rank and file.

FACTIONAL COMPETITION

The strategies of entrenchment examined above are essentially strategies that reproduced or expanded the initial political capital of the ALP leaders at the expense of the masses. On the other hand, the strategies of factional competition are strategies of accumulation that reproduce this expanded political capital at the expense of some of the leaders. These strategies are based on conflicts between the leaders themselves as they struggle to monopolize the informally augmented and entrenched power of the positions of leadership.

As noted earlier, the formation of personal networks was an early strategy of accumulation within the ALP. With the passage of time and the increase in the power of the more charismatic individuals, these networks crystallized into very definite factions within the party. Factional competition within the party took many forms. Sometimes it manifested itself in the making of appointments on the basis of strengthening a particular factional interest. At other times, it took the form of spreading rumours or voting for positions with the express aim of weakening an opposing faction. But the events that are most revealing of this aspect of the life of the ALP are the periodic purges or factional eliminations it experienced throughout this phase of one-party dominance.

The first significant case of this type of factional conflict occurred as early as 1943 when the party was just four years old. The president at the time was Reginald Stevens. Stevens was a member of the middle class who had gravitated toward working-class causes. But at the same time he was committed to working-class struggle, he was overly concerned about incurring the wrath of the local colonial elite. He thus appeared to many as a weak leader, an image that was further reinforced by his heavy reliance on Sir Walter Citrine, the general secretary of the British Trade Union Congress. Because of this aspect of Steven's leadership, the question of militancy as a strategy in challenging colonialism became a major issue. In 1943, this issue became a contest between competing factions when Stevens agreed to the request of the colonial government for a ban on strikes until the war was over. Opposition to the decision was led by the Bird faction. This opposition developed into a challenge to Stevens's leadership. The power struggle that resulted ended with Bird replacing Stevens. Bird was by far one of the more charismatic leaders and was a man of great oratorical skill. However, this ascension to the top was only the first of many other factional fights that he would have to endure.

Another expulsion of a similar type occurred in 1946 with the preparation for the elections. The issue at stake was the candidates to be selected. Disagreements arose concerning particular choices and the processes by which candidates were to be selected. These disagreements resulted in a power struggle between the leaders of the Bird faction and the chairman of the political committee, Oliver Davis. This struggle was further intensified by class differences—Davis being of a more middle-class background. At the end of the confrontation Davis was forced out of the party.[2] In addition to the specific issues involved, the conflict was important as it increased control of the Bird faction over the candidate selection process.

Much more important was a third purge that occurred in 1948–49. Once again the fight was precipitated by policy differences. This time the specific issue was an appropriate response to complaints of plantation owners about "the dilatory manner" in which workers had been reaping the sugar crops. Even more than in the previous cases, the struggle was factional in nature. The issue is one that could have easily been resolved but it pitted two of the most charismatic leaders in the party against each other. These leaders were Vere Bird and Douglas Roberts. Roberts was often referred to as the Bustamante of Antigua,[3] which was suggestive of his style and popularity. Also an important leader in the faction with Roberts was Samuel James, who was the general secretary of the ATLU. In that capacity, James had a lot of day-to-day contact with the masses, hence his popularity. But despite this popularity, the leaders of this faction were not able to defeat the Bird faction. At the end of the struggle, Roberts, James and a number of their strong supporters were forced out of the party.

The fourth and final purge discussed here occurred in 1967. In terms of its ramifications, it was by far the most important. The issues of this struggle were also two factors that Michels recognized in the case of European working-class parties: the accumulating of functions and conflicts between the objective needs of different branches of the organization.

In the course of staying on top of all these internal fights, the Bird faction had acquired a tight control over both union and party. The executives of one were the executives of the other. However, as decolonization progressed, the importance of party-based roles increased dramatically to the point of eclipsing union-based roles. It was in the darkening shadow of this eclipse that some members of the union executive began to make an issue of party leaders also being union leaders. They protested strongly this wearing of "two hats."

This opposition was lead by George Walter who, like James, was the general secretary of the union. This was clearly an important issue, but its discussion was never separated from the political aims of Walter and his close supporters. Viewed in these terms, the conflict degenerated into a power struggle in which Walter and two of his close supporters were forced out. However, as we will see shortly, the results of this purge were very different from those of the previous one.

The purges described above point to the persistent pattern of factional conflict within this union-party combination. In addition to the specific issues involved, these conflicts were at the same time struggles between the more charismatic leaders to monopolize the increasing power that was accumulating in the leadership roles of the organization. The primary outcome of this pattern of factional conflict was the essential monopolization of power within the union-party by the Bird faction between 1943 and 1967. During this period, the expulsion of potential rivals enabled this faction to maintain its exclusive control over the political resources of the party that decolonization and the various strategies of accumulation were expanding. This monopoly, in turn, expanded the social base for authoritarian decision-making within the party.

THE ACCUMULATION OF FUNCTIONS

The final strategy of accumulation that was important in the period of one-party dominance was the accumulating of functions by the Bird faction. This strategy was also crucial for their monopolization of power as it concentrated power in their hands not only at the expense of the masses but also of other leaders.

The primary new functions that these leaders sought to acquire were the new positions that were being generated by the process of constitutional decolonization. This process initiated a series of changes in Antigua's constitution that increased the number of elected seats in the Legislature and expanded the franchise. For example, the constitutional changes of 1951 increased the number of seats from five to eight and introduced universal adult suffrage. In 1956, the ministerial system of government was introduced. In 1967, the constitutional status of Antigua was changed from a colony to an associated state. With this new status, the country was internally self-governing while Britain remained responsible for defense and foreign relations. In short, the process of constitutional decolonization produced an array of new and important positions that required an increase in the organizational complexity of the party.

It was this extension of the role structure of the party that created new opportunities for the further accumulating of functions by the leaders of the Bird faction. As this faction already controlled the top positions in the union, the absorption of these new party positions amounted to an accumulation of functions. Thus, by 1967, Vere Bird had achieved the status of a maximum leader. He was both Premier of Antigua and president of the ATLU while his ministers were the executives of the union. This was the phenomenon of wearing two hats that led to the purge of 1967. However, until that event, this practice served as another important strategy of political accumulation on the part of the Bird faction.

THE PERIOD OF TWO-PARTY DOMINANCE

Political accumulation in the period of two-party dominance can be analyzed in terms of two important developments. The first was the emergence of a new major party—the Progressive Labour Movement (PLM). The second was that the emergence of the PLM resulted in equally matched electoral contests for the control of state power. These two developments produced significant changes in the nature of party competition, which, in turn, made the politics of this period very different from the previous one. By contrast, this was the period in which clientelism and other strategies of accumulation at state level emerged, culminating in the phenomenon of political tribalism.

THE PROGRESSIVE LABOUR MOVEMENT

The creation of the PLM was one of the major political developments that followed the purge of 1967. The expulsion of the leaders of the Walter faction from the ATLU/ALP was not taken as easily as previous expulsions. Not long after the expulsion, Walter formed a new union, the Antigua Workers Union (AWU), which opened its doors in July 1967. Its executives included the dismissed leaders while the rank and file was drawn largely from ex-ATLU members who were outraged at the dismissals.

But, to survive the competition with the ATLU, the AWU very quickly discovered that it needed a political arm. The need for this political ally was one of the major factors leading to the formation of the PLM. In addition to this factor, the PLM emerged as a result of the efforts of three other opposition groups. These were the Antigua People's Movement (APM), a group led by middle professionals; the Antigua and Barbuda

Democratic Movement, a party led by landed interests; and a left-wing group led by middle-class intellectuals. Thus, at the time of its creation in 1968, the PLM represented the coming together of four groups that were opposed to ALP leadership.

Because of its close alliance with the AWU, the organizational structure of the PLM was similar to that of the ALP. Both parties were, in fact, union-party combinations with centralized democratic systems. However, despite the close association between the AWU and the PLM, they were organizationally separate. Ideologically, the PLM was also very similar to the ALP in that its dominant position could be described as a laborist one.

But despite these structural and ideological similarities, there were some important differences between these two parties. Of these, the first is already noted plurality of groups which made up the party. The second was a commitment to reducing the tendencies toward factional oligarchy. This commitment included emphasizing democratic norms, the opening up of all positions of leadership to contestations and the introduction of primaries to break the hold of factions on the candidate selection process. In short, the early PLM was significantly more democratic than the ALP and had a more diverse set of ideological positions within its centralized democratic framework.

ACCUMULATION WITHIN THE PLM

Political accumulation within the PLM can be divided into two phases. The first covers the formative years of the party before it gained power in 1971. The second covers the years after the gaining of power and is also the period in which clientelism and the other new strategies of the two-party period really emerged. The strategies that dominated the first of these two phases were largely similar to those we have already analyzed in the case of the ALP.

As noted above, the PLM emerged out of the coming together of previously organized groups. The important processes of developing personal followings and establishing one's reputation as a leader had already been accomplished in three of the factions. The AWU faction was lead by Walter, the ABDM by Robert Hall and the APM by Rueben Harris. The left-wing faction under the leadership of Tim Hector firmly crystallized shortly after the birth of the party. Consequently, the PLM started its career with distinct and well-developed factions. This, in turn, meant that processes of self-entrenchment began at a more advanced stage.

Within the party, some leaders immediately sought to secure their positions from serious challenge. Like their counterparts in the ALP, the strategy employed was that of cultivating an image that could only be challenged at very high costs. As leader of the dominant AWU faction,

Walter very quickly achieved this status. Others such as Donald Halstead, Rueben Harris and Robert Hall succeeded to lesser degrees. Like its counterparts in the ALP, the Walter faction used its dominance to exercise undue informal influence on the candidate selection process. This influence soon smothered the sparks that led to the introduction of primaries. So strategic became this pattern of control that no more primaries were held after the first set. Thus, within the first year of its formation, the PLM manifested very definite tendencies toward factional self-perpetuation and entrenchment. The conflicts that resulted would, in time, undermine its attempts to be more internally democractic than the ALP.

Like the ALP, strategies of factional competition were very prominent in the development of the PLM. This competition resulted in two purges within a year of the formation of the party and another in 1983. Only the first one is examined here.

The first of these two purges resulted in the departure of important leaders and a sizeable portion of the followers of the APM faction. The conflict was largely between this faction and the AWU faction. The specific issue at stake was the filling of the positions on the party's steering committee that were left vacant by the by-election of 1968. In the effort to fill these positions with individuals from their own ranks, the AWU faction rejected all non-union candidates that were nominated. This strategy was most violently opposed by the APM faction. This opposition resulted in an all-out fight which ended with the departure of leader Rueben Harris along with a significant portion of this faction in the middle of 1969. With Harris's departure, leadership of this faction fell to Oliver Davis (purged from the ALP), Toby Derrick and Henderson Stevens.

Later in the same year, a second purge resulted in the departure of the left wing of the party, which would later become the socialist ACLM. Once again, the conflict was with the leadership of the AWU faction. It was fueled by definite ideological differences and the fears of the latter concerning Western reaction to the presence of the former elements within the party. The particular form this conflict took was the attempt by the AWU faction to bring the Political Action Committee, which was controlled by the left faction, more directly under the control of the executive. Because the executive was controlled by the AWU faction, the left faction saw it as an attack on their power base. The confrontation that ensued produced the departure of the party's left wing.

So, as in the case of the ALP, political accumulation went beyond the use of mere self-entrenching strategies. It openly embraced the use of factional competition as leaders struggled among themselves to monopolize the political resources of the party. This competition resulted in the clear dominance of the Walter faction just as it had produced the dominance of the Bird faction in the ALP.

Finally, although they were present, strategies of accumulating important executive functions were weaker in the development of the PLM. Most striking was the reappearance of the tendency of "wearing two hats," despite its role in the formation of the PLM. However, the practice was rather quickly eliminated. Again, this lesser role of strategies of this type can be related to the particular democratic ethos of the early years of the PLM.

In sum, the PLM that became the primary rival of the ALP emerged from a formative process that included recognizable patterns of internal political accumulation. That is, the securing and augmenting of the power of delegated positions by leaders was as integral to the formation of the party as they were to the ALP. In both cases, processes of accumulation were made possible by the use of similar strategies. The isolating of these processes and the strategies that facilitate them are important as they constitute the social base for the authoritarian tendencies observable within these parties.

CLIENTELISM AND STATE-LEVEL ACCUMULATION

The twin phenomena of political accumulation and authoritarianism I have been analyzing are not exhausted at the party levels of Caribbean political systems. Rather, as suggested earlier, they can also be observed at the state level. Their existence at this level is additionally significant because of their increased societal scope and their transformation into bases for the self-constituting of dominant class fractions. At this level, periods in which evenly matched parties compete for the control of state power have tended to be the ones in which party (factional) competition have been the most important generators of authoritarian tendencies. The activities of an equally strong opposition party are seen as the primary threat to continued control of state power. Thus, more than other self-entrenching strategies, the attempts to control these activities becomes the focus of party competition. This competition makes use of a variety of instruments including repression, job discrimination and electoral manipulation.

In Antigua, the analysis of this type of evenly matched party competition coincides with the second phase in the development of the PLM. That is, the period which started with the latter's quest for and assumption of power between 1970 and 1976. However, throughout the period of competition with the ALP, which lasted until 1982, the most systematic generator of authoritarianism was the accumulative strategy of clientelism. Consequently, my analysis of this phase of PLM development and of accumulation and authoritarianism at the state level will focus on this particular strategy.

As Stone has pointed out, "clientelism in the Third World is more than a device to win votes for competing parties" (Stone 1980: 93). At the same time that it serves this function, it is also a "mechanism by which to institutionalize a power structure" (Stone 1980: 93). In the language of the theoretical perspective being elaborated here, it is also a strategy of exchanging political capital in the interest of further accumulation.

In Antigua, the turn to this type of clientelistic politics began with the ALP's gradual shift from the anticolonial politics of advocacy and confrontation to machine politics based on the control, exploitation and administration of state power. The PLM made a similar shift soon after gaining power in 1971. That is, party leaders abandoned the fight for further democratization as a basis for political mobilization and replaced it with the exploitation of state power. With this shift in the orientation of both parties, the state was now set for the emergence of clientelism on a large scale.

As in the case of other strategies of political accumulation, the practice of clientelism was based on an exploitative privatization of public offices and the discriminatory use of their power and resources. Generally, positive resources such as jobs, recognition of civil rights, speedy services, protection of union rights, cheap access to land, etc., have been passed from these offices to supporters via the patronage machine. At the same time, negative resources such as the state's ability to repress, to fire, to deny civil rights, to weaken unions, etc., have passed to opponents through the victimization machine. The setting into motion of these machines were the primary processes responsible for the structural ambiguities and authoritarian practices that characterized the Antiguan political system throughout this period. Practices such as party manipulation of the police, the judiciary and the civil service, the arbitrary denial of civil rights, the attempts to curtail the freedom of expression, to eliminate opposing parties and unions can all be related to the operating of these machines in the interest of holding on to state power.

The use of these machines as instruments of accumulation began to intensify within the first months of the PLM's coming to power in 1971. A good example of this party's victimization machine at work was its firing of a number of workers from state-owned utilities companies (*The Worker's Voice* 1971: 1). The case of these workers was taken up by the ATLU, as it represented most of the workers in these companies. The response of the new administration was to not recognize the ATLU as the legitimate bargaining agent of these workers. This response toward the ATLU was not an isolated incident. At several other workplaces where the ATLU was likely to have the majority of workers, the new regime refused to conduct the voting that would determine which of the two unions would be the bargaining agent (*Antigua Times* 1971: 1).

This practice, in general, and the case of these workers, in particular, were seen as instances of victimization. For example, the leaders of the

ATLU interpreted these actions as political moves that were designed to weaken and eventually eliminate their organization. Similarly, the workers felt that their union rights were being undermined and their jobs taken away because they had been opponents of the new regime. Quite naturally, the response of the ATLU leaders and the workers was one of loud opposition. This opposition produced an extended period of picketing which included several clashes between PLM/AWU members and ALP/ATLU members.

At the same time, the PLM's patronage machine was also in operation. Jobs in the expanding tourist industry were going to party supporters and members while the union rights of AWU members were carefully protected. In some of the more celebrated cases, civil service rules of promotion were violated or manipulated to ensure that particular appointments were made (*Antigua Times* 1973: 1).

As these patterns of patronage and victimization continued, the power of party leaders increased as the competition permitted them to demand and accumulate greater amounts of loyalty. As these demands increased, the lower-middle and working classes in particular became more and more polarized. The symbols of this polarization were the colors red and blue, the colors of these two parties. Within the first six months of the PLM administration, there was hardly an area of public life that had not been affected by the rivalry. Even the annual carnival did not escape. The 1971 carnival was boycotted by many ALP supporters to protest the discriminatory manner in which the jobs associated with it were distributed. Political tribalism had by this time become a dominant feature of the Antiguan political system. However, it never got to the levels reached in Jamaica but approximated the levels reached in St. Kitts-Nevis during the period of competition between the People's Action Movement and the St. Kitts Labour Party.

Upon its return to power in 1976, the ALP pledged not "to tolerate or encourage any political reprisal or victimization" (*ALP White Paper* 1976: 8). This pledge was indicative of the importance of the victimization issue. However, this promise did not last very long. After a short grace period, the practice began to escalate once again, declining in intensity only after the near destruction of the PLM in the years following the 1980 elections. This destruction of the PLM, temporarily restored the hegemony of the Bird faction over the ALP and the dominance of the latter over the state, although not as solidly as in the period of one-party dominance.

In sum, it was this rivalry that gave the two-party period its particular political color. In terms of outcome, clientelism as a strategy of accumulation allowed the Bird faction to gain a monopoly on state power in much the same way that factional competition enabled it to monopolize its party's political resources.

THE POST-TWO-PARTY PERIOD

The period (1980–90) that I have called the post-two-party period is difficult to describe because, except for marked declines in clientelistic competition, its distinguishing features are still in the process of emerging.
Consequently, the best I can do at present is to characterize it in relation
to the two-party period. Among the more important changes that set the
1980–90 period apart, I include the following: the collapse of the PLM, the
decline of political tribalism and the rise of the four new parties—the
ACLM, the UPM, the NDP and the UNDP.

THE UPM

The collapse of the PLM and the rise of the UPM were two closely related
events. The former was largely the result of the increased intensity of
political struggles both within the PLM and with the ALP. Within the
party, the struggles of the AWU faction to stay in control of the party
intensified between 1976 and 1984. This intensification was brought on
largely by the corruption charges that the ALP brought against members
of the PLM leadership after the former returned to power in 1976. Among
those charged were Walter and his ministers of Home Affairs and Public
Utilities. For those factions within the party that were dissatisfied with
Walter's leadership, this became an opportunity to push for a change. On
the other hand, Walter and his close supporters saw it as a time for
closing the ranks and being solidly united. Once again, the resulting conflict ended with the departure of the AWU faction in 1983. Under Walter's leadership, this faction formed a new party, the UPM, which was
closely affiliated with the AWU.

   This departure of the AWU faction reduced the PLM to a shell of what
it used to be and ended its political career. In the 1984 elections it received only 1.9 percent of the popular vote while the UPM and the ALP
received 23.5 percent and 69.2 percent, respectively. As the UPM merged
shortly afterward with the NDP, its accumulative impact is considered
when the UNDP is examined.

THE ALP VERSUS THE ACLM

Between the crippling of the PLM and the rise of the UPM in 1983, opposition to the ALP was maintained largely by the socialist ACLM. Prior to
openly declaring itself a party in 1980, the ACLM had been a critical,
activist movement dating back to the late sixties. Through its primary
publication, *Outlet*, it gained national recognition and credibility. As a
party, the ACLM has been even more vocal, its visibility peaking in this
period of PLM decline. This growing presence of the ACLM contributed

to the deformation of the two-party period in that it helped to weaken the red-blue polarization by replacing it with the capitalist-socialist polarization. This shift in the ideological orientation of local politics became all the more significant with the revolutionary seizure of power by the New Jewel Movement (NJM) in Grenada.

But, despite its prominence, the ACLM has not been able to translate this advantage into votes or a large persistent following. In the 1980 elections, it polled only 1.1 percent of the popular vote, did not contest the 1984 elections and in the 1989 elections polled only 2 percent of the popular vote. Consequently, its status as a contender for power remains in doubt.

What are the authoritarian consequences that have followed from ALP competition with the ACLM? Because of its small popular base, the ACLM never constituted an electoral threat to the ALP. Thus, for all practical purposes, competition at this level had been suspended, making practices such as large-scale victimization unnecessary. In other words, this relative security produced a relaxing of some strategies of state-level accumulation that were intensively employed in the competition with the PLM. However, despite these differences there was competition with ACLM, which forced the ALP to adopt a number of defensive strategies.

Modeled after C. L. R. James's small revolutionary group, the ACLM has not developed the complex bureaucratic structures of the major parties. Consequently, the generating and exercise of power within the party has largely been communicative in nature. As a result, accumulative behavior within the ACLM has largely been restricted to the oratorical and the strong image varieties. However, its impact on inter-party competition has significantly affected patterns of accumulation at the state level.

As in its battle with the AWU faction within the PLM, the ACLM presented the ALP with an unbeatable ideological challenge. Through its dominance of the print medium, the force and clarity of its ideological positions, the ACLM was better prepared than any other party to attack the ALP in its most vulnerable spots. But as spectacular as the ideological victories of the ACLM were, their electoral consequences were small. As a result, the responses of the ALP leadership to the ACLM were motivated more by fears of spontaneous uprisings, saving face and covering up corruption than by the perception of fatal threats to their electoral hold on the state apparatus.

Not surprisingly, the primary object of their response was the silencing of the ACLM leadership. Using Section 33(a) of the Public Order Act, the ALP began bringing charges against the editors of *Outlet*. As early as 1977, charges were filed against editor Ellerton Jeffers. These continued over the years and culminated in the 1985 case against Tim Hector for supposedly making false statements that could stimulate suspicion regarding the conduct of public affairs. The case went all the way to the Antigua High Court and Privy Council, both of which declared the above section of the Public Order Act unconstitutional. In short, the authoritarian practices that followed from the competition with the ACLM derived largely from these and other attempts at ideological containment. In the absence of an ACLM machine, the continued expansion of the ALP machine led to increasing corruption without the widespread victimization of the competition with the PLM.

FACTIONAL CONFLICT IN THE ALP

A third important consequence of the deformation of the two-party period has been a very sharp increase in the level of factional conflict within the ALP. The period between 1971 and 1990 has so far been the longest that the ALP has gone without factional fights leading to expulsions. The collapse of an equally strong electoral rival has been accompanied by a dramatic increase in accumulative behavior (factional competition) at the party level. Open factional fighting has occurred over a number of issues such as ministries, appointments and policy positions. However, by far the most significant source of intra-party fighting has been over the future leadership of the party.

Since his rise to power following the purge of 1943, Vere Bird has been the party's leader. However, particularly following the 1984 elections, Bird's advancing age has made the issue of his successor an urgent matter. The possibility that the 1984–89 term may have been his last gave rise to a number of self-declared or suggested candidates. Thus, by early 1985, four distinct factions were in competition for this prospective position: one was led by Adolphus Freeland, minister of labor; another was a group that suggested and supported the candidacy of John St. Luce, minister of finance; a third was led by Lester Bird, deputy prime minister and son of the prime minister; the fourth was led by Vere Bird, Jr., minister of communications and also a son of the prime minister.

Between 1976 and 1984, Lester Bird was seen as the one most likely to be the successor. However, as the pressure from the PLM and the UPM declined following the ALP sweep of 1984 elections, conflicts between these factions began to intensify. One consequence of this intensification was the eroding of the certainty of Lester Bird's succession. By the middle of 1985, St. Luce, because of his reputation for moderation and honesty, had won the support of many within the cabinet and thus emerged as a possible challenge to the deputy prime minister. However, St. Luce's tolerance for political infighting is not very great and so never openly challenged the deputy.

As a result, the real fight between these two factions was led by Rueben Harris, minister of education. Harris, after being forced out of the PLM, joined the ALP as a part of the latter's merge with the Antigua People's Party (APP), a small, middle-class-based party. The feuding between Harris and Lester Bird reached the media early in 1986 over the tour of an English cricket team, members of which had recently played in South Africa (*The Worker's Voice* 1971: 1). Bird opposed the tour while Harris not only welcomed it but supported the arrest of some protestors who had actively opposed the tour. Tensions between these two peaked with the publication between May and July of a series of articles on the leadership problems of Antigua's major parties in *The Herald*, the paper of the deputy's faction. One article in the series that dealt rather directly with Harris was withdrawn from publication at the last moment on the threat of legal action by the minister of education. Adding fuel to these fires were the repeated calls by the ACLM leadership for the charging of one or both of these ministers for making statements likely to undermine confidence in the conduct of public affairs.

The next major outbreak of factional fighting occurred at the start of 1987. This time it pitted the Freeland faction against the deputy and the prime minister. The precipitating event was a cabinet reshuffle which in the mind of the minister of labor produced a weakening of his position and a reinforcing of the deputy's. Freeland not only refused his new portfolio but proceeded to go public with the conflict. In his statement to the press, he attacked the deputy saying, "he is not the leader we want for the Labour Party" (*The Herald* 1987: 1). However, after a few days of holding out, Freeland retracted his statement and accepted his new portfolio. With this capitulation also went his chances for being the successor. At the same time, it was the closest the party had come to another factional expulsion.

In the face of all this private and public feuding, several unsuccessful attempts were made to contain them. The first was the prime minister's intervention following the publication of the articles in *The Herald*. In his address to the nation on this crisis, he sought more to reaffirm his leadership than to resolve the issues. He argued that there were many who wanted to lead the nation, but they would have to wait their turn. The address stopped the articles but not the feuding.

A second attempt to resolve the leadership crisis was constitutional in strategy. An amendment to the party's constitution was proposed which would have created the position of deputy political leader. Its holder would then be the successor following the departure of the political leader. This solution, however, was opposed by the prime minister and came to naught.

A third attempt was made at the party's annual convention later that year. It produced a series of eloquent pleas for unity but no solutions. Hence, the important fourth attempt: a specially organized series of retreats early in 1987. However, despite being a good effort, it produced only a brief truce.

Perhaps more important than any of the above attempts was the Cabinet reshuffle mentioned earlier. It produced the coming together of the

Harris and Lester Bird factions under the latter's leadership. As a result, the major conflicts have been this coalition led by Lester Bird and the Vere Bird, Jr., faction (*Caribbean Contact* 1987: 8–9). The outcome of this unresolved conflict between the two brothers has so far been shaped by two important events. The first was a major scandal in 1987 regarding the role of Vere Bird, Jr., in the allocation of money for the resurfacing of Antigua's airport. The second was an even more disastrous scandal in 1990 which linked Bird Jr., to the sale of Israeli arms to the Medellin drug cartel of Colombia. This affair has led to his resignation from the cabinet pending the results of a commission of inquiry. Given these circumstances, Lester Bird appears once again to have the upper hand. In short, this sharp increase in intraparty fighting supports my contention that the post-two-party period produced an intensifying of accumulative behavior at the party level.

THE UNDP

Finally, in this analysis of the post-two-party period, I take a brief look at the UNDP, Antigua's newest political party. As noted earlier, this party was the result of a merger between the NDP, a small, middle-class party, and the UPM, which was a major splinter from the PLM. Although the executive of the latter voted to stay out of the merger, many individuals from the PLM joined the UNDP. Consequently, this party can be viewed as a regrouping of the opposition under new leadership. At the head of this leadership is a very prominent Antiguan surgeon, Dr. Ivor Heath, who was also the leader of the short-lived NDP. Ideologically, the regrouping has produced a rather unintegrated mixture of an abstract middle-class liberalism and a more concrete working-class laborism. In the case of the PLM, this tension resulted in the expulsion of middle-class elements (the APP faction) and a clear dominance of the laborist position. In the UNDP middle-class liberalism has so far played a more prominent role than it did in the PLM.

In addition to the above differences, the second incarnation this opposition group has so far been considerable weaker than the first. The primary reason for this drop in strength are the comparatively weaker social roots of the UNDP. Because of the importance of the UPM elements in the party, the primary roots of the UNDP are in the history of party splintering and of intra- and inter-party conflict, rather than in a social movement. In contrast, the ALP had the anticolonial struggle; the PLM, the struggle for the further democratization of unions and parties; and the ACLM, the socialist struggle. These struggles have given their parties distinct causes, identities and symbols to which people have committed themselves emotionally and ideologically. So far, the UNDP has found no such distinct social cause. Consequently, it has relied primarily on the crises and scandals of the ALP regime for its critiques. But, even if these could serve as a social base, the UNDP has had to fight to be heard on these issues because of the strength of the ideological critiques produced by the ACLM.

Given these features of the UNDP, it is not surprising that it did only slightly better in the 1989 elections than the UPM did in the 1984 elections. The party gained one of the sixteen seats in parliament. It was won by the deputy leader, Baldwin Spencer, a trade union leader and ex-member of the UPM. Out of a total of 21,548 votes cast, the UNDP received 6,896, or 32 percent of the popular vote. The ALP received 14,218, or 66 percent of the popular vote.

However, it needs to be pointed out that this was the most irregular general election in Antigua's history. Ballot paper was not available in some constituencies for the start of voting and remained so in some cases for up to seven hours. The results in one constituency were declared null and void by the High Court as a result of a challenge brought by the UNDP. But, in spite of this victory, the party did not follow through with a re-contesting of the seats on the grounds that without electoral reform it could not win.

The implications of this electoral performance are rather inconclusive for the UNDP's status as a major rival for the ALP. Will it become as strong as the PLM or remain a distant second of the ALP? This will depend on its relationships to the social problems of Antigua, its own factional tensions and those within the ALP. So far, the struggle for state power and the opposition to the ALP have kept factional tensions in check.

If this continues to be the case, it could lead to the start of a new period of two-party dominance, assuming the ALP survives its own factional conflicts. If there is splintering in the ALP, the splinter group could easily join the UNDP thus making the two more evenly matched. Without major political reforms, such a development could result in the return of large-scale clientelistic competition and a resurgence of inter-party tribalism. This, in turn, could mean a return to levels of authoritarianism of the first two-party period. In other words, the rise of this party should not be seen as a solution to the above problems. On the contrary, without major reforms it is likely to be an additional base of accumulative and authoritarian practices.

CONCLUSION

In this paper, I have tried to identify the processes of building and defending informal power structures that have had authoritarian consequences for the Antiguan political system. These processes were isolated and analyzed under the rubric of political accumulation. I used this concept to refer to political behavior that was motivated primarily by surplus extraction. If this conceptualization is correct, it suggests that the authoritarian features of the Antiguan democratic system can be analyzed within a neo-Michelsian framework.

Even though the data were drawn exclusively from the Antiguan case, it is reasonable to suggest that the strategies of political accumulation analyzed are employed by political elites throughout the region. However, the importance of this behavior and the consequences it produces will vary with specific patterns of political growth, the elite and class formation. For example, party splintering produced by factional conflicts have been lower in Jamaica than Antigua. However, the violence produced by party competition has been greater in the former. This centrality of political accumulation could change with a significant break in the present patterns of class and elite formation. A rapid expansion of the military, a dramatic increase in the ability to attract foreign capital or both could be the start of a whole new period. Under these conditions, explaining regional authoritarian tendencies may require the use of theories closer to the bureaucratic and military authoritarian models. Without such changes, the dominant classes in formation in the region will continue to be without strong bourgeois or military factions, thus making the current hegemony of the political fractions possible. This in turn will keep their behavior in a primary relation to regional authoritarian tendencies.

ACKNOWLEDGMENT

I would like to thank Jorge Heine (Universidad Interamericano) for his helpful comments on an earlier draft of this paper.

NOTES

* First published as "Political Accumulation and Authoritarianism in the Caribbean: The Case of Antigua," *Social and Economic Studies* 40, no. 1: 1–38.

1. The historical details for the analysis of these two sections are drawn primarily from my book *Peripheral Capitalism and Underdevelopment in Antigua* (1985).
2. Interview with Oliver Davis, 24 August 1978.
3. Alexander Bustamante was the fiery labor organizer who became founder and leader of the Jamaican Labour Party (JLP) in the early 1940s.

SEVEN

Caribbean Dependency in the Phase of Informatic Capitalism

The plantation model of Caribbean economies, as formulated by Kari Polanyi Levitt and Lloyd Best (Levitt and Best 1975), took as one of its central concerns the persistent problem of Caribbean economic dependence.[1] The model made this problem more explicit and hence more visible than earlier approaches to Caribbean economies. With the neo-liberal turn in Western economic theory, the plantation model, along with similar dependency approaches in Latin America and Africa, entered a period of eclipse. The paradox of this eclipse is that as the plantation model has receded, the problem of dependency has only become more stark, urgent and visible. This paper is an attempt to explore this paradox. In the course of its exploration, the paper will establish four basic claims: (1) that the rise of Asian capitalism has forced the advanced capitalist countries into a new or informatic phase; (2) the continuing relevance of plantation theory in this new phase of advanced capitalism; (3) that in this informatic phase Caribbean plantation economy has gone through a fourth "ratooning"—a reference to the practice of reusing already cut stalks of cane rather than uprooting them and replanting new slips for the next crop; and (4) that in addition to structural factors, this fourth repeating of the plantation pattern may also be linked to persistent effects of the colonial capture of the auto-poetic processes by which Caribbean economic and entrepreneurial identities were established. By "auto-poetic," I am referring to the creative processes of symbolic self-representation, affirmation and negation by which we establish identities and differentiate them from other identities. The paper concludes with the notion of a mobilized entrepreneurial sector that cuts across classes, as a possible structure that could break this repeating pattern and prevent a fifth ratooning.

CARIBBEAN DEPENDENCE BEFORE THE PLANTATION MODEL

Although Levitt and Best were the first to put the problem of economic dependence at the center of the theoretical stage, the problem was well recognized by many, such as C. L. R. James, Arthur Lewis, and Eric Williams, who were involved in the reforms that followed the uprisings of the 1930s. The problem of dependence was recognized by all three as a dark shadow that Western imperialism had cast over regional economies. However, it was never systematized and made explicit as the plantation theorists would later do. All three saw imperialism as the hostile cocoon out of which Caribbean colonial economies emerged. The restrictive aspects of this imperial cocoon led to features such as overspecialization, domination by foreign capital, and foreign technological expertise. However, they differed among themselves about how to overcome the legacies of this restrictive colonial birth.

In the case of James, the imperial roots of Caribbean economies and the dependence it produced on plantation agriculture was well established in his classic text, *The Black Jacobins*. In this work, James is critical of Toussaint L'Ouverture's decision to re-establish the plantation system in spite of the resistance of the ex-slaves that he had freed by defeating the French and the British. James writes:

> The ultimate guarantee of freedom was the prosperity of agriculture. This was Toussaint's slogan. The danger was that the blacks might slip into the practice of cultivating a small patch of land, producing just sufficient for their needs. . . . He confined the blacks to the plantations under rigid penalties. (James 1989: 242)

That produced what James called the new despotism. In contrast to the plantation theorist, James's objections focused not so much on the negative developmental consequences for the Haitian economy, but the policy's suppression of the economic impulses and self-organizing activities of the laborers.

This inability to make the badly needed move beyond the plantation system and trust the economic creativity of the masses is a theme that recurs through James's writings on Caribbean economies. It is most clearly seen in the two models that James developed for transforming Caribbean economies (Henry 1992d: 158–65). The first was an industry-led strategy of transformation, while the second was a peasant-led strategy. In the course of outlining the latter, James asserted that "no economic regime has had so demoralizing an effect on the population as the sugar estates" (Lewis 1983). Here, too, his economics was shaped by his search for a modern form of political organization that could accommodate the self-organization of workers and peasants as classes. Thus the key feature of both alternative models was the participatory form of economic organization, rather than the strategy of development, that would institutionalize principles of worker control of production. This was James's socialist answer to the imperial origins of Caribbean economies.

In the case of Williams, *Capitalism and Slavery* was the text that established his view of the imperial origins of Caribbean economies and the colonial legacies of over-specialization and dominance by foreign capital. In an earlier (1943) essay on Caribbean development, Williams wrote: "Colonialism, there is the enemy of Caribbean diversifications" (James 1983: 154). The diversifications that Williams had in mind were local food production and industrialization within a federated Caribbean. Thus, he made the following special note of peasant crops such as limes in Dominica or bananas in Jamaica: "these democratic crops stand out in striking contrast to the dictatorship of foreign capital and foreign management which characterizes the sugar industry" (Williams 2004). The dictatorship of foreign capital was not only responsible for the lack of agricultural diversification but also the lack of industrialization. Williams wrote:

> the most natural industry of the Caribbean, sugar refining, was and is deliberately prohibited by foreign competitors. The prohibition began in England in 1671, and was a part of the general colonial policy in the eighteenth century which banned iron and textiles industries in colonial America. (Williams 2004: 22)

Here we can recognize some of the themes that the plantation school will develop in a much more systematic fashion.

Before turning to the case of Arthur Lewis, whose work bore more directly on the emergence of the plantation school, it is important to note that the theme of Caribbean dependence can also be seen operating implicitly in the work of scholars from outside of the region who were also involved in the discussions that followed the uprisings of the 1930s. This was true even of some British and American scholars who were involved in these discussions. A good example of the latter is Annette Baker Fox's 1949 text, *Freedom and Welfare in the Caribbean: A Colonial Dilemma*. This work has as its main theme the tensions and contradictions inherent in a still colonized Caribbean demanding autonomy and economic development at the same time. In her view, the nature of colonial societies was such that the "satisfaction of one demand was very likely to prejudice the fulfillment of the other" (Williams 2004: 23). In other words, given the colonial history of economic exclusion in the region, autonomy might bring on economic collapse, while continued economic aid from the West would extend and possibly increase existing patterns of dependence. She insisted that as long as "social and economic development takes place mainly through outside aid, there can be no real independence" (Fox 1949: 3). Not surprisingly, she saw the region as being caught in a vicious circle from which there would be no easy exit.

In response to this dilemma, Fox discussed in detail the shifts in both British and American colonial policies that occurred after the uprisings of the 1930s. The shift in the American position she described as a "new deal" and in the case of the British "development and welfare" (Fox 1949: 220). Both were marked by a Keynesian shift from *laissez-faire* to state intervention in a number of economic fields including direct production, land reform, subsidies, and increased educational opportunities. The result was a containing of the violence of the uprisings and significant moves toward political independence. Although a strong supporter of these initiatives and the policies of planned economic development put forward by the Caribbean Commission, Fox was only guardedly optimistic that these would solve the problems of economic dependence, even though the region might succeed in gaining political independence. Needless to say, Fox was correct in this assessment.

ARTHUR LEWIS AND CARIBBEAN DEPENDENCE

The restrictive shadow that Western imperialism had cast over Caribbean economies was established in Lewis's early works such as *Labour in the West Indies*. However, as in the cases of James and Williams, the external dependence it produced was not explicitly thematized. Lewis's response to the problems of Caribbean dependence remained implicit in his Fabian or democratic socialist response to his own question regarding "what can be done" to realize the transformative goals of the new labor movement of the 1930s (Lewis 1977: 44). For Lewis that realization required two basic changes in Caribbean economies: first, total income "must be considerably increased and in the second place, it must be more equitably distributed" (Lewis 1977: 44). This redistributive but growth-oriented view of democratic socialism remained with Lewis most of his life. Thus in 1971, he wrote that the aim of democratic socialism is "to combine political democracy with . . . economic equality" (Lewis 1977: 44). He then proceeded to defend the view that there were no irreconcilable conflicts between democratic socialism and economic development, although there were real tensions.

However, in spite of the permanence of these two poles of income growth and redistribution, Lewis's thought went through several stages of development. Norman Girvan has suggested a division of Lewis's thought into three basic phases: the first was that of Caribbean industrialization; second was the phase of the dual economy; and third, that of trade and development (Lewis 1983: 669–70). Further, Girvan convincingly shows that over time Lewis moved closer to some of the positions of the dependency approach—particularly those of Raul Prebisch (Girvan 2005: 219). However, Lewis's Ricardian views of trade remained a basic source of difference with the dependency view of the relationship between trade and imperialism. In the following short review of Lewis's work before the rise of dependency theory and the plantation school, my remarks will cover only the first two of the three phases suggested by Girvan.

In both of these phases, to increase total income, Lewis insisted on both the industrialization of Caribbean economies and the expansion of agriculture. However, given commodity prices of the 1930s and the emergent nature of the Caribbean bourgeoisie, Lewis saw two crucial areas in which his two-part strategy for transformation would be in need of immediate but hopefully short-term assistance. As in the case of Fox, the first was for increased preferential treatment, grants and loans from the West; unlike Fox, the second was a carefully worked-out strategy of industrialization that would include the problematic requirement of importing a foreign capitalist class to lead the associated process of capital accumulation. The rare skill possessed by members of this class was "the technique of managing large undertakings." This skill was rare because it cannot be learned in colleges or universities but "only in the practice of managing businesses" (Lewis 1970: 204–10). The role of this imported capitalist class in the expansion of national income, Lewis would develop with great care and brilliance in classic essays such as "Economic Development with Unlimited Supplies of Labour" (1954), and "The Industrialisation of the British West Indies" (1950). Only with assistance in these two areas did Lewis see total income increasing, which could then be more equitably redistributed.

However, without naming them as such, assistance with both price and entrepreneurial support pointed to two crucial areas in which the success of this Caribbean workers' movement would be dependent on the cooperation of the very capitalist and imperialist forces that it had been fighting. This contradictory but necessary bringing together of opposites such as capitalism and socialism was one of the defining features of Lewis's thought. For him, there were no absolute economic laws, only partial principles and empirical generalizations whose limits he always kept in mind when applying them to concrete situations. In this case, capitalism and socialism were not treated as absolute principles, and neither were market and plan or peasant and bourgeois entrepreneurship. For Lewis, all of these partial principles of economic thought conditioned each other, at the same time that their general scope was being constantly challenged by new concrete cases. This unusual approach is particularly evident in his book, *Principles of Economic Planning*. Thus to understand Lewis's concept of democratic socialism is to grasp the manner in which it was changed by the capitalist imperatives of the economic growth needed to increase total income. In more poetic terms, we have here the proletarian tradition of Caliban risking deeper entrapment in the capitalist imperatives of Prospero to achieve a desired expansion and redistribution of national income.

In the course of making the imported capitalist the primary agent in the process of increasing total income, Lewis was forced to confront two important factors bearing on Caribbean dependence: (1) "the sociological problem of the emergence of a capitalist class" (Lewis 1970: 258); and (2) "the relative efficiency of peasant and plantation production" (Lewis 1970: 301). The strategy of importing a capitalist class necessarily raised questions about existing levels of entrepreneurial capability in Caribbean societies. These inadequate levels Lewis assumed to be fairly common for newly developing countries. However, in *The Theory of Economic Growth*, Lewis assumed that this form of entrepreneurial dependency would end fairly soon with the rise of a local capitalist class (Lewis 1977: 49).

With regard to the expansion of agriculture, Lewis strongly supported programs of land redistribution to increase the size of peasant farms and peasant output. With the appropriate institutional support, Lewis saw "no reason why the West Indian peasant should not learn to utilize the land as capably as the planter." In short, Caribbean peasants also had an important role to play, along with the imported capitalist class, in the project of increasing and redistributing national income. The coordinating of these strategies of industrialization and expanding peasant output would be the job of the state, as it had to provide the combination of incentives and protection to foster the growth of both an industrial bourgeoisie and a more viable peasantry.

Lewis's democratic socialist ideas on industrialization, increased peasant output, and income redistribution became the foundations of economic policy in much of the region. Programs of industrialization and peasant land settlement were undertaken in territories such as Jamaica, Trinidad, Barbados and Antigua. In these more concrete forms, because of the difference in the power values of its opposing socialist and capitalist dimensions, Lewis's proposals pushed the political economy of the region in the direction of state-coordinated capitalism. Only in the cases of Trinidad, Guyana and Jamaica did the latter go beyond mere coordination and approach real forms of state capitalism. This new direction made this third phase distinct from the second—or post-slavery—phase of the plantation model, but also not the democratic socialist order that Lewis envisaged.

For this third phase in the history of Caribbean dependence, four important outcomes emerged from this state capitalist turn in Caribbean political economy. First, Caribbean state-coordinated capitalism did significantly increase national income (Lewis 1970: 280); second, it did not succeed in redistributing it according to the ethics of Lewis's democratic socialism; third, it did not succeed in developing an independent peasantry; and fourth, while it did succeed in stimulating the growth of a local bourgeoisie, this class has not achieved the assumed capability of being able to replace the imported capitalist class. This local bourgeoisie sprang from the merchant classes at a time when the planters were breathing their last. This rising bourgeois class was primarily English, Middle Eastern and Indian in ethnicity. The names that we associate with this further evolution of the Caribbean bourgeoisie are firms such as Kirpalini, Neal & Massy in Trinidad, and, in Jamaica, the Matalons, the Ashenheims, and Desnoes & Geddes. The aspirations and outlook of this class were those of Ariel rather than Caliban. The former identified with Prospero and worked to further his imperial project, while the latter resisted it. Thus in Jamaica after the upheavals of the 1930s, this emerging bourgeois class formed a party with the declining planter class in an effort to block the workers from gaining control of the state. Such were the ambiguous outcomes of the attempts of local political parties to implement Lewis's democratic socialist response to the problems of Caribbean dependence.

PLANTATION THEORY AND CARIBBEAN DEPENDENCE

As these ambiguous outcomes of the attempts to implement the Lewis model of transformation left the problem of dependence very much unresolved, they determined to a large degree the issues that the plantation theory of Levitt and Best would have to address. At a minimum, the new theory would have to account for the failure of the peasantry and the local bourgeoisie to perform in the manner suggested by Lewis. It would also have to account for the more obvious continuities in the overall structure between the earlier plantation capitalism and the newer state-coordinated capitalism.

To understand these and other crisis tendencies of Caribbean state-coordinated capitalism, Levitt and Best shifted their gaze from the industrialization of regional economies and their local classes, and focused more directly on the anti-developmental consequences of the behavior of imported capitalist classes. Consequently, they would attempt to show that there were aspects of their behavior that were inhibiting the growth of local classes and making investment decisions that not only reinforced dependence but also transferred excessive portions of the region's surplus to the metropole. We can sum up these aspects of the behavior of imported capitalists under the thesis of the imperialism of trade. As we will see, this thesis linked the imperial aspects of trade to the simultaneous production of development in the center countries, and underdevelopment in the peripheral countries.

As in the case of Lewis, the plantation theory of Levitt and Best was grounded in a historical/institutional approach that divided the history of Caribbean economies into three broad phases: (1) the phase of pure plantation economy; (2) plantation economy modified or the plantation in the post-slavery period; and (3) plantation economy further modified or the plantation in the period of state capitalism. This historical approach was a backward glance in historical time in order to see more clearly the paradoxes of the third and then present phase.

Within the framework of this historical perspective, Levitt and Best recognized four variations in the ways in which Caribbean economies made the transition from phase 2 to phase 3. First, there was the variant in which imperial ties were cut, but the old export sector was retained, as in the case of Cuba. Second, was the one in which, again, imperial ties were cut, but the old export sector collapsed, as in the case of Haiti. Third, was the variant in which old metropolitan ties were broken but new ones established through quasi-staples such as tourism. Good examples of this case are Barbados and Antigua. Fourth and finally, we have the variant in which a new staple such as oil or bauxite was added without breaking older ties as in the cases of Trinidad, Guyana and Jamaica. Yet in spite of these variations in the transition to the state-coordinated capitalism of the third phase, there were really no successful cases of industrialization to report. None of these economies moved from "subsistence production to small scale, wage employing business serving a national market, and from there to large-scale corporate enterprise" (Girvan 1971: 41–3; Henry 1985a: 127–36).

For Best and Levitt, the primary cause of this failure to industrialize was to be found in the assumption of the Lewis-based policy makers that the developmental consequences of using imported capitalists would outweigh the anti-developmental ones. Plantation theory was an attempt to show the major problems that were now associated with that assumption. It attempted to show the manner in which this cornerstone of Caribbean state-coordinated capitalism was a carryover from earlier phases that was still inhibiting the growth of local entrepreneurship, local capital markets, and thus more autonomous links between local savings and investment decisions. By inhibiting or weakening these links, the use of imported capital and capitalists reinforced rather than undermined Caribbean dependence.

At the most general level, plantation theory pointed to the existence of fundamental continuities between the three basic phases of Caribbean economies with regard to both structure and their less-than-viable functioning. These continuities were in five crucial areas. First was the continuing subordinate role of the manager or resident capitalist in the larger net of metropolitan capitalists, merchants and financiers who made the crucial surplus distribution and investment decisions affecting the developmental outcomes of this new staple or quasi-staple. Second, was the reappearance of the old staple cycle—a foundation period, a golden age, and a period of maturity and decline—in the new staples of the state capitalist period. Third, was the continuing dependence of Caribbean economies on metropolitan demand, capital, and entrepreneurship for its growth dynamic. Fourth was the persistence of incalculability in the transactions of these newer plantations and their parent companies. Fifth and finally, we had the continuing dominance of the further modified plantation sectors of the state capitalist period over the "residentiary sector" or what Levitt and Best sometimes referred to as the "national econo-my" (Levitt and Best 1975: 45). Indeed, it was the negative effects of this dominance of the further modified plantation sectors on the national economies that constituted the heart of the Best/Levitt critique of the Lewis approach.

For Best and Levitt, the overall effect of these newer plantation sectors on national economies has been that "the national propertied class is born in circumstances which restrict its capacity for innovation and self-asser-tion and stunt its growth. The national economy emerges with a bias toward production of output requiring traditional plantation skills and serving traditional markets" (Levitt and Best 1975: 45). Because of this, "when a new national resource is discovered or an old one is revived, the national economy has neither the capital nor the entrepreneurship nor the international marketing experience to organize production" (Levitt and Best 1975: 49). The financial sector is also inhibited in a similar way:

> The fractured and partial nature of the capital market of the hinterland countries is not due to low levels of income, or a low rate of saving from domestic product. It is the result of mercantilist relations of pro-duction with metropolitan corporations, and a system of financial intermediaries which is similarly characterized by the free flow of funds between branches of metropolitan commercial banks and their head offices. (Levitt and Best 1975: 53)

In short, Levitt and Best argued that when the imperialist trade rela-tions of the state capitalist period are superimposed on those of the previ-ous periods, "the barriers to the emergence of indigenous enterprise are reinforced" (Levitt and Best 1975: 52). Further, the classes of this circum-scribed national economy cannot really mature. These underdeveloped classes—"the quasi-proletariat, the quasi-peasantry, and the quasi-bour-geoisie—are creatures of the plantation export sector" (Levitt and Best 1975: 46). Confined in this manner, these classes are unable to give the national economy the internal dynamic that it would need to replace the dynamic supplied by imported capitalists. Thus in spite of the Haitian case, Levitt and Best recommended a breaking with this model that based industrialization on the developmental consequences inherent in mercan-tile relations of production and trade: "a severance of the metropolitan ties is a precondition of structural transformation" (Levitt and Best 1975: 47). This was the sharp break that Levitt and Best made with the Ricar-dian views of international trade that informed Lewis's model. Hence we get the statement by Best that the real differences between plantation theorists and Lewis are to be found "in the causes we adduce to explain mal-distribution of gains from trade which had so agonized him along with Myrdal and Singer" (Best 1999: 43).

THE MODEL AND ITS CRITICS

As well-known as the model itself are the criticisms that have been made of it. These criticisms have been of two types: negative and positive. The negative criticisms have come from two groups of scholars: first, the positivist economists who are uncomfortable with the historicism of Best and Levitt, and would like a more scientific theory with greater predictive power and more testable hypotheses. Second, were the more orthodox Marxists who insisted on a clearer specifying of a proletarian change agent and more definite strategies of transformation. The constructive criticisms came from neo-Marxist scholars, such as George Beckford, Norman Girvan, Clive Thomas and me, who attempted to extend the theory in various ways. Thus, in my case, the attempt was to develop in detail the suggestion that the transition to state-coordinated capitalism in Antigua was of the third or quasi-staple variant (1985a), and also the cultural dimensions of the problem of dependence—in particular, philosophical dependence (2000a).

GEORGE BECKFORD

Beckford's contribution to plantation theory was a detailed comparative analysis of Caribbean agriculture in the third phase of plantation further modified, or what we have been calling state capitalism. What was new about agriculture in this phase was its thorough integration into the organizational structures of transnational firms that were processing and transporting plantation outputs. Consequently, Beckford was concerned about the developmental impact of this corporate reorganization on both Caribbean agriculture and the larger economy.

For Beckford, the corporate consolidation of plantation agriculture was twinned with the growth of the Caribbean peasantry that followed the ending of slavery. This was the sector of the "national economy" that he focused on, describing in detail its determined struggles to develop in spite of constraints and competition coming from the now corporate plantation sector. Particularly in the case of Jamaica, Beckford showed that these constraints included plantation control of the best lands and local financial institutions, strong dominance over local labor markets, and also the new national government. Like Best and Levitt, Beckford argued that these continuities with earlier phases outweighed the discontinuities:

> the emergence of the vertically integrated corporate plantation enterprise has really served to preserve the character of the slave plantation system. Three characteristics of that earlier institutional environment—appendage in overseas economy, total economic institution, and incal-

culability—have been preserved and strengthened since Emancipation. (Beckford 1972: 48)

In spite of these inhibiting effects of corporate consolidation, however, the Caribbean peasantry was able to grow. Beckford argued that they diversified production by introducing new crops, and created an internal marketing system and rudimentary banking and credit systems. This growth in peasant production in spite of plantation constraints led Beckford to the following important claim: "it is this expansion which has been the chief source of economic development of the West Indian economies since emancipation" (Beckford 1972: 48). In other words, even with the corporate reorganizing of the plantation sector, Beckford argued that the really dynamic sector of Caribbean economies was the peasantry, and that national resources and government policies should be steered much more strongly in their direction.

For Beckford, the peasantry was therefore the crucial agent of change and development that could supply the missing entrepreneurial dynamic and end the excessive dependence on imported capitalists. On the point of which of these two sectors is more dynamic, Beckford is most explicit in his disagreements with Lewis and comes much closer to the Best/Levitt position on the "national economy." In his view, the corporate plantation sector, like its predecessors, continues to release its developmental dynamics in the center and its anti-developmental dynamics in peripheral areas like the Caribbean.

NORMAN GIRVAN

Girvan's contribution to plantation theory was an intense focus on the fourth variant of the transition to Caribbean state capitalism in which the new staples of oil and bauxite were added to the old in the economies of Trinidad, Guyana and Jamaica. Consequently, there is a definite shift from the strong focus on agriculture to the transnational, corporate organization of mineral exports. Yet, in spite of this shift, it is the continuities between the imperialism of trade between all three phases that is the center of Girvan's argument. This argument rests on the claim that while anticolonial movements of the 1950s severely weakened political imperialism, the new relations between postcolonial states and transnational corporations have in fact strengthened the practice of economic imperialism. This new form of the imperialism of trade, Girvan referred to as "corporate imperialism," and the response of the region to it as "economic nationalism" (Girvan 1976: 5).

For Girvan, as for Best and Levitt, the primary channel through which imperial strategies work is the subordinate position of the manager of the local subsidiary in the overall hierarchy of corporate decision making. In addition to this weak position of the manager, Girvan analyzed problems of incalculability in inter-company transactions and other channels through which the transfer of surplus to the center from the Caribbean took place. He summed up his analysis as follows:

> it is the imperialism of the parent over the subsidiary, as embodied in the power relationships and economic transactions characteristic of the transnational firm, which, when reproduced on a world scale and transposed onto the center-periphery pattern of the international capitalist economy, gives rise to the phenomenon that we have called corporate imperialism. (Girvan 1976: 25)

The economic nationalism of Caribbean state capitalism is, in Girvan's view, an attempt to assert sovereignty over the resources of the region. However, he also suggested that this push for sovereignty was not necessarily an attempt to overthrow the corporate imperialist order, but to improve the positions of Caribbean states within it. This stance was linked to the declining quantitative importance of Third World minerals in corporate processes of accumulation, as distinct from their qualitative importance. In spite of this declining strategic position, Girvan insisted on a more radical subverting of corporate imperialism that would require a "genuinely revolutionary socialist change" (Girvan 1976: 9).

CLIVE THOMAS

In Thomas's *Dependence and Transformation*, we find the most comprehensive attempt to outline a socialist alternative to the plantation system. As with Beckford, the peasantry is a very important change agent in Thomas's extension of the Best/Levitt plantation model. However, in this case it was not just the peasantry, but workers and peasants in alliance with a socialist state that was the suggested agent to replace the imported capitalist and to supply the missing internal dynamic.

Thomas's insistence on a socialist state points to a significant difference with Beckford on the role and capability of the peasants in this process of transformation. Thomas's estimate of the ability of the peasants to fill the entrepreneurial gap left by the displacing of the imported capitalists was different from Beckford's. To fill this gap, Thomas saw a very definite need for his socialist state to engage in the practice of "class creation." All of the major classes of Caribbean societies were underdeveloped in relation to the challenges of economic transformation. Thus, Thomas's socialist state was in the paradoxical position of having to create the functional equivalent of a capitalist class, a state bourgeoisie. Here Thomas is confronting the same-problem of an entrepreneurial deficit that Lewis attempted to solve by importation. In other words, it is a state bourgeoisie leading a worker/peasant alliance in a centrally planned process of transformation that would end the ratooning of the plantation and establish the autonomy of the national economy in relation to the appropriating and reinvesting of the Caribbean surplus.

These ideas about transformation came closest to being implemented with the writing of "The People's Plan" by George Beckford, Norman Girvan, Louis Lindsay, and Michael Witter (1985). This plan was submitted in 1977 to the Michael Manley regime that had been re-elected in 1976 on a democratic socialist platform. However, on grounds of feasibility, the regime did not implement the plan.

THE BEST/LEVITT RESPONSE

In spite of building in very creative ways on the foundations of plantation theory, these transformative extensions of the theory were never really embraced by Best and Levitt. Thus, it is on the issue of the practical policy implications of the thesis of the imperialism of trade that the theory has really floundered. Levitt has noted the incompleteness of the theory because of their failure to elaborate a model in which the national economy was either dominant or independent (Levitt 2005: 67–68). In response to this particular challenge, four responses can be observed on the part of Best: first, a distancing from the failures to implement some of the delinking policies of plantation theory in the contexts of the Bishop regime in Grenada and the Michael Manley regime in Jamaica. Second is to shift from economics to the need for a genuinely participatory politics that would be educative for the masses in the Jamesian sense. Third is a shift to the level of culture and the problem of Caliban's and Ariel's continuing entrapment in the economic discourses of Prospero. Fourth and finally is a shift to an improvisational stance that sees calls for plans, strategies, and more scientific theories as dogmatic.

A good example of Best employing all of these strategies can be seen in the indirect and elusive manner in which he presents his position in the paper he wrote for the Fourth Sir Arthur Lewis Memorial Lecture (1999). In particular, we can see the shifts to the political and cultural levels in his attempt to explain the failures of the Lewis model. With regard to the cultural shift, Best links Lewis's failure to adequately grasp the specific realities of the region to his long absence from the Caribbean, and his intellectual entrapment in the categories of the British economic tradition. Drawing on Wilson Harris, Best portrays Lewis as a creolized Afro-Saxon, a poignant case of Caliban's entrapment in the economic discourses of Prospero. It is this entrapment that leads Best to the startling assertion that Lewis was "not a West Indian economist at all" (Best 1999: 28). This cultural and epistemic alienation in turn not only forced Lewis into theorizing the British situation but also prevented him from seeing clearly the political dimensions of Caribbean economies (Best 1999: 37). For Best, the core of this political dimension remains the contradiction between the plantation and residentiary sectors. However, in this paper, we do not get a direct stating of the combination of political, epistemic and economic strategies that will remove or resolve it.

However, in spite of this less than enthusiastic response on the part of Best and Levitt, the visionary significance of these above extensions is undeniable. If the imperialism of trade has been and still is our reality, then we have nowhere to go but in the direction pointed out by the extensions that have been made by Beckford, Girvan, Thomas and others. The way forward can only be extensions or combinations of these extensions. However, before taking these up more directly, we now have a new theoretical problem to confront: whether or not we have entered a fourth plantation phase as a result of the emergence of yet another phase in the history of metropolitan capitalism—a phase that I have called informatic capitalism. This new phase shows all the signs of once again adding new staples and shifting the location of overseas production but incorporating these changed peripheral sites in very dependent ways.

INFORMATIC CAPITALISM

To understand the shift in our current economic gaze, to grasp why our eyes are now on economic survival rather than economic nationalism or radical transformation, we must come to terms with the peripheral implications of the major restructuring of Western capitalism that has been taking place over the past 25 years. The rise of the informatic phase has been the result of the coming together of two major forces: (1) a severe crisis of accumulation in the Western economies in the 1970s; and (2) the rise of Asian capitalism fed by an expanding revolution in information and communications technology. The informatic phase has been emerging from the responses of Western capitalism to these two major challenges.

The crisis that gripped the American and Western European economies in the 1970s is well recognized by economists of widely differing persuasions. On the left, it has been well documented by economists such as Paul Sweezy (1978) and Gérard Duménil and Dominique Lévy (2004). On the right, it has been analyzed by scholars like Roger Alcaly (2003), economist and also the manager of a hedge fund. This crisis, which continued into the early 1980s, was evident in rising rates of inflation and unemployment, declining profit rates and rates of labor productivity (Duménil and Lévy 2004; Alcaly 2003: 6–7). In addition to the phenomena of stagflation and growing international competition, what was also unusual about the crisis of the 1970s was its resistance to established doses of Keynesian stimulation.

The basic response of Western elites to this crisis or accumulation was led by finance capital as they were being hurt by rising inflation. Consequently, they pushed for higher interest rates and reform of corporate governance that would make it more sensitive to stockholder interests. In short, the initial response to the crisis took the form of a revolt by angry investors who were dissatisfied with the ways in which corporate managers were responding to inflation and foreign (particularly Asian) competition.

The ideology of this revolt was shareholder value. In the U.S., the leaders were the takeover entrepreneurs such as Irwin Jacobs, Carl Icahn, Michael Milkin, and Ivan Boesky. Their primary weapon was the hostile takeover, which had the effect of putting corporate managers on the defensive. It also forced them to deal more effectively with foreign competition through mergers and enlarge rewards to stockholders by increasing the price of company stock. Closely related to these changes was the making of managers also into shareholders. As owner/ managers, CEOs would now share the views of stockholders.

The American state, which after 1980 had turned sharply to the right, supported these initiatives of finance capital in two important ways: (1) by deregulating banking and broadening the range of activities deposit banks could engage in by repealing the 1933 Glass-Steagall Act in 1998, and (2) by supporting finance capital's drive to globalize and liberalize financial markets. It was in this new policy context that finance was able to stimulate the U.S. economy in the second half of the 1980s. However, this ballooning of the financial sector also created a speculative bubble in the economy that would cause problems later. This bubble was evident in the "dot com" phenomenon, rapidly rising stock values, and skyrocketing increases in corporate remuneration. In 1970, the average American CEO made 69 times the wage of the average worker. In 2000, that figure had risen to 300 (msn.com).

Although the shift to finance eased the crisis somewhat, the pressure of foreign competition only increased. Thus the decade of the 1990s was marked by a turn to the information sector as a strategy for coping with foreign competition. This competition was coming primarily from Japan and the larger Pacific Rim. Drawing on the new information technologies, Japanese capitalists, particularly those at Toyota, pioneered what today has come to be known as high-volume flexible production and just-in-time production (Cohen 1996: 105–20; Womack et al. 1990: 12–20). The former was a mode of production whose internal structure was significantly different from that of the Fordist mass production assembly line that still dominated American and European auto companies. This post-Fordist or Toyotaist mode of production had an assembly line that was capable of making many more stops for quick changes and so was better able to make small batches of customized products. In other words, to mass production this new mode of production added mass customization. To deal with the pressure of foreign competition, it was this shift from the Fordist to the Toyotaist assembly line that would have to be successfully executed in the West.

Making this transition has not been easy for the major Western firms of the monopoly era. They have responded in six basic ways: (1) making themselves bigger through mergers and acquisitions; (2) partnering with Japanese firms; (3) developing new informatic technologies of their own; (4) breaking the post-war pact with American labor in order to lower labor costs and in some cases reneging on pension commitments. This has destroyed the classic Galbraithian firm which was the centerpiece of the monopoly phase; (5) the globalizing of commodity markets, particularly in peripheral areas; and (6) the reorganizing of their peripheral operations, relations and locations.

These still-ongoing changes, together with the initial response of financialization have been sufficiently profound for us to speak of a new era in the history of Western capitalism—the informatic phase. Because it is still developing inside the financial bubble of the 1980s it is the combination of these two sets of forces that have been behind this transition to a new phase. In this new economy, it is companies like Walmart, Microsoft, and Dell Computers rather than General Motors, Ford or IBM that have emerged as the new model companies. Indeed, the troubles of the latter, particularly Ford and General Motors—classic Galbraithian firms—have been extensively reported in the press. Particularly in the cases of Walmart and Dell, it is the new informatic technology along with the new labor and peripheral regimes that have given them their competitive advantage over the dominant firms of the monopoly phase. This transformation is an ongoing one, the outcome of which is still not certain. However, my argument for a new and distinct informatic phase of Western capitalism rests on the assumption that informatic production will at some point in the future gain control over or significantly lessen the current dominance of finance capital.

THE CARIBBEAN PERIPHERY IN THE INFORMATIC PHASE

When we look at the globalizing of financial and commodity markets and the reprioritizing of peripheral areas in the informatic phase of Western capitalism, we find a lot that should be of interest to plantation theorists. In particular, Levitt and Best focused quite intensively on the adjustment strategies of metropolitan capital in the declining phases of the growth paths of peripheral plantation economies. They suggested that these metropolitan responses included divesting from old staples and old peripheral sites, while shifting investments to new staples or to new terrains, which offered virgin soils, cheaper labor, and better technological possibilities. Keith Nurse has developed very insightfully this aspect of the original model. The Best/Levitt strategies of adjustment certainly help us to understand the shifts in location and patterns of divestment and investment that have emerged in the peripheral areas of informatic capitalism. With regards to the Caribbean, we can note five important changes in its peripheral relations with Western capitalism.

First, there has been a decline in overall peripheral importance with the emergence of China as the most attractive peripheral site and India a rising second. Indeed, the model firms of the informatic phase such as Walmart and Dell would be inconceivable without access to these Asian peripheries but very conceivable without access to the Caribbean periphery. This decline in Caribbean peripheral importance has resulted in major contractions in Lewis-style programs of industrialization which have added to the difficulties of Caribbean state-coordinated capitalism, particularly in countries like Barbados, Antigua and St. Lucia, which had attempted to build industrial sectors on the Lewis model. However, the interest of metropolitan finance and real estate capital in the region's beach front areas remains very strong. In many islands these have indeed become the new plantations. Hence we get the persistence of external interests in Caribbean tourism. However, this interest has not been strong enough to avoid an overall decline in peripheral importance. The semi-peripheralization of China, which officially is still a communist state, has important implications for both socialist theory and plantation theory. It raises anew the old question of the necessity for a capitalist phase in the formation of modern societies. However, we cannot deal with that issue here.

A second important change in the Caribbean mode of peripheralization has been the decision of metropolitan capital to divest from plantation agriculture in the region, impacting very significantly territories like Dominica, St. Lucia, St. Vincent, and Jamaica, where there were significant investments in bananas. From the perspective of plantation theory, this withdrawal of metropolitan capital should have been a welcomed opportunity. Instead, however, we had the mounting of a major effort to preserve this classic plantation sector and the system of preferences upon which it would have to depend. From the point of view of informatic capital, it was a doomed attempt to keep alive a practice from the second phase of Caribbean plantation economy in this new and fourth phase that has been brought into being by the changes in the organization of metropolitan capital.

The third important Caribbean peripheral change of the informatic phase has been the addition of the new staple of natural gas in Trinidad and the new informatic quasi-staples of electronic data processing, internet gaming, call centers, and hospitality centers. Thus Trinidad, which has continued its pattern of adding new staples without divesting from old ones, has been the site of the most dynamic changes, and thus has moved more deeply into this fourth phase. At the other extreme is Haiti, whose situation has only deteriorated, along with Dominica and St. Vin-

cent, which did not really develop strong state-coordinated capitalist regimes based on new staples or quasi-staples. The latter two countries are
now standing between the collapse of plantation agriculture and an alternative that is yet to emerge. In economies like those of Antigua, Barbados
and St. Lucia, the persistence of metropolitan investment interest in tourism along with the new informatic quasi-staples has been the basis of this
fourth restructuring of their plantation sectors.

The fourth important change has been the preference of finance controlled informatic capital for open financial and commodity markets and
for private sector leadership in the Caribbean periphery. This has meant
pressure on Caribbean states to downsize, to weaken their already weak
developmental roles, and to support the role of the market in determin-
ing economic outcomes. The consequences of these pressures were seen
very clearly in the Seaga, the second Michael Manley, and Patterson regimes in Jamaica. Thus for Caribbean economies that made strong state-
coordinated capitalist turns, they are now wavering rather undecidedly
between private and state-led capitalism. On the whole, however, these
attempts to reverse the roles of the state and private sector have been
strikingly unsuccessful.

Fifth and finally, informatic capitalism's return to market fundamen-
talism has brought with it a direct theoretical and ideological challenge to
plantation economy's thesis of the imperialism of trade. The major effect
of this neoliberal/informatic view of markets has been a relegitimizing of
the position that trade between center and periphery is not only free and
fair but also the primary route to development. As such it sanctions as
good for the Caribbean the investment, pricing, and relocation policies of
metropolitan capital that plantation theory has so severely criticized. Because of the failures that have accompanied the attempts to implement
the policy recommendations of both Lewis and the plantation theorists,
a theoretical and policy vacuum opened up and was filled by these neoliberal theories and policies. Consequently, the region has experienced a
significant loss of autonomy in economic thought, as it has been forced to
affirm ideas and policies that are alien to its own economic imagination
and tradition of thought.

These in brief are the major changes that the informatic phase has
made in the status and organization of its Caribbean periphery. These
changes are significant enough to constitute a fourth phase, a fourth ratooning of the plantation sector of Caribbean economies. If this is indeed
the case, then it really puts the pressure on plantation theory to come
up with a model of transformation that could interrupt this repeating
pattern that it has systematically thematized and thus eventually eliminate it. It must build on the attempts of Girvan, Beckford, Thomas, and
others to develop this transformative dimension of the theory.

TRANSFORMING PHASE 4 OF CARIBBEAN PLANTATION ECONOMY

The fourth ratooning of the Caribbean plantation in the informatic phase raises a number of questions about the persistence of this pattern and how it is reproduced. I want to suggest that our poets and novelists, whose focus has been Caribbean identities, may be of great help here. In *Caliban's Reason*, I argued that the philosophical foundation of plantation theory was historicism. However, one of the major limitations of Caribbean historicism has been its reluctance to fully embrace its philosophical twin—Caribbean poeticism. The latter has produced a vast literature on the formation of colonized identities and self-consciousness that can usefully supplement the more insurrectionary views of the Caribbean economic subject held by plantation theorists. We have not thematized as systematically as the poeticists the structures of individual and class consciousness that the plantation has produced. Kamau Brathwaite has described this distinct colonial field or consciousness as an "inner plantation." [2] The value of integrating these poeticist accounts is that they focus much more directly on the forces that limit the growth, horizons and capabilities of colonized subjects, including entrepreneurial subjects. There are hints of such a synthesis in Best's many references to the works of V. S. Naipaul and Wilson Harris.

From our earlier analyses of the failed attempts at transformation, we can conclude that Caribbean economies have equilibrated around a crisis-ridden state-coordinated capitalism beyond which it has been difficult to move them either to the left or the right. Further, we can also conclude that there is no single class in its present form that is really up to the task of replacing the foreign bourgeoisie. Most recently, the persistence of this external dependence has been dramatically exposed by the figure of Allen Stanford in Antigua, and who was threatening to extend his influence regionally. [3] This vacuum points to an inescapable entrepreneurial problem that has to be addressed more directly if the entrepreneurial dynamic of these economies is to be localized. Such a transfer would require the creating of a designated entrepreneurial sector that would cut across the major classes and also include the state. The mobilizing of this sector would have to include both its technical training and consciousness-raising in an effort to bring its capabilities up to the task of shifting and controlling the entrepreneurial dynamic. It is in the areas of changing entrepreneurial identities and raising self-consciousness that poeticist accounts of Caribbean subjects can be helpful.

Poeticists such as George Lamming and Sylvia Wynter have argued that transformation in the region has been hindered by retrogressive responses to postcolonial challenges that are linked to the reproductive logics of colonial identities. As W. E. B. Du Bois noted, colonized and racialized identities are divided formations, marked by what he called "double consciousness" (Du Bois 1969: 16). Colonized subjects see themselves through their own eyes but also through the eyes of their colonizers. The latter view is very often what Wynter has called a liminal gaze, such as "the negro" or "the coolie" that stereotypes and limits the capabilities of the colonized (Wynter 1984: 19–70). This stereotypical identity constitutes the colonized as "the other" of the colonizer and establishes hierarchical and non-interchangeable roles between these two. In spite of their negativity, once they are internalized these liminal values and roles become integral parts of the reproductive routines of these identities — thus ratooning these externally imposed limitations. These self-limiting dynamics of colonial identities need to be more carefully included into our analyses of the subjective formation of Caribbean classes and their puzzling entrepreneurial performances. Thus what follows is a socio-philosophical contribution to this problem of entrepreneurial under-performance and how it contributes to the ratooning of the plantation sector. The socio-philosophical nature of this contribution builds on some of the themes of cultural and epistemic entrapment raised earlier by Best in his comments on Lewis. Thus, no attempt is made here to deal with the specifically economic aspects of the proposed entrepreneurial sector.

ENTREPRENEURIAL ABILITY AND THE COLONIAL SUBJECT

The formation of the Caribbean entrepreneurial subject cannot be separated from the broader socio-discursive processes that have produced the more general conceptions of the Caribbean subject. As a culturally plural society, the economic self-consciousness of the classes of Caribbean society has been shaped by quite different cultural, racial and political experiences. More precisely, these differences also represented different ways of framing what Lewis called "the will to economize" (Lewis 1970: 23). Further, these culturally different ways of structuring and expressing this will were subjected to very different patterns of identity-based exclusion from engaging in specific business practices. In short it was the combination of these culturally distinct expressions of the will to economize and the colonial/racial negations or affirmations they encountered in the market place that determined the entrepreneurial identities of individuals in these different groups.

Drawing on Lewis, I will define entrepreneurial self-consciousness as the size and nature of the undertaking that one will attempt to manage. As noted earlier, entrepreneurial identities and capabilities, unlike many others, are not learned in colleges and universities. Rather, they are developed within families or apprentice-style relationships. Thus entrepreneurial outlooks and capabilities are uniquely dependent on how these identities are constructed and reproduced over the generations. The "I" or self-consciousness of the entrepreneurs who continue to control the commanding heights of Caribbean economies were shaped by the cultural traditions, the racist practices and the self-organizing strategies of the Western bourgeoisie. Further, they encountered strong legal and political affirmation as they entered various marketplaces. On the other hand, the framing of the will to economize among the smaller middle-tier capitalists was shaped by Middle Eastern traditions of trading along with their exposure to both the entrepreneurial and racist practices of the dominant Western capitalists. Third and finally, the economic self-consciousness and will to economize among the professionals and workers who occupied the lower-middle and working-class positions were framed by African and Indian traditions of farming, trading and manufacturing, along with the intense legal and political negation they encountered in the Caribbean marketplace. In spite of this culturally plural background, however, our focus here will be primarily on the formation and deformation of entrepreneurial consciousness among the Afro-Caribbean and Middle Eastern groups.

ENTREPRENEURIAL SELF-CONSCIOUSNESS AMONG AFRO-CARIBBEANS

The roots of the Afro-Caribbean "I" and hence its will to economize are of pre-colonial West African origin. From Africa, future Afro-Caribbeans brought with them cooperative traditions of farming that were rooted in communal/lineage and tribute-paying modes of production. In these modes of production, land was owned either in common or by the state (Reid 2002: 98–108; Polanyi 1966: 33–59). Further, economic production was embedded in social norms of reciprocity and redistribution in the interest of reducing inequality. Markets were specific places where goods were sold and not abstract deterritorialized invisible hands coordinating economic signals and decisions. They were socially regulated spaces in which activities were coordinated by principles of social interaction, reciprocity and state-sponsored redistribution (Polanyi 1966). Consequently, in the pre-colonial African context the will to economize and to accumulate was not framed primarily by the calculus of markets abstracted from all notions of social space, but by an economic calculus that was encoded within and subordinated to other systems of meaning.

Enslavement on the plantations of the Caribbean radically disrupted these African economic and entrepreneurial traditions. By the latter, I am referring to the individuals who take responsibility for initiating things and regimes such as the pre-colonial kingdoms of Dahomey and Buganda (the latter now a part of Uganda) that took responsibility for long-term planning to avoid famines or shortages in dry seasons. As plantation workers, they acquired new economic identities that conflicted with the older ones. African women became primarily domestic workers but also field slaves. African men became house slaves, field slaves and urban slaves for hire. Thus began the plantation redefinition of Africans as agro-proletarians, urban workers and domestics. These restricted economic identities constituted the contours of Brathwaite's inner plantation that relations with Prospero had established in the entrepreneurial self-consciousness of Caliban. As such economic subjects, they were being created for a surplus extracting relationship with Western capital. These identities as various forms of labor power were economic definitions of self that were created and imposed by the needs of the plantation sector. It was the colonizer's view of the African economic subject and not the latter's view of him/herself. As a worker and a black, the African by definition would not be socially recognized as being capable of performing the roles of the white capitalist. This is what it meant in this case to be defined and "othered" by the liminal gaze of the planter. However, once internalized, this restricted conception became a part of the economic self-understanding of Africans that would now be reproduced along with other aspects of their economic identities.

However, in spite of the imposition of this predominantly agro-proletarian identity, some of the old ones survived. These could be seen in the small plots that slaves were allowed to cultivate and in marketing practices such as higglering. Thus I am suggesting the emergence of a double economic identity—one based on African traditions of farming and entrepreneurship, and the other on plantation constructions of agro-proletarians. The former has been the basis for the strong drive among rural Afro-Caribbeans to reconstitute themselves as an independent peasantry, as the cases of Jamaica (Beckford 1972) and Haiti (Dupuy 1989) have made particularly clear. The agro-proletarian identity has been the basis upon which others have sought to insert themselves more satisfactorily into local labor markets. In the oppositional tensions between these two economic identities and the difficulties of realizing them, the entrepreneurial traditions of Afro-Caribbeans struggled to assert themselves.

In the decades after the ending of slavery, the Caribbean masses continued to move rather unproductively between these two identities. Positively they were able to reassert some of the old farming traditions and apply them to the production of crops for local consumption and also for export. On the negative side, they were unable to overcome the structural constraints of the plantation on their economic activities or to effectively break the entrepreneurial constraints that came with an agro-proletarian identity. Consequently, they were unable to surge into the entrepreneurial spaces of the middle and big capitalists.

However, important changes came with uprisings of the 1930s. The latter made the insurrectionary consciousness of Caliban visible among the Caribbean masses once again. This consciousness was given organizational form by the trade unions and political parties that were formed in the aftermath of these uprisings, and which eventually gave Afro-

Caribbeans access to state power. However, in the decades following this access to state power, classic Michelsian oligarchic patterns (Michels 1968) began to develop within these mass organizations, which instrumentalized and clientelized relations between leaders and led. The result has been a partyist capturing of this insurrectionary consciousness of workers and a channelling of it into the electoral and other strategic concerns of leaders. The essence of partyism is the absolutizing of the creative agency of the party and its election to power. As such an absolute, one's party becomes the precondition for economic success. The will to economize, whether in proletarian or peasantist form, became deeply politicized, but did not produce any great increase in the entrepreneurial dynamism of this class. It did result in the growth of small one- or two-person enterprises by members of this class, but no major increase in entrepreneurial capability that would have enabled it to assume major responsibilities in localizing the productive dynamic of Caribbean economies.

From the foregoing brief account, it should be clear that the economic and political self-organization of workers and peasants in the post-insurrectionary period did not sufficiently break down the structural barriers of the outer plantations or the inhibitions of the inner plantations. These have continued to lock workers and peasants into subordinate wage roles in ways that make it particularly difficult for them to move into more entrepreneurial and economically independent roles. It was these weak impulses toward taking control of production in the movements or Caribbean workers that led James, in *Party Politics in the West Indies*, to outline an intermediary program of state capitalism for workers in Trinidad (Henry 1992d: 233–39). Consequently, if workers and peasants are to play significant roles in a model of transformation aimed at transferring the entrepreneurial dynamic from the peripheral sector to the national economy, they are going to have to break out of their current partyist entrapment, reorganize themselves more autonomously, and expand the horizons and capability of their will to economize. To the extent that they do not, they will contribute to the ratooning of the plantation sector and to the entrenchment of the current crisis-ridden forms of state-coordinated capitalism.

THE MIDDLE EASTERN CAPITALISTS

The inability of the bourgeois classes of colonial societies to replace its metropolitan counterpart has been given classic formulations by James (James 1962). In 1961, Fanon argued that the colonial bourgeoisie "is in no way commensurate with the bourgeoisie or the mother country which it hopes to replace. . . . The psychology of the national bourgeoisie is that of the businessman, not that of the captain of industry" (Fanon 1968:

149–50). This difference in psychology has led many on the left to dismiss this class as irrelevant for any process of socialist transformation. However, given the above assessments of the entrepreneurial capabilities of Caribbean developmental states, workers and peasants, strategic necessity requires a rethinking of this position. It suggests the inclusion of nationalist elements of this class into an entrepreneurial sector that can be mobilized around bringing a phased transfer of the productive dynamic of the economy into effect. Thus, rather than dismiss the possible contributions of this class, I will suggest a poeticist reading of its underperformance that could possibly help us to understand it better.

As already noted, the local bourgeoisie in the Caribbean has been for the most part racially/ethnically distinct from both the big capitalists and the masses of Indo and Afro-Caribbean peasants and workers. Their ranks have included businessmen of Jewish, Lebanese, Syrian, European ethnicity, and more recently businessmen and women of Indian and African backgrounds. Many of these individuals rose from positions of itinerant traders to become successful merchants who would occupy and then dominate the intermediate economic positions between the European planters and the Afro- and Indo-Caribbean masses. Unlike the latter case, the liminal gaze of the colonizer confirmed the basic economic view that Middle Easterners had of themselves as traders. However, this gaze also inscribed their identity in a racial hierarchy that established it as intermediary between black and white, workers and plantation capitalists. This was the bounded space in which their will to economize would be recognized. Here, this space outlined the perimeter of the inner plantation that relations with planter Prospero established in the entrepreneurial self-consciousness of this Arielist stratum. The latter's will to economize would not be recognized as capable of transcending this intermediate space and entering the terrain of the planters. Such moves were forbidden by the racial hierarchy into which their identities were now embedded. Once this place in the hierarchy was internalized, it became a part of the reproductive dynamic of their own identities, converting these external prohibitions into internal, self-limiting inhibitions that facilitated their long and static adjustment to their designated place as merchants.

As in the case of workers, the insurrections of the 1930s were also important turning points in the formation of the economic consciousness of these intermediary classes. These uprisings made the Arielist tendencies that resulted from the internalizing of their place in the colonial/racial hierarchy more explicit. However, the failure of their attempts at alliance with Prospero forced them into new relations with the African and Indian masses. These new relations produced a politicizing of their will to economize that was different from—but comparable to—the cases of workers and peasants, as it made them also integral parts of the then emerging state-coordinated capitalist order. Earlier, we noted the rise of their more corporate identity and their limited industrial responses to the

state incentives of the Lewis era. As a result of these policies and movements, merchants became merchant-manufacturers, producing commodities like cement, soft drinks, garments, beer and rum. These shifts toward manufacturing also produced the conglomerate structure that has
become typical of the major Caribbean corporations. This structure is one
of family-based shareholding groups owning controlling interests in
these merchant-manufacturing combinations.

The rise of the informatic phase has been the next major turning point
in the formation of these bourgeoisie classes, as it introduced policies in
support of private sector as opposed to state leadership of the economy.
Adapting to the reality of globalization has not been easy for these
classes. There were many casualties, making the corporate terrain of the
region quite different from what it was before 1980. As noted before, the
attempts to push these classes more deeply into manufacturing was not
successful. Indeed, the major expansion of their activities during this
period has been in the areas of finance and the financial sector. Commercial banks, development banks, insurance companies and building societies increased in number, adding finance to the conglomerate structure
of major Caribbean corporations. In Jamaica, this expansion was too rapid, leading to a major collapse of the sector and a rescue by the state. This
event foreshadowed in many ways the global collapse of financial sectors
in 2008. In Trinidad, the growth of this sector has been steadier, with
major forays across the region.

As expected, this brief account of the formation of the Caribbean bourgeoisie has not been the portrait of a dynamic developmental class such
as the Taiwanese or the South Korean bourgeoisie. Indeed, in many ways
it confirms Fanon's portrait of it. It is important, however, to take note of
what movements have taken place and their significance for a project of
mobilizing the entrepreneurial potential of the region. Further, this class
is as much a part of the national economy as the productive activity of
workers. Not only do we need to take note of these movements, but we
also need to understand as best we can why they have been so slow and
cautious. Here I think that we can see evidence of self-inhibiting patterns
that block or limit responses to market signals and investment opportunities. It is as though these patterns block out signals coming from the
terrain of the planter and let in only those coming from intermediary
terrains and that are of intermediary proportions. In other words, market
signals and investment opportunities are still being interpreted through
the lens of the liminal restrictions placed on the trading activities of this
class by the plantation sector. Thus, there is significant inertia coming
from the self-reproducing patterns of bourgeois identities that is limiting
the entrepreneurial activities of this class. As Fanon noted, this class "is
unable to give free rein to its genius, which formerly it was wont to
lament, though rather too glibly, was held in check by colonial domination" (Fanon 1968: 151). This inability to be creative, to surge into the

terrain of planter Prospero, has been both a puzzle and an embarrass-
ment even to these classes themselves. To unravel this puzzle, we need to
grasp the extent to which the entrepreneurial identity of this class is still
caught in the dynamics of the relationship between Ariel and Prospero.
To the extent that these identities have remained Arielist they will continue to reproduce their need for Prosperean complements. The continued
reproduction of these needs, together with those of Caliban's inner plantation constitutes an important socio-psychological base that has enabled
the outer Caribbean plantation to go through its fourth and current ratooning.

CONCLUSION

Given that Caribbean economies are now well into the long cycle of their
fourth ratooning, the question that we must confront is: can we prevent a
fifth? In the last sections of this paper, I emphasized the need to raise the
level of entrepreneurial performance by mobilizing a sector drawn from
all of the major classes, on whose local shoulders the productive dynamic
of the economy would rest. From past experience, I have concluded that
at present, this sector would not be ready for such a takeover. Training
and consciousness-raising for such a mission will therefore be a necessity.
The performance of this entrepreneurial sector would be part of a larger
model of transformation that targeted specific industries for phased competitive takeovers. The persistent functioning of such a sector could significantly expand the national economy and thus break the pattern of the
repeating plantation.

We need to work out the economics of such an entrepreneurial sector
carefully. From a sociological standpoint, economics has consistently
been the rationalization of the productive practices and capabilities of a
particular class—landlords, merchants, industrial capitalists, financiers,
and so on. Thus, a new challenge before Caribbean economics would be
the improving and rationalizing of the productive activities and capabilities of the combination of classes that constitute such a sector. The economics of such an entrepreneurial formation need to be carefully worked
out in a model that reverses the sectoral dynamics of the Lewis model by
specifying the first, second, third, and consequent sets of industries that
will be competitively transferred from the plantation to this sector and
thus to the national economy. The ideological framework of such an economic transfer must also be determined by careful readings of current
insurrectionary tendencies among the masses if it is to have both legitimacy and efficacy.

We should begin with those economic resources over which we have
control or could easily control. Initially the focus should be on low-tech
industries like tourism and those in which we have a cultural advantage.

Decolonizing, and hence raising, levels of entrepreneurial self-conscious-ness and capability will also be very important. In particular, I have suggested that current readings of investment opportunities and other economic signals by our entrepreneurs tend to be distorted by Prosper-ean deferrals that put certain undertakings off limits. Changing these patterns will involve focusing on practices and faculties over which we have control. At present, this control is sufficient to enable us to change the cultural constructions that limit or distort entrepreneurial readings of investment opportunities and other economic signals. In his *General Theo-ry of Employment, Interest and Money*, Keynes showed that there is no simple market relationship between savings and investments (Keynes 1964: 125–35). Working relations between the two are in part a result of new ways of seeing oneself and the risks in one's environment, as well as the result of actions of the state. Consequently, there must be more that we can do in this fluid region to make the entrepreneurs in our sector take more risks and respond more positively to opportunities in the Car-ibbean environment. By doing something like this, we just might be able to avoid a fifth ratooning of our plantation heritage.

NOTES

* First published as "Caribbean Dependency in the Phase of Informatic Capitalism," in Brian Meeks and Norman Girvan (eds.), *The Thought of New World, The Quest for Decolonisation* (Kingston, Jamaica: Ian Randle, 2010), 172–205.

1. I would like to thank Norman Girvan for his very helpful comments on an earlier draft of this paper. However, I take full responsibility for the claims made and the positions taken in the paper.

2. Since my paper was completed, this financial bubble exploded with unprece-dented force in the fall of 2008, producing the biggest crisis of global capitalism since the great depression of the 1930s. Ironically, it has been massive doses of Keynesian medicine that have helped to stabilize and contain the destructive effects of this "eco-nomic tsunami." Although my paper had grossly underestimated the size and the forces within the bubble, its containment after the collapse of the financial sector, and the information policies of the new Obama administration in the U.S., have only strengthened my argument regarding the informatic future of global capitalism.

3. Fortunately or unfortunately, Mr. Stanford's financial empire collapsed in early 2009 as part of the larger crisis of the U.S. financial sector. His empire was brought down by the Securities and Exchange Commission on the charges that Mr. Stanford was running a Ponzi scheme rather than making genuine investments.

EIGHT

C. L. R. James, Walter Rodney and the Rebuilding of Caribbean Socialism

After gathering considerable momentum in the 1970s, Caribbean socialism entered a period of dramatic decline following Michael Manley's abandoning of his democratic socialist agenda and the collapse of the revolution in Grenada in the early 1980s. Reinforced a few years later by the fall of state socialism in the Soviet Union and Eastern Europe, the socialist project seemed as though it was all over. Mesmerized by this dramatic turn of events, some went so far as to declare "the end of history" and the arrival of "TINA" — "there is no alternative" to Western capitalism.

However, the Great Recession of 2008 and the ongoing challenges of its aftermath have significantly reversed these views, by throwing up, in another powerful seismic drama, the crisis tendencies and other negative features of capitalism that generations have found objectionable. As a result, both academics and policy makers have been forced once again to take seriously the basic concerns of classical political economy, such as the extraction of surplus value, the distribution of that surplus, its relation to wealth and poverty, and to the simultaneous production of developed and underdeveloped economies.

As major theorists in the field of Caribbean political economy, C. L. R. James and Walter Rodney were proponents of complex dialectical discourses between class, race and political economy; further, both James and Rodney fell within a regional tradition of thought that I have called Caribbean historicism. As such thinkers, both men have been major figures in bridging the epistemic and political cleavages between economics, class and race within the school of Caribbean historicism, and thus, important contributors to the larger field of black political economy.

In addition to helping to bridge this class/race divide, James has also been a major bridge figure who navigated well the epistemic divides between Caribbean historicism and its twin, Caribbean poeticism. The latter is the school that has given us Wilson Harris, George Lamming, Sylvia Wynter, Vidia Naipaul, Kamau Brathwaite and other literary luminaries of our Caribbean region. At the heart of Caribbean poeticism we find a creative realism that takes the inherent creative powers of the human self as its metaphysical point of departure. What was distinctive about James's creative realism, and hence his poeticism, was the bold manner in which it included the creativity of the public self of the masses as well as individual creativity (Henry 2009b: 188–198). As a result, there are much stronger poeticist elements in James's dialectic of class, race and political economy than in the case of Rodney.

In spite of these differences in their poetics, I will argue that the dialectical frameworks of the thought of both Rodney and James shared as a primary concern the full humanization of Caribbean and other workers. In other words, the goal of their political economy was the full development of the collective subjectivity and individual agency workers. Both men placed great importance on the transformative powers of the creativity inherent in the human self, and of workers as a group. For James in particular, the notion of a public or collective self, which was a potential carrier of creative powers of great imaginative and transformative capability, was central to this project of full humanization. Indeed, the creativity of this collective self determined the subjective conditions for socialist transformation. Consequently, any social structure, pattern of organization or practice of production that inhibited the creativity of this public self had to be opposed and removed if possible.

The central thesis of this paper is that since the collapse of socialist regimes in the Caribbean region, China, the Soviet Union, Eastern Europe and Vietnam, the ensuing patterns of global economic organization and practices of capitalist production have been placing a rising mountain of obstacles in the way of the creativity of the public self of Caribbean workers. The nature and magnitude of these technological and neoliberal obstacles have been such that long-standing Left goals of worker freedom, autonomy, self-management and full humanization embraced by James and Rodney are now receding ideals. It is precisely these dramatic shifts in global social forces that constitute the objective conditions grounding the current crisis of the Left. At the same time, these adverse conditions have become real material bases for a reconstruction of the Caribbean Left as a significant oppositional force in the current or post-2008 conjuncture.

This conjuncture now includes the first major crisis of the globalized neoliberal economic order that Western capitalists have been attempting to put in place since the major collapse of socialism in the late 1980s. This crisis has a lot in common with earlier crises of Western capitalism, but also features that are quite distinctive. The most important of these distinct features include the following: first, an important dimension of the present crisis has been the de-industrialization of the West at a pace that far exceeded that of the creation of the new high-tech economy that was to replace its industrial predecessor. Second is the overlapping of the crisis of neoliberal globalization with the collapse of state socialism. Third, this crisis includes the rise of a new hegemonic power, China, and its possible ascent to the center of our increasingly globalized economic system. Fourth, this crisis has brought to a halt the various rounds of negotiation between world trade ministers through which markets for various commodities have been liberalized and globalized. Fifth and finally, for the past five years this crisis has returned the central steering mechanisms of the major Western economies to their states, whose leaders have had to rescue entire banking systems and to take over some companies at the cost of trillions of dollars and trillions of Euros.

This is the context in which I would like to revisit the political economies of both James and Rodney, to look at how they viewed the obstacles challenging the full humanization of workers, and how helpful they can be to us as we navigate our way through this receding of Left ideals and state formations. The time has come for us to both embrace the spirit of James, Lee, and Chaulieu's text, *Facing Reality* and to re-imagine it for our time. In particular, I will examine James's notion of state capitalism and Rodney's notion of peripheral capitalism, the similarities and differences between the two, and the implications of this comparative exercise for a reconstruction of the Left in our present conjuncture. I will argue that the failures of the past thirty years of Caribbean leadership, however defined, have demonstrated a clear need for a more transformative turn if regional economies are to move in more autonomous and productive directions; and that a democratic socialist state represents the best option for getting this needed change in political organization and state agency.

RACIAL CAPITALISM AND CARIBBEAN WORKERS

With specific regard to the Caribbean, the major obstacles between workers and their full humanization were the surplus extracting practices of a racial capitalism, their changes over time, and their power over local governing elites. Consequently, an anti-imperial political project had to include not only national independence but also the creation of worker-controlled states in which the identity of the state was no longer tied exclusively to the identities of white capitalists, but would reflect the identities and aspirations of the Africans and Indians, who made up the majority in Caribbean societies. For Caribbean workers of African descent, full humanization also meant liberation from the negative white supremacist stereotype of "the negro" or worse, "the nigger." For Caribbean workers of Indian descent, full humanization also meant liberation from the negative racial stereotype of "the coolie." Thus the de-coolietizing of Indian identities and the de-negrification of African identities were vital parts of the political economies of Rodney and James. In other words, full humanization had to go beyond the de-proletarianization of worker identities to include de-racialization. Both men also saw the realization of this project of full worker humanization as taking place only in a socialist society. Some of the clearest statements on the nature of this socialist society are to be found in some of James's texts such as *Every Cook Can Govern, The Invading Socialist Society,* and *Facing Reality.* For example, in the second of these texts, James noted: "the struggle for socialism is the struggle for proletarian democracy. . . . Socialism is the result of proletarian democracy" (1972: 4). Further, this long-lasting racial dimension of Western capitalism requires that we ask: what does it mean to be black or brown in the second decade of the twenty-first century?

Although quite similar, Rodney and James had different accounts of the changing nature of the political economy of Western racial capitalism and thus of the changes in the obstacles that it placed in the way of the full humanization of Caribbean workers. For James, the changing political economy of Western capitalism was conceptualized as a back-and-forth movement between the ideal of liberal market capitalism and varying degrees of state capitalism. For Rodney, this changing political economy was grasped through the tensions between central capitalism and peripheral capitalism within an increasingly integrated global capitalist system. To address the concerns and demands of our conjuncture, we must also take into account the implications of the collapse of state socialism and the Great Recession in the capitalist world for these crucial concepts of state capitalism and peripheral capitalism. Let us look first at James's notion of state capitalism.

JAMES'S STATE CAPITALISM

State capitalism was for James a very complex, intermediary formation that was of very polyvalent significance. First and foremost it was a fallback or compromise politico-economic formation adopted by liberal capitalism when its attempts to reach for the ideal of completely self-regulating markets goes into crisis and is forced to re-introduce practices of state ownership and regulation of the economy. James sometimes referred to this move as "the stratification of production" (1972: 20). The period since the onset of the Great Recession of 2008 can be seen as one of those. In the United States, where the crisis began, the TARP program of the conservative Bush administration began the rescue process with $700 billion. This was followed by the Obama administration's purchasing of large shares of equity in companies like General Motors, and AIG, and three rounds of quantitative easing. In the last of these rounds, the Federal Reserve Bank has been pumping $85 billion a month into the financial sector for the past two years. Thus as in the case of the Great Depression, the Great Recession has once again turned the U.S. economy into what James called "a vast state-capitalist and military syndicate" (1972: 30).

But for James there was much more to the phenomenon of state capitalism. It is also a compromise position to which state socialist regimes could fall back as their attempts to plan state-owned economies and to empower workers entered crisis phases in which they are forced to re-introduce the market along with practices of private ownership and capital accumulation. In the case of the Soviet Union, after a period of state-administered rapid industrialization that mobilized large numbers of workers and vast quantities of natural resources, a number of problems continued to plague this economy, and eventually brought growth to a virtual halt. These included, real difficulties in the mathematics of central planning, the devastation of agriculture that resulted from the emphasis on industrial production, the now legendary problem of shortages, the neglect of social services and mass consumer demand. The retarding effects of these difficulties, which were never really addressed, began to inhibit growth in the early 1970s (Aganbegyan 1988: 1–6). As the growth rate continued to fall, this combination of circumstances reached crisis proportions in the early 1980s, leading to Mikhail Gorbachev's announcement of the reforms of *uskorenie* (acceleration), *perestroika* (restructuring) and *glasnost* (opening). Perestroika in particular contained the major market and cooperative reforms that Gorbachev had in mind. These reforms were not carried out, as Gorbachev was overthrown and replaced by Boris Yeltsin, whose project was the complete conversion of the Soviet Union to capitalism.

In the case of China, similar problems leading to a crisis of growth were major factors motivating the 1978 reforms introduced by Mao's successor, Deng Xiaoping. These economic problems had their roots in the Great Leap program of 1958, which included the setting of production targets for industry by the state and the collectivization of agriculture. By 1960, the state had a major agricultural crisis on its hands, plus major industrial shortages due to inter-industry imbalances. Abandoned in 1960, the Great Leap was followed by measures of decentralization, which empowered provincial authorities. The conflicts generated by these failures set the stage for the ideological purges and excesses of the Cultural Revolution, which further exacerbated the problems of the Chinese economy. This was the divided milieu out of which Deng rose to power with his plans to re-introduce the market and practices of private accumulation (Vogel 2011: 217–265).

Thus, from a Jamesian standpoint, we can in the main define state capitalism as a heightened systemic re-introduction of practices of state ownership and regulation of production in an economy of private accumulation, or the systemic re-introduction of practices of market regulation and private accumulation in a socialist economy based on state ownership and state accumulation of capital. Both share the effect of putting the goal of a worker-controlled state on the back burner or making it some distant future goal. In addition to China in 1978, the Soviet Union, Eastern Europe, Vietnam and most recently Cuba have to varying degrees re-introduced markets and practices of private accumulation. In the majority of these cases, the impulse to make these changes came from crises brought on by difficulties in central planning, persistent shortages in key consumer goods, capitalist pressures, declining growth rates, definite tendencies toward economic stagnation, and the impact of the convergence of interest between the U.S. and China.

For James, these tendencies for both liberal capitalism and state socialism to make these state capitalist turns raised a very disturbing specter from the point of view of workers. This specter was that of a state capitalist convergence of interest between the elites of major capitalist and state socialist societies leading to converging practices and mutual exchanges that would preserve these varying mixed socio-economic orders in which workers are still proletarianized, racialized and disempowered. James feared greatly such a convergence of interest between the United States and the Soviet Union, and what that would mean for workers and their full humanization in a socialist society. In *World Revolution 1917–1936*, James suggested that such a convergence would set back this global proletarian movement several decades.

Today the reality that we are facing is not a convergence between the United States and the Soviet Union, but one between the United States and China, that some have referred to as Chimerica (Karabell 2009: 3). The convergence between these two economies is the major politico-economic development produced by the crises of state socialism and neoliberal globalization. Without it, we cannot understand the decimation of trade unions and the falling of wages in the U.S., the de-industrialization and corresponding financialization of central capitalist economies with the rise and fall of regional political economies in these core countries. At the same time, we also cannot account for the dramatic shifts in patterns of industrial relocation and financialization in Asian economics over the past three decades. In short, the politico-economic reality that we are facing is a major state capitalist convergence between China and the United States that has resulted from the crisis of state socialism in the former and from the crisis of neoliberalism in the latter. In terms of global impact, it has become the biggest filler of the hole opened up by the end of the Cold War between the U.S. and the USSR. In short, facing reality today means facing the new set of obstacles and setbacks that this type of convergence, which James feared so intensely, has placed and is placing in the way of workers liberation.

But even the above complexities do not exhaust James's concept of state capitalism. To the above involvements in both private and state models of accumulation, James added yet a third dimension to this multi-faceted concept of state capitalism. This third dimension stretched the notion to include the experiences of colonial economies that were trying to break the chains of imperial domination and to modernize. In postco-lonial economies such as those of the Caribbean and Africa, James saw state capitalist formations as transitional political economies that were facilitating the movement from chiefdoms, kingdoms, and colonial states to de-racialized representative democracies with modernizing economies trying to find their way in a global order that was dominated not by Europe but by the United States and the Soviet Union. To the extent that these postcolonial regimes, such as those of Kwame Nkrumah, Julius Nyerere or Eric Williams, were facilitating these transitions, James viewed them as progressive in contrast to the regressive nature of the state capitalist formations of the developed economies. Particularly in *Party Politics in the West Indies*, James did not see these new ex-colonial nations moving immediately to socialist political economies, but to tran-sitional phases in which state ownership and regulation of economic ac-tivity would be high. These were the outward features that led James to refer to them as state capitalist. With the receding of the colonial era, these once progressive regimes have become obsolete and thus regres-sive. Thus ours is a conjuncture that is dominated by a converging of three streams of potentially regressive forms of state capitalism. Howev-er, it is important to note that the institutional content and projects of transformation in each of these three uses of the concept of state capital-ism are significantly different.

RODNEY'S PERIPHERAL CAPITALISM

Coming a generation after James, and reaching maturity in the post-inde-pendence years, Rodney saw the changing political economy of global capitalism through a different lens. He saw it primarily through the con-cept of peripheral capitalism that was developed by Latin American and Caribbean schools of dependency theory. This is the school that gave us scholars such as Lloyd Best, Norman Girvan, Clive Thomas and George Beckford. The impact of this school on Rodney is very clear in his influen-tial book, *How Europe Underdeveloped Africa*. Further, it is well known that both Rodney and Girvan were members of a study group with James when they were graduate students in London. Thus, in spite of this first hand exposure to James, this new generation of radicals, who came to be known as the Caribbean New Left, blazed a path of their own as they had a new reality to theorize.

This reality was not the death crisis of the colonial/plantation economies and their transition via state capitalist regimes to market-oriented,
industrializing representative democracies. Rather, the crisis that the Caribbean dependency school was confronted with was that of the actually
existing capitalism in the region that the transitional state capitalist regimes had produced. These new post-plantation formations the members
of this school theorized as instances of dependent or peripheral capitalism. The periodic crises of the colonial/plantation economies were interruptions in capital accumulation that were brought on by conditions of
over-supply in the international markets for their commodities. The strategies for managing and adjusting to these crises were combinations of
firing workers, lowering wages and seeking guaranteed places in these
markets that were tending toward oversupply. It was the insurrectionary
responses of Caribbean and other workers to crises of this type in the
1930s and 1940s that motivated James's socialist writing. With the ascen-
dency of the United States in the period after the Second World War, a
more liberalized and competitive global order came into existence in
which guaranteed markets became harder to come by. The challenges of
becoming more competitive were the new realities confronting the transitional state capitalist regimes of the region. On the home front, as democratically elected regimes, they were subject to greater pressures from the
masses and their trade unions and parties for wage increases and other
social benefits.

Under the pressure of these new imperatives peripheral capitalism
developed its own pattern of crisis tendencies that were different from
those of classic colonial capitalism and also from the crisis tendencies of
central capitalism. The peripheral economies of the Caribbean are technologically dependent on the central economies, and this technology enters
these formations through the foreign-dominated process of capital accumulation. Consequently the major weapon of these peripheral capitalist
economies in the competitive fight they must now engage is still primarily cheaper labor. As a result, Caribbean economies have not made a very
successful adaptation to the American dominated world of more competitive markets. These competitive challenges have only gotten more difficult with the onset of neoliberal globalization in the 1980s.

Although the new technologies introduced into Caribbean economies
generated rounds of increasing productivity, the broader failure to insert
themselves competitively in the global order has produced unstable and
interrupted patterns of capital accumulation, as companies leave when
profits begin to decline and there are fewer protected markets to be had.
In addition to being subject to these interruptions, the surplus generated
by the above increases in productivity was very unevenly distributed.
The lion's share usually traveled abroad with the transnational corporations, with significant portions going to small, educated elites and to the
state. The masses gained access to a portion of the surplus by pressuring

the state for jobs, wage increases and a variety of other social programs through their unions and parties. The extent to which they were successful depended on how strong and organized they were. In this way, Caribbean states have attempted to compensate for the inability of the private sector to incorporate the vast majority of workers by processes of continuous investment.

Because the process of private accumulation driving these economies has high leakages and major interruptions, the above increases to labor soon surpass the technologically produced reductions in costs of the foreign ventures. Profits begin to decline and are made up by increases in prices. This is then followed by demands for wage increases by workers, leading to persistent inflationary spirals that further contribute to interruptions in the process of capital accumulation and additional investment. The political conflicts, power plays, the strikes, the intense elections, and the coups that have come to mark political life in the Caribbean today have these crisis tendencies as their backdrop.

These were the crises of actually existing capitalism in our region— peripheral capitalism—that the dependency school was attempting to come to grips with. As the peasant/worker upsurges of the 1930s and 1940s signaled for James the intensifying of the crises of the colonial/ plantation economies, so the upsurges of the 1960s and 1970s alerted Rodney, Girvan, Thomas and others to the intensifying crises of Caribbean peripheral capitalism. As the crises of the 1930s and 1940s produced the trade union and parties that ushered in the independence period, so New Left organization such as New Beginning, NJAC, ASCRIA, NJM, ACLM, and the WPA, of which Rodney was a leader, embodied the new aspirations for and visions of a black socialist-oriented alternative to the first major manifestation of the crisis tendencies of Caribbean peripheral capitalism. This was the set of core experiences that led this generation of radicals to move away from James's theory of state capitalism and to develop their own theory of peripheral capitalism in a bold effort at facing reality in the Caribbean of 1960s and 1970s.

PERIPHERAL CAPITALISM AND SOCIALISM

Prior to the late 1980s, there were several peripheral capitalist countries that went through periods in which they identified themselves as socialist in response to the maturing of crisis tendencies similar to the ones described above for the Caribbean. In Africa, these included countries like Algeria, Ghana, Tanzania, Mozambique, Angola, and Zimbabwe. In the Caribbean region, there were the cases of Cuba, Nicaragua, Jamaica, Guyana and Grenada. In all of these cases, regimes had come to power that were attempting transitions to socialism from widely varying sociopolitical conditions. In the case of Grenada, the People's Revolutionary

Government was made possible by the coming to power of the NJM, one of the radical New Left groups noted above. For these groups, regimes such as those of Eric Williams, Hugh Shearer, Eric Gairy, V. C. Bird, and Forbes Burnham were no longer the progressive formations that James saw in the late 1950s and early 1960s. Thus they were as opposed to Williams, Bird, and other leaders of their generation as James had been opposed to the earlier colonial/plantation regimes.

Where Rodney stood in relation to these Caribbean regimes can be gauged from his involvement with and strong support of Nyerere's Ujamaa socialism in Tanzania. Rodney embraced Nyerere's famous Arusha Declaration of 1967 and its program of nationalizing the major sectors of the economy and re-communalizing agriculture. These moves represented for Rodney the beginnings of a socialist worker-controlled state. The real challenge now was the efficient and productive executing of this project. But before long, many of the crisis tendencies of the peripheral capitalist order began to re-appear in this new socialist order and would eventually overtake it. Most striking was the continued dependence on external technology and managerial skills, which entered Tanzania through a foreign-dominated process of capital accumulation. These foreign capitalists were supplemented by a small cadre of local bureaucrats who were not particularly committed to ideas of socialist transformation. Rodney was particularly distrustful of and instinctively opposed to this petit bourgeois stratum, and was quite critical of Nyerere's reliance on them. His fear was that they would put more effort into making themselves into a propertied stratum than the difficult but important transition to socialism. However, as Rupert Lewis has pointed out, Rodney was never clear on how this worker controlled state would be able to manage the Tanzanian economy without these inputs from abroad and from the local petit bourgeoisie (1998: 143).

By the mid-1970s, the Tanzanian socialist experiment was in the grip of a major crisis that was brought on by difficulties in the state's ability to manage efficiently the enterprises that it had nationalized and also by difficulties with the project of re-communalizing agriculture. The combination of these two production crises severely interrupted both private and state processes of capital accumulation, and thus the ability of the regime to ensure good wages for workers and maintain the social benefits to which they had become accustomed. Caught in this older peripheral capitalist crisis tendency, the regime was forced to abandon its project of Ujamaa socialism and to seek help from the IMF and the World Bank. Tanzania was now back to its earlier state capitalist formation and trying to create a new form of peripheral capitalism that would be better able to manage the crises and interruptions in the process of capital accumulation.

In Mozambique, the socialist experiment led by the revolutionary party, Frelimo, ended in a similar fashion. In 1975, after a similar process of economic nationalization in both agriculture and industry, the challenge was once again that of effective execution of economic goals and strategies for a transition to socialism. On this crucial challenge Mozambique did not fare much better than Tanzania. By 1985, a combination of shortages on state farms, stagnation on private ones and poor performance in other state-controlled sectors, forced the government to seek the assistance of the IMF and the World Bank. Thus it too was soon making use of the fall back position of state capitalism to make another attempt at building a peripheral capitalist economy.

In the Caribbean, the case of Jamaica in the early 1970s is instructive with regard to these issues of the crisis tendencies of socialist experiments in the peripheral countries. Here too, we can see similar tendencies for peripheral experiments in socialism to collapse under the weight of economic, managerial and political pressures, and having to fall back on the earlier transitional formation of state capitalism. After coming to power in 1972, Michael Manley embarked on a project of democratic socialism in 1974 as a response to continued declines and disequilibria in the Jamaican economy. These negatives—balance of payments deficits, increasing debt, and slowing growth rates—were severe enough to have moved the Jamaican economy quite close to the edge of a cliff. Overwhelmingly re-elected in 1976 on a democratic socialist mandate, Manley teamed up with leading members of the Caribbean dependency school, including Norman Girvan and George Beckford, to plan and implement the transition from actually existing Jamaican capitalism to democratic socialism.

This plan, "The People's Socialist Plan," called for the nationalizing of key industries in banking, construction and energy. Food production linked to agro-industrial production would be the core of the agricultural sector and not the plantations. State and "community enterprises" were to be the primary units of production in this sector. A community enterprise was "a business organization in which the means of production are socialized and controlled by a community, under the administrative direction of community councils" (Beckford et al. 1985: 37). With the state in control of these crucial areas of production, it would then be possible to implement a transition to a socialist economy. The plan had a lot in common with its counterparts in Tanzania and Mozambique, and was driven by similar motivating passions. However, after consideration by Manley, the plan was rejected. He chose instead to seek assistance from the IMF, suggesting the magnitude of the short-term pressures on the Jamaican economy, and thus the questionable feasibility of undertaking at that moment the major medium and long-term reforms suggested by the People's Socialist Plan.

In Grenada, the attempt to go beyond post-plantation peripheral capitalism went significantly further than in the case of Jamaica. The transitional plan of the People's Revolutionary Government outlined a clear three-sector model of the economy: state, cooperative, and private with strong participatory norms and ideals. The nationalizations undertaken were in keeping with the state managerial capabilities and the cooperative sector was buoyed by a strong participatory and collective ethos that the revolution had generated. Unfortunately, this promising experiment in socialist transformation was cut short by exploding political differences between the leaders, which gave the United States the excuse it needed to invade and return the state capitalist steering mechanism to the peripheral capitalist path.

With Guyana's experience of Forbes Burnham's cooperative socialism in his mind, Rodney's perspective on many of these Caribbean socialist experiments was a very critical one. This followed very clearly from his position on Tanzania that we examined earlier. Because of the petit bourgeois leadership of most of these experiments, Rodney was also quite skeptical of their aims and prospects. Indeed, he referred to them as pseudo-socialist regimes in which power would remain in the hands of the petit bourgeoisie in spite of all the talk about workers. As Rupert Lewis has noted, "C. L. R. James' very strong support of Julius Nyerere and Michael Manley was, however, never Rodney's position" (1998: 214).

At the same time that socialism in the Caribbean, with the exception of Cuba, was going through these oscillations with its state capitalist midwife, the market reforms in China were beginning and the socialist crisis tendencies of the Soviet Union and Eastern Europe were maturing at an accelerating pace. As these began to burst and market reforms were undertaken, the oscillations in these longer-standing socialist societies began to echo those of the more fragile and short-term socialist experiments in the Caribbean and Africa. Were there common factors in these oscillations or were the similarities just passing surface mirages? These are some of the difficult theoretical questions for which the Caribbean Left must find answers if it is to come to grips with the reality facing it. Since 2008, the answers to these questions have gotten both easier and more complicated. The crisis of neoliberal globalization has exposed in very dramatic ways the difficulties and limits of the project of establishing the global economy on principles of self-regulating markets. The corresponding turn to a state capitalist steering mechanism in order to navigate this deep and prolonged crisis helps to make clear the role that states can and must play in the post-crisis period. However, the crucial challenge for the Left is to theorize this role more accurately than we did in the past.

SOCIALISM, PERIPHERAL CAPITALISM AND THE CRISIS OF NEOLIBERAL GLOBALIZATION

The period of collapse for socialism in many Caribbean and other peripheral countries was soon followed by the collapse of state socialism in the Soviet Union and Eastern Europe. The vacuum created was filled by processes of global adjustment and restructuring, which were driven by the conservative Western project of neoliberal globalization. The material basis for this project was the exhaustion of the post-war Keynesian solution of state management of aggregate demand to the crisis of accumulation that produced the Great Depression of the 1930s. Rising labor costs that were integral to the "virtuous cycle" of Keynesianism had reduced profits and income inequality to points where it led to shareholder revolts with demands for corporate restructuring. These revolts brought on the decline or death of many of the major corporations of the Keynesian period and the rise of a new breed of corporate units, which broke the social pact with American labor, as they attempted to peripheralize new areas of the globe in search of cheaper labor. This search for new sources of cheap labor was directed primarily at Asia and Eastern Europe. With this new round of peripheralization, we had projects such as the Latin Americanization of Eastern Europe and the many rounds of negotiations that extended the liberalization of some markets that was started earlier by the United States. Thus began the dramatic de-industrialization of the West, the attempt to replace this industrial base with a new informatic foundation, and the launching of the second attempt by the West to organize the economies of the world on the principle of self-regulating markets in which they were the most competitive.

With all of these adjustments taking place in the wake of the collapse of socialism, not only was Caribbean socialism further eclipsed but also the region's peripheral status—its investment value to central capital—declined sharply. Compared to China, Caribbean labor was expensive and over-unionized. It was during this period that we also lost the battle for the survival of the Caribbean banana industry and the last remnants of the system of protected access to European markets that were a part of that industry. The unmediated global competition that our region had been running from since the 1840s was now staring us directly in the face.

However, just when this neoliberal train seemed unstoppable, fueled particularly by the globalization of financial markets and the creation of bubbles, its projects of peripheralizing new areas of the globe were quite unexpectedly brought to a dramatic halt. This very loud screeching halt was the result of two major factors: the inability of American homeowners to pay their mortgages, which was a significant part of the financialization of the U.S. economy; and, second, China's success in turning the tables on this second Western attempt to peripheralize its economy.

In order to grasp clearly the nature of the challenges of the post-crisis period, it is important that we recognize very clearly that the mortgage difficulties of American homeowners did not cause the crisis, but were indeed its major triggers. Rather, it was the rapid financialization of both the American and British economies in the 1980s, at the same time that de-industrialization was increasing and the birth of the new informatic economy began to stall, which were the real causes of the crisis. The financialization of these two economies was an accumulative strategy by the big Wall Street banks to fill the economic vacuum created by a rapidly departing industrial sector and a slowly rising informatic one. These big investment banks started this process with funding the hostile takeovers, mergers and acquisitions that came out of the earlier shareholders revolt. From funding these mergers and acquisitions, they moved to massive amounts of speculative trading, which became major business opportunities after the U.S. abandoned Bretton Woods and currencies started floating against one another. Trillions of dollars could now be made from the buying and selling of currencies, other financial and real assets on the basis of manipulating price differences or betting on anticipated price shifts. This type of speculative trading very quickly eclipsed more traditional banking activities such as making money from interest on loans for investment or home building. This was money making on a massive scale without ordinary processes of production—it was Marx's formula for finance capital, m-m', in motion.

With mergers and acquisition going and speculative trading replacing traditional banking activities, other institutions in the financial sector also had to be changed. The new relations with savings and commercial banks that came with the repeal of the Glass-Steagall Act brought these traditional institutions into the speculative orbits of these big investment banks. With this growing monopoly over the entire system of credit, money markets had to be drawn into these orbits along with the creation of new financial institutions such as hedge funds, special investment vehicles (SIVs) and other elements of what has come to be known as the shadow banking system. Together, these changes amounted to the complete re-organization of the entire financial sectors of the American and British economies under the direction and control of a small number of investment banks. So re-organized, the entire credit system was turned into the major engines of capital accumulation that needed massive increases in global indebtedness to fuel its turbines. To function well, these engines of financial accumulation had to create attractive bubbles in areas such as emerging markets, commodities, education, oil, and housing, so that individuals and major investors would go into debt so that these banks could make even more money from interest and other payments.

This was the new model of financial accumulation into which American homeowners got caught via Wall Street's opaque and shady techniques for creating mortgage-backed securities and selling them as triple-A investments to the world. Without these dramatic transformations in the banking system to fill the accumulative void created by increasing de-industrialization and the stalling of the new informatic economy, it is impossible to understand why the failure of American homeowners to meet their mortgage payments could have been the trigger for such a major collapse. The bubble dynamics inherent in this model of accumulation help us to understand why Wall Street has been pushing so hard for the privatization of social security. Finally, the dramatic collapse of this financial model of accumulation lets us know that the U.S. economy is stuck between a growth engine in severe crisis and a new informatic one that is having great difficulty monetizing itself and thus getting big accumulation started.

Further aggravating, but at the same time also helping to contain, this hole that has opened up in the U.S. economy is the related factor of China's success in turning the tables on the second Western attempt to peripheralize its economy. Since the start of Deng Xiaoping's reforms in 1978, which were motivated in part by a slowing Chinese economy, American multinational companies have been investing in China hoping to repeat what they had done many times in Latin America, Africa, and the Caribbean. The arrival of these companies was an integral part of Deng's policies of re-introducing markets, legalizing private accumulation and opening China to foreign investment. However, the commanding heights of the Chinese economy would remain in state hands, making this new experiment some form of market socialism. However, it should be noted that Deng was not one for ideological labels that would be imposed on concrete Chinese realities. Rather, it is more accurate to see him as attempting to bring market and plan together in a push for Chinese development and seeing what emerges from this hybrid.

Among the first American companies to enter Deng's China were Avon and Kentucky Fried Chicken (Karabell 2009: 57–96). The stories of the successes of these two companies quickly became legendary. Soon the trickle of foreign companies became a flood. In the 1990s, major industrial companies such as IBM, General Electric, Caterpillar, General Motors, and many other American, European and Japanese companies had established major investments in China, attracted by its cheap or what Arthur Lewis would call, its "unlimited supplies of labor" (1954). Starting in 2001, we had the arrival of the big Wall Street investment banks. On the surface, this massive influx of Western companies looked very similar to well-known earlier instances of economic peripheralization, which have resulted in further cases of the vicious peripheral capitalist cycle.

But this has not been the case with China. On the contrary instead of the vicious peripheral capitalist cycles that we described earlier, between 1992 and 2012, China has experienced the highest growth rates for any twenty-year period on record. It is now the world's second largest economy, has trillions in reserves, and has become America's major creditor as the latter's debts continue to rise. This is yet another dimension of the Chimerican state capitalist convergence that has become the dominant politico-economic feature of our current conjuncture. But in spite of this problematic convergence, the question that must now be asked is: has China's market socialism broken the peripheral capitalist cycle? And, if it has, how did it manage to benefit so much from what appeared to be just another peripheral relationship?

First and most important is the unusual parity that China as a strong state was able to establish with the Western economies. Deeply aware of the imperial dimensions of trade between unequal central and peripheral countries, Deng and his economic advisors worked hard at countering these aspects that were potentially there in this new relationship with the West. In exchange for all of the advantages that would accrue to the West from having access to Chinese labor, the Deng administration insisted on being able to dictate and enforce the terms under which Western capital would enter the Chinese economy. For example, foreign companies in China had to partner with either a state-owned enterprise or a private Chinese entrepreneur; they had to put down at least 25 percent of the initial capital, and very early in this experiment were restricted to certain areas of the Chinese economy. Further, the products of these companies had to be exported so as not to compete with Chinese producers. In short, it was the highly unusual terms under which Western capital entered China that immediately sets it apart from other cases of peripheralization by the West. This is an important lesson here for all postcolonial states still caught on the treadmill of the peripheral capitalist cycle. This turning of the peripheral tables by China at a time when the U.S. and Europe were caught in the throes of the Great Recession has produced a dramatic shift in the global balance of power and thus the international context for a rebuilding of Caribbean socialism.

REBUILDING CARIBBEAN SOCIALISM

Thinking about rebuilding Caribbean socialism requires us to imagine ourselves and many other countries working through and moving beyond this crisis and the state capitalist convergence of interests that it has produced between China and the U.S. To get past this crisis, the U.S. must move beyond its flawed model of financial accumulation and restore its productive base with new technology and much more American labor. China is hard at work attempting a transition of its economy from what many Chinese economists now call its Lewisian phase to one in which industrial production is directed primarily at domestic markets. As the cost of labor in China continues to rise, the Lewisian phase will decline even more rapidly, ending the current convergent of interests and opening up many new possibilities for the reorganization of global industrial production. Japan is struggling to get out of its long period of stag-nation; and, in spite of persistent attempts, it is still not clear what the path out will be for Europe. If China succeeds in its transition ahead of Europe, Japan, and the U.S., it could be the economy that will determine what the post-crisis global economic order will be like. This is still very much an open race, and any one of these major contenders could be the bringer of the new era. In my view, it will probably be some combination of them that will finally bring the reluctant informatic phase of the global economy on board.

Equally important will be the form that the political economy of these contending countries will take in the post-crisis years. Will the U.S. be able to move beyond financialization and return to another and more productively based form of neoliberalism? Will Japan continue with its strong state-coordinated market economy, while at the same time resum-ing growth? Will China be more market oriented or more socialist orient-ed after its transition? Will Europe's social market economies survive the crisis and emerge stronger? And amid all of these possible changes, what is likely to be the political economy of the Caribbean as this new infor-matic order replaces the crisis-ridden one that is on its way out? Clearly we are not among the contenders who will usher in the new era. Our challenge is a different one: is this transitional period an opportune one for breaking out of the peripheral capitalist cycle?

After the stunning defeats that Caribbean socialism has experienced, the question could be asked: why rebuild this politico-economic tradi-tion? The most basic and obvious reasons for such a rebuilding are that many of the objective and subjective conditions for it may be present. With regard to the former, we have shown that the global trends pro-duced by the crises of both neoliberal capitalism and state socialism have adversely affected the region, lowering its peripheral status, destroying its already weak industrial sectors and thus creating hardships for work-ers. This increasing marginalization is an objective condition that calls for a response that would aim to reverse this trend and break the larger cycle of which it is a part.

With regard to the subjective conditions for rebuilding, this tradition of a socialist-oriented response to the above type of economic marginal-ization is alive in us, it flows out of us, and left to ourselves it is the kind of politico-economic order that we would create. A problem could arise here only if something in the current conjuncture has permanently si-lenced this long-standing response of ours. Our politico-economic imagi-nation is heavily state-centered. Unlike Americans, we have more faith in state institutions than we do private market oriented institutions. This state-centered orientation clearly has a lot do with our history of planta-tion slavery and the dominant role of the planter classes of the region in that practice. Further, it was through the agency of the state that the rule of the planters was overthrown and Caribbean societies were able to move from the oppressive stagnations of colonial economies to the economic treadmills of peripheral capitalist cycles. This is the experience that has established us in state-centered politico-economic traditions of thinking and acting.

Further, the Caribbean political tradition is inseparable from the larger Africana political tradition and has its roots in 17th-century regional maroon communities in which attempts were made to recreate African chiefdoms and kingdoms. This early phase in our political history also saw 18th-century slave uprisings that were national in scope and vision in which the goal was to throw out the colonizers and establish African kingdoms over whole territories as opposed to marooned parts (Gaspar 1985: 321). The 18th century also gave us our first political theorist to put his thoughts down on paper, Ottobah Cugoano (1757–?). A slave in Grenada, Cugoano turned that experience into his fiery and uncompromising text, *Thoughts and Sentiments on the Evils of Slavery*. Cugoano was one of a small number 18th-century African political theorists and writers that included Anton Amo (1703–1759), Phillis Wheatley (1753–1784), Lemuel Haynes (1753–1833), and Olaudah Equiano (1745–1797), who were articulating the deep resentment that African peoples had against the system of plantation slavery and the planter classes who organized these units of production.

A second important phase in our political history was marked by the late 18th- to early 19th-century Haitian Revolution, and the presidential monarchism that it produced. This was a creole political formation that was a peculiar mix of African monarchism and European republicanism. However, it is important to note that this revolution also produced the tradition of an independent peasantry that resisted very strongly this presidential monarchism of Toussaint and his generals as the latter's economic base required the re-introduction of the plantation system.

Throughout the remainder of the 19th century, the Africana political tradition moved in a black nationalist direction as its attention was focused on ending slavery in Caribbean territories other than Haiti, and also in the United States and Brazil. The success in the fights against slavery only set the stage for more direct confrontations with the plantations system, the planters and the racist colonial states that made their control of Caribbean economies possible. Throughout much of the Caribbean these confrontations took the form of struggles for land that would establish the tradition of an independent peasantry. However, in contrast to the case of Haiti, these battles were not against a creole system of presidential monarchism but against systems of white colonial rule. In this regard, the peasant struggles of Dominica, Jamaica and Antigua make instructive comparative cases with Haiti (Trouillot 1988; Green 1999; Beckford 1972; Henry 1985a).

Looking at the broader Africana political tradition, the dominant figure that emerged from this post-slavery period was the African American conservative assimilationist, Booker T. Washington. His influence extended to the Caribbean reaching such important Caribbean figures as Marcus Garvey. In contrast to the independent peasantry model, Washington outlined a self-help, enclave political economy for African Americans in which they exchanged security for the surrendering of all political rights. However, the failure of this model by the start of the 20th century set the stage for the socialist turn in the Africana political tradition. Dissatisfaction with Washington's leadership and influence produced two types of criticisms: the Pan African criticisms of one time admirer, Marcus Garvey, W. E. B. Du Bois, Sylvester Williams and others; and the socialist criticisms of Hubert Harrison, W. A. Domingo, Richard Moore, Cyril Briggs, and African Americans such as A. Phillip Randolph. This first generation of Caribbean socialists were soon followed by George Padmore, C. L. R. James and Claudia Jones, who were in turn followed by the rise of democratic socialists such as Arthur Lewis, trade unions and political parties under the leadership of democratic socialist figures like Norman Manley, Grantley Adams, Cheddi Jagan, Eric Williams, and V. C. Bird. It was the failures of these democratic socialist regimes to break out of the peripheral capitalist cycle that gave birth to the Caribbean New Left, symbolized by Walter Rodney, Tim Hector, Clive Thomas and many others. The latter's equally unsuccessful attempts to break the grip of this cycle created the stage on which the collapsed neoliberal drama is being played out.

As we think now of attempting another break, the question that we must ask ourselves is whether or not this tradition is still alive in us. Do these black/brown socialist themes accurately represent our political passions, the depths of our political subjectivity? Have the new patterns of inter-regional migration, the changing relations between Indo-Caribbeans and Afro-Caribbeans, and the fuller entry of women into the workforce and the political arena so transformed today's working classes that they no longer carry these passions? When the next popular upsurge erupts onto the historical stage, will it pick up and carry forward these themes that have long animated us or will we discover that they were crushed during the neoliberal onslaught or went down with the collapse of state socialism? Indeed, only that next popular creative and insurrectionary upsurge will be able to say for sure, but I am confident that these socialist oriented passions are still with us in the political impulses that I continue to see ordinary Caribbean people display.

This state-centered politico-economic identity is not one that we should apologize for or attempt to deny. Rather, it should be the identity that we seek to build on and to expand. It is because of its persistence that the project of rebuilding Caribbean socialism makes sense and rings of subjective authenticity. It would be foolish for us to attempt to affirm an American politico-economic identity that sees states as the enemy and the private sector as agents of freedom who are also capable of doing everything better than a state. In spite of a fairly long exposure to this liberal tradition it is not one that we can readily practice. Although not identical with it, we are closer in spirit to the European social market position on political economy. Here, the fear of the state is significantly less than in the case of the Americans and closer to us. However, Europeans are more embracing of markets than we are. So the precise mix that supports their social market economies is significantly different from the mix that our political tradition has consistently produced. Both the Japanese and the Chinese have even stronger states than we have recently become accustomed to, although there are very significant differences between the Chinese and Japanese states. However, both of these countries are now more embracing of markets than we are. In looking at these comparative differences in politico-economic identities we should become more fully aware of our uniqueness, more confirmed in it and embracing of its strengths and also more determined to address its weaknesses.

Assuming that the above are adequate objective and subjective justifications for rebuilding Caribbean socialism our next concern has to be what must the future Caribbean Left do differently so as to avoid the mistakes of Left groups of the 1940s and the 1970s, and to respond creatively and constructively to the new global environment in which this rebuilding will take place. First, the broad theoretical and ideological vision for such a rebuilding would not be the socialist vision that James outlined in *The Invading Socialist Society* or *Facing Reality*. That strong sense of a rising global proletarian movement that informs these works, we do not have at this moment. Rather, what we see are solidarity and political participatory eruptions such as the Solidarity Economy movement in Brazil. Further, the economic self-managing capacity of Caribbean workers beyond the framework of the independent peasant model has not really manifested itself in a major creative upsurge. On this point, I know that I differ from the position of Matthew Quest, who thinks that workers are indeed ready for James's proletarian democracy. Also, I do not think that this broad theoretical vision can be that of Rodney's complete state control without the cooperation of the local bourgeoisie.

Consequently, in my view, this broad socialist vision for the Caribbean, must be closer to the one James outlined in *Party Politics in the West Indies*. Indeed, I will argue that it would have to be that of a brown/black democratic socialism capable of embracing the independent struggles of Indo-Caribbean and Afro-Caribbean women. However formulated, this broad vision should be a guide and not a blueprint that leaders would attempt to impose on Caribbean realities. At the same time that we are using it as a map we must always bear in mind that we are really creating something new, a new territory that none has yet seen, and that the crucial clues reside in the creative upsurges of the masses.

Undertaking such a project of black/brown democratic socialism today will clearly be a very different endeavor from those of the 1930s or the 1960s. The ending of the Cold War, the new global status of China, and its membership along with Russia in the G20 all point to the dramatic changes that have been produced by the collapse of state socialism and the financial meltdown of Western neoliberal capitalism. It is conceivable that as the current convergence of interests between China and the U.S. decreases, some form of a cold war could develop between the two. But even this would be different from the previous one.

For the project of rebuilding Caribbean socialism in this changed context, one of the first questions that this new global order requires that we answer is that of the nature, scope and effectiveness of central planning. The reintroduction of markets in Cuba and in just about all of the other state socialist societies is the driving force behind this question about the central planning of economies by states. The retreat of these societies from this model of macro-economic organization points to major technical difficulties with it, and also to the case that in making such reductive moves these states are indeed acknowledging that they took on much more than they could handle.

Does this mean that democratic socialist states should not plan? Not at all. Rather, what these dramatic retreats from central planning suggest is that states need to estimate very realistically their capacity to steer and plan economies, and also the kind of cooperation that they will require from the private sector. Thus it seems to me that the problem is not so much planning itself, after all private corporations do a lot of planning, but with socialist states being able to resist the impulse to plan and steer more areas of the economy than they can effectively execute. Within the Caribbean tradition, Clive Thomas has outlined some models of planning that he thought would be appropriate for peripheral capitalist economies making the transition to socialism (1974: 177–84). When compared to the planning responsibilities undertaken by the People's Revolutionary Government in Grenada, we can see the significant gap between the two. This raises the question as to whether or not there must be some minimal levels of managerial and planning capabilities for a socialist state that will be in control of only certain sectors of the economy.

If the state's steering and planning of the economy is going to be a limited undertaking, then this is clearly going to have to call for new and clearly defined relations between the planned sectors and those that are coordinated by market signals. During the colonial era, entrepreneurial activity—whether by peasants, workers or petit bourgeois individuals— was effectively stifled. Given the resulting underdevelopment of entire local entrepreneurial sectors produced by colonial/plantation regimes, the reliance on neo-mercantile protected markets that they encouraged, and the much more competitive international order we will be facing, the new relations between market and plan must include the creating of an expanded and more dynamic entrepreneurial sector that will be devoted to the upgrading of the entrepreneurial and managerial capabilities of both states and private sectors. Without a concerted effort in this direction old patterns of entrepreneurial dependence will be certain to reappear. Vital to this project of upgrading entrepreneurial and managerial capabilities must be a carefully planned program to reduce the high rate of outflow of trained professionals and intellectuals. According to the IMF, the Caribbean is the region with the highest percentage of its trained professionals abroad (Mandle 2010). Reversing this drain must be a part of the general upgrading of the organizational and performative capabilities of our societies. In the post–Cold War era, a wider variety of mixes and strategies of cooperation between market and plan have been emerging in countries like Vietnam and Russia. So on this point we should be very open, observant of what is taking place in other countries that are also struggling with similar issues while at the same time being true to our political traditions.

From the experiences of countries like China and Russia, it is clear that the retention of markets and opening them up globally will bring significant increases in social inequality and persistent levels of unemployment, tendencies that are in direct contradiction of socialist goals of class equality and full employment. In any form of market socialism there are definitely going to be problems of proletarian exploitation and issues arising from the exclusion of the unemployed. Thus to deal with the class problems that will inevitably arise as both state and private systems of accumulation get going special arrangements will have to be made to deal with the rights, aspirations and concerns of these two strata of our populations.

As James has consistently tried to show, exploited workers and the unemployed build bonds and institutions of collective solidarity to deal with their marginalization. In the post-crisis years, these patterns of worker marginalization are very likely to increase. Thus in any rebuilding of Caribbean socialism, there must be departments of state with primary responsibilities of supporting, legitimating, and legalizing where necessary the cooperative and solidarity oriented institutions that will emerge among these strata of the population. Particularly important in this regard, will be the providing of strong support and encouragement for the participatory dimensions of these institutions of collective solidarity and cooperation. These aspects open up the educational potential incorporated in these institutions. Further, these particular participatory practices must be connected to broader democratic and political ones that are not so directly tied to issues and conditions of employment.

In addition to addressing these class issues a new incarnation of Caribbean socialism must also deal with persisting issues of race that are still embedded within the practices of Western capitalism. These have been evident in the racial issues that have plagued the presidency of Barack Obama, relations between blacks and the police, increasing patterns of residential segregation in the U.S., the image of blacks in the media, the number of blacks going blonde, and what Antiguan writer Althea Prince has called "the politics of Black Women's hair." With the receding of the black power movement, the effects of these persisting racialized capitalist practices have been increases in the Fanonian phenomenon of blacks wearing white masks. The fact that the reparations issue made it onto the 2013 agenda of the Caribbean Heads of Government meeting is a significant indicator that the race issue is far from being a settled one.

Further, a new Caribbean democratic socialist project must also deal much better than its earlier incarnations with the sexist difficulties surrounding full entry of women into the workforce and into the political arena. There is a lot of work to be done here, as in the current conjuncture issues of race, gender and class have tended to move in separate directions and often find themselves in conflict with each other. Unity and solidarity around these issues are vital for any rebuilding of Caribbean socialism. An important step in this regard must be the fuller integrating of Anna Julia Cooper, Claudia Jones, Sylvia Wynter, Rhoda Reddock, and Cecilia Green into the tradition of black political economy.

Given this broad theoretical framework linking issues of planning, markets, employment, class, gender and race, the missing piece in this outline is the new model of state accumulation that would enable us to break the peripheral capitalist cycle in the context of the informatic order that is likely to follow these years of crisis. As Arthur Lewis has suggested, we have not yet found a path to economic development and wealth creation that is not based on some form of surplus extraction from the direct producers of goods and services (1954). This is the fundamental problem with the independent peasant model. It does not generate a significant surplus that can be collected and reinvested in the ongoing transformation of the economy. This was a problem of which Toussaint was very keenly aware; hence his opposition to the model. In *World Revolution*, when James spoke of the immaturity of workers and their dependence on elites, this inability to self-organize the collective extracting of a surplus from themselves, pooling it and productively investing it in their own growth was one of these continuing dependencies. Thus the whole thrust of a democratic socialist model of accumulation must be a transparent process of surplus extraction by the state in the interest of workers as long as they are unable to do this for themselves. This of course opens up the possibility that James feared of sure elites monopolizing the surplus and betraying the workers. In capitalism, this process of surplus extraction is of course the right and privilege of the capitalist. Between the claims of *State Capitalism* and *World Revolution* and those of *Party Politics in the West Indies*, we can see James oscillating on this important issue of the dependence of workers on such elites.

Thus we have got here five basic options for surplus extraction: a capitalist mechanism of private extraction with little or no sharing with workers; an independent peasant model that does not extract a surplus;

a fully worker-controlled process of surplus extraction; a completely state-controlled one; and a partially state-controlled one with the risk of betraying workers. My choice is for the fifth of these options with deep structures of transparency.

Assuming this state-centered mechanism of surplus extraction, what should the overall model of accumulation look like and what should be its primary goals? Let us begin with the latter of these two questions. The immediate aim of this model of accumulation cannot be the placing of the control and transformation of Caribbean economies in the hands of workers. Rather, a much more intermediate step should be the immediate aim of the model of accumulation. That step should be the disrupting and breaking of the earlier noted pattern of cost-cutting technologies entering Caribbean economies through foreign-dominated processes of capital accumulation. This as we have seen has been the key driver of the peripheral capitalist cycle that has devoured the earlier incarnations of Caribbean socialism. To break the above pattern the state must gain control of key sectors that are the sites of such investment with the goal of running them as or more efficiently and at the same time retaining those portions of the profits that would usually go abroad. This would of course mean gaining control of sectors and industries that the specific state in question could manage or learn to do so fairly quickly. In effect, the state must gain control of practices of surplus extraction and accumulation that were formerly in private hands. What it does with this surplus and how transparently and democratically it reinvests it will determine just how socialist that state is.

For territories like Jamaica, St. Lucia or Antigua and Barbuda, the tourist industry would be the one the state should seek to gain control of. This is not a high-tech industry. After 60 years of operating under foreign control it is about time we make it a national goal to master all aspects of this industry so that it becomes one that is predominantly run by locals, with the lion's share of the profits staying local. In conjunction with state control of industries like tourism the state will also have significant control over the banking sector if it is to have the capacity to steer investments in new directions and further develop the economy. Entrepreneurial and managerial moves such as these must be done with higher levels of state capacity and efficiency than in the past, at the same time that state officials are ideologically and institutionally constrained to remember on whose behalf they are extracting surplus, accumulating and investing capital. These higher levels of performance will require a careful rethinking of the internal organization of Caribbean state-owned enterprises as corporate units of production. Periods of crisis, such as the one that we are going through, often bring with them new patterns of corporate organization. If the Chinese succeed in their process of transformation, it could indeed change our views of state-owned enterprises as distinct corporate units.

CONCLUSION

The above are some general outlines of the foundations upon which I think we can rebuild the project of Caribbean socialism. I did not get into the politics of re-launching such a project, but that must be the subject of another paper. I must reiterate here that this model will generate class inequality and unemployment and hence the importance of a complement of cooperative institutions to counteract and compensate for these tendencies. The Caribbean needs a vision of itself beyond the difficulties of this crisis period. Let us not repeat old patterns and simply wait for the return of external demand to revive our industries. If we do, we will find ourselves a decade from now still shuttling between James's transitional state capitalism and the peripheral capitalism of Rodney and the members of the Caribbean dependency school.

NOTE

* First published as "C. L. R. James, Walter Rodney and the Rebuilding of Caribbean Socialism," *C. L. R. James Journal* 19, no. 1 & 2 (Fall): 458–84.

Part III

A Homeward Turn:
Antigua and Barbuda

NINE

V. C. Bird's Political Philosophy

Unlike the case of Caribbean literature or Caribbean history, we are only now beginning to give Caribbean philosophy the attention that it deserves. It has been the hidden discourse that we live and breathe, but have not taken the time to systematize or celebrate. Yet it is a crucial lens for grasping ourselves and for understanding a public figure like V. C. Bird. The primary aim of my book, *Caliban's Reason: Introducing Afro-Caribbean Philosophy*, was to break this pattern of philosophical neglect. I very intentionally devoted it to making visible the most hidden dimensions of this already hidden discourse. Thus it is a work that unearths Afro-Caribbean ontologies—the discourses in which we have taken up the question of the ultimate nature of being—as opposed to the more visible areas such as political and social philosophy. It was an unusual approach to the study of an anticolonial philosophy, so much so that my former high school teacher and good friend, Tim Hector, took me to task for it and also for leaving out the area of metaphysics (*Outlet* 2000: 6).

By focusing so intensely on Caribbean ontology, I was going against a very prominent defining mark of colonial, anticolonial, and early nationalist philosophies: that is, the tendency to de-center subfields like ethics, ontology, metaphysics and epistemology and to give the center to social and political philosophy. We can see this characteristic shift very clearly in the case of the United States, the first modern postcolonial nation. In early America, there certainly were the prolific Christian philosophers, Jonathan Edwards and Cotton Mather. However, these religious thinkers were soon eclipsed by the political philosophers: Thomas Jefferson, Alexander Hamilton (originally from Nevis), James Madison and John Adams. This higher visibility of political philosophy over ontology and ethics can also be seen in Haiti, the second modern postcolonial nation. The political philosophy of revolutionary Haiti has been named and immortalized by C. L. R. James as a "Black Jacobin" philosophy. In other words, it was a creole political philosophy that combined elements of the Jacobin wing of the French revolutionary Left with elements of an indigenous discourse about racial liberation.

Given these examples of American and Haitian philosophy, we should not be surprised that philosophy in the region has been primarily social and political philosophy and not metaphysics or epistemology. However, it is important to note that in spite of being de-centered, these subfields of ethics, ontology, metaphysics, etc. do not simply disappear from colonial philosophies. Rather, they resurface in the arguments used to justify a race-first, a class-first, a trade union–first or a nation-first position. Thus within the framework of colonial philosophies, metaphysics no longer takes the form of justifying the priority of Spirit over matter or the reverse, but the justifications for the ranking and prioritizing of factors such as race, class, gender, trade union, party or nation. As we will see, it was no longer metaphysical questions like how many angels can dance on the head of pin that engaged our early nationalist philosophers, but those of weighing and debating the importance of the various dimensions of the liberatory process.

The hybrid nature of the Haitian Black Jacobin discourse reflected a broader creole pattern in regional political thought that we will see at work in Antigua and Barbuda and also in V. C. Bird. In other words, to locate Bird philosophically, we simply need to ask ourselves the question: what was his equivalent of Toussaint's Black Jacobinism or of Jefferson's revolutionary republicanism? As we will see, initially this equivalent was Bird's variant on another regional political philosophy, black democratic socialism. But first we must turn our attention to Bird's emergence as the president of the ATLU.

Even though the waterfront strike of 1940 gave the ATLU its big opportunity, all did not go well with this attempt to represent the workers and to channel their insurrectionary Weston-type vision into the ideological and organizational mold of trade unionism. Workers were still taking actions on their own that did not have union approval. The executive of the union had agreed with Governor Letham's call for a ban on strikes for the duration of the Second World War. Thus the strike of 1940 was a clear indication that Antiguan and Barbudan workers had not accepted the governor's call. The leadership of the union, headed by Reginald Stevens, and its new rank and file were not on the same page. Indeed, they were on very different pages. The two would have to be brought closer together if this new experiment was going to work. Comparable problems were also being experienced by the St. Kitts Trades and Labour Union where a similar waterfront strike was taking place.

In Antigua and Barbuda, the worker-initiated strike was against the shipping firm of Bryson and Company. However, as it dragged on it eventually became a major concern for the colonial state. This turn of events was indicated when on May 3, 1940, Acting Governor J. D. Harford (Governor Letham was away) told an emergency meeting of the legislature that "at noon on the 1st of this month (Wednesday) a ship chartered by His Majesty's Government in the UK was anchored in St. Johns Harbour to load 3000 tons of sugar, which had been purchased by the British Government. Now it is reported to the local government that the men were unwilling to load the ship because no decision had yet been reached in a certain negotiation, up to now, in train" (CO 152/494/2). The responses of the workers to the ban on strikes and to the war were clearly indicated in these refusals. It was not a response of which the leadership approved.

Because of the urgency of the matter, Acting Governor Harford called all of the representatives of the parties to this conflict to meet with him in an effort to settle the dispute. As president of the ATLU, Reginald Stevens was invited as the representative of the workers. Bryson and Company initially resisted this act of state intervention but eventually sent their representative, T. F. Burrows, a lawyer who was openly opposed to trade unions. At the meeting it was the performance of Stevens that was particularly lacking. First, it took him 24 hours to make himself available and later in the afternoon, after consultations with others in the union, he rejected the governor's offer of a 4-cent increase to the lighter men as a temporary measure to get the ship loaded as part of the war effort. Harford then called for another meeting. To this Stevens wrote in reply: "I regret being unable to meet with your Excellency's request as I am very busy at this time with my business and other duties which are now demanding my immediate attention" (CO 152/494/2). This was indeed a poor and tactless excuse. Not only was Harford incensed, the entire office of the Secretary of State for the Colonies in London was in an uproar. This was not the way in which one responded to British imperial authority even if it is in the process of withdrawing.

Going over Stevens's head, Harford took the decision to load the ship with other workers. Stevens was completely outplayed. When Governor Letham returned, he stood firmly behind Harford's actions. In his report to the Secretary of State, he noted that Stevens had apologized profusely by letter to Harford, and that he "verbally admitted his failure to me" (CO 152/494/2). The Governor then went on to describe him as a "man of small physique, and un-impressive in appearance, a sense of inferiority, little or no superior education, and he is filled with the suspicion of the West Indian planter and employer common of his class . . . He has many deficiencies but is not a fool, and he has some shrewdness . . . He has a very difficult and irresponsible train to drive" (CO 152/494/2).

This swift and decisive intervention on the part of the colonial state brought the strike to a very unsatisfactory conclusion for the union. It was the first major setback for workers in a while and made clear the different responses they could expect from actions directly affecting Brit-

ish imperial interests and not just those of the declining planters. Not
surprisingly, Stevens's letter to Harford brought nothing but criticism
from the imperial center, from the planters, the local state and also from
many inside his very young union.

Unfortunately, the available historical sources do not enable us to say
much about Stevens's consultations before he rejected Harford's initial
offer. However, it seems reasonable to conclude that he encountered
great resistance and competing views on cooperating with the imperial
authorities even in the case of loading this one ship. We cannot say for
sure what exactly were these differing views but they suggest that there
was still a major gap between Stevens's procedural and non-confronta-
tional style of leadership and the insurrectionary mood of the masses of
workers who were now in his union. This could have been the "difficult
and irresponsible train" that he had to drive, which Governor Letham
referred to earlier. In any event, the whole incident was of a very high
cost to Stevens and contributed to his decline as a leader.

The official rejection of Stevens as president of the ATLU came in
September of 1943 at the union's annual conference. At this historic gathering a much more confrontational V. C. Bird, who already had a strong
loyal following within the organization, was elected president by an
overwhelming majority. Stevens took his defeat very hard and slowly
drifted away from the union. As noted in chapter 1, Bird's appeal was his
more confrontational style and a greater determination to find a place in
the union's practice for the insurrectionary impulses of the masses and
their Weston-type vision.[1] Indeed, it was Bird's ability to better align the
institutional capabilities and legal rights of the union with the insurgent
impulses of the mass for change that would be one of the big differences
between his leadership and Stevens's. As we have already seen, Govern-
or Letham saw in Bird a man and a leader of a very different type—one
that tended to over- rather than under-reach himself. In short, it was the
problem of establishing a better fit between the objective practices of the
union and the living Weston-type subjectivity of the masses that led to
the decline of Stevens and the rise of Bird.

With Bird at the helm, it now becomes very crucial for us to return to
his philosophical vision for the union, and in particular the type of social
changes that he thought it could bring about. In other words, it is time for
us to take a detailed look at V. C. Bird's black democratic socialism and
also the philosophies of other key figures in and around the organization.
These political philosophies would be the Antiguan and Barbudan equivalents of the Black Jacobinism of early Haiti or the revolutionary republicanism of early America.

As with most people, Bird's political philosophy developed and
evolved slowly over time. We have already noted its beginnings in the
ethical discourse of bad mindedness. This discourse has its origins in the
Afro-Christian dichotomy between good and evil. These are irreconcil-

able opposites in which good must cut down and destroy evil. Bird's initial grasp of the planters was in terms of the evil half of this dichotomy. Consequently, they were seen as people with evil intentions. They acted toward Black Antiguans and Barbudans out of bad motives—their minds, their very natures were bad. Seeing them in this manner helped to determine Bird's well-known uncompromising attitude of resistance to that class.

A classic example of how the British colonial elite as a whole appeared when viewed from the perspective of ethical bad mindedness can be seen in Jamaica Kincaid's *A Small Place*. Kincaid says to the British: "You came. You took things that were not yours, and you did not even, for appearances sake, ask first . . . You murdered people. You imprisoned people. You robbed people. . . . There must have been some good people among you, but they stayed at home" (Kincaid 1988: 35). Kincaid then poses this pointed question to herself: "is the Antigua I see before me, self-ruled, a worse place than what it was when it was dominated by the bad-minded English and all the bad-minded things they brought with them?" (Kincaid 1988: 40). However, it is important to note that for Kincaid Afro-Antiguans and Barbudans were also included in the practice of bad mindedness. This theme is very clearly developed in her novel, *The Autobiography of My Mother* and its main character, Xuela. ("To encounter Xuela," she wrote, "is to know bad mindedness first hand.")

Another powerful treatment of ethical bad mindedness in the context of Antiguan and Barbudan society can be found in Edgar Lake's masterful novel, *The Devil's Bridge*. In contrast to Kincaid's focus on the female subject, Lake examines the discourse and practice of ethical bad mindedness in the lives of Antiguan and Barbudan males. Lake's unnamed main character is a working-class man of the 1950s who lives near the Bridge, a gritty area of St. Johns that was a lot like Bird's old neighborhood. He is a man on the edge, just barely surviving by doing many things including being the head of a band of clowns who dance in the streets for money at Christmastime. Lake's character sees his lot as the fault of all the bad minded people who are doing better than him. Thus he carries a deep resentment against much of society and is able to justify preying on most of its members. His distance from these evil citizens who are making his life so hard is indicated by his experience of himself as a "lost" or "fallen" individual. So low is his fallen state that he makes a pact with the Devil and invokes the identity and voice of another dead clown by the name of Harsh Ryder in order to survive. But even with the aid of the Devil and the borrowed identity of Harsh Ryder his survival remains on the edge. Unable to hold body and soul together, he and his band strike out against all of the bad minded people they held responsible for their plight while pretending to be just dancing clowns. Like Xuela, Lake's character is a study in the polarized world of bad mindedness and how its evil category gets projected onto others. It was an ethical and oppositional projection of the evil category onto the planters such as this one that was the foundation and first phase of Bird's political philosophy.

From these oppositional beginnings in the local discourse of ethical bad mindedness, Bird's political philosophy began to take on more positive features. That is, a statement not only of what it was against but also what it was for and how it was to be achieved. In making this move, Bird was clearly going against the implicit mode of philosophizing typical of the Antiguan and Barbudan working class that would then express itself in the language of collective action. Bird was here joining a group of black working-class thinkers such as Hubert Harrison, Marcus Garvey, George Weston, and Uriah Butler, whose abilities in articulating their political visions made them working-class leaders and heroes.

A political philosophy is a statement of one's conception of freedom and order, the kind of state that would embody one's conception of these two key political coordinates, and the roles of leaders and citizens in the resulting political community. It was a positive vision of this kind that was now taking progressively more concrete form in Bird's mind. As he moved from the religious side of working-class leadership to its political side, Bird began to connect more directly with the insurrectionary political philosophy of masses that called for an alternative to the post-slavery order and the rule of the planters. Although not very clear at first, Bird's new social order had to be more worker centered. However, as an urban dweller, the agrarian orientation of the Weston-type solution did not come naturally to Bird. This would be an important divide that he would have to negotiate.

The next important step in the development of Bird's political philosophy was of course his conversion to trade unionism and democratic socialism. To understand this conversion, it is necessary to go beyond the speech by Sir Walter Citrine. This is in no way to deny the historic importance of this speech. Rather, what I want to argue is that its real function was that of a catalyst to a strong unionist tendency that was already developing.

In addition to speaking about the history, principles and functions of trade unions in England, Citrine also felt the need to establish his "claim to credibility" as a speaker on behalf of trade unionism. In doing so, he talked about his life as a worker: "I started work at the age of 12 and a half years. I went to work in a flour mill from six o'clock in the morning till six o'clock at night and received six shillings a week . . . That work nearly killed me. Within six months I had inflammation of lungs and kidneys as a consequence of working in a dusty atmosphere" (*Antigua Magnet* 1939b: 2). Citrine then went on to describe how he left that job and went to work as an electrician first in the glass-blowing business, then in the building trade and finally in the ship building industry. He concluded this brief autobiographical sketch with the following: "so I say therefore from the point of view of early association and from that of my actual working career I know something of what poverty means" (*Antigua Magnet* 1939b: 2).

These revelations of his roots in poverty and of his experiences as a worker brought loud cheers from the audience. Other occasions that brought loud cheers from the audience were those in which Citrine affirmed some central principle of trade unionism and of the dignity and humanity of working people. Thus loud cheers followed when Citrine said: "in that capacity, it has been my work and my study and my constant endeavor to try to understand the problems of working people all over the world. I have had the great privilege of being the President of the greatest international organization of trade unionists in the world" (*Antigua Magnet* 1939b: 2). Cheers also were heard when Citrine reported of 19th-century English workers that "it was at that stage that the workingmen started to combine. It was when they saw quite clearly that if they were going to get for their wives and children and themselves a decent standard of existence they had to rely on themselves and not on others" (*Antigua Magnet* 1939b: 2). From these and other points of loud cheers and "here here," it seems very reasonable to conclude that Citrine was really preaching trade unionism to the already converted. That is, this philosophy was already familiar to many in the audience, who were responding in much the same manner that they did when their pastors affirmed some key Christian or Afro-Christian principle. These cheers were the *Amens* of the already converted. Citrine's moving address was the catalyst that turned them into trade union activists and evangelists. Among those so moved was clearly a maturing V. C. Bird.

But to grasp the broader context of Bird's transition from ethical bad mindedness to a trade unionism that was cast within a broader framework of black democratic socialism we now need to get a better sense of where the pre-Citrine roots of trade unionism in Antigua and Barbuda came from. These roots are to be found in some of the new international networks that were created by Caribbean immigrants to the major cities of the imperial centers around the turn of the 20th century. These new networks integrated Antigua and Barbuda into new information flows that included ideas about trade unions, revolutionary socialism, Pan-Africanism and critiques of the accommodationist style of black leadership represented by the dominant figure of Booker T. Washington. Washington had replaced the more radical Frederick Douglass as the leader of black America.

Although a very small territory, Antigua and Barbuda was not an isolated presidency in the 1930s. Colonialism had already integrated them into the British imperial economy, and to the flow of ideas that traveled along those channels. However, since the turn of the 20th century, labor demands in the global capitalist system had created reverse migratory trends that were now bringing both skilled and unskilled workers from the Caribbean and other colonies to the major cities of the imperial centers. Thus, by the 1930s, substantial Caribbean immigrant or diasporic communities existed in cities such as London, New York and Paris. The bonds that were subsequently established between these diasporic communities and Caribbean territories such as Antigua and Barbuda came to constitute a new set of links connecting these islands to the imperial centers. As the effects of the international women's movement are evident today in the lives of Antiguan and Barbudan women, so in the 1930s the effects of the international workers movement reached Antiguan and Barbudan workers through the above diasporic networks.

Although it was still very difficult, Caribbean migrants to these metropolitan areas were freer to organize politically, to join trade unions, and to publish papers that were critical of racism and colonialism. Consequently, in solidarity with African Americans, these diasporic communities became major sites of Africana and Caribbean ideological productions that were regularly sent back to the region via networks of black seamen. This diasporic internationalism became a major political force affecting the activities of the lodges and friendly societies of the Caribbean masses. Indeed, as Corey Walker has shown, the lodges were the first organizational bases of these diasporic links that date back to the 18th century. He notes that in many of these lodges, such as African Lodge #459 of Philadelphia, significant numbers of the members were from the Caribbean (Walker 2008: 58).

A good example of this diasporic internationalism at work was the mobilization of people all over the Africana world against the 1935 invasion of Ethiopia by Italy. Black organizations in the diaspora organized demonstrations, published papers and sent them to African communities all over the world. *The Voice of Ethiopia*, the paper of the African American organization, Ethiopian World Federation, was one of these papers that reached Antigua and Barbuda regularly via the networks of seamen. In short, early 20th-century diasporic internationalism was a new link connecting Antigua and Barbuda in a very different way to life in the metropole. The infamous Sedition and Undesirable Publications Act of 1938 was an attempt by the planters and colonial elites to stop this flow of information into Antigua and Barbuda along these networks, particularly the newspapers *The Voice of Ethiopia*, *The Golden Age*, and Garvey's *Black World*.

In the decades between 1900 and the 1940s, the increasing flow of ideological and political information along these networks of diasporic internationalism took four basic forms: (1) the ideas of the New York–based New Negro Movement of Hubert Harrison, who was originally from St. Croix; (2) the Pan-African ideas of the New York–based Garvey movement; (3) the Moscow/London-based communist movement of George Padmore and C. L. R. James; and (4) the New York/London–based Marxist-feminism of Claudia Jones, who was also the organizer of the first Caribbean carnival in London. Behind these new information flows was the resurgence of three major social movements against the same capitalist order that workers in Antigua and Barbuda had been rising up against. These three movements were the international working class movement, the Pan-African movement against racism and colonialism, and the international women's movement.

An important feature of the work of the leaders of these new diasporic flows of information is that they all represented post–Booker T. Washington conceptions of black leadership that included trade unions and the fight for black political rights. Harrison arrived in New York in 1900 at the age of 17. He quickly established a reputation for his editorials on race issues that were published in the *New York Times*. Harrison, along with the African Americans W. E. B. Du Bois and William Monroe Trotter, was among the earliest critics of Washington's model of political leadership that accommodated the denial of black political rights. Harrison joined the Socialist Party, formed his own organization, the Liberty League, and edited its paper, *The Voice*, which traveled the networks of black seamen. There were many Antiguan and Barbudans in Harrison's League including William Derrick, owner and editor of *The West Indian Abroad*. Harrison's wife, Irene Horton, was from Antigua (Perry 2010: 55). Marcus Garvey was also critical of Washington's model of black leadership although he was a great admirer of Washington. Indeed, Garvey left Jamaica for the United States with the express purpose of meeting Washington. However, in his calls for African American political rights, and political independence for African and Caribbean nations, Garvey was clearly breaking with this black leader that he had admired. There were many Antiguans and Barbudans in the Garvey movement. George Weston and Bishop George McGuire are two of the best known. McGuire was the moving force behind the concept of a black Christ that was part of the theology of the movement. Weston returned to Antigua in the late 1940s and throughout the decade of the 1950s organized Black History Week, following the example of the African American historian, Carter G. Woodson.

As a communist and head of the International Trade Union Committee of Negro Workers, Padmore had not only moved beyond Washington but was also critical of the leadership styles of more progressive figures such as W. E. B. Du Bois and Garvey. In 1933, Padmore broke with the Communist International and moved from Moscow to London, where he founded the International African Services Bureau with his boyhood friend from Trinidad, C. L. R. James.

Claudia Jones, a long-eclipsed but now resurfacing working-class intellectual, arrived in New York from her native Trinidad in 1924 at the age of eight. Like Harrison, she rose to prominence through writing columns in local newspapers. In 1936, Jones, like Padmore earlier, joined the American Communist Party, became the editor of its *Weekly Review*, and also one of its major theoreticians on women's issues. A strong supporter of trade unions, Jones represented a model of black female leadership that we would not see again until Angela Davis. Like C. L. R. James, after her arrest and deportation, Jones moved to London where she edited the influential *West Indian Gazette* and worked with the London branch of the Caribbean Congress of Labour (Davies 2008: 30).

These were some of the new political currents and their creators that had been bringing news of trade unionism to Antigua and Barbuda and making leaders like Governors Best (1915–19) and St. Johnston very uncomfortable. These ideas were challenging the Washington type accommodation to the colonial denial of black political rights and putting forth nationalist and socialist alternatives. This post–Booker T. Washington turn in Africana political philosophy and leadership will constitute the core of what Cedric Robinson, Anthony Bogues, Rupert Lewis and others have called the black radical tradition. In the main, it has been a critical race/class discourse that has fashioned original syntheses out of Left European theories of class and indigenous theories of race. To this creole mix, Claudia Jones was among the first Caribbean women to systematically add gender.

Thus long before Citrine, there was this vibrant tradition of Africana political thought. Padmore and Jones had been strong advocates of trade unionism—although of a more radical type than Citrine. But nonetheless, the literature that Padmore's organization distributed throughout the region was all about workers getting organized, joining trade unions and standing up for themselves. The Garvey movement represented a new phase in the long and historic struggle of Africana people against slavery, colonialism and racism. Before Citrine, Garvey had visited Antigua and Barbuda and spoke in that same Cathedral School room in which Citrine spoke. These were all powerful diasporic influences that were changing the political outlook of individuals like Luther George, Bird, Stevens and many others who would form or join the ATLU. Indeed, Bird's black democratic socialism emerges within this political tradition and constituted his home-grown contribution to its body of thought. However, the fact that Citrine has completely eclipsed the black radical tradition in the popular accounts of the origins of the Antiguan and Barbudan labor movement points to the problem of visibility from which this tradition and its diasporic influences still suffer.

In the case of a Caribbean leader like Eric Williams, these diasporic influences of the black radical tradition were much more direct. In the early 1940s when Bird was in the thick of his struggle for power with the planters, Williams was a celebrated professor at Howard University. He worked with many of the leading African American scholars of the day including the philosopher Alain Locke and the sociologists Charles Johnson and Ira de Augustine Reid. One of Williams's well-known essays on the rise of "the University of Woodford Square" and of his party, the People's National Movement, carries the title "I Cast Down My Bucket"—a clear invoking of a famous image from Booker T. Washington. Williams combined these themes of racial liberation with those of class to produce his own version of a black democratic socialism. His was of course a more scholarly version than Bird's. Yet both are philosophizing in response to similar sets of forces and influences.

In addition to the above diasporic organizations advocating worker resistance to both classism and racism, there was the regional organization, the Caribbean Congress of Labour. Many in this organization had been influenced by the ideas of Padmore, Garvey, and Jones, and they in turn had a direct influence on many Caribbean political figures including Bird and other leaders of the ATLU. In sum, it was this steady flow of ideas about working class organizing that traveled along these networks of diasporic internationalism and the actual experiences of Antiguans and Barbudans who had been members of trade unions in the metropoles that helps us to understand why Citrine's lecture fell on such receptive ears and was able to be such a powerful catalyst.

Citrine's lecture represented the flow of a new type of information along a fifth network: the imperial channels that reflected the impact of a reinvigorated British working-class movement. Thus on many points Citrine's arguments converged not only with what was coming in from the diasporic grapevine, but also with what workers in Antigua and Barbuda were feeling very strongly. In Citrine's political philosophy and also that of the British Labour Party, trade unionism was ideologically framed within the discourse of Fabian or middle-class-directed socialism. This was quite different from the working-class-led socialism of Padmore's and Jones's trade unionism or the racial framing of Garvey's views on trade union organizing.

Thus in addition to deciding for trade unionism there was also the broader question of the larger political philosophy in which it had to be placed. Making this crucial choice would be the third important stage in the development of Bird's own political philosophy. The context in which Bird would make his philosophical choices was clearly that of a lively debate between these three positions of Pan-Africanism, democratic socialism and communism. As we will see, the radical feminism of Claudia Jones did not make it into these circles. Evidence of these competing views can be found in the ATLU's paper, *The Worker's Voice*. Particularly in its editorial columns the paper gave voice to three of these political philosophies and also to the principles of trade unionism.

In the Pan-African tradition, articles and editorials in the paper would critique apartheid and racism, would celebrate the achievements of outstanding individuals of African descent or publish extracts from their writings. Thus, in its January 12, 1949, issue, the paper celebrated the achievements of the African American congressman, William Dawson who became the chairman of a committee in the U.S. House of Representatives. The article took great pride in the fact that he was two generations away from slavery, and that he had worked as a porter to pay his law school tuition at Northwestern University.

In its June 15 issue of the same year, there was an article on Garvey. It said in part: "he was born twenty years before his time. So new and revolutionary were his ideas, that even his own people, the people for whom he suffered imprisonment, disgrace and premature death—even they could not grasp the significance of what he was telling them." There were articles covering the activities of Pan-Africanists such as W. E. B. Du Bois, Paul Robeson, Langston Hughes and Shirley Graham. In short, the Pan-African view was more than adequately represented.

In the January 19, 1949, issue of the paper, there was an editorial, "Why Communism?" by someone writing under the pseudonym of "Benny." He defined communism as the "doctrine that all goods, means of production, etc. should be the property of the community." He then went on to describe it as "a dangerous seed." This description led to the following question: "who is responsible for planting that seed in the heart of the nation?" The reply was indirect but quite clear:

> we do not want communism in the West Indies, but it has been forced down our throats for years now, and we are just on the verge of swallowing, if the situation is not changed. The merchants are amassing all the wealth of the island . . . The Syndicate [Estates] is going around with a few cheap Montserratians . . . in an effort to block every tradesman from work. All these things are sewing the seed of communism in the hearts of starving people.

Seven days later, Benny returned with another editorial reinforcing this position: "every right thinking person will understand that when a man is convinced in himself that he is not being treated right, he has no hope of being treated right . . . What next? Will it stop there? I say a thousand time no. Something is conceived in his heart, and that thing is communism." Thus, like the Pan-African philosophy, the communist one was also given voice.

By far the best represented was the black democratic socialist position. The paper in the 1940s was filled with articles on economic nationalization and other policy moves that were being made by the labor government in England. The June 9, 1949, issue of the paper carried an editorial on nationalization in Antigua and Barbuda:

> Should sugar be nationalised? There are at least two schools of thought: the Liberals feel that each individual should have his opportunity to better himself, that private individuals should be allowed to use their initiative and intelligence to forge ahead if they can . . . It can easily be seen that if only the man with capital decided to pay fair wages and to divide profits equally, all would be well, Unfortunately, it does not work out that way. The few who have try to get more—at the expense of the many—the masses . . . This is where socialism or state ownership

comes in . . . If nationalisation is properly carried out, it would solve all the problems of unequal distribution. Sugar is the chief industry of these islands, and it should be so controlled that everyone gets his rightful share of the proceeds.

However, clearly missing from these debates are the strong feminist influences that were coming from the networks around Claudia Jones. Although many women were encouraged to join the ATLU, the editorials in its paper did not reflect the radical and progressive positions on women's issues as they did on issues of class and race. On the contrary, we can find a number of very regressive positions being taken on issues of gender equality.

Other important contributors to these early philosophical debates were the ethical submissions of L. U. V.; A. W. H. Rock, a distinguished musician; and S. A. Henry. Like Jonathan Edwards and Cotton Mather in the case of early America, these staunch ethicists and philosophers of love as the binding force of political communities would be eclipsed by the more political voices that made power, force and struggle the basis of political community. This was an instance of the basic tension within colonial philosophies with which we began. L. U. V. in particular, developed the good half of the dichotomy that grounded the discourse of bad mindedness. He identified what he called a "cultural lag" that was producing deep divisions and suspicions with the ranks of the union. To counter these destructive tendencies he called for a "cooperative campaign" that would improve relations not only within the union but also the union's relations with capital. The new cooperative exercises in what we can call good mindedness, were to be based on the principle of regarding the other's freedom as we regarded our own. These were the ideas that Bird's colleagues were debating as they were putting the ATLU together.

Not only were these political philosophies intensely debated, they were also very different in spirit from the earlier editorials and articles that appeared in the *Magnet*. A generational gap separated the writers for the *Worker's Voice*, from Harold Wilson, the editor of the *Magnet*. In spite of his trenchant critiques of both the planters and the colonial state, Wilson remained a man of the post-slavery order. In spite of being instrumental in getting both Garvey and Citrine to speak at the Cathedral School room, Wilson never really joined the new socialist wave of working-class insurgency that was occurring all over the world. His individualist outlook blocked him from fully appreciating the power of collective action that was now surging through the region. In his criticism of the government, Wilson was bold and direct. He came out strongly against the Sedition and Undesirable Publications Act, seeing in it "the powers of a dictator." Highly critical of Governor Letham, he wrote: "Sir Gordon has been absent so often from the Colony during his tenure of office that it has gradually been forced on the thoughtful that the services of a Governor could be dispensed with or merged with some other office" (*Antigua Magnet* 1938: 2). This criticism calls to mind Letham's absence during the crisis produced by Stevens's poor handling of the 1940 waterfront strike against Bryson and Company.

Another strong feature of Wilson's journalism was the articles he wrote on the dire living conditions of the poor both in and outside of St. John's. He described the neglect of Garling's Land, Bird's old neighborhood, by the government: "Ovals is, comparatively speaking, new compared to the settlement known as Garling's Land; yet greater attention has been paid to the thoroughfares in the first named area than the latter. Two or three highways on Garling's Land seem to have been completely forgotten by the roadmenders as Sea View Farm's lanes have been" (*Antigua Magnet* 1939: 3). Furthermore, Wilson described what he called "the Bucket Brigade," which was a line of people with buckets between Gray's Farm and Green Bay to transport water due to shortages (*Antigua Magnet* 1939: 2).

But in spite of these consistently sharp portraits of the conditions of the working class, Wilson was unable to see what the writers for *The Worker's Voice* were seeing quite clearly. He could not see that the moment had arrived in which it would be possible to change the order of society through the collective action of the working class. Thus instead of the socialist and communist positions that were being taken in *The Worker's Voice*, he continued to push the liberal line of advance by individual effort and good character that Mathurin had criticized in his editorial on democratic socialism.

From the above available choices of a broader philosophy for his commitment to trade unionism, Bird was clearly drawn to the Fabian or democratic socialism of the British Labour Party and the Pan-Africanism of Garvey. In his *Democracy by Diplomacy*, Ambassador Lionel Hurst noted: "Bird long embraced Marcus Garvey's African-centered philosophy. Bird was sure that his role was to continue the dismantling of the white man's burden" (Hurst 2007: 103). This was the distinct mix of European Left thought and indigenous race discourse that would produce Bird's *creole* political philosophy of black democratic socialism. However, this borrowed Fabian philosophy would have to be revised and reworked to deal with the class and racial realities of political life in Antigua and Barbuda. In particular, the middle-class bias of Fabian socialism, its failure to deal with the race problem, and the high level of state capacity that it presupposed would all turn out to be areas in need of major redress.

Consequently, Bird's early democratic socialism would undergo a series of adjustments and revisions that would force it to go through a number of significant transformations. First, the race issue made Bird's Fabian socialism a black democratic socialism. Second, the limited entrepreneurial capacity of the Antiguan and Barbudan state placed major obstacles in the way of nationalizing the economy. This would eventually lead to compromises that would push Bird's political economy in a state capitalist direction rather than a socialist one. Thus before it could even get off the ground, Bird's black democratic socialism slowly began changing into a political philosophy of black laborism in the context of a capitalist society. Finally, after the break with George Walter, the split in the working class, and the rise of a rival party, the Progressive Labour Movement, partyism or ALPism took precedence over all of these broader political philosophies and also over the trade unionism they were originally designed to frame. In short, Bird's political philosophy was a complex discursive formation that went through four crucial phases: (1) ethical bad mindedness; (2) black democratic socialism; (3) black laborism; and (4) partyism or ALPism.

We have already examined the first of these phases. In the remainder of this chapter we will examine the second and third phases. In chapter 6, we will return to the last of these phases in which all of the philosophical fragments from these earlier periods were clashing rather violently inside of Bird's political party. But for the moment, our focus will be on the initial black democratic socialist phase of Bird's political philosophy, as it was his solution to the crisis of post-slavery Antigua and Barbuda, and thus the philosophy that guided him through the period of his struggle for power. This struggle will be the subject of the next chapter.[2]

As already indicated, Bird was not a writer like Eric Williams or Michael Manley. He was primarily a speaker and a man of action. He was very much at home in the oral traditions of Antigua and Barbuda. Verbatim accounts of his speeches from the 1940s are extremely difficult to find. Hence our reconstruction of his early political philosophy is based on the following sources: the few accounts of his speeches that are available, his dissenting submission to the Soulbury Commission—which was set up to look into the sugar industry in Antigua and Barbuda, a collectively signed memo of the Political Action Committee of the ATLU, and the 1956 manifesto of this committee, which had earlier been transformed into the Antigua Labour Party.

The break with the ban on strikes for the duration of the war was just one of several changes that Bird made upon assuming the leadership of the ATLU. In addition to these and other actions that brought the union more in line with insurrectionary impulses of the masses, Bird hammered out with his colleagues on the executive and on the Political Action Committee, a broad vision of changes in the position of workers and the role of the union in the realization of that vision. This was a black democratic socialist vision, which he shared with a significant number of people on the executive including Novelle Richards and Louis Lockhart—the latter had not long returned from London very much the Fabian socialist. This position though dominant was clearly not the only position that was being taken within the inner life of the union.

The first clear indication of this emerging democratic socialist position can be seen in the 1947 memo that the Political Action Committee of the union wrote to the Secretary of State for the Colonies in preparation for the already noted 1947 meeting in Montego Bay, Jamaica. The memo was signed by V. C. Bird, Bradley Carrot, Hugh Pratt, Samuel James, Ernest Williams, Emmanuel De Suza, Alexis Francis, E. H. Lake, Clarence Christian, Novelle Richards, and Rolston Williams. These were key individuals in Bird's inner circle with whom he shared this emerging black democratic socialist vision.

The memo covered a number of issues that its authors saw as being very important. First and foremost was the national or political status of the English-speaking Caribbean as a whole, including that of Antigua and Barbuda. The memo reiterated their earlier opposition to the policy of "closer union" between the Leeward and Windward Islands. Instead, its authors made the case for a loose federation of all the islands of the English-speaking Caribbean that would be a sovereign state. In other words, a strong regional nationalism was one of the important pillars of Bird's developing political philosophy. The signatories went on to assert that "we feel, and we are sure that you will realize before you leave the forthcoming conference, that we are just as prepared to take over the reigns of Government as Canada was in 1867, Australia in 1900, South Africa in 1909, and India and Burma today" (CO 152/538). Here the nationalist and anticolonialist thrust is unmistakable.

Indeed, the authors rounded out this section of the memo on the national question with a very insightful comment on the federation that they had in mind:

> We beg to point out that the conditions obtaining in these islands indicate the necessity for a loose type of federation rather than a closely knit unit. The long distances, the lack of adequate communications, the differences of tradition and custom—evidenced by the Spanish traditions of Jamaica, the cosmopolitan outlook of Trinidad, the large Indian minority in British Guyana and the ultra-British tendencies of Barbados and Antigua—together with the that strong insular feeling so peculiar to inhabitants of small islands, are factors that must be taken into consideration in any attempt to federate the West Indies. (CO 152/538)

Following closely behind this discussion of the national question was that of the economic question. The writers of the memo began by acknowledging the chronic state of crisis into which the Antiguan and Barbudan economy had fallen. The prime indicator of this crisis-ridden condition was that, unlike St. Kitts, Antigua and Barbuda had become a "grant-in-aid" presidency. In other words, as the memo noted, the island has become "dependent to a great extent on annual grants from the

Mother Country." The primary reason the authors gave for this crisis state was the competition from non-British Caribbean territories in the production of sugar for the British market. Bird and his colleagues were very unhappy with this situation for two reasons. First, it made them feel like "unwelcome burdens on the British taxpayers." Second, this continuous acceptance of gifts was "hardly conducive to that independence and high moral stamina so necessary for self-governing Dominions." The suggested solution to this grant-in-aid problem was "government control of all our staple industries, the majority of which are now in the hands of absentee proprietors, and which is causing a perpetual outward flow of large portions of the resources of the Islands" (CO 152/538). This suggestion clearly contained the beginnings of a state socialist thrust that will be even more fully developed in Bird's minority report to the Soulbury Commission.

This turn toward the state reflected the failure of the planters to make markets work as dynamic engine of growth that could keep the Antiguan and Barbudan economy moving and lift it out of the depression. In their defense of the private privilege of controlling the economy, the planters never made a case based upon their ability to use the market principle to expand or give a new area of growth to the economy. Rather, they made cases on the basis of race and protectionism. This is the profile of a regressive and crisis-ridden private sector that is afraid of the market principles that it is supposed to affirm and live by. This total collapse of private-sector-dominated markets in the face of the poverty and hardships that the masses were experiencing made the state a very attractive option and also the socialist ideas that legitimated its intervention in the economy.

The third major issue that this memo from the Political Action Committee took up was the race question. Along with the previous two, these three social issues usually occupy the foreground of anticolonial philosophies rather than the metaphysics, ethics or epistemology of more settled times. In particular, Bird and his colleagues attempted to bring to the attention of Mr. Creech-Jones the ongoing practice of racial discrimination in the civil service. Without hesitation they wrote: "promotions and appointments are governed by the color of the applicant, his standing in the community, or to any 'Godfather' he may have to say a word in the right quarters for him, than by any ability or qualification that he may possess" (CO 152/538). Racism as a social problem in Antigua and Barbuda was clearly being put on the political agenda for change, along with those of political independence and economic reorganization. It was a rather comprehensive vision for change that clearly indicated the direction in which Bird's political philosophy was developing. It was the black socialist orientation of this memo that separated it from the petitions of the planters and the teachers to the Secretary of State, and also from the editorials of Harold Wilson.

Even more revealing of this political philosophy was Bird's now famous minority report to the Soulbury Commission of March 8, 1949. This commission was appointed on July 7, 1948, by Governor Baldwin and reported its findings in February of 1949. Bird's dissenting opinion created quite a stir both at home and abroad. The report was widely read in the colonial office and garnered very sympathetic responses from the Left circles of the British political establishment. This text is clearly one of Bird's finest pieces of writing. Antiguan economist Vincent Richards said to me that this was "the one piece of writing without which you cannot write this biography." Indeed, it represented the peak of Bird's radicalism.

At the heart of Bird's minority report was the economic question. It expanded upon the Political Action Committee memo as it made a strong case for the nationalization of the sugar industry of Antigua and Barbuda. It is precisely in the arguments leading to this crucial policy position that we can see the influences of the democratic socialist tradition on the evolution of Bird's thinking. The political economy that opens and pervades the whole of Bird's statement to the commission was one regarding the justice of land rights and land use in the context of the economic crisis that was still gripping Antigua and Barbuda. That is, although the 1939–45 war had lifted some countries out of the depression, it did not do the same for Antigua and Barbuda, as distressing poverty remained the lot of the vast majority of the population, even among those who could find gainful employment. It was with this persisting failure of the planter-controlled economy that Bird began his report, and in particular the high levels of unemployment and underemployment to which it gave rise.

On this pressing problem of what today we would call structural unemployment, Bird noted: "Mr. Moody Stuart has repeatedly asserted from the floor of the legislative council that the sugar industry cannot employ all of the people who are in need of work . . . Under the present set up, out of 10,000 available workers, more than half receive no employment from the end of the crop (usually June) to the beginning of the next crop (usually January). Those fortunate enough to be employed are allowed to work only two or three days a week during the six months off season" (CO 152/538/13). This was the unsatisfactory employment outcome that led Bird to raise the question as to whether or not this woefully inadequate outcome justified planter control of so much of the best productive land in Antigua and Barbuda.

Indeed, Bird went on to point out that "to assist those without work during the six months between the crops, the Governor has often had to institute various forms of relief, but these schemes have only given about four weeks relief over the whole period at the prevailing rates" (CO 152/538/13). In short, something beyond these short-term relief programs needed to be done, if these problems of structural unemployment and under-employment were to be resolved.

To go beyond the relief programs of the governor, Bird suggested that the land question be put back on the political agenda. That is, the issue of land rights, what justifies them, land use, and the social obligations that go with them—all of these basic issues of social and political philosophy needed to be re-examined. Bird wrote: "the first decision that must be taken, with due regard to all of the circumstances, is whether the comprehensive well-being of the island can afford to permit the continuation of a situation in which the land, the only source of wealth in the country, is concentrated in the hands of a few landlords to be used as to suit their own economic ends without regard to the economic and social needs of the community as a whole" (CO 152/538/13). This statement made it quite clear that existing patterns of land ownership and distribution had arrived at a point where they were without adequate moral or productive justification. As such illegitimate and under-productive patterns of ownership they constituted "a social problem which can no longer be ignored with impunity" (CO 152/538/13). Here Bird had struck at the core justifications of the planter-ruled post-slavery society as he had been able to sense that it had reached its limits.

However, changing these post-slavery patterns of land rights and land use would be an extremely difficult undertaking, given the intensity of planter resistance. For Bird, this resistant "attitude of the plantation owners is deeply rooted in slavery, and that they are interested, not in seeing the land reorganized for production which will accrue to the benefit of the community of the whole, but actually in opposing and obstructing any arrangement of land ownership which will assist in building up an independent peasantry likely to deprive them of using a large standing body of unemployed, serflike, landless workers to keep down wages with the object of keeping sugar profits up" (CO 152/538/13).

In support of this critique of the planter economy from the perspective of economic and social justice, Bird provided a very detailed and factual account of that economy. Indeed, so engaging was this factual analysis that John Randall, an official in the office of the Secretary of State in London wrote to the Colonial Secretary in St. Johns inquiring about "Bird's material." In this detailed analysis, Bird examined the structure of the Syndicate Estates, the process of centralization and mechanization that they were going through, the reductions in employment, and their ownership of the best lands. He then provided data on peasant land settlement schemes from the government's Land Settlement and Development Board. The primary result of these empirical demonstrations was a picture of stark inequality. This inequality led Bird to suggest the "need for balance between the peasants and the plantations." Consequently, the key question became: how to achieve this vital balance?

It was around this issue of achieving a balance between the peasant and planter classes that Bird made most of his specific recommendations. These recommendations can be summarized as follows: (1) government should limit ownership of land by individuals and corporations; (2) government should seek to acquire some of the lands now owned by the Syndicates Estates; (3) increase the power of the Lands Authority so that it can acquire land; (4) use the Lands Authority to expand peasant land settlement schemes; (5) nationalize the sugar factories; (6) establish alternative industries; and (7) introduce measures to improve industrial relations in Antigua and Barbuda. These were the comprehensive political and economic measures that Bird suggested for dealing with the persistent problems of unemployment and underemployment that still plagued the Antiguan and Barbudan economy after the war. The strong democratic socialist influences on this program of economic change should be very clear in the role that Bird was suggesting that the state should play in the economy.

Needless to say, the most controversial of these recommendations were the proposals for the nationalization of the two sugar factories and for the redefining of property rights. These were challenges to the existing system of private property and the liberal conception of the state that supported these rights in Antigua and Barbuda. However, in the context of a resurgent international working-class movement and the ascendancy of the British welfare state these proposals did not sound strange or too radical. Indeed, Bird's suggestion for the nationalization of the sugar factories represented the addition of another voice on the British Left that had been advocating the nationalization of the sugar industry in the English-speaking Caribbean. Consequently, the real impact of Bird's minority report was to reignite the debate over such an economic policy choice within the office of the Secretary of State, and to put it back on the political agenda.

In response to the Commission and to Bird in particular, the Secretary of State drafted a memo titled "Nationalisation of Leeward Islands Sugar Factories." In this memo he noted: "the trade union leaders in both St. Kitts and Antigua have made it plain by consistent advocacy that they consider that the factories should be nationalised. By implication it appears that they should be able to influence their control and that the workers in the industry would have a greater share in the factories profits" (CO 152/538/13). The Secretary expressed no surprise or shock at the socialist orientation of Bird's proposal. This was because he had heard similar proposals several times before from democratic socialist in parliament and other areas of the British political establishment. However, his response to the Commission's report as a whole was a threefold one.

First, he noted the majority opinion of the Commission, which stated: "there was agreement that the technical efficiency was owed to white capital and managers," and that the majority was wary of tampering with this efficiency. Second, he recalled an earlier (1942) memo written by a Mr. Caine on "The socialisation of the St. Kitts Sugar Industry." Third, after weighing Bird's and Cain's arguments against the efficiency arguments he decided to delay his decision and to hear what others had to say on the matter.

The Caine memo was interesting because of the ways in which it was both similar to and different from Bird's dissenting report. Unlike Bird and Bradshaw, Caine rejected the notion that workers were being exploited in spite of the sizeable profits and the payments to shareholders of the St. Kitts Sugar Factory. Thus worker exploitation was not the basis for his recommendation that the industry should be socialized. Rather, Caine's basis was that "it can perhaps with justice be argued that the original subscribers of the capital put up in 1912 have now had a very reasonable return on their money and that there is no reason why they should continue through all time to draw their present tribute from the island" (CO 152/538/13). In other words, Caine was arguing for a definite value to be placed on the return to the original capital that is used to start any business or to make subsequent expansions. After the owners had realized that exact return, the rights to the subsequent profits of the business would have to be significantly reordered. This was the argument that the Secretary placed right alongside Bird's and over against the white efficiency arguments.

The importance of these commentaries and exchanges around Bird's minority report is that they help us to locate the Fabian socialist turn in his political philosophy. Even though different from Caine's, it was part of a family of ideas about the role of the state in a reorganized economy that challenged capitalist property rights and rules for distributing profits. As such, these ideas questioned the legitimacy, the justice and the morality of British capitalism and of the post-slavery order of society in Antigua and Barbuda. With this socialist turn, Bird was making a number of innovative moves in the tradition of black political leadership. He was clearly joining the post–Booker T. Washington trend established by Du Bois, Harrison, Garvey and others. At the same time, he was moving away from the strong capitalist economic outlook of the Garvey movement, and also from the strict independent peasantist positions of Major Hugh Hole and the masses of insurrectionary peasants. In doing so, Bird was able to bring the insights and solutions of the international working class struggle to bear more directly on the problems of Antigua and Barbuda.

However, as someone deeply influenced by the Garvey movement, the issue of race remained very much on Bird's agenda. Further, the Weston-type vision of a social order of independent peasants coming from the rural masses was also a pressing reality that he had to acknowledge. Juggling all of these competing dimensions of the struggle for liberation was not easy. Indeed, it had become the big metaphysical issue of the day. Nevertheless, it was one of the challenges with which Caribbean leaders were confronted. These were the on-the-ground factors pushing Bird's socialism in a different direction from that of the Fabian tradition.

Further complicating Bird's black democratic socialism was a significant decline in British elite support for it in the colonies as the Cold War between the U.S. and the USSR got underway. Thus there were growing conservative elements in the British political establishment, who, although willing to accept the socialism of their British colleagues, were not prepared to do the same for their colonial subjects. Edward Mathurin made this point very clearly in an editorial in *The Worker's Voice*. "For years now, leaders in the West Indies have come to regard themselves as socialists . . . When Britain's socialists—the Labour Party—came into power there was joy throughout the West Indies . . . Socialism is the answer to our prayers—now we will get. So said the poor deluded 'colonials.' They forgot or did not know one thing: socialism may be an excellent thing for the British people but it is not for export. It is not for the colonies . . . British socialism and colonial socialism are two widely different things" (*The Worker's Voice* 1949: 3).

As time passed the problems of juggling these competing dimensions of the transformative process and the above external pressures on Bird's black democratic socialism would only get worse with no signs of genuine resolution. The gap between British Fabian socialism and Bird's struggling political philosophy would only grow wider. By the mid-1950s, this gap had widened significantly as a result of the pressure from local discursive and political realities on Bird's thinking. This pressure pushed his philosophy in the direction of a more equitable synthesis of democratic socialist ideas with those of Pan-Africanism and those of an order of independent peasants. This synthesis, again not very clearly worked out, can best be described as black laborism as it retained the vision of an empowered working class but without the nationalization of the economy, along with the race issue and the peasant question. The crucial difference separating black laborism from Garveyism and also from more revolutionary forms of socialism was Bird's commitment to a program of state led development as a response to the poverty that was still gripping Antigua and Barbuda. This emphasis on the state as the primary entrepreneurial actor to move the economy forward was the contribution he incorporated from the democratic socialist tradition into this new synthesis of black laborism. At the same time it also meant that the confrontations with the planters would not be revolutionary as in more radical forms of socialism nor would there be the racial separation advocated by Garveyism.

This new political philosophy of black laborism with its emphasis on the national, economic and racial questions was further developed in the 28-page 1956 manifesto of the Antigua Labour Party. The manifesto, which was prepared for the upcoming elections, featured as candidates,

V. C. Bird (St. Johns Rural West), Edmund Hawkins Lake (St. Johns City South and Barbuda), Lionel Hurst (St. Johns City North), Denfield Hurst (St. Johns Rural North and St George), Novelle Richards (St. Johns Rural South), Bradley Carrot (St. Mary), Ernest Williams (St. Paul) and Donald Shepherd (St. Phillip and St. Peter). The manifesto is a collective document that expresses the ideals of the candidates and also reflects the internal life of the party.

The document opens with a preamble that covers the major projects that are being administered by the party. These included arrowroot and cornmeal production, the growing of cotton and pineapples, a peasant land settlement program, and plans for a deep-water harbor. In his comments on this manifesto to the Secretary of State, Governor Blackburne said about the plans for the deep-water harbor: "this is news to me" (CO 152/538). Bird and his colleagues had by this time moved ahead of the Governor demonstrating that they were indeed the real force behind the push out of the depression. These developmental thrusts dominated the manifesto as its primary response to the economic question—having clearly eclipsed the earlier demands for the nationalization of the sugar factory as the primary strategy for economic transformation.

Revealing this growing developmental thrust, the preamble declared: "Antigua has entered a new era in which there are possibilities for the fulfillment of many of our early hopes and aspirations. The developments of the past five years have issued a greater challenge to us—a challenge that exacts sacrifice and the highest capacity of service" (CO 152/538). Here we can sense the easing of the high winds and the lifting of the dark clouds of the Great Depression that hung over Antigua and Barbuda long after they had lifted in other countries. In addition to the above economic projects, the manifesto also pointed to constitutional and other changes in the political system that included the ministerial system of government, and the majority of the seats on the Executive Council being elective rather than nominated. With these changes and the receding of the economic pressure of the depression Bird's democratic socialism was slowly being replaced by his black laborism.

Emphasizing the progress being made on the national question, the manifesto noted: "the developments in our political system of Government have given greater measures of responsibility to our people. In fact, we are on the threshold of internal self-government, which should come in a matter of time and as such we have an obligation to see that the stewardship of Government remains in the hands of those who are imbued with the ideals of charity and brotherhood, equality of opportunity, equal justice under the law, and who will steer the ship of state through troubled seas into a safe anchorage" (CO 152/538). This statement with its reference to the hands that should be guiding the ship of state was clearly a broadside against the planters with whom they were still in competition for the control of state power. On this point of the continuing struggle, the manifesto was very clear: "we intend to press for the removal of the nominated members of the Executive Council so as to bring us in line with other territories with similar or more advanced constitutions. The next stage is full internal self-governance and we hope to attain this standard before long" (CO 152/538).

Although quite muted, the racial and the socialist question were still very present in the manifesto. Clearly in reference to the race question, the writers declared: "the labour party asserts the right to the dignity of man and will not retreat from the course it has pursued to remove the contemptuous status of the workers of Antigua" (CO 152/538). This theme was a continuing one throughout the document, which showed how race and class were inextricably mixed in Bird's political philosophy.

Receding even more rapidly behind the projects of economic development was the socialist question of economic nationalization. As these economic projects required the cooperation and entrepreneurial capabilities of thousands of agricultural workers and a small number of middle-class businessmen, Bird and his colleagues had to accommodate the vision of a social order of independent peasants that was very strong among these workers. This was more immediately within their grasp than the socializing of the Antigua Sugar Factory. Consequently, a very real tension developed between the initial Fabian socialist orientation and the actual economic activities that were taking place on the ground. Further, the more conservative voices in Britain carried the day on the discussions regarding the nationalization of the Caribbean sugar industry. It was under the pressure of these internal and external forces that Bird's black democratic socialism moved more and more in a capitalist direction—becoming a political philosophy that would attempt to center black labor within the framework of a white capitalist economy.

However, at the time of writing this manifesto the ideological commitment to democratic socialism was still very much there. It can be seen in the following statement regarding the upcoming federation of the territories of the English-speaking Caribbean: "federation is going to demand greater efforts and greater vision from all of us. To this end, we support a federated socialist movement throughout the Caribbean so the parties and organizations with aims akin to ours can plan a common programme of activity to enable us politically to pursue the course of welding our peoples spiritually and materially for the forward march against poverty and other economic and social deterrents that stunted our growth in the past" (CO 152/538).

However, this still active commitment to democratic socialism would not last much longer. As we will see in subsequent chapters, this philosophy will fall victim to several forces. The most important of these was the partial nature of Bird's victory over the planters in the struggle for land, the erosion of British Left support for nationalizing the sugar factory, a heavy inflow of foreign capital to the tourist sector, and the splitting of the working class into two rival camps in 1967. As this socialist component receded, its political economy was replaced by that of state capitalism. This in turn produced Bird's philosophy of black laborism as a product of the merging of this new state capitalism with Pan-African discourses on race. The persistence of these Pan-African elements in Bird's thought was clearly visible in his 1960 invitation to the African American opera singer, Marian Anderson, to perform in Antigua and Barbuda after she was barred from singing at Carnegie Hall. It was also evident in Bird's now famous 1967 speech that he gave at the Princess Elizabeth Hall (where the National Archive is now situated) on his visit to Kenya, his meeting with Jomo Kenyetta, and his views on the Mau Mau uprising. There was a clear line of continuity between this talk and the statements on race expressed in the memo of the Political Action Committee, Bird's minority report and the 1956 manifesto of his party. The need for and the continuing importance of fighting for racial liberation is a common thread connecting these statements that are decades apart.

Bird's re-election in 1976 after his defeat at the polls by the Progressive Labour Movement (PLM) in 1971, brought with it the last set of significant changes in his political philosophy. These changes took him in a decidedly conservative direction. As the power of foreign capital in the tourist industry pushed Bird in a capitalist direction, the competition from a strong rival party pushed him in an authoritarian direction. From a philosophical standpoint, it was the emergence of partyism or ALPism that was the big shift produced by the increased political competition. This partyism was a discourse that elevated the party to a position of supremacy and thus deserving of absolute loyalty. Equally absolute had to be the opposition displayed toward its rivals. These rivals, even though former working-class colleagues, now had to be seen through the evil category of the ethical discourse of bad mindedness that was formerly reserved for the planters. This supremacy of the party made it even more important than the union and all that it stood for—in short, it ontologized the party.

The party became the center, the starting point of all political thinking and of all conceptions of political order. Reinforced by the rise of similar thinking in the PLM and later in the United Progressive Party (UPP), partyism eclipsed all other political philosophies. Whether in the form of ALPism, PLMism or UPPism, this rather myopic philosophy came to dominate the ideological and political imaginations of the masses. It was during a major crisis of this partyist period in the ALP that the insider and ghostwriter, Patriot, described the philosophical crisis that had developed within the party. He wrote: "the party has no set of principles which bind its members together. . . . Some have described the party as 'socialist,' others as 'democratic socialist,' and still others as 'conservative.' The ALP has become a party for all men, all things and all seasons. Opportunism rules the roost" (*Antigua and Barbuda Herald* 1986: 7).

As we will see, this making of the electoral and organization imperatives of the party the supreme concern generated the conservative political currents that marked this period. As they got stronger they began to
freeze and consume the insurrectionary creativity of the workers that it
was originally designed to support and cultivate. In this partyist phase,
worker creativity was mesmeratically contained, manipulated and
steered in the direction of middle-class consumption. This is the partyist
condition in which working-class subjectivity and creativity in Antigua
and Barbuda are still trapped today.

These in brief were the major phases and changes in Bird's political
philosophy. As we have seen, it was a journey from ethical bad mindedness to partyism, and on the way making major stops at the stations of
Pan-Africanism, democratic socialism, and black laborism. It was the first
three of these philosophies that guided his struggle against the planters
and the colonial state, while it was the last two that guided his exercise of
power. We turn next to Bird's heroic struggle for economic and political
power against the monopoly of the planters.

NOTES

* First published as "V. C. Bird's Political Philosophy," from *Shouldering Antigua and
Barbuda: The Life of V. C. Bird*, 2nd ed. (London: Hansib, 2010), 77–104.

1. Henry is referring to "Meet V. C. Bird," chapter 1 of *Shouldering Antigua and
Barbuda: The Life of V. C. Bird*, which is not included in this volume [editors].
2. *Ibid.* [editors].

TEN

Philosophy and Antigua/Barbudan Political Culture

In his incendiary "Fan the Flame" column in the *Outlet,* journalist and scholar Tim Hector repeatedly asked a question that I found particularly challenging. That question was the following: "where is our philosophy?" It brought to my attention the postcolonial absence or non-recovery of a Caribbean philosophy that was in sharp contrast to disciplines such as literature, music, history, economics or politics. Compared to these disciplines Hector's point was undeniable. As such, it made clear an intriguing feature of postcolonial cultures: the different rates at which specific disciplines or discourses are able to make their individual recoveries.

Our philosophy has been one of the last disciplines to make its recovery. However, this is not to say that it was literally dead. Rather, it is to say that it remained a subtext in the texts of the disciplines that made earlier recoveries. Today, I am happy to report that Afro-Caribbean philosophy has moved out of this subtextual position and is presently going through a period that can be compared to that of Afro-Caribbean history, literature and economics in the late 1950s and early 1960s. My primary goal in this paper is to examine these developments in Afro-Caribbean philosophy and also some of the ways in which they may be able to contribute to the demands for transformation in Antigua/Barbudan political culture.

The history of Antigua/Barbudan political culture can be divided into three broad periods: (1) a heritage of African monarchism; (2) a colonial plantocratic phase that began in the late 1600s; and (3) a postcolonial proletarian phase that began in the 1930s. The African political heritage was a tradition of constitutional monarchism in which the powers of chiefs and kings were limited by the powers of popular councils. This

political heritage was crushed by the strategy of direct rule, which provided no institutional space for it in the structures of the colonial state
that marked the start of the second period.

The ideological orientation of this second period was based on a philosophy of European imperial right. That is, the European right to rule
Antigua/Barbuda and other territories in the hemisphere. This political
philosophy took the form of a white supremacist liberalism that centered
the interests of agrarian capital, and affirmed the freedom of white Europeans, while marginalizing the interests of labor and negating the freedom and humanity of black Africans. These fundamental principles were
spelled out in a series of legally binding constitutions that both outlined
and established the early political order of Antigua/Barbuda.

The ideological orientation of the third or proletarian period was in
many ways an inverting of the priorities of the second period. The political philosophy of our proletarian tradition has been a black laborism that
has sought to center the interests of workers and to re-establish the humanity, freedom and rights of black Antigua/Barbudans that had been
negated in the second period. This centering of the interests of labor and
the rights of black Antigua/Barbudans was accompanied by the rejection
of white supremacy, the de-centering of the interests of agrarian capital,
and the rejection of the philosophy of European imperial right. Thus the
patterns of political affirmation and negation that marked the third period were quite different from those of the second and also the first. In the
language of Shakespeare, the third period has been the insurrectionary
tradition of Caliban as opposed to the earlier imperial tradition of Prospero.

However, in spite of its definite successes, this proletarian tradition is
now in a state of crisis that has been brought on by a number of factors
such as its own authoritarian tendencies, the upward class mobility of
leaders, the globalization and regionalization of its economic environment, and rapidly changing patterns of gender relations. Dealing with
these issues, particularly in the context of Antigua/Barbuda's continuing
economic dependence, has not been easy. Thus the question arises: how
must the social philosophy of black laborism be expanded and transformed so that it can keep pace with the changes around it and emerge
from its current state of crisis? The primary aim of the philosophical
analysis contained in this paper is to provide a new lens through which
to look at this question.

PHILOSOPHY AS A DISTINCT DISCOURSE

As a distinct discipline, philosophy's area of special interest is not the
economy, the social structure, or the class or gender relations of a society.
Rather, it is the consciousness, and in particular the self-consciousness of

the people of that society. Therefore, we can say that the distinct point of departure of philosophy is the "I" in the phrase, "I am." In the Western philosophical tradition, this "I" has been variously referred to as the ego, the knowing subject, the willing subject or the ethical subject. In the Afro-Caribbean tradition, one of the most distinctive formulations of the "I" of self-consciousness is the Rastafarian one. Phrases such as "I and I friend" point to a formulation that minimizes the concepts of "me" and "mine." The "I" of self-consciousness is a gendered formation as feminists have forced philosophers to admit. Further, self-consciousness is not a fixed or fully formed achievement. Rather, it is, as Wilson Harris insists, a fluid and incomplete formation that is always capable of further growth and awareness (1987: 1). It is through this lens of self-consciousness and its formation that philosophy as a discipline sees and acts upon the world.

The concerns of this self-conscious "I" with its own ultimate foundations have given rise to the subfield of ontology. Its concerns with truth and knowledge production have produced the subfield of epistemology. Similarly, its moral concerns have given birth to the subfield of ethics, while problems in relation to its social order have been the basis for the subfields of social and political philosophy. In short, the discipline of philosophy links the "I" of self-consciousness to a number of distinct subfields that permit the exploring of a variety of possible problems in its formation. Philosophy is not the only discipline that deals with the formation of the human subject. Psychology, literature and other arts also do. In the case of psychology, the focus is more on the emotional make up of the subject. In narrative arts like the folktale, Édouard Glissant suggests that the emphasis is upon accounts of specific events that cannot be generalized into comprehensive pictures. In the novel, the explorations of the "I" are more detailed and do make comprehensive pictures possible (1992: 94). Thus there are important areas of overlap between the novel and philosophy as the latter is also interested in comprehensive portraits. However, in the case of philosophy, these comprehensive accounts are more abstract and conceptual rather than narrative in nature. Thus one of the primary divergences between the two is the different internal orders they have established between narration and conceptualization.

THE AFRICAN ROOTS OF ANTIGUA/BARBUDAN POLITICAL CULTURE

Given the above definition of philosophy, Afro-Caribbean philosophy must therefore be about the "I" of Afro-Caribbean self-consciousness and the ontological, ethical, social, aesthestic, epistemological, and other discourses to which its patterns of formation have given birth (Henry 2000a). Consequently, it must be different from Indo- or Euro-Caribbean philosophies. A Caribbean philosophy would therefore consist of all three and their various mixtures.

The roots of the Afro-Caribbean "I" and hence of Afro-Caribbean philosophy are of pre-colonial West African origin. Very briefly, the precolonial West African conception of a person was a complex unity of several parts that in the case of the Akan of Ghana consisted of the honan or body, the sunsum and the Okra. The sunsum was the rough equivalent of the Western ego, and the Okra that of the Christian soul. Although the sunsum was often unaware of its Okra, the latter was the spiritual foundation of the Akan "I." The Okra is the spark of divinity in all of us. It is the carrier of our destiny and our direct connection to the creator of the universe.

In addition to having this spiritual twin, the Akan saw the susum or the "I" of everyday consciousness as being open to a number of other spiritual influences both good and bad. These spiritual influences were primarily the actions of departed ancestors, nature gods and goddesses, and evil spirits. Therefore, the Akan individual was not a single and closed entity in spite of his/her experience of self as a singular "I." This singularity is an illusion of limited self-consciousness, as one is in reality a twinned or multiple subject who is both embodied and open to a variety of spiritual influences. This Akan individual is also subject to the influence of socio-historical forces, but these were seen as less important. Similar accounts of the West African "I" can be found among the Yoruba of Nigeria and the Fon of Dahomey, ethnic groups that contributed significant numbers to the Afro-Caribbean population.

This spiritual conception of the West African "I" was correlated with an equally spiritual conception of the West African state. For example, the spiritual dimensions of the Akan state can be seen in the symbols that defined its two primary centers of authority: the king or Omanhene, and the queenmother or Ohemmaa. The Omanhene was the earthly representative of the sun god, Nyankopon, and his color was gold. The Okra of the Omanhene was believed to be the recipient of special energies from the sun god, which he in turn passed on to the nation. Because of this important spiritual responsibility, the Omanhene had to perform the weekly ritual of washing his Okra in order to ensure its spiritual receptivity.

The Ohemmaa or queenmother was the representative of the moon goddess, and her color was silver. Embodying the feminine principle of the cosmos, the Ohemmaa was the one who symbolically gave birth to the Akan state. Thus an Akan state could be founded without a king but not without an Ohemmaa. The latter had her own court to which cases involving women could be transferred from the court of the Omanhene.

However, in spite of being spiritually legitimated through their roles as representatives of these gods, there were definite limits on the powers of the Omanhene and the Ohemmaa. Their powers were constrained by an intricate system of checks and balances that Kwame Gyekye has referred to as "proto-democratic" (1997: 115–31). First, the Omanhene and the Ohemmaa were checks on each other's powers. Second, below these two was the Berempon or the Council of Heads of States. This council included the heads of the major states that constituted the Akan Confederacy. The Omanhene would also have to act in concert with the concerns of this council. In addition to the Berempon, each head of state within the Confederacy had to rule in concert with his Mpanyimfo, or council of elders. This council consisted of non-military chiefs of clans or smaller sub-groups within these societies. These chiefs in turn had to rule with the aid of councils of their own in which the voices of the elderly, women and youth had to be represented. It is particularly at this level of the chieftancy that Gyekye sees the proto-democratic elements of the Akan political system. In particular, he calls our attention to the role of these popular councils in the processes by which a chief was enstooled and also those by which he could be destooled. This in brief was the state that corresponded to the spiritually constructed "I" of Akan individuals. It is also the constitutional monarchism of which we spoke earlier, and which Afro-Antiguans attempted to revive with the crowning of King Court in the period before the abortive insurrection of 1736.

AFRO-ANTIGUA/BARBUDAN PHILOSOPHY

In the Caribbean, this West African conception of the "I" has gone through four essential transformations. It has been (1) Christianized, (2) racialized, or more specifically negrified, (3) re-historicized, and (4) re-poeticized. More recently, it has been undergoing two additional transformations: a regendering by Caribbean women and an increasing of its existential awareness through the works of scholars like Lewis Gordon (1995a; 2000). Consequently, the archeology of the Afro-Caribbean self-consciousness has six crucial layers that can be tapped into or unearthed. Christianization and racialization took place within the context of European colonization. Re-historicization and re-poeticization took place within the context of decolonization and nationalist recovery in the late and postcolonial periods. The contemporary Afro-Caribbean subject is the product of these major transformations of the inherited West African "I."

Good examples of the Christianizing of this "I" are Vodou, the Rastafarians, and communities of black Methodists, Anglicans and other Christian denominations. Racialization was most evident in the transformation of Akans, Igbos, Yorubas and other Africans into negroes, a label that identified them by the color of their skin rather than the conceptions of the "I" they used to identify themselves. The re-poeticizing and re-historicizing of this Christianized and racialized West African "I" occurred around the same time, starting in the late nineteenth century. Good examples of the first can be seen in the works of many Afro-Caribbean writers such as Wilson Harris, Sylvia Wynter and George Lamming. Here in Antigua/Barbuda, the results of this poeticist re-inscription can be seen in the works of writers like Jamaica Kincaid, Edgar Lake, Joanne Hillhouse and Althea Prince. Good examples of the second are to be found in the works of Anténor Firmin, Marcus Garvey, C. L. R. James, Frantz Fanon and Elsa Goveia. In Antigua/Barbuda, two significant representatives of this historicist re-inscription of the doubly transformed African "I" have been the black Marxism of Tim Hector and the black laborism described by Novelle Richards and Keithlyn Smith that constitutes the philosophic core of the political culture of party politics in Antigua/Barbuda. Let us look a little closer at these historicist and poeticist re-inscriptions of the subject as they bear more directly on the current crises of Antigua/Barbudan political culture.

NOVELLE RICHARDS AND ANTIGUA/BARBUDAN HISTORICISM

Historicism is a philosophic approach to the "I" of self-consciousness that makes the undertaking of an historical project the primary medium for its formation and development. History and history making are thus vital for the self-consciousness of the human subject. It is through changes in repressive social orders brought about by collective action in support of historical projects that advances in self-consciousness are achieved.

Novelle Richards's *The Struggle and the Conquest* is a short text that outlines the historicist philosophy of black laborism that developed in Antigua/Barbuda in the 1930s. This philosophy inherited and transformed the Pan Africanism of George Weston and Marcus Garvey. Like Pan Africanism, black laborism saw the "I" of Antigua/Barbudan self-consciousness as being essentially an insurrectionary, anticolonial one. Whatever the other faces that it wore sometimes, these were only masks covering that essential core. This image of the Antigua/Barbudan working-class subject emerged from its history of insurrectionary upsurges such as the ones of 1918 and 1939. In the telos of these uprisings, Richards and other black laborists saw solutions to the poverty and unfulfilled lives of this class. For them, the primary solution was the collective organization of the Antigua/Barbudan working class so that it would have legitimate sources of power other than force to change the classist and racist social order established by the ruling planters.

Unlike the Pan Africanists, the chosen mode of collective organization would be a trade union rather than an antiracist organization. In other words, as a mobilizing and organizing strategy, class would be first with race in the background. Consequently, Richards's text is the narrative of the channeling of the insurrectionary drives of the 1939 and 1940 uprisings into the organizational structure of the Antigua Trades and Labour Union (ATLU). As this struggle against the planters progressed, the need for two other organizational structures emerged. These were the political party and the nation-state. Both were crucial if workers were to gain control of state power and use it to change their social and material circumstances. The details of the rise of this union, its affiliated Antigua Labour Party, and the coming to power of V. C. Bird are chronicled by Richards, and are too well known to be repeated here (Henry 1985a: 141–61).

What is important for us in Richards's text is the activist, morally justified, and insurrectionary image of Antigua/Barbudan men and women. They are heroically perceived as a collective force using the stage of history to reorder the class/race and colonial institutions of Antigua/Barbudan society. It is a political and strategic re-historicizing of the "I" with the clear message that historical transformations of oppressive social structures was the way to eliminate the material poverty and limited self-consciousness of this group of colonized subjects.

KEITHLYN SMITH AND ANTIGUA/BARBUDAN HISTORICISM

Keithlyn Smith's, *No Easy Push-o-ver*, continues the historical narration of the rise of black laborism in Antigua/Barbuda and brings it to 1994. The primary focus of this continuation is the story of the rise of a second trade union to better serve the insurrectionary aspirations of the workers. This union was the Antigua Workers Union (AWU) and its affiliated party, the Progressive Labour Movement (PLM). Again, the details of these developments and the rise to power of George Walter are very well known and will not be repeated here (Henry 1985a: 141–61). However, from the standpoint of the insurrectionary view of the Antigua/Barbudan working-class subject, a new dimension was added to the philosophy of black laborism: the rather ambivalent picture of how this insurrectionary subject behaved when in positions of power. Smith described this image as one of "despotic rule" dwelling at the center of all the good efforts to improve the life of the working class. It was as though the latter was being held hostage by the former.

As a result, there emerged two competing organizational expressions of black laborism: the ATLU/ALP and the AWU/PLM versions. The latter saw itself as the more democratic expression of this philosophy and committed itself to the elimination of the despotic tendencies that spoiled the insurrectionary image of the workers and cast such a dark shadow over its major political rival. Apart from this important concern, Smith's account shows very clearly the very high degree to which the AWU/PLM shared the basic principles of the philosophy of black laborism.

TIM HECTOR AND ANTIGUA/BARBUDAN HISTORICISM

Black laborism was not the only form of historicism to emerge in Antigua/Barbuda. Indeed, the black Marxism of Tim Hector was and still is the most extensively elaborated of all Antigua/Barbudan philosophies. Hector's black Marxism shared with Smith and Richards's black laborism the insurrectionary view of the "I" of the Antigua/Barbudan working class. Hector's portrait of this class in his "Fan the Flame" column included not only its own uprisings but also those of its counterparts in other Caribbean islands, including the Haitian revolution.

Hector's differences with black laborism went beyond the issue of despotic tendencies in working-class rule noted by Smith. They extended beyond that to include the form of the collective organization that would best channel the insurrectionary energies of the working class, and to the vision of the new society that should replace the old colonial order.

The type of collective organization, whether a party, union, or small revolutionary group like the ACLM, that Hector thought most appropriate was that of direct democracy. In other words, organizations in which the roles of leaders, delegated representatives, and other governing elites were minimized or ideally eliminated and replaced by the self-organization and popular control of the workers. Like C. L. R. James, Hector saw the high ideal and demanding discipline of the principle of self-organization as crucial for the long-term education, growth and maturation of this recently decolonized class (1976: 4). In spite of his love of books, Hector was convinced that book knowledge was not going to be the primary route to learning and transformation of self-consciousness for the Antigua/Barbudan working class. Rather, it would be self-organized practical activity of an expressive and creative nature that at the same time addressed their pressing material and existential needs.

For Hector, the new society that should replace the colonial order was a socialist one (1983: 27). By that he meant a society with institutions of direct democracy into which the workers could pour their insurrectionary goals and have them returned in organizationally empowered forms. In short, Hector's black Marxism drew inspiration from the works of C. L. R. James, Marx, and Lenin, in contrast to the black laborists who were more influenced by the tradition of Fabian socialism.

These divergences were important concerns that became the markers of significant differences between the ACLM on the one hand, and the ALP and the PLM on the other. But in spite of these important differences, Hector, Smith and Richards shared the historicist re-inscribing of the "I" of the working class in insurrectionary terms. This re-inscription brought with it a greater emphasis on the transformation of social structures through working-class organizations that have been a vital source in the formation of contemporary Antigua/Barbudan political culture. Indeed, the contemporary political culture of Antigua/Barbuda is hard to imagine without the contributions of these three organizations. However, before taking a more critical look at this historicist legacy, we must examine some of the alternative accounts of the "I" by those Antigua/Barbudan writers who have re-poeticized rather than re-historicized our self-consciousness after its negrification and Christianization.

JAMAICA KINCAID AND ANTIGUA/BARBUDAN POETICISM

Unlike historicism, poeticism approaches the transformation of self-consciousness more directly and not indirectly through the transformation of social structures. Its direct focus is on the internal dynamics of our self-formative processes, the conflicts and blockages to which they are subject, and their implications for the order of our society and its transformation. The basic thrust of the poeticist position is that only a new or changed self-consciousness will produce a new society. A divided or conflict-ridden self-consciousness can only produce an equally divided and conflict-ridden society. Thus it is extremely important to pay close attention to the blocks that inhibit our self-formative processes as they are reflected in the nature of our society and the difficulties we experience in changing it.

In the works of Jamaica Kincaid, we find a very comprehensive treatment of the formation of the Afro-Antigua/Barbudan female subject. Kincaid's methodology is the forging of a vital link between the symbolic or cultural dimensions of our self-formative processes and the poetics of the novel. That is, the establishing of analogical parallels between the self-information and the grammar by which figurative devices such as metaphors, plots, allegories, images, analogies are brought together by the writer to produce narrative texts. Kincaid's account of the female Antigua/Barbudan "I" begins with the birth of this self somewhere on the border between the eternity of spirit and earthly life in Antigua/Barbuda. It continues with detailed explorations of life in Antigua/Barbudan society, and also includes the diasporic life of this subject beyond the shores of this society. *At the Bottom of the River* is the text in which the more spiritual phase of this treatment is explored in greatest detail. The heroine of this work is the unnamed daughter who is inseparably twinned with an archetypal mother figure rather than a biological mother. The spirituality of both mother and daughter are evident in the fluid ways in which they move between the corporeal and incorporeal worlds. These movements echo those of African spirituality as well as its conception of the human self as multiple and open to direction from the spiritual realm. This explicit thematizing of the spiritual foundations of the Afro-Antigua/Barbudan female self, together with Kincaid's direct references to the Obeahist traditions of this society, establishes the connection to the African layer of this female self that she is exploring.

In both *Annie John* and *The Autobiography of My Mother*, Kincaid's black female subject has left the more ethereal realms for the more oppressive realities of Antigua/Barbudan society. In *Annie John*, it is the existential possibilities and non-possibilities that exist with the framework of the mother/daughter relationship in this society that Kincaid explores with great skill, insight and mastery. In *The Autobiography*, Kincaid places this mother/daughter relationship more in the background, giving the foreground to the impact of patriarchal and class/race oppression on the self-formation of the main character, Xuela. Her roots are much more working class than those of Annie. Consequently, she shows many more of the injuries of black working-class life. Both Annie and Xuela are female subjects whose self-formative processes have been severely interrupted and blocked. However, the reasons for these blockages are very different. In Annie, it stems from the internal dynamics of the mother/daughter relationship. In Xuela, the sources of her blockage and related bitterness are to found in the patterns of gender and class/race inequality in her society.

The clear message that emerges from this poeticist examination is that the "I" of many women Antigua/Barbuda is fragmented and conflict-ridden below the surface. These cleavages are such that they block the achievement of high levels of self-consciousness, leaving aggression, bad mindedness, and resentment as primary motives for action. To encounter Xuela, is to know bad mindedness, that negative motive so often attributed to each other by Antigua/Barbudans. Like Annie, many migrate, a phase in their lives that Kincaid explores in *Lucy*. Before taking up the implications of this poeticist re-inscription, we must examine the case of the men.

EDGAR LAKE AND ANTIGUA/BARBUDAN POETICISM

A different but also very instructive example of a poeticist re-inscription of the Afro-Antigua/Barbudan "I" of self-consciousness is Edgar Lake's recent novel, *The Devil's Bridge*. Lake embeds his narrative in a continuous flow of breath-taking metaphors that also demonstrate so clearly the constitutive powers of the poetics of the novel. The sustained focus of this visionary and densely symbolic text is the blocked self-formative process of working class Antigua/Barbudan males. Lake's account reinforces Kincaid's portrait of conflict-ridden female subjects that are unable to achieve a relatively stable "I" through which to navigate their way in the world, and be recognized by others. At the narrative level, *The Devil's Bridge* is the story of a band of dancing clowns who, instead of their usual Christmas performances, decide to use the occasion to extort money from the villagers of the countryside.

The roots of these men are in the gritty, competitive and tough world of working-class steel bands such as Hell's Gate, Brute Force and Red Army. They are often in conflict with each other as drives to dominate or to just survive result in attempts to manipulate or control the agency of another. These men are aware of their proletarian situation, but only fleetingly. Thus the narrator says of his group: "we were the salt and tobacco, the cotton and sugar of crumbling empires; now we sought to create our own with these faltering steps, avoiding our own whips and billowing capes and masks" (2004: 34). However, this proletarian self-recognition leads not to insurrectionary but criminal forms of resistance.

In their own Afro-Christian terms, these are "fallen" or "lost" men. They have been forced by the struggle for survival to live on intimate terms with crime and other practices that they know are morally wrong. Lake represents this fallen state as a spiritual turning to a pact with the Devil in order to survive. With the Devil as hero and leader, these men joined his red army of antinomial and anti-social behavior. Having made this turn, these men find it extremely difficult to embrace moral alternatives to the predatory, daredevil, and hell-raising lifestyles that they have adopted. They can only keep repeating these scheming patterns even when they fail. Amidst all of this infernal mayhem, we can certainly find some of the staple negatives of Antigua/Barbuda such as bad mindedness, bad talking and downhousing. Thus, in a very real way this novel is an important exploration of the problem of evil in the "I" of the Antigua/Barbudan working class, and particularly concentrated in that part of St. Johns we call The Bridge, and which Lake will re-poeticize as "The Devil's Bridge."

The clowns are led by the unnamed main character, who is also the narrator. With the aid of the devil, he invokes and speaks through the voice of Harsh Ryder, a dead clown who had deceptively seized control of Red Army. He is thus a twinned rather than a solitary subject, part evil ghost and part working-class Antigua/Barbudan male. Like Ryder, the man whose voice he has taken on, the main character is a predator born of poverty and has been to prison several times for robbery. Further, he extorted not only money from his victims but also "frightful cries" for their lives. He says: "as I felt their pulses of ambition die and forced their dancing feet to a grinding halt, my own appetite grew with each corresponding morsel" (2004: 16).

The journey of this band of twelve clowns from *The Bridge* through the countryside is an allegory of the doomed search of these men for a stable selfhood that hopefully would make unnecessary the heroic pact with the devil. On this journey they go through villages such as Hamilton, Greencastle, Old Road, and Sweets. In each of these villages, the attempts at extortion fail, forcing the band to examine their motives and projects. These failures lead to flashes of insight, moments of conscience, and fleeting possibilities of self-reconciliation, particularly in villages where one of the clowns grew up. But they were unable to grasp these possibilities for self-transformation and thus for saving themselves.

Because of these unresolved existential problems, the laughter, dancing, and artistry of the clowns all became masks that concealed the scheming games these problems necessitated. Consequently, the artistic talents of these clowns were held hostage in very destructive ways to the unresolved material and self-formative needs of these men. In contrast to working class artists or sportsmen like Arnold Prince, Short Shirt, Obstinate or Vivian Richards, the "devil-may-care" ways of these clowns overwhelmed their art and made it into an instrument of predatory survival. As they continued their journey across Antigua behaving as marauding badjohns, the deeper antinomial layers of themselves slowly rose to the surface, pursuing them openly as leprous ghosts. Thus, this doomed journey across the countryside becomes a very ghostly affair reminding one at times of words from that old calypso, Jumbee Jamboree: "back to back, belly to belly/ Ah don't give a damm, Ah, done dead a'ready/ back to back, belly to belly/ it was a jumbee jamboree."

Lake's allegorical account of the "I" of the Afro-Antigua/Barbudan male is a classic example of what I mean by the re-poeticizing of the Afro-Christian version of this center of our self-consciousness. There are important continuities between the Afro-Christian account and Lake's as the themes of evil, the figure of the devil and quest for salvation make clear. The major difference introduced by the poeticists is the challenge that these self-formative problems can be resolved in this earthly life if we took the time to recognize and address them more carefully. Further, they have suggested that without their resolution, postcolonial Antigua/ Barbuda and other Caribbean societies will not find the order, development and nationhood for which they are seeking. Rather, these will continue to be comparatively chaotic societies with large numbers of their citizens migrating.

DOUBLE CONSCIOUSNESS, HISTORICISM AND POETICISM

Now that we have extracted the philosophical subtexts of these influential works, we are in a much better position to see at least the outlines of the philosophical landscape of Antigua/Barbuda. After filling in some more details of these outlines, we will be in a much better position to look at our political culture from a distinctly philosophical perspective. The value of such an exercise is that it should enable us to see things in this culture that we did not see before, and to see in a new light those things that we had already seen. However, before turning to the crisis of contemporary Antigua/Barbudan political culture, we must first attempt to resolve the rather sharp historicist/poeticist opposition that springs from the very foundation of the philosophical perspective that we are offering as a new lens. This is an important detail that must be filled in before we can really use this new philosophical lens.

What are we to make of the two contrasting historicist and poeticist accounts of our self-consciousness offered by the above outlines of Antigua/Barbudan philosophy? Is one false and the other true? Are they complementary and at some deeper level constitute parts of a larger whole? These are still unsettled issues that have been raised by several Caribbean scholars but not given sufficient attention. For example, in Derek Walcott we find some of the strongest arguments for the dominance of the poeticist position over the historicist (1995: 34–48). In Wilson Harris, we find a position that is less polarized but definitely establishes the priority of poeticism. George Lamming, whose poeticism is a very balanced one, has supplied the credo of the poeticists: "the sovereignty of the imagination" (2004). On the other hand, in Marcus Garvey, C. L. R. James, George Padmore, and Eric Williams we find positions in which the value of both is recognized but they clearly give priority to historicism. The issues that are at stake in these positions are, I think, also present in the differences between the Antigua/Barbudan writers examined above. Indeed, I see these unresolved issues as also being important features of our specific philosophical landscape.

My position on this cleavage between Afro-Caribbean historicism and poeticism is that it is indeed very real but that there are deeper levels of our own self-formative process at which they do come together. Hints of this deeper unity can be found in the fact that one is often a clear subtext for the other. In Kincaid's *A Small Place*, the historicist subtext of her fiction is most explicit. In Hector's writing there was a consistent turning to our poeticists as vital supplements in the making of his arguments. In other words, these two seemingly opposed philosophical positions constitute a unity that we have not yet been able to make a living reality. In my view, there are two major obstacles blocking the path to this philosophical unity.

The first is the ontological problem of the ultimate foundations of the Afro-Caribbean "I" that is at the heart of our self-consciousness. For writers like James, Hector, Richards, and Smith, these ontological foundations of the self are rooted in the world- and self-constituting powers of sociohistorical action. For Walcott, Harris, Kincaid and Lake, these foundations are clearly located in the powers to constitute and name reality that come from the poetics of the creative imagination. My contention here is that the real extent of the differences and areas of convergence between these two ontological positions have not been examined as carefully as they should have been. Such an examination, I think, would significantly reduce existing degrees of polarization and divergence between the two.

The second and more difficult obstacle to the unity between the positions of Afro-Caribbean historicism and poeticism is related to the subjective impact of negrification on the African "I" that W. E. B. Du Bois called

double consciousness (1969: 16). With this concept, Du Bois was attempting to thematize a very specific division in both the psyche and the consciousness of the racialized African subject. At the level of the psyche,
racialization produced what Du Bois called a "veil" between the negrified self and the white other. This dividing veil gave rise to a twoness
within the African subject that Du Bois represented by questions such as:
am I a negro or an African? Am I a negro or an American? Can I be both?
Do I have to cease being a negro in order to be Antigua/Barbudan? In
other words, the nature of the negro identity was such a negatively
marked one that it could not be easily brought into a relationship with
any of the modern socio-political identities created by the West. This was
the inner division at the level of the psyche.

In addition to this splitting of the psyche, Du Boisian double consciousness also referred to a splitting of the self-consciousness of the
racialized African subject that divided its ways of knowing itself. In other
words, negrification brought with it "double vision." This double vision
Du Bois analyzed in terms of first and second sight. First sight is the
ability to see one's self through one's own eyes, that is, as an African or
an Afro-Antigua/Barbudan. It is the mode of self-perception that we had
before colonization and negrification. Second sight is the ability to see
one's self through eyes of the white other, that is, as a negro. Consequently, it's a mode of self-perception we acquired after negrification. This
movement from first to second sight was dramatically portrayed in the
scene of the movie *Roots* in which the young Kunta Kinte, after many
beatings, finally answers to the name Toby. To see one's self exclusively
through the eyes of another is to lose true self-consciousness. It is to lose
one's self to a false consciousness. In the context of colonialism, the second sight of seeing one's self only as a negro was a particularly deadly
form of false consciousness as it made one a cooperative partner in his/
her own domination. Instead of identifying with Africa and its diaspora,
such a mentally colonized African will identify or, more precisely, mis-
identify with Europe and be driven to whiten his/her existence. This is
indeed a profound state of loss of true self-consciousness from which
some, like V. S. Naipaul, see no recovery.

But this is not the whole story on second sight. There is also what we
can call potentiated second sight. This is a related but quite different way
of seeing from ordinary second sight. Potentiated second sight is the
result of a double transformation of ordinary second sight. First it takes
the image of the negro not as a true statement about the "I" of the continental or diasporic African, but one about the dehumanizing capabilities
that are embedded in the "will to power" of the imperial European subject. This lived statement on the destructive depths of the European subject is combined with varying degrees of recovery of first sight or the
capacity to see one's self as an African or diasporic African. The combination of these two often produces the effect of an angry awakening from a

nightmare ready to strike at all those responsible for one's negrification and loss of true self-consciousness.

In Antigua/Barbuda, good examples of the recovery of first sight can be seen in the art works of Errol Edwards, Zucan Bandele and Mali Olatunji. First, by answering to African names they are reversing the path traveled by Kunta Kinte. Second, Edwards's carvings, Bandele's dancing, and Olatunji's photography all display an impressive ability to create in distinctively African idioms. The woodist aesthetic that currently informs Olatunji's photography draws directly on African conceptions of the ancestors and is an attempt to portray the vision of those departed ancestors who remain close to earthly life and make their home in trees. Woodism is their way of seeing the world through the wooded textuality of trees. Such recoveries of an African-oriented first sight, have served as one of the two transformations needed for the potentiating of ordinary second sight.

It is the working of these complex dynamics between first, second and potentiated second sight that I think has been the major block to dialogue between Afro-Caribbean historicists and poeticists. The specific complications introduced by the second of these ways of seeing one's self, have made it very difficult, from either the poeticist or the historicist perspective, to grasp simultaneously these two opposing views of the "I" of the negrified African. The poeticist perspective captures very well the African who is trapped or lost in the conflicts, mis-identifications and false consciousness of ordinary second sight. The condition of ordinary second sight illumines quite clearly the life of Kincaid's Xuela and also of Lake's clowns. On the other hand the historicist position captures very well the African subject who is in the awakening state of potentiated second sight and struggling to get out of the nightmare of a negrified and colonized existence. The condition of potentiated second sight illumines quite clearly the lives of the insurrectionary subjects of Hector, Richards and Smith. It is this inability of either of these two philosophical perspectives to grasp simultaneously both halves of our racially divided self-consciousness that has kept them apart and at loggerheads.

This grasping of both halves of this racially induced divide is precisely what Du Bois's theory of double consciousness offers us. Similarly, Fanon's ability to move between these two traditions stemmed from his psychoanalytic and existential readings of this inner divide that arose with negrification. Thus, if we very explicitly insert theories such as these that are able to grasp the receding unity in the racial dualizing of the African self-consciousness, then very important bridges could be established between our poeticist and historicist perspectives. Such insertions would make present the deeper unity that is not visible from within either of these two positions. In helping us to see how and why each of these two philosophies grasps only one side of our racially divided subjectivity, Du Bois's theory can bring us to a better understanding of the difficult communications that have transpired between the two. Each was operating on the basis of a single subject when there was a divided and doubled one before them. With this resolution of the contradictions between the claims of the poeticists and the historicists we now have a more complex and coherent philosophical perspective from which to continue our look at the crisis of Antigua/Barbudan political culture.

ANTIGUA/BARBUDAN POLITICAL CULTURE

As noted earlier, more than any of the above philosophies, black laborism has been the discourse that has guided the rise to power of our proletarian state and its related political culture. At the center of this political culture has been the trade union based political party. Because of the highly restricted nature of the franchise in the second of three major phases in our political history, the independent candidate rather than the political party was the key to elected office. Within the party, the center of de facto, as opposed to de jure, order was the party leader. Indeed, the emotional, charismatic and mesmeratic bonds established between the leader and the members have constituted the foundational core of life in Antigua/Barbudan political parties.

To grasp the importance of this leader/led relationship we must look a little more closely at how the concept of the political leader has been imagined and constructed by us. The political leader is a complex formation that emerges from a mixture of formal definitions and projected meanings. The formal definitions of the party leader are spelled out in the party's constitution. But these de jure definitions tend to take second place to the meanings that party members project onto the leader. In the early years, the party leader was a heroic male figure who embodied the anticolonial and antiracist feelings of the masses and their aspirations for freedom, autonomy and material improvement. He had to be bold, courageous and effective in his commitments to the cause of redistributive justice and social advancement for the working class. To the extent that the masses could project such hopes and feelings onto their leader, these projections were also accompanied by feelings of binding loyalty and unending gratitude for debts that could not be repaid.

Added to these heroic layers of meaning was an additional set that encoded the relationship between leader and led in the categories of parental or kinship discourses. An analogy was established between the authority and life-supporting activities of the leader and those of parents. As a result, many of the feelings party rank and file had toward their parents were transferred to their party leader.

When we pull together these projected components of the conception of a party leader, the portrait was one of a very strong authoritarian male figure who was committed to upsetting the colonial social order that had denied workers freedom, justice and social advancement. The authoritarian dimensions of this heroic leader were also shaped by two additional sources: the model of the colonial governor and that of the traditional African chief, monarch or warlord. All of these are strong authoritarian male figures that have left definite traces on Afro-Antigua/Barbudan conceptions of political leadership.

Given this conception of the party leader, it follows that changing leaders in our political culture has not been an easy or routine task. Because of the intensity of the heroic, parental, monarchical, life-long loyalties and other meanings that we have projected onto our early political leaders, separating from them or replacing them has been particularly difficult. We want them to be there for as long as possible, and experience as ingratitude the ending of their term as leader before they are ready to step down. Thus term limits are not part of our political culture in spite of the abuses of power that have followed directly from leaders being in power too long. This strong attachment to leaders has consistently given rise to destructive factions within parties and to equally destructive patterns of competition and fighting between rival union-based parties.

The importance of this culture that was forged within the confines of our parties is that it provided the basic repertoire of practices and strategies that working-class leaders would bring to the managing of state power and to the building of a national political community. The constructs of the party leader became the basis for the model of the national leader. As party politics was all about class-based redistribution, so also was national politics. As it was difficult to remove party leaders, it was also difficult to remove national leaders. Prime ministers approximated quite closely monarchical conceptions of leaders. Further, regime change (for the opposition) and regime continuity (for the ruling party) have become the conditions for progressive change in Antigua/Barbudan society. Thus the eyes of both citizens and party elites are never far from the next election. This absolutizing of the creative agency of the party and its election to power has been the basis for the emergence of the discourses of partyism within the broader philosophy of black laborism.

As this political culture reached maturity and the heroic actions of the decolonizing period began to recede, there has been a distinct tendency for the heroic dimensions of the leader to be replaced by his ability as patron of an ever expanding patronage machine. This slow but definite transformation of leader and led into patron and client has been the basis for the corruption that became such an integral part of our political culture. To the extent that parties in power gain some measure of control over portions of the economic surplus, there has been a long-term tendency for state investment decisions and development plans to be subordinated to the imperatives of staying in power or winning the next election. This gives rise to short-term horizons and political priorities in the making of important investment decisions. This subjecting of national development to logics of political accumulation represents a political form of surplus extraction whose distortions can be compared to those produced by transfers of economic surplus by metropolitan capital. Given these distorting tendencies, it is not surprising that this political culture and its philosophy of black laborism have entered periods of profound crisis.

In the history of this proletarian phase, two periods of crisis stand out quite sharply. The first was the crisis period of 1967–1971 during which the black laborism of the ALP degenerated into the parliamentary authoritarianism of de facto one-party rule. This was the practice of "despotic rule" about which Keithlyn Smith spoke earlier. Recovery from this first period of crisis came with the formation and rise to power of the PLM. This party not only established a genuine two-party system of governance in Antigua/Barbuda but also attempted to find alternatives to the despotic tendencies of the ALP. However, after a strong start at deepening the democracy of black laborism, the PLM was soon overtaken by the very despotic tendencies that it had set out to reform. It lost power in the elections of 1976 to the ALP, which would remain in power until 2004. In short, its attempts to re-democratize black laborism produced very mixed results.

The second crisis period extended from 1986 to 2004, during which despotic tendencies again overtook the ALP producing a corrupt and authoritarian form of de facto one party rule. The period from 1976 to 2004 was one of successive electoral victories for the ALP against the ACLM, the PLM and the parties that replaced it, the United People's Movement (UPM) and the United Progressive Party (UPP). These victories occurred in spite of growing corruption and the return of despotic rule.

A second attempt at recovery from the despotism that has dogged both versions of black laborism came with the victory of the UPP in the elections of March 2004. Crucial for this victory was the ending of the monopoly that the ALP had on the electronic media by the Observer Radio Station. This has profoundly altered the nature of public debate in our society by creating equal space for voices and views that are different from those of the ruling party. Indeed, it is no exaggeration to say that the ending of this monopoly has been the major recent change in our political culture. It is in this new context of "talk as you like" that the UPP has been attempting to pick up some of the reforms begun by the PLM. Thus the key question that arises at this point is whether or not it will succeed where the PLM failed.

In launching its reform of the ALP's black laborism, the UPP passed very quickly three crucial pieces of legislation: (1) the freedom of information act; (2) the prevention of corruption act; and (3) the integrity in public life act. In addition, the UPP has reintroduced income tax, which had been eliminated by the ALP in 1976, as part of the former's effort to get Antigua/Barbuda's financial house in order. The UPP has also signed agreements with various companies for new investments in the tourist industry.

In spite of these initiatives, the overall response to the first two years of UPP rule has been quite mixed. This has been largely due to too many perceived similarities in policies and practices with the ALP. The practice of victimization, policies toward foreign investors, and UPP responses to what oppositional voices are saying via the media are just some of the factors. This mixed response to the UPP has been quite aptly summed up in the popular phrase, "I voted for change not exchange." Thus at the moment it is not at all clear that the UPP will be able to rid black laborism of the despotic tendencies and economic problems that have repeatedly thrown it into crisis.

In addition to showing these strong signs of sharing the long-standing crisis of black laborism, there is also the feeling that events in the global arena are moving at such a pace that we are not keeping in step and could be falling behind. For example, there are the policies of globalization and regionalization that the Western countries are pursuing. Another is the replacement of UNCTAD by GATT and the WTO as the main forums for international trade negotiations. These changes will liberalize trade and make it more competitive, but it is still not clear what will be Antigua/Barbuda's response to this changing economic environment. In short, from both within and without, black laborism under the leadership of the UPP is swimming against a strong tide.

PHILOSOPHY AND THE CRISIS OF BLACK LABORISM

Given this impasse in the political culture of black laborism, can a unified discursive field of the philosophies of historicism and poeticism be of any help in overcoming its stasis? Can the writings of Lake, Kincaid, Hillhouse, Prince, Hector and others help to restore the insurrectional creativity of black laborism? I definitely think that they can. From a philosophical standpoint, what is striking about the current state of black laborism is that its creative "I," its political center of self-consciousness has been captured and excessively subjected to the internal dynamics and competitive needs of its two organizational vehicles. Further growth in self-consciousness through creative activity has been severely curtailed by the demands for electoral success through competitive and strategic action. This state of capture in which self-consciousness now exists has been further reinforced by the performative crisis of its liberal proletarian state in the context of the neoliberal globalizing of markets. In other words, black laborism is currently caught in a crisis of partyism and statism: that is, the premature freezing and fixing of its sense of the Antigua/Barbudan "I" and its related categories of socio-political understanding around the organizational, financial and ideological resources that its two parties will need in the competition for state power. Indeed, both ALPism and UPPism have equated its party's specific conditions for gaining state power with the fulfillment of the philosophy of black laborism. In both cases, there is a Michelsian type substituting of partyism for the living inner movements of the masses whose insurrectionary intentionality and creativity gave rise to the philosophy of black laborism.

Philosophically speaking, these partyist discourses of ALPism and UPPism have been hardened into ontological absolutes out of strategic necessity. As such they have become primary markers of identities, rigid determinants of self-consciousness, and sources of intense identity-based partisan conflicts, which have severely divided the Antigua/Barbudan working class. With identities and ideologies locked in these polarized partyist constructions, changing or expanding the sense of "I" and its related categories of thought in order to meet changing circumstances has been extremely difficult. Because of its partyist containing of this need for more continuous transformations in the levels and horizons of self-consciousness, black laborism appears, from the philosophical standpoint, as a significant fetter whose grip needs loosening. It is precisely to help in the unsettling of the partyist structure and horizons of the self-consciousness of the rank and file that Afro-Caribbean philosophy is needed if black laborism is to get beyond its current impasse.

The fateful grip that these partyist identities and ideologies have had on the self-consciousness of the working class has been amply demonstrated by the despotic tendencies that overtook the democratic reforms of the PLM, and which now hang over the current attempts by the UPP. In both of these cases, a major impediment to success was the very real entrapment of the self-consciousness of masses and leaders of these parties in the ontologized or absolute versions of PLMism and UPPism. The inhibiting effects of the grip of these partyist discourses have become very evident in the hold that they have secured over the creative imaginations of many calypsonians. This was particularly clear in the calypsos of 2004, which carried all the paralyzing marks of being entrapped in the stalemate generated by the conflicts between the ALP and the UPP. A distinct aesthetic feature of these calypsos was a very flat political realism that was unable to rise above the stalemate or to suggest solutions to issues raised. Consequently, this aesthetic was in sharp contrast to the much more imaginative social realism of the calypsos of King Short Shirt.

From this entrapping of political self-consciousness in partyism, it is easy to grasp many of the ethical shortcomings that have plagued black laborism and continue to do so. The ethics of this philosophy were rooted in two fundamental principles: (1) the moral condemnation of the colonial order of economic exploitation and white racism; and (2) the moral affirmation of redistributive justice and racial equality for the working class and the colonized masses. Although these ethical principles identified the morally blind and selfish motives of European colonizers, it had no clear program for dealing with similar motives within its own ranks. Ethical matters only got worse as party loyalty soon took precedence over the founding ethical principles. This shift fueled rather than controlled selfish and amoral impulses. The growth of the latter impulses was further fed by rising levels of consumerism, which has taken working class self-consciousness in post-insurrectionary and middle-class directions. Consequently, black laborism has had a very difficult time expanding its ethical capabilities in order to deal with the epidemics of greed, corruption, and lust for power that have broken out within its two parties. Such a needed ethical expansion could only have come through a change in self-consciousness that was achieved through qualitative changes in the educative and practical lives of the rank and file.

The current crisis of black laborism can be seen from a different angle through a comparison with Hector's black Marxism or the poeticism of Lake or Kincaid. In contrast to the black laborism outlined by Richards or Smith, Hector's black Marxism, as noted earlier, is easily the most extensively elaborated of all of Antigua/Barbudan political philosophies. This emphasis on discursive elaboration was not a case of writing for writing's sake. On the contrary, it was a case of writing for the sake of self-consciousness. The cultivation of the latter was first priority for the ACLM. This emphasis on conditions that encourage the growth of self-consciousness explains its extensive use of philosophical texts. At the same time, the ACLM is a good example of how the organizational vehicle of a political movement can remain underdeveloped from excessive subjection to the concerns with the cultivating and raising of self-consciousness. In this sense, the ACLM stood in sharp contrast to the ALP, the PLM, or the UPP.

In the case of philosophies such as the poeticism of Lake and Kincaid or Olatunji's woodism, we have primarily aesthetic discourses that for the most part have remained without politically oriented organizational vehicles. Thus there have been no parties attached to them that would make them contenders for state power. Yet, they have important contributions to make to the overcoming of the current crisis of black laborism. The primary concern of these philosophies has been the discursive elaboration of ideas and the exploration of feelings for the sake of raising self-consciousness. However, unlike Hector's black Marxism, the focus is not on the active, insurrectional intentionalities of the working class but on the blocked and inhibited ones that interrupt the further growth of self-consciousness. In other words, they help us to understand the negative factors that limit the scope of our actions and our vision. Thus, in the light of these Antigua/Barbudan philosophies, we are able to see the crisis of black laborism from a very distinct vantage point.

In addition to providing this distinct lens through which to view the crisis of the political culture of black laborism, Afro-Caribbean philosophy can make at least three other important contributions to the resolution of this crisis. First and foremost, the rise of Caribbean philosophy as a distinct discourse suggests that we put on the political agenda the problem of producing the self-knowledge necessary for the liberation of our sense of "I" from its current state of partyist entrapment. The body of self-knowledge that is capable of transforming the architecture of our self-consciousness is one that is able to keep pace with and maintain its autonomy in the context of constant expansions in the production and deployment of technical and organizational knowledge. In my view, there is a direct relationship between the effective use of a given volume of technical/organizational knowledge and the existing level or volume of self-knowledge. A shortage of the latter not only hurts the growth of self-consciousness but also limits our ability to use our technical/organizational knowledge effectively. Thus the first contribution of Caribbean philosophy to the crisis of black laborism is the principle that a change in the volume or social organization of our existing stock of technical/organizational knowledge requires corresponding changes in the stock and organization of self-knowledge. At the present moment, there is a significant imbalance between the two that is making growth in self-consciousness difficult when it is urgently needed.

The second contribution of Caribbean philosophy to the crisis of political laborism is the suggestion that the correcting of this imbalance can begin with the de-absolutizing of the ideologies of ALPism and UPPism. The goal of this de-absolutizing should be to make clear that these two political discourses are ideologies and not confirmed ontologies. As ideologies, ALPism and UPPism need to be recognized and treated as carefully elaborated but provisional accounts of the values, goals and visions of the broader philosophy of black laborism, rather than iron-clad truths to which submission is the only appropriate response. Further, this process of de-ontologizing partyism should make it clear that the real foundation of black laborism is the self-creativity of the masses in its insurrectionary moments. Thus it is this creativity that must be valued and cultivated above all else. It is the source of new beginnings, shifts in directions and other creative transformation demanded by changes in our overall circumstances. This is the creativity of the masses of which James and Hector spoke. It can take many forms, one of which James called "the invading socialist society," suggesting the priority of this creativity of the masses over the specific organizational forms they produce (1972). Thus it is the continued growth in creative capacity that this de-ontologizing exercise must have as its primary goal.

The de-ontologizing of partyism is essentially an exercise in self-critique. Such exercises require the kind of textual and dialogical environment that would facilitate honest discussion and a love of the truth. Such an environment would have to be freer of the pressures of party organization than is presently the case. The processes of exchange, discussion,

reading and writing that this exercise would entail are not to be undertaken for the purpose of creating an intellectual elite within the party, but
for increasing the party's awareness of its deep roots in the self-positing
creativity of the masses in spite of its growing organizational structures
and involvement in the exercise of state power. Such a de-ontologizing of
the discourses of ALPism and UPPism could help to liberate and reinvig-
orate the current state of self-consciousness and prevent it from being
recaptured so totally by its organizational vehicle.

The third important contribution that Caribbean philosophy can make
to the crisis of black laborism is an illumination of the latter's particular
state of double consciousness. As noted earlier, one of the major findings
of Afro-Caribbean philosophy is the subterranean unity of the twinned
philosophies of poeticism and historicism. One has always been implicit
within the other. Yet, as we have seen there have been very strong tendencies for us to seek out one and reject the other. Black laborism with its
emphasis on collective action is clearly rooted in the historicist wing of
this double philosophy. As such it has exhibited strong tendencies to
reject its poeticist half. With the ontologizing of ALPism and UPPism, the
separation from the creative inputs of its poeticist half has increased significantly. The strategic demands of party organization and state administration have largely been responsible for this increased separation. Thus
as forms of historicism, ALPism and UPPism are more deeply cut off
from the creative streams of its poeticist wing than many other forms of
Caribbean historicism. Self-consciousness is here more alienated from its
own spontaneous modes of poetic expression than in the black Marxism
of Hector, Fanon or James. As noted earlier, these poetic modes of expression are particularly sensitive to the blockages in our self-consciousness
that continue to arise from practices of class, race and gender domination.
Such contributions are very necessary if our self-consciousness is to continue to grow and not remain in old conflicts and habits of thought. In
short, a more open embracing of the other (poeticist) half of the philosophy of historicism is vital for the production of the self-knowledge necessary for better balances with the rising volumes of technical/organization-
al knowledge.

A fourth contribution is the providing of a discursive context for examining the ethical dimensions of party life and the interactions between
the parties. As we have already noted, greed, corruption, excessive party
loyalty, and consumerism have overwhelmed the ethical lives of both the
parties and the state. In addition to these, bad mindedness is often seen
by the public as the dominant intention motivating interactions within
and between the parties. Thus there are major ethical problems to be
addressed. First, this popular ethical category of bad mindedness needs
to be more closely examined, so we can know more precisely the nature
of the ethical judgments it performs. One thinks immediately of the Sartrean concept of bad faith that Lewis Gordon has used so effectively in

his analyses of anti-black racism. Second, new ethical ideals for the parties or how to restrain the impulses toward greed and corruption must be discussed. If not, it will be difficult to know exactly where the principles of redistributive justice and racial equality stand today, or what will be their future.

CONCLUSION

Finally, it is important to note that the needed increases in self-knowledge must also come from the contributions of disciplines other than philosophy. Thus the contributions of philosophy that we have outlined above will be most effective when taken as part of a larger interdisciplinary field of self-study for purposes of revealing and reflecting our self-consciousness back to itself, and for keeping it free, creative, and growing. Such an interdisciplinary mirror we can call the field of Antigua/Barbuda studies—a field that would clearly be part of the larger mirror and field of Caribbean studies.

NOTE

* First published as "Philosophy and Antigua/Barbudan Political Culture," *C. L. R. James Journal* 13, no. 1 (2007): 239–64.

ELEVEN

Badminded Nikki

A Review of Joanne Hillhouse's Oh Gad!

Before I get into my close-up on Nikki Baltimore, the main character of this novel, I must say up front that *Oh Gad!* is a major artistic triumph of which all Antiguans and Barbudans can be justly proud. I certainly am delighted by the publication of this novel, and I thoroughly enjoyed reading it. As a work of fiction, it is beautifully written and flows like a river on its way to the sea. The conversations between the characters are well-crafted dialogues, often very sharp, with verbal darts that pierce the thick armors of several of the characters.

Along with being very well written, this is a very Antiguan and Barbudan novel. Hillhouse's fiction bears and reflects the cultural marks and tensions of our society, its patterns of in and out migration and its dependence on metropolitan cities like New York. *Oh Gad!* very artfully encodes in its characters and plot lines rich slices of the culture of Antigua and Barbuda. As the novel unfolds and we meet the characters, we can see ourselves as clearly as if its dramas were projected onto a large screen. We encounter very directly the cultural values, proverbs, practices, and everyday crises that make up life in our twin-island state. Many of the difficulties that challenge her characters, Hillhouse links to slave past and the matrifocal family structure that it has left us. Thus, among the major achievements of this novel is the extent to which the social and cultural life of our society gets woven into its most basic fabric.

A good example of this rich cultural embedding is the title of this work. It is taken from a particular moment in the manufacturing of coal pots and other utensils from clay in the pottery industry of the village of Grays Farm. It is that delicate and fragile moment when something could go terribly wrong in the manufacturing of a clay coal pot. The moment in which it could crack or, worse, fall to the ground. Such were the moments that produced the "frantic exclamation of *Oh Gad!*" and which Hillhouse has made the title of her very Antiguan and Barbudan novel.

Other revealing examples of this rich cultural embedding of characters and actions in the novel are Hillhouse's extensive use of Antiguan and Barbudan proverbs and also of our notions of spirituality. A rather humorous, but significant incorporation of spirituality is in one of Nikki's conversations with her deceased mother, whose grave the daughter visits regularly after return to Antigua and Barbuda. Nikki talks to her mother as though she was alive and able to hear her. Indeed, her mother became her "confessor-confidante" (175). On this particular occasion, Carlene, the Jamaican girlfriend of Nikki's nephew Tones, joined her at the gravesite. Invoking the Jamaican notion of a duppie or the Antiguan image of a Jumbie or ghost, Carlene said to Nikki: "jus wondering what you goin do the day she do answer back. New story! Me never know say that one from foreign can run so. She come down de hill, speed pass the car, pass bus stop everything, run clean ah St. Johns" (177). As a Jamaican, Carlene's presence here also reflects currents patterns of inter-regional migration that have been shaping the postcolonial period in Antigua and Barbuda. This use of the image of the jumbie and of our proverbs made me think of the photographs and aesthetics of Mali Olatunji, whose book of breathtaking images, *The Art of Mali Olatunji: Painterly Photography From Antigua and Barbuda*, is now available.

However, the particular feature of our culture in this work that I will focus on is our notion of bad mindedness. It is an ethical and existential notion that we often use to read human motivations and distinguish good people from bad. Thus, we use it to identify or name social encounters in which we experienced the other person as acting out of spiteful, evasive, deceptive, exploitative or overtly hostile motives. These motivations are unethical because the other person is being used, stereotyped, or degraded in some way, and thus not being treated as an equal or as an end in him or herself. Such bad-minded actions often lead to destructive conflicts that only further complicate or defeat the aims of the individual employing them. My focus on the main character, Nikki, is an effort to explore this theme.

A CHARACTER-DRIVEN NOVEL

In spite of its carefully embedded cultural riches, *Oh Gad!* is a character-driven novel. Its characters are very well developed, clearly delineated, and very artfully kept alive by Hillhouse. There are also a lot of dramatic events—interpersonal conflicts, deaths, pregnancies, and births—that help to keep the novel going. But ultimately, it is the strong female characters—Nikki, Audrey, Mama Vi, and Jazz—that drive *Oh Gad*'s powerful narrative. At the same time that these female characters are strong and assertive, they are very recognizable as being from Antigua and Barbuda. Indeed, this quality is true of all of Hillhouse's major characters, so much so that even when they try they are unable to escape from the lure and hold of their island home.

Of these strong, often tough and well-defended female characters that drive the novel, the most important is clearly Nikki Baltimore. When we first meet her, Nikki is living in New York. However, she is not doing very well. Nikki is working in the basement office of a less-than-profitable nonprofit organization doing various things from fundraising to dealing with tenant complaints. Her personal life is not faring much better. She is estranged and very emotionally removed from her father, who she calls "the professor." He, too, lives in New York. Nikki is even more disconnected from her mother, Mama Vi, who lives in Antigua and is a master of pottery making in the village of Grays Farm. Further, Nikki is living with her boyfriend, Terry, but he is having an affair with a new associate at his firm. Not surprisingly, Nikki is very unhappy. However, she is strikingly unable to understand why or figure a way out of her unhappiness.

This inability to figure a way out of her dilemma brings us to an important feature of several of the novel's female characters that Hillhouse sketches with great skill and sustains very effectively. This feature is the strong need in these characters to have their defenses up at all times. The armor provided by these defenses protects an emotional core, keeping it at a distance from others and thus making it extremely difficult for others to touch or get to know them. At the same time, these defenses also enable these women to evade or put aside issues from their past that they don't want to feel or are unable to deal with at the present time. Consequently, they are also out of touch with their real feelings about important things in their lives. In the case of Nikki, these include the problems in both her personal and professional lives. Because she is out of touch with how she is really feeling, Nikki is unable to formulate a clear response that would enable her to deal with them in more constructive ways. Her feelings about Terry, her father, her mother, and her work are all part of a larger complex of feelings that Nikki is driven to evade and disown. To disown, mask and evade these feelings, she, like several of the other major characters, had to develop this tough exterior, a virtually impenetrable wall that keeps others and herself at a definite distance from this emotional core of troubled feelings and relations. Thus, an opportunity to escape from herself and her social situation in New York would be a welcome gift.

Such an opportunity to further escape her emotional core, Terry, her job and her father came with a phone call from her older sister in Antigua and Barbuda, Audrey. Without warning or preface, Audrey announces very abruptly, "Mama Dead" (1). Audrey is even more well defended, and hence a tougher character than Nikki. Getting beyond Audrey's heavily reinforced armor was just about impossible, and, as we will see, Nikki seldom succeeded in getting past, around or under it. After getting over shock and abruptness of Audrey's phone call, Nikki makes a phone call of her own. She calls her slightly older half-sister, Jazz, who also lives in New York, and persuades Jazz to travel with her to Antigua and Barbuda to attend her mother's funeral. This persuading she does in a rather casual fashion, suggesting that they also make the trip a fun getaway. Nikki and Jazz have the same father, the professor, but different mothers. Leaving Terry behind in New York, the two sisters travel to Antigua and Barbuda, where the dramatic action of the novel will unfold as they meet long-separated relatives.

NIKKI'S COMPULSIVE SELF-EVASION

We have already seen that one of the unmistakable features of Nikki's personality is her defensiveness, her need to keep people at a distance and the related need to disown, evade and not experience how she really feels about a lot of things that are going on in her life. Closely related to this need to evade her emotional core is another very noticeable feature of Nikki as a person: she is unable to formulate, and thus lacks, a positive project of selfhood that would enable her to define more positive goals for herself and to be more proactive on behalf of their realization. In the absence of such a positive projection of self, Nikki's career choices and her involvements in personal relations are the results of external events that have somehow managed to penetrate her self-protective armor, to have gotten under her skin and get some emotions flowing in spite of her need to keep others and the world at bay.

Being made to engage with others in spite of herself is something that Nikki both resents and welcomes. Thus, it should come as no surprise that her responses in situations like these are very ambivalent ones. At the same time, she needs to both push the new person or situation away, and also to give in to the emotions that they have stirred in her. One the one hand, a part of Nikki must resist and put up defenses against such external intrusions and the blocked or denied feelings that they might awaken in her; on the other hand, once some of these emotions are aroused, Nikki is unable to control them. They overwhelm her defenses and surprise her as she had been out of touch with them. In short, Nikki's need to evade and conceal her emotional core from herself and others makes her into a young woman with strong inhibitions on her emotions and who is thus unable to be present in conversations, or to give herself fully to the personal and professional undertakings in which she is involved.

Nikki's self-evasiveness and how it affects her ability to relate honest-ly with others emerges quite clearly in his conversation with her sister, Jazz: "'I wanted to be my own person,' Nikki said. 'But I guess I never decided who that was'" (291). She continues: "There were times when I fantasized about doing nothing, contributing nothing, just being, not any particular shape or color or texture, something impossible to hang on to or to pin down" (291). These sentiments make clear Nikki's inability to formulate a positive project of selfhood, which follows quite naturally from her need to evade so much of her emotional core.

This desire to be "something impossible to pin down" shaped very profoundly Nikki's attitude toward marriage. To Aeden, her love interest toward the end of the novel, Nikki declares: "I dreaded it" (359). This intense dread was elicited by "the impossibility, it seemed, of fitting with someone else, your rhythm with theirs. Sitting down to breakfast with them every day, turning around and always finding them there, sharing a toilet, cleaning the toilet we shared" (359). Nikki's ideal of marriage was "separate lives, separate spaces, uncomplicated but accessible compan-ionship to fill the inevitable loneliness. It was a selfish kind of loving. It was all I thought I was capable of giving. And it was easy, too easy to live with him (Terry) and yet keep myself locked away from him" (359). Here we can see clearly some of the ethical and psychological flaws in Nikki's character that followed directly from her self-evasive and other-exclud-ing behavior. This behavior severely limited how much she could be present in her relationships, how much of herself she could give, and how honest and genuinely forthcoming she could be. These failings are among the first signs of Nikki's bad mindedness.

NIKKI'S SELF-EVASIVE CONVERSATIONS WITH JAZZ

As her inability to fashion a definite identity and the related desire to be something that could not be pinned down had framed Nikki's attitudes toward relationships and marriage, it also shaped and determined the nature of her interactions and conversations with her family members in Antigua and Barbuda, who she had not seen in thirteen years. Because of this absence of a positive project of selfhood that would allow her to reach out to others and to be reached by them, Nikki can only converse with and relate to others negatively. That is she must often evade normal-ly penetrating questions or reinforce existing defensive walls to repel these overtures from friends and family. This negative style of conversing with others is Nikki's stock in trade. Because they occupy such promi-nent places in the novel, I will focus here on her conversations with her sisters Jazz and Audrey.

The first extended conversation between Nikki and Jazz on which we can eavesdrop is the one that followed the call from Audrey announcing the death of Mama Vi. We have noted the rather matter-of-fact manner in which Nikki persuaded Jazz to travel with her to Antigua and Barbuda. She expressed no thought or feeling about the passing of her mother other than her decision to attend the funeral. Jazz, who is a much more open character, is not taken in by Nikki's removed, matter-of-fact attitude toward Mama Vi's passing. Jazz recognizes the inhibited and edited nature of Nikki's response. She knows that there has to be more that Nikki is actually feeling and therefore refuses to let her get away with this clear case of evading her feelings for her mother, and also for the decaying state of her relationship with her live-in boyfriend, Terry.

Reaching out to Nikki, Jazz asks in a soothing tone, "How are you doing?" On the defensive, Nikki blocks Jazz's attempt to reach her with the following reply: "God, Jazz, don't give me 'The Voice'" (4). The latter refers to the tone that Jazz often adopts when she wants to get past Nikki's strong defensive armor. Reinforcing her first evasive move, Nikki then attempts to change the subject by talking about the tickets to Antigua and Barbuda that Terry had already paid for. Jazz again sees through this defensive move and says to Nikki, "Don't do that." Still determined to remains unreached by her sister and good friend, Nikki shoots back with an even more pointed and evasive denial: "Do what?" Standing her ground, Jazz replied, "Don't bury your feelings like you always do." Still refusing to open to her sister and let her know what she is feeling, Nikki replies: "I don't always do anything" (4). This is Nikki at her defensive best, unable to share a substantial part of her emotional core, and therefore must shut out even her sister and best friend.

This negative style of conversing with Jazz is not peculiar to this specific dialogue. On the contrary, it is present in the conversations between these two throughout the novel. To see this, let us eavesdrop on another of their conversations—the one in which Jazz, just before returning to New York, tries to get Nikki to talk to her about why she is staying in Antigua and taking a job as a tourist consultant, which she had been offered to her by Minister Hensen Stephens, who she had only recently met. A smooth, fast-talking politician, Hensen had somehow managed to get under Nikki's defenses and thus, in spite of her armor, was able to get her emotions flowing rather uncontrollably in his direction. The surprising eruption of this relationship revealed one significant way in which Nikki remained vulnerable to some types of individuals, in spite of her carefully mobilized defenses.

Concerned about Nikki's decision to stay in Antigua, Jazz opened the conversation with the following strong statement: "Nikki, this doesn't make any sense" (52). A little further on in the conversation, Nikki countered: "That is just the thing, Jazz. I have not felt much of a yearning for anything." She continued: "But when Hensen opened this door, I could see the possibilities. I mean, what have I done since college? Just rolling along. Maybe it is time I held onto something solid" (54). Jazz could not see what was solid about the job and remained convinced that Nikki was hiding even from herself the real motives behind her decision to stay in Antigua and Barbuda. "I am not getting it," she said to Nikki. Getting even more defensive, Nikki refused to budge. She went silent on Jazz and then closed the conversation: "I am on the fence, she said inadequately. This is the way I choose to jump" (55).

From the above, the similarity between the patterns of self-evasion and keeping Jazz at bay in this conversation and the previous one should be clear. A rather sharp contrast to Nikki, Jazz is clearly the more open of the two and is without the heavy armor guarding her emotional core that her sister wears. Jazz is the one who is always trying to reach out, to get Nikki to face herself and to share herself. But Nikki remains unable to be emotionally present and thus, unable to share. Her defenses are stronger than Jazz's gestures of reaching out, touching and engaging. Consequently, Nikki is unable to converse with Jazz in good faith. This need to be absent, to be unavailable and to conceal her emotional core is the source of Nikki's dishonesty, her bad mindedness in her relationship with Jazz.

NIKKI AND AUDREY

Abruptness, the firing of fast-moving verbal darts, and their instant repelling by strong defensive armors are the patterns that characterize the interactions and conversations between Nikki and Audrey. In contrast to her exchanges with Jazz, Nikki is consistently the one who is overpowered and pushed away in her conversations with Audrey. The latter sister is clearly the one with the stronger armor, and is significantly more bad minded than Nikki. In addition to being even more self-evasive than Nikki, Audrey often acts out of feelings of resentment and spite. She also projects much greater images of strength, toughness and aggressiveness. Hillhouse tells us that Audrey "was tall like Mama Vi, but also thick" (15). These features all help to make Audrey a powerful portrait of what Antiguans and Barbudans mean by bad mindedness. Indeed, Nikki is quite intimidated by Audrey's bad mindedness for which her own is no match. The evasive practices that worked so successfully with Jazz will fail miserably in Nikki's exchanges with Audrey.

We already caught a glimpse of the commanding image of dominance projected by Audrey in the terse and abrupt manner in which she told Nikki the news of Mama Vi's death. It left the very quick and capable Nikki without her usual counter punches. The first meeting between the two sisters occurs when Nikki and Jazz arrive at the family home in Grays Farm after settling in at their hotel. At this home they meet long-separated brothers and sisters, nieces and nephews. Audrey arrived at the house shortly after the two sisters from New York. She has only two words for Nikki: "You reach" (15). Hillhouse tells us that Nikki's stomach tightened in response to the impulses behind those two words. Regaining a measure of composure, Nikki attempted to introduce Jazz and to explain to Audrey that she was just about to fix something to eat, as it was lunchtime. Audrey does not acknowledge Nikki's attempt to introduce Jazz, dismisses her attempts at lunch, and proceeds to take complete control of the kitchen. In making these moves, Audrey has very effectively out-maneuvered Nikki and put her in her place both emotionally and physically. In Audrey's emotional world Nikki belonged at a distance and physically she was to be out of what is clearly Audrey's kitchen. Bad mindedness pervades the very fabric of this conflicted relationship, which is driven by Audrey's resentment and sustained by the self-evasive needs of both women.

After the above initial encounter, Nikki avoided Audrey. The next time they met was at the Christening of Carlene's son, Toni. At the church, Hillhouse tells us, "No words were exchanged between Nikki and Audrey" (107). However, at the party that Audrey organized the older and bigger of the two sisters took it upon herself to announce her displeasure at Nikki's now romantic relationship with Minister Hensen Stephens, and to warn her about him. In her often terse and abrupt manner of speaking, Audrey noted: "So, is like that now" (108), referring to the fact that Nikki had arrived with Hensen Stevens. Feeling intimidated, Nikki could only say, "What?" To this Audrey replied very directly: "The boy Stevens, what he hanging 'round here for? . . . Is you he sniffing 'round? Is that you come back here for?" (108). This addition of acerbic distrust to disapproval left Nikki again with only one word, "What?" In short, as Hillhouse tells us, Nikki was speechless.

Even more telling is Nikki's next encounter with Audrey. It began with a voicemail from Audrey on Nikki's phone: "This is Audrey; give me a call" (157). Nikki was terrified by the message and did not call back right away. However, in the meantime, her brother, Fonso called to let her know that Tones was in the hospital, and that he had been in an accident. Figuring that this was the reason for Audrey's call, Nikki got to the hospital as soon as she could. At the hospital, as at the church, no words were exchanged between Audrey and Nikki.

Just as revealing is a later encounter between the two when Nikki is visiting the family home with the hope of seeing Carlene, but encounters Audrey. "You can wait, if you want" (170), was Audrey's way of greeting Nikki. But not long after, Audrey spoke again: "So you working with Kendrick Cameron now, I hear" (170). Nikki did not want to speak, as she would have to get into her public and embarrassing breakup with Minister Hensen. It was a major part of the reason why she was now working for Kendrick. After all, Audrey had warned her about him. But the older sister had a very different concern on her mind that surprised Nikki: "That Blackman Valley project is trouble" (171). This was a tourist development project that would require the converting of agricultural land in the Grays Farm area that Nikki was now working on with Kendrick. Upstaged and forced once again on the defensive by Audrey's savvy aggressiveness, Nikki could only reply: "How do you know about that?" (171). Without missing a beat, Audrey counters: "Is Antigua this, new travels fast" (171). Able to muster only a weak response, Nikki replies: "my business is not your business." With more sting on her tongue, Audrey counters: "one thing I know 'bout life, though: picknee who na hear wha dem mooma say drink pepper water, lime and salt" (171).

This dart from Audrey had more pepper water, lime and salt in it than the saying itself. It took just about everything out of Nikki's counter punches, leaving her almost speechless once again. Audrey was not interested in getting Nikki to face her suppressed feelings, she was not giving her "The Voice" in the way Jazz would. Rather, she is interested in maintaining a position of dominance that she inherited with the passing of Mama Vi. In striving to maintain this sense of self, Audrey is more determined, ruthless and bad minded than Nikki in her efforts to be something that cannot be overthrown and pinned down. Audrey is female "macha" and female "bravado" all rolled into one bad minded character.

HILLHOUSE AND THE TRADITION OF ETHICAL BAD MINDEDNESS

From the foregoing sections, it should be clear that in Nikki Baltimore, Hillhouse has undoubtedly created a highly original character. Nikki will easily find her distinct place within the Antiguan/Caribbean cast of great literary characters. The greatness of Hillhouse's fictional achievement here is the authenticity, distinctness and depth of Nikki's bad mindedness while at the same time making this lead character capable of reflecting a lot of the very real social issues impacting the lives of Antiguan and Barbudan women of working-class origins.

Because of the significant ways in which Nikki reflects the broader social context of family and immigrant life, she calls to mind a number of other original and well-developed female characters in Antiguan and Caribbean literature. The intensity and persistence of her evasiveness made me think of female characters in the novels of Jamaica Kincaid, Althea Prince, and Edwidge Danticat. For example, the character Xuela, in Kincaid's *The Autobiography of My Mother*, is a woman whose motivations for acting are overwhelmingly negative. Indeed, she is much more bad minded than Nikki, and is closer to Audrey. Kincaid also makes extensive use of the notion of bad mindedness in her latest (2012) novel, *See Now Then*. It is the lens through which the main character, Mrs. Sweet, sees the hateful motivations of her husband as their marriage is breaking up.

Of course, all of Hillhouse's talk about Grays Farm and Mama made me think of Monica Matthew's moving memoir, *Journeycakes*. In Edgar Lake's *The Devil's Bridge*, we can see the forms that bad mindedness has taken in the lives of Antiguan and Barbudan men of working-class origin. Lake's main character, Harsh Ryder, is particularly revealing with regard to actions motivated by feelings of resentment, and desires to deceive and exploit others. When we compare Nikki to these characters, and to Audrey, it should be clear that hers is a mild case of bad mindedness, driven primarily by her need to evade and hide from others large portions of what she is really feeling. This inability to be emotionally present forces her to lie, to be deceptive to those she is in relationships with, and thus to ethically compromise herself.

At the same time, much of the suspense and sense of drama that lifts from the pages of *Oh Gad!* turns on whether or not Nikki will be able to get past her defensiveness, open up to family, friends, and lovers, and thus find her way to a more fulfilling life. However, this dependence of the novel's dramatic tension on Nikki's fate raises important questions regarding the relationship between the art of fiction and the demands of surrounding social reality. From the perspective of creating and sustaining the dramatic tension of this novel it is clearly more engaging to have Nikki keep her defenses up and thus to continue creating their associated mini dramas. On the other hand, if we look at Nikki as a social type, and thus a window into the lives of real Antiguan and Barbudan women of working-class origin in our postcolonial period, then it should be most instructive to address the possible resolution of Nikki's bad mindedness. By exploring the possibilities of such a resolution, she could become a light or a guide to other women struggling with similar issues of evasiveness or other forms of bad mindedness. On this dilemma of the right or appropriate balance between art and social reality, I think that Hillhouse's fictional or compositional strategy is one that falls between these two important positions, but with a definite lean toward the aesthetic and dramatic demands of her novel. As a sociologist, my interests lean in the opposite direction—toward the resolution of Nikki's bad mindedness and its significance for other men and women. So let us see what Hillhouse has to say about this sociological aspect of her novel.

If Nikki's bad mindedness means that she is not or cannot be emotionally present in conversations, relationships and work projects, then where is she? What is she doing? What is preoccupying her and thus making it difficult for her to be available in the present moment? Artfully addressing this issue of Nikki's emotional absence as a living social issue, Hillhouse suggests that she is preoccupied with and distracted by unresolved conflicts, fears, doubts and pains from fissures and breaks in her earlier relations with her family. In other words, Nikki is emotionally trapped in the past and thus is unable to fully participate in her present as a young adult. Her evasiveness, her need to conceal her emotional core—the sources of her bad mindedness—have their roots in unresolved conflicts from her childhood. The blocking effects of these unresolved conflicts compromise Nikki's relationships, her conversations and her professional performances.

Getting a little more specific, Hillhouse hints at and makes repeated references to severe economic pressures within the matrifocal families of the Antiguan and Barbudan working class. This is a family structure that the laboring men and women of Antigua and Barbuda inherited from the period of our enslavement by Europe. In particular, Hillhouse hints that this combination of economic poverty and a matrifocal family structure has produced the phenomenon of itinerant or absent fathers, and mothers who have to be strong because they also have to father the children. Referring to her own mother, Mama Vi says: "Mama bring us up hard, to make sure we have the mettle. Beat you like you name donkey so that when life fire it blows an' dem is like mosquito bite" (183). Reinforcing this image of the difficulties of life within working-class families, Hillhouse has "the Professor" report the following observation in his field notes: "That was a constant of life in the former slave societies of the 'new' world, not only this little island in the Caribbean—the transient male, the stable female family head, generations of women, men with many families. A legacy of slavery, a twisted version of the polygamy practiced in Africa, a bastardized hybrid of the two" (183). Jazz, who is the furthest removed these poor economic conditions in matrifocal families, is the least bad minded of all, the most open, the most capable of being emotionally present, and of acting in good faith.

The above insights that we glean from these sociological aspects of the novel suggest that within these economically strapped families too often many of the children did not get the emotional support and sense of solidarity that they needed to have with both of their parents. These broken family ties often left their growing members with real feelings of incapability, inferiority, insecurity and resentment, which they must either conceal or act out. Both of these responses lead to practices of bad mindedness, which will make it difficult for them to be fully present in the adult phases of their lives.

Reinforcing this hint that bad mindedness is connected to family ties that were broken in childhood is the fact that in the second half of the novel, Hillhouse has Nikki attempting to repair the broken relations with her mother. This the latter does through regular visits to Mama Vi's grave, where she talks to her as though she were alive and letting some of those long-repressed feeling from her childhood flow. Similarly, Nikki also begins the process of reconciling with her father through the close reading of journals that he had given her from his years of doing ethnographic fieldwork in Antigua and also of knowing Mama Vi.

But, in spite of these very real efforts at reconciliation, of pulling together the broken pieces of her childhood family life, Hillhouse still does not allow for any major degree of change in Nikki's need for bad minded practices. Her evasiveness remains the most striking feature of her personality and a major source of dramatic tension right up to the end. Thus in the relationship with her new lover, Aeden, Nikki remains just as evasive and off-putting. Consequently, Hillhouse leaves it up to the reader to imagine Nikki's life in the years ahead. Besides the need to sustain the dramatic tension of the novel, this lack of change in Nikki could also be an indication of how difficult Hillhouse sees the challenge of uprooting these personality inheritances of bad mindedness. Which of these interpretations is the correct one is yet another question that Hillhouse leaves the reader of *Oh Gad!* to decide for him or herself.

NOTE

* First published as "Badminded Nikki: A Review of Joanne Hillhouse's *Oh Gad!*" *Antigua and Barbuda Review of Books*.

TWELVE

The Socialist Legacy of Tim Hector

Since the turn of the 20th century, Caribbean people have been thinking of the economic transformation of their colonial societies through two primary lenses: those of capitalism and socialism. The former was seen as a modernization of the plantation capitalism of the colonial era. The latter was viewed as an alternative to these two forms of capitalism. Antigua and Barbuda has been an integral part of this tradition of seeing itself, and the larger region, as being located between these two alternative poles of capitalism and socialism. However, since the closing decade of the 20th century, the socialist alternative in the region and abroad has been in a state of steep decline and collapse. Since the close of the first decade of the 21st century, the capitalist alternative, after gathering new strength through strategies of neoliberal globalization, is still in the process of recovering from a major financial meltdown that has come to be known as the Great Recession of 2008. It is the convergence between these two formerly alternative systems that followed their periods of crisis, which defines the current conjuncture that we are muddling through. The focus of this paper is on the impact of this ambiguous conjuncture on the Antiguan and Barbuda Left, and in particular the socialist legacy that it inherited from Tim Hector.

When I think of the socialist legacy of the Caribbean, I think of the revolutionary socialism of George Padmore, Hubert Harrison, C. L. R. James, Cyril Briggs, Claudia Jones, W. A. Domingo and others. This part of the legacy was forged in Caribbean diasporic communities in the early decades of the twentieth century. I also think of the Fabian or democratic socialism of Norman Manley, Eric Williams, V. C. Bird, McChesney George, Novelle Richards, and others, which these individuals attempted to implement in the middle decades of the twentieth century. Tim Hector's place in this legacy of Caribbean socialism was his central role in reviving the revolutionary socialism of C. L. R. James in the 1960s, which came to be known as the Caribbean New Left. Thus in the political history of Antigua and Barbuda, two types of socialism have taken root: first, a black democratic socialism that was introduced by V. C. Bird and others in the Antigua Trades and Labour Union (Henry 2009a); and second, a Jamesian socialist tradition that was introduced by Tim Hector and the Antigua Caribbean Liberation Movement (ACLM).

Like many other territories in the region, the birth of this Jamesian or Caribbean New Left tradition of socialism in Antigua and Barbuda was triggered by the imploding of the earlier Fabian tradition, under the weight of its internal contradictions and limitations. These performative difficulties resulted in a series of gradual moves toward forms of foreign-dominated state capitalism as solutions to the crisis tendencies of Caribbean Fabian socialism. In addition to not clearly articulating the nature of these crisis tendencies, these particular state capitalist solutions, Antigua and Barbuda included, reinforced white economic control without solving problems of high unemployment, poverty, and racial inequality that were leftovers from the colonial period.

Consequently, the intellectual and political challenge to the Caribbean New Left was a new formulation of the socialist project and a political practice by which it could be implemented. Hector made this clear in his review of my book, *Peripheral Capitalism and Underdevelopment in Antigua*: "it is for this reason that ACLM exists, called up by history to remove a century old blockage" (1985: 7). Both the objective and subjective conditions for such a reformulation were present. The strength of the dissatisfaction with the receding colonial order was still very palpable in the hearts and minds of many in Antigua and Barbuda—and across the Caribbean. Also very palpable was the growing feeling that the desired national development was moving further away rather than closer under the leadership of the post-independence regimes. In other words, there was a widening gap between popular projections of self into the future and where national development was going with the state capitalist turn.

In response to these objective and subjective conditions, individuals on the Left in Antigua and Barbuda began producing "black power" or "black nationalist" critiques of V. C. Bird's tourism-centered state capitalist response to the crises of his earlier black democratic socialism. Individuals such as Barry Stevens, Mali Olatunji, and Lestroy Merchant began criticizing what they perceived to be its unsatisfactory cultural ethos, its racial attitudes and anti-worker biases and practices. Many from this group joined together and organized themselves into a co-operative, the Outlet Co-operative Venture. Their primary goal was to produce the journal, *Outlet*, and to further articulate their views of an alternative to Bird's state capitalism. In the co-operative spirit, articles were written more often by a collective "We," than they were individually authored. But in the leadership were clearly Barry Stevens, Lestroy Merchant, Everett Christian and Fitzroy Christian.

What was most striking about the group's alternative vision were its roots in the long co-operative tradition of Antigua and Barbuda and the wider Caribbean. This was a co-operative tradition with roots in West Africa, which was revived during the post-slavery period. It is also important to note here that this was also the economic tradition that V. C. Bird drew on in his initial black democratic socialist alternative to colonial capitalism. In explaining their return to the co-operative tradition, the Outlet group wrote: "a co-operative is owned by those who use it. Its purpose is to provide SAVINGS not profits. It differs from commercial enterprise in that the aim is not to get the highest possible remuneration for capital but to SERVE THE INTEREST OF ITS MEMBERS" (1969: 1).

Out of this body of co-operative ideas, the Outlet group argued for developing a strong co-operative sector for the Antiguan and Barbudan economy: "time and again, the need for co-operation and the institution of co-operative business in Black Communities to establish a balance to the private business as far as the people are concerned has been stressed . . . We have suggested before and we suggest again that we all look to co-operatives for we believe therein lies our salvation, our freedom from the exploitation of the masses" (1969: 1). In contrast to firms in the capitalist sector, the Outlet group saw the co-operative as "an institution with human aims and spiritual goals" (1969: 2). However, they did not see this co-operative sector as replacing the capitalist sector. Rather, they saw it as "a counterforce to monopolistic practices" coming from both the state and private sectors. In short, their alternative view of the economy was a three sector one, which as we will see was quite similar to Bird's original black democratic socialism. The Outlet Co-operative then did a critique of the tourist industry in Antigua and Barbuda, and went on to list a number of enterprises that had been co-operatively organized. These included banks, credit unions, agricultural marketing, grocery stores, housing and health services.

TIM HECTOR AND THE OUTLET CO-OPERATIVE

From the above, it should be clear that before Hector's 1967 return to Antigua and Barbuda from studying in Canada, the foundations of a black co-operative critique of Bird's state capitalism were being laid. It was coming from deep within the political imaginations of members of the middle and lower strata of Antiguan and Barbudan society. In spite of being only partially formulated, its similarity in broad outline with Bird's original black democratic socialism point to some of the well-established categories and ideals of the popular political imagination. After joining the Outlet Co-operative, Hector quickly ascended to the position of leader. His major contribution as leader was to give this emerging black co-operative alternative a more rigorous and comprehensive socialist reformulation. This he did by recasting it within the categorical framework of the Jamesian tradition of socialism (Henry 1992d: 239–50).

For James, socialism was first and foremost the popular institutionalizing of the creative visions and projected alternatives of the future produced by the masses of the people. The creative responses of workers to their laboring condition, their oppositional projections of self in response to their de-humanization are the foundations of his socialism. Its primary aim is to find the answers and alternatives to the problems of this class that are embedded in these creative visions and self-projections. For James, the latter were the textual foundations of socialism. For Hector, socialism was "the institutionalization of people's power, over production and politics" (1978: 3). It was in this Jamesian spirit that Hector read these initial articulations that were coming out of the Outlet Co-operative, and thus saw them as indicators and barometers of the political sentiments in large segments of the population. The Jamesian recasting provided by Hector changed significantly the political economy of the black co-operative alternative.

In filling out its political dimensions, Hector reframed them in terms of more direct forms of democracy that would give the people much greater control over elected representatives and much more active involvement in the day to day affairs of the state. The people would be organized in assemblies or popular councils. These councils would have the power to recall representatives, and to intervene effectively in cases of misrepresentation by elected officials. In other words, Hector proposed a system of government in which real power was located in popular councils as the alternative to the parliamentary system of representative government in which elected officials often abused the power and trust given to them by the masses.

The economic dimensions of the black co-operative alternative were refashioned along similar lines. The earlier three-sector model remained the core of Hector's economy. This was going to be a national economy, but not one in which huge government bureaucracies controlled everything. Rather, it was going to be a national economy in which there would be "the direct voice of the people in the organization and development of every major enterprise that is the property of the nation" (1978: 3). At the center of this popular involvement in the economy must be the working class, as dominant agent and major entrepreneur.

In the state sector there would be a planning committee, "made up of technicians, workers and farmers" (1978: 3). However, this was definitely not going to be a centrally planned economy. The goal of this planning was to launch and coordinate the transition from the neocolonial/tourist economy to the new national economy and how this state sector would relate concretely to the private and co-operative sectors. However, in both the co-operative and state sectors, assemblies or popular council models of governance would be introduced. For example, "ACLM will organize large co-operatives on government agricultural land, with state farms in each zone to give support and technical guidance to each co-operative" (1978: 3). To further support these co-operatives, an Agricultural and Savings Bank would also be established, as well as a co-operatively run marketing company.

In the area of industrial development, the ACLM's plan was "to establish industries, manufacturing industries, which have a direct linkage with primary production in Antigua, e.g. textiles, food processing, pottery, etc. These agro-industries would be located in rural areas, to reverse the steady drift toward the capital and thus avoid the insoluble problems created by that drift. In the commercial sector, the planning committee would encourage the formation of worker controlled co-operative import-export enterprises with some state owned ones to support and guide them as in the case of the agricultural co-operatives" (1978: 3). Through these linkages between agriculture, manufacturing and commerce, the ACLM hoped to eliminate unemployment even if it required the imposing of an unemployment levy. To further support workers and farmers in these productive and political ventures, Hector called for significant expansions in the educational and training opportunities available to the members of these classes. Drawing on the work of Caribbean economist, Sir Arthur Lewis, he called for an appropriate set of agricultural and technical institutes to support the productive activities of the masses in Antigua and Barbuda (1977: 6).

Thus workers and farmers, through their assemblies, would be in charge of significant areas of production, making key decisions, regarding output, wages, benefits, unemployment, and the distribution of the surplus and its investment. Indeed, these were the councils or assemblies that would in most cases also have the power to recall poorly performing political representatives from state offices. Thus Hector's critique of Libya's experiment with direct democracy was that its assemblies were "not based on production, but on residence" (1982: 9). For Hector, socialism was the unity of working people organized in associations of co-operative producers, which clearly established the control of workers over both politics and economics.

From the Jamesian standpoint, a key question arises here: how accurate was this socialist formulation as an interpretation of the creative responses and oppositional self-projections of the workers and farmers of Antigua and Barbuda? It certainly was an insightful and plausible reading of these popular political sentiments, and a brilliant formulation of them into a plan of social transformation. But given the fallibility of all interpretative readings, it is by the effectiveness of its practice and the response of workers to it that we must judge this reading. Looked at in the light of its practice, this initial model went through a number of changes, which suggest that it might have been a little too big for the hands and feet of Antiguan and Barbudan workers; that is, when they tried it on there was not a close enough fit for immediate use. The workers of Antigua and Barbuda were certainly engaged and tempted by this program of the ACLM, but never made it their own. Also important here is the fact that, being more the scholar, Hector did not have the charisma and closeness to the masses that Maurice Bishop or Michael Manley had.

Over the years, the key changes and adjustments that Hector and the ACLM made to their socialist program were in regard to how immediately and how completely the workers of Antigua and Barbuda would be able to take direct democratic control of the state and substantial areas of the economy. From the more immediate position of the late 1960s and 1970s, Hector and the ACLM shifted to a less immediate one. This latter position called for the building of the national economy and the politics of the postcolonial state on the notions of mass party democracy developed by James in his book, *Party Politics in the West Indies*. This less immediate reformulation introduced a preparatory period during which party life was to be built around cultivating practices of direct democracy in both politics and economics (1983: 1–3). The transition to the earlier vision of direct democratic control in politics and economics would have to wait a while, at least until the next major upsurge by the working class. Hence the turn after 1980 to the electoral route to power and away from the idea of coming to power on the wave of an insurrectionary upsurge by workers and farmers.

Unlike the case of Maurice Bishop in Grenada or Michael Manley in Jamaica, the Caribbean New Left never came to power in Antigua and Barbuda, even though they tried. In other words, the ACLM never acquired the quantum of power needed to attempt a socialist transition. Unable to break the grip of the two major parties on state power, Hector and the ACLM were forced to further rethink their positions in the face of declining popularity and influence. This rethinking led to a major split in the party, as some, including Hector, decided to form a coalition with the opposition United Progressive Party, headed by Baldwin Spencer, while others remained opposed. Needless to say, the split further weakened the Left. This political decline marked the beginning of the turning of ideological tables such that soon it would be this New Left Socialism and not state capitalism that would be asked to justify itself. However, in order to fully grasp this crisis of Antiguan and Barbudan socialism, we must take a quick look at the collapse of Jamaican and Grenadian socialism, African socialism, and state socialism in China, the Soviet Union and Eastern Europe to see how they match up against the experience of socialist decline in Antigua and Barbuda.

THE COLLAPSE OF CARIBBEAN, AFRICAN, CHINESE AND RUSSIAN SOCIALISM

In addition to Bird's firm grip on the reigns of state power in Antigua and Barbuda, events in the surrounding socialist world began moving the balance power in adverse directions for Hector and the ACLM. First, there was the 1980 electoral defeat of Michael Manley's democratic socialist regime in Jamaica. Among the many and complex reasons for this defeat was the economic difficulties of the regime and Manley's decision to turn to the IMF. The Jamaican defeat was followed in 1983 by the tragic implosion and collapse of the socialist revolution in Grenada. In this case, it was the internal political clashes and how they were handled that led to this destructive outcome. This violent end to a very promising socialist experiment devastated the image and credibility of the Left in the hearts and minds of the Caribbean masses. It was an implosion that has left deep scars, many of which have not yet healed. Also contributing to the changing image and political position of Hector and the ACLM was the defeat in 1990 of the popular Sandinista Revolution in Nicaragua, which had received a lot of attention in the wider Caribbean.

Also making their own contributions to the weakening position of the ACLM were the economic difficulties that had begun to overwhelm some well-known socialist experiments in Africa. The most important of these were the Ujamaa socialism of Julius Nyerere in Tanzania, and the socialist experiments of the revolutionary party Frelimo in Mozambique. Tanzania in particular attracted a lot of Leftists from both North America and the Caribbean, including Walter Rodney and Clive Thomas. In the cases of both Mozambique and Tanzania, the regimes were overwhelmed by economic difficulties such as shortages, which forced them, like Jamaica, to turn to the IMF and to undergo a capitalist restructuring. In short, the evidence from other developing countries where socialist regimes had come to power pointed to serious internal and external difficulties standing in the way of realizing these alternatives to capitalism.

As if these difficulties of Caribbean and African socialism were not enough, the late 1980s brought the dramatic collapse of Soviet and Eastern European state socialism. These were indeed momentous events with far-reaching implications for the credibility of the Left in Antigua and Barbuda, as well as the wider Caribbean. These tremors within the socialist bloc began even earlier with the 1972 start of détente between President Nixon and Chairman Mao, which paved the way for the market reforms of Mao's successor, Deng Xiaoping. Were there any similarities in the collapse of Caribbean and African socialism and the ones in China, the Soviet Union and Eastern Europe? Indeed, such was the impact of these dramatic events that many quite rightly began to ask: "what is left of the Left?" This, in short, was the larger context that resulted in Caribbean New Left socialism finding itself on the defensive and having to justify its claims to power and popular support.

Hector's answer to the above question was simple and direct. He was highly critical of responses like Francis Fukuyama's end of history and victory of liberalism thesis, Margaret Thatcher's "there is no alternative" (TINA) thesis or Samuel Huntington's view that the collapse of state socialism would be followed by a "clash of civilizations," mainly with Islam. Hector based his rejection of these views on the persisting problems of labor's exploitation and alienation by capital in the post–Cold War period. These objectively and subjectively impoverishing experiences would continue to generate resistance and thus the projecting of alternatives by workers, which would provide precious substance for new socialist alternatives. In short, all of the major problems of capitalism—exploitation, poverty, periodic crises, etc.—would continue after the fall of socialism in Jamaica, Grenada, Tanzania, Mozambique, China, Russia and Eastern Europe.

Although Hector was certain of another major crisis of Western capitalism, he did not live to experience the Great Recession of 2008. This certainty regarding another major crisis of Western capitalism came from many sources. One in particular was the 1985 book by the Indian economist Ravi Batra, *The Great Depression of 1990*. Batra based his predictions on rising levels of inequality in the West, and on the growth of high-risk investors, such as Allen Stanford, and major banks and insurance companies, such as Lehman Brothers and AIG. Although he was off by a decade or so, Batra's book made a strong impression on Hector. It helped to confirm his belief that the period following the dramatic global collapse of socialism would be a return to more "savage" forms of capitalism with higher levels of exploitation, greater inequality and more dramatic periods of crisis.

The dramatic unfolding in 2008 of such a finance-driven crisis, which took Western capitalism to the brink of collapse, was a game-changing event. To avoid complete collapse, Western leaders had to make dramatic turns toward thicker forms of state capitalism, which have left their economies in the hands of their central banks with their policies of low interest rates, quantitative easing and stress tests. These banks, along with other government agencies, have been the chief organizers of the trillion dollar rescue missions that have pulled Western economies back from the brink. Figuring out when central banks will end these life-support measures has been one of the biggest concerns in the lives of major Western banks and corporations. It is important that this crisis of Western capitalism should not be seen in isolation, but rather as one of a series of financial crises around the world that followed the globalization of financial markets. These crises include the 1980s Latin American debt crisis, 1990s financial meltdown in Jamaica, and Asian financial crisis of the 1990s.

The form of state capitalism to which Western neoliberal economies turned was clearly quite different from that to which Bird turned following the crisis of his black democratic socialism. But what they shared in common was an un-prescribed mixing of principles of economic organization. As the collapse of socialist regimes in the 1980s pointed to their major crisis tendencies, the Great Recession of 2008 pointed equally clearly to the return of old crisis tendencies in Western economies now that many of the Keynesian supports had been removed during the post–Cold War period. The exploding of these crisis tendencies and the state-directed manner in which they were contained and dysfunctional markets repaired, soon made clear some of what was still left in the Left.

However, in spite of such potent reminders, the Left cannot extend its correctness on the crisis tendencies of capitalism to the correctness of its socialist alternative. The experiences of the 1980s have made it quite clear that the time has come for the Left to fully acknowledge and work on the crisis tendencies of its socialist alternative. These must now be boldly and transparently addressed if the Left is to be once again a credible political force. In other words, as capitalism has had to explain its turn to the state when its markets go into disarray, socialism has now to explain its even more dramatic turns to markets when its central planning by the state has been overwhelmed by shortages, slow growth, and other economic problems. This dramatic turn to markets has occurred in China, Russia, Eastern Europe, Vietnam and most recently Cuba. In the cases of these socialist economies, the resulting forms of state capitalism have been quite different from the state-directed measures that have rescued Western capitalism but have been closer to the form that rescued Bird's black democratic socialism.

THE CRISIS OF ANTIGUAN AND BARBUDAN SOCIALISM

If there is anything that the above experiences of socialist regimes and movements make clear, it is the fact that implementing socialism is a very difficult and complex undertaking. Yet many on the Left have been reluctant to fully acknowledge these difficulties, or the crisis tendencies to which socialist orders are prone. In many cases, failures are attributed to the intentions, absent capabilities, or betrayals of leaders, while ignoring the many technical and structural difficulties faced by young socialist orders. Marx, Engels, and Lenin did not solve all of the problems associated with the building of socialist orders. Indeed, it would have been impossible for them to have foreseen the major ones with which we are now confronted, hence the very pressing need for us to face these problems honestly and to address them with all of our intellectual and political resources. Thus from the point of view of this paper, any account of the global crises of socialism must begin with factors that overwhelmed the two socialist movements here in Antigua and Barbuda: V. C. Bird's attempts in the 1940s and Tim Hector's in the 1960s.

Drawing on Bird's experiences three factors strike us immediately. First, it should be clear that leaders of socialist movements and young socialist states must accumulate and sustain a sufficient quantum of power, popular and institutional, in order to undertake the transition in spite of resistance and push back from established centers of capitalist power. Without such a strong political position, the experiment will most likely be prematurely stopped by the powers of the old order.

Second, given the additional experiences of Tanzania, Jamaica, China, and the Soviet Union, it should be clear that the specific crisis tendencies of centrally planned and co-operatively organized economies can lead to the collapse of these socialist experiments. In particular, the problem of shortages, poor coordination between different sectors of the economy, and maintaining the growth rates necessary to meet the increasing demands of members or consumers. At this particular juncture in the history of socialism, these problems need to be anticipated and met with probable solutions. In short, the economics of socialism has to be established on new foundations if we are to move forward on the waves of future upsurges.

Third and finally, particularly in the light of the experiences of Grenada, the ACLM, and the Soviet Union, it should also be clear that the politics of socialism has to be established on new foundations and practices. To start, Grenada made clear the crises of political accumulation and competition that can develop around ideological differences and their potentially explosive nature. This set of differences is particularly important in periods of transition where rules for leadership and regime change are themselves undergoing change. From the experiences of the Soviet Union and Eastern Europe, it should be crystal clear that an authoritarian state cannot be the basis of the politics of socialism. From the experiences of the ACLM, we have learned to pause and look carefully at the real agency of which workers are capable before assuming that the masses in a given society are ready for an immediate transition to forms of direct democracy. This is an extended debate that I have been having with my friends and fellow James scholars, Matthew Quest and Ellorton Jeffers, a former vice chairman of the ACLM. In short, the political economy of socialism must take its cues and not stray too far from the collective self-projections of workers. These must be it contents and foundations. As workers are always projecting themselves into the future, there will always be content for us to build on and articulate. Thus the present challenge is to do that in this moment with all of its contradictions and ambiguities.

In its earliest and most comprehensive phase, Bird's 1940s attempt at building a black democratic socialist Antigua and Barbuda was centered on the nationalizing of the sugar industry—including its lands—and reorganizing it on a co-operative basis. However, although his socialist movement had a strong popular base, it never acquired the additional elements of institutional power within the colonial context, which was needed for such a major change. As a result, the suggestions for nationalizing the sugar industry had to be dropped when this idea lost the support of democratic socialists in the colonial office in London. However, the significance of this political challenge was not fully grasped by the New Left in Antigua and Barbuda, as our focus was on Bird's character and intentions and much less on the challenges of implementing socialism. Hector recognized the radical nature of Bird's early socialism, noting that "V. C. Bird from 1943 to 1962 was a socialist in the grand manner" (2002: 9). However, following such statements of recognition were oft-repeated statements on Bird's "betrayal" of his socialist legacy and of the workers (1987: 6–7). This thesis of betrayal was present in some of Hector's last written essays from his sickbed in Cuba. In one of these he wrote: "Bird's betrayal, his climb down from public ownership of the commanding heights was not accomplished overnight" (2002: 9). Hector then proceeded to argue that this betrayal was the result of Bird allowing himself to be seduced by the titles conferred on him by the British and the capital that the Americans were pouring into Antigua and Barbuda's tourist industry. In other words, Hector attempted to explain Bird's turn to state capitalism without reference to any of the difficulties that Bird and other socialist leaders had been experiencing with the implementing of socialism that may have led them to turn to capitalism. Whether or not there was such a betrayal, we cannot let it obscure this crucial issue of whether or not Bird had secured the critical quantum of power needed for executing a transition of such magnitude.

Equally important were the lessons that the New Left in Antigua and Barbuda failed to learn from the economic difficulties Bird experienced with his co-operative and state-run enterprises. In addition to his plans to reorganize the sugar industry on a co-operative basis, Bird also attempted to build a state-run industrial sector as an integral part of his socialized Antiguan and Barbudan economy. This industrial sector was conceived as an extension of the agricultural/peasant sector. Arrowroot starch, cornmeal, and cottonseed oil factories were established, which were to be supplied by increased peasant output of arrowroot, corn and cottonseed. The idea here was to orient the economy more toward increasing peasant output, improving agriculture and the material well being of peasants.

These state-run industrial undertakings failed for a number of reasons at the technical, managerial and productive levels. In the case of the cornmeal factory, the primary problem was the quality of the meal. With the cottonseed oil factory, the major difficulty was that of meeting projected volumes of output. In the case of the arrowroot starch factory, it was the unreliability of peasant supplies of arrowroot. This was a well-intentioned industrial program, designed to empower agricultural and industrial workers, and to further socialize the economy (Henry 1985a: 108–21). Yet by the 1960s, this plan from the 1940s had just about collapsed as it morphed into a tourism-dominated form of state capitalism. Exactly how this happened was not something that the New Left examined in detail as we attributed it to Bird's betrayal of his socialist heritage. Today, we need to go beyond this betrayal argument and look more carefully at some of the stubborn structural and performative difficulties.

The pressing need for this detailed study of the failures of Bird's experiments becomes obvious when we look retrospectively at the socialist program of the ACLM. They both spring from a common co-operative root that is deep within us as a people of West African descent. It is this common root that accounts for the striking similarities between these two socialist programs. To concretize the co-operative model of a socialist economy outlined above, the ACLM established its East Antigua Commune and the West Antigua Co-operative Farm. In an interview with Harold Lovell, a former vice chairman of the ACLM, Anthonyson King, the West Farm's manager, said: "Though we are aware that a new society will create a new man, the farm and the organization of work demonstrates the possible. Further, it is from experiences in this type of activity that people acquire the skills to run a country" (Lovell 1982: 13).

However, in spite of getting off to a good and widely publicized start, these co-operative experiments were overtaken by economic difficulties, which have not been clearly analyzed by its members. When interviewed, one gets widely differing accounts of the causes of their eventual collapse. From my perspective, there were definite production problems, which gave rise to issues of steady growth, and thus of the ability of the co-operatives to support its members as they acquired growing families.

Given this outcome, as well as the co-operatives encouraged by Bird, the need for a much better understanding of the economics of co-operative enterprises, their growth problems in particular, should be crystal clear. This new understanding should include careful studies of co-operatives in Antigua and Barbuda that have failed and those that have succeeded. Probably the best-known and most successful co-operative in our country is the Community First Co-operative Credit Union. This co-operative began in the 1950s as the Antigua and Barbuda Teachers Credit Union, and has expanded to include other professionals in order to secure continued growth. Any future mobilization of the Antiguan and Barbudan Left must include this firmer grounding in the economics of co-operatives, as well as state sector economics. These lessons do not apply to just the case of Antigua and Barbuda. On the contrary, they can help us to understand the global crisis of socialism and the key factors in getting out of it.

THE CRISIS OF SOCIALISM: A GLOBAL PERSPECTIVE

As the crises of Antiguan and Barbudan capitalism have consistently reflected those of global capitalism, it should be clear from the foregoing that the current collapse of the socialist movement in our country reflects the global condition of socialism. As already noted, the features of the global crisis of socialism are the dramatic turns that socialist regimes have had to make toward markets in order to revive their economies. It is important to note that this trend began in the third world countries such as Antigua and Barbuda, Jamaica, Tanzania and Mozambique to be followed by China, the Soviet Union and Eastern Europe.

In the case of China, it is now clear that the 1978 market reforms of Deng Xiaoping were motivated by major economic problems that had been slowing China's growth. In particular, both he and Zhou Enlai became quite dissatisfied with the Soviet-style project of centrally planning the entire Chinese economy, and thus contributing to the historic "Sino-Soviet split." More specifically Deng was dissatisfied with the outcomes of state-managed programs of industrialization as well as the state-run collectivization of agriculture. Within a few years of introducing these policies, Mao and his comrades had a massive agricultural crisis on their hands in addition to major industrial shortages due to inter-industry imbalances. These crises set the stage for the break with the Soviet model, the deterioration of relations between the countries, and the putting out of diplomatic feelers to the U.S. at a time when President Nixon was very interested in "opening" China to Western business interests, and having it as an ally against the Soviet Union. These developments set the stage for the conflicts of the period known as "the Cultural Revolution" out of which Deng emerged as leader and started his market reforms. The intricate details of this complex coming together of geo-political and economic forces are still emerging, but they are extremely important for any understanding of the current collapsed state of socialism.

In the case of the Soviet Union, we can identify similar sets of growth-inhibiting problems that contributed to the re-introduction markets. Even clearer than in the case of China were problems associated with the mathematics of central planning, difficulties with state-run collectivized agriculture, major shortages in many industrial goods, the neglect of services, and mass consumer demand (Aganbegyan 1988: 1–5). By the 1970s, the failure to address these problems severely reduced the growth rate of the Soviet economy. It was the sharp worsening of these trends in the 1980s that led to Mikhail Gorbachev's announcement of the reforms of *uskorenie* (acceleration), *perestroika* (restructuring), and *glasnost* (opening). *Perestroika* in particular contained the major market and co-operative reforms that Gorbachev had in mind, while *glasnost* contained the political ones. These reforms, together with the earlier Chinese rejection of the Stalinist turn its revolution took, marked the end of the economics and politics of the classic Soviet model. What then would be the new politics and economics of the socialist alternative of workers in power? These reforms were not carried out, as Gorbachev was overthrown by Boris Yeltsin, whose project was the complete return of the Soviet Union to capitalism and the restoration of old Russia. Thus we had the dramatic fall of the Soviet Union.

Similar factors were also behind the collapse of state socialism in Eastern Europe, the re-introduction of markets, and their turning to the capitalist West, many joining the European Union and in the case of Poland, NATO. But for us in the Caribbean, the case that is particularly instructive are the market reforms of Raúl Castro in Cuba, and the attempts of the Obama administration to normalize relations with that Caribbean nation. The 2011 *Draft Economic and Social Policy Guidelines* of the Cuban Communist Party is a document that specifies the areas of the Cuban economy that will be re-privatized and function on market principles. Consequently, this is a set of reforms that can be usefully compared to those of Deng and Gorbachev, and also to the internal changes that the ACLM made to its original program. The information from such comparisons would be vital for grasping where socialist policies and programs are at the current moment. It is still much too early to say what will be the outcomes of the reforms in Cuba. The Chinese have become quite influential in Cuba, and the latter's reforms seem to be closer to the Chinese model than the Russian. However, my guess is that we will be seeing a form of market socialism with distinct Cuban characteristics.

These three cases of reform make clear the global features of the current crisis of socialism as well as the unique characteristics and problems of New Left socialism in Antigua and Barbuda. These global features point to the emergence of hybrid political economies that mix principles of partial planning, governed or restricted markets, and co-operatives. These mixed political economies will be with us for a while as we work our way through the after life of both the Great Recession and the fall of state socialism. Between the fall of Lehman Brothers, the fall of the Soviet Union and the rise of Deng's China, we have the major reference points for the world in which we now live. It is a world of convergence and rapprochement, which has brought these formerly opposed types of societies into unexpected relations of cooperation and complementarity.

The most striking case of such convergence is that between the China and the U.S. The symbiotic relationship that has developed between these two economies has been both deep and far-reaching. China has become America's biggest creditor and source of cheap labor, while America has become the largest market for Chinese industrial goods. This symbiosis is now so deep that some scholars have referred to it as "Chimerica" (Karabell 2009). In his 1947 book, *The Invading Socialist Society*, C. L. R. James explored the implications of a period of crisis-driven convergence between Western capitalism and state socialism such as this one. This tendency for both market capitalism and state socialism to move toward each other in times of crisis was at the core of what James called state capitalism. He thought that such a state capitalist convergence was most likely to occur between the U.S. and the Soviet Union. Such a convergence, whether with China or the Soviet Union, James thought would be a most unfortunate development as it would set back the struggle for a people's socialism at least forty years. In any credible account of the current weakened position of labor and the collapsed state of socialism, this Chimerican convergence along with Western policies of neoliberal globalization must occupy major places. The question that arises here for all inheritors of Hector's socialist legacy is: can this legacy survive this period of neoliberal globalization and the state capitalist convergences between a crisis-ridden neoliberal capitalism and an equally crisis-ridden state socialism? Before we can answer this question we must take a brief look at neoliberal globalization and Hector's response to it.

HECTOR, GLOBALIZATION AND SOCIALISM

Departing from us in 2002, Hector's last writings caught only the onset of this period of unprecedented state capitalist convergence. These writings began with his responses to the fall of the Soviet Union, his rejection of "the end of history" and TINA theses, and ended with some detailed analyses of the phenomenon of neoliberal globalization. This process of globalization began in the early 1980s as a response of Western capitalism to rising wages and the increasing power of organized labor at home, and also to intense industrial competition from Japan, Hong Kong, and Singapore. This increased competition saw these Asian countries capturing sizeable shares of U.S. markets without the U.S. being able to make compensatory inroads into other markets abroad. Neoliberal globalization has been a Western effort to negotiate, through the WTO, the removal of all trade barriers in commodity and financial markets. These included systems of protected markets that had been left over from the period of European empires, upon which Caribbean sugar and bananas still depended. The West, particularly the U.S., was confident that in this more open system they would gain or regain needed market shares.

Although the process of globalization remains incomplete, the area in which it has allowed the West to gain significant market shares overseas has been finance. This was the change that led to the financialization of the American and British economies in particular. This globalization of financial markets led to the creation and growth of stock markets around the world including the Eastern Caribbean Stock Market on which shares of Antiguan and Barbudan companies are traded. This growth in stock markets increased dramatically the mobility of capital as it now crossed national borders, entering and leaving stock markets at will. Further, both in the West and abroad, this globalization of financial markets fundamentally altered the nature of banking, such that banks would make much more money from betting on the changing values of currencies than lending for investment purposes. The result of all of these changes has been financial capitalism on a scale even Lenin could never have imagined. The best image of these globalized financial markets is still that of the character Arthur Jensen in the 1976 film, *Network*. He declared: "There are no nations! There are peoples! There are no Russians! There is no Third World! There is no West! There is only one holistic system of systems, one vast interwoven, interacting, multivariate, multi-national domain of dollars—petro-dollars, electro-dollars, Reich marks, rubles, pounds, and shekels. It is this international system of currency that determines the totality of life on this planet." To this globalized system of currencies, Jensen could have added the Eastern Caribbean, Jamaican, Barbadian and Trinidadian dollars.

Other markets, such as those for agriculture, shoes or educational training, have not been as completely globalized as finance, but are more so now than they were in 1980. Thus, although globalization remains an incomplete project, it has provided the economic framework in which Western economies have been able to capture shares of overseas markets in banking, real estate development, tourist development, consumer and government debt. Together with the convergence with China, Lloyd Best, in typical fashion, likened this globalization policy response by the West to a googlie that Caribbean leaders and masses have not yet found a way to hit out of the park.

At the same time that Hector rejected the TINA and "end of history" theses, he also expressed serious concern about this googlie of globalization that the West was now bowling. Like Best, he knew that it would clean bowl, with stumps down, most of the Caribbean governments that were at the wicket of state. This deep concern of Hector was very clearly expressed in at least three "Fan the Flame" columns, "What is Globalization? Why Socialism?" (2002) "Globalization and Us" (2001), and "From Chattel of Globalization to Globalized Chattel" (1999). In these three essays, Hector identified six crucial features of Western globalization. First, it did not begin in the 1980s. On this point, he noted: "we in the Caribbean are the first products of the first stage of globalization, which obviously did not begin yesterday. For, since the 15th century, we were brought here from Africa, through the suffering and death of the Middle Passage" (2001: 8). The neoliberal restructuring of the 1980s was thus the latest installation in the global project of the West. Hector suggested that this phase of "globalization is a phenomenon with which we must contend for at least, I suspect, the next two decades" (2001:8). In short, there was not going to be a quick fix available to us.

Second, Hector saw neoliberal globalization as the work of the 1000 top Western corporations, who, in his view, controlled the WTO, the

OECD, and many presidents and prime ministers. At the heart of this attempt to open up global markets, Hector saw an effort to further "the concentration of capital in the hands of fewer and fewer global corporations." At the same time, he saw this more intense concentration bringing with it "the degradation of the earth's eco-system all over the globe, the growth of inequality, with the rich getting richer and the poor more impoverished, with the world itself more impoverished in terms of community values and commitments" (2001: 9).

Third, Hector was convinced that the financialization of many economies produced by neoliberal globalization would make the major economies of the world more unstable and prone to the erupting of periodic crises—recessions and depressions. We have already made reference to the influence of the Indian economist Ravi Batra on Hector regarding this point. Further, Hector saw the financialization of the Antiguan and Barbudan economy as bringing it well within the orbit of this new set of rolling financial crisis tendencies moving through the global economy. In 1990, he saw three threatening clouds on our financial horizon. The first was personal indebtedness: "in the boom years, personal loans in Antigua leap-frogged from $EC 125.2 million in 1985 to $215 million in 1989 without any significant increase in productive capacity" (1990: 10). Second was a devaluation of the Eastern Caribbean dollar that he thought would follow the neoliberal ending of protected markets for sugar in St. Kitts and bananas in the Windward Islands: "this devaluation will dramatically increase inflation without the corresponding capacity to increase wages. This devaluation will not make Antigua's exports more competitive. The fact is, we have no export sector worth the name" (1990: 11). Third and finally was state indebtedness: "in 1988 Antigua was $68.3 million in arrears on its debt payments . . . Antigua is caught in a debt-trap. Its credit-worthiness is non-existent. Yet it needs to borrow. Yet it cannot pay. We are in a bind" (1990: 14). The Great Recession of 2008 would not have taken him completely by surprise, and neither would the financial meltdown it produced in Antigua and Barbuda—a meltdown that took us to the IMF.

Fourth, Hector saw globalization as leading to an unprecedented era of global finance capitalism, such as we described above. Thus he noted that in 1975, nearly 80 percent of foreign exchange transactions were connected to the real economy, while in 1998 that number had fallen to 2.5 percent (1999: 8). It was as a miniscule part of this 2.5 percent of foreign exchange transactions that he located the financial transactions that support the Antiguan and Barbudan economy. In the period since the Great Recession, the big banks that markets had condemned for failure, along with Lehman Brothers, are now bigger than before the crisis and their rescuing by European and American governments and central banks. Thus a widening gap between the financial sector and "the real economy" continues to be a striking feature of both Western economies and our own.

Fifth, Hector saw globalization as greatly increasing the power of capital to exploit and extract surplus value from workers. With capital being able to cross national borders at will while labor cannot, an imbalance arose that has made the relocating of industries to escape the power of well-organized labor a dominant practice. This imbalance has not only dramatically weakened the power of unions but also placed national working classes in fierce competition with each other. The most striking example of this heightened competition has been between Chinese and American workers. For Hector, this increased exploitation was of special concern to the cause of socialism.

Sixth and finally, Hector saw globalization as further marginalizing and eroding the power position of the Caribbean region as a whole. This trend he thought would indeed continue until we found a way to hit this googlie out of the park.

WHAT WAS TO BE DONE

Given the above features of neoliberal globalization, Hector realized that effective resistance by the Caribbean Left would require major changes in both theory and practice. The economic base of this expanded and reinforced resistance by the Caribbean Left would still be the three-sector model outlined earlier. However, to protect and make it work, the Left in all of the islands would have to significantly increase their power base— both popular and institutional.

In regard to this political dimension of an appropriate response to the googlie of globalization Hector wrote: "from the Caribbean perspective, it necessitates a Regional State—all 28 states and all 36 million people— Cuba to Guyana" (1999: 9). The insular and territorial states that we have so far developed have been made even less viable and more obsolete by globalization. The latter has thus increased the pressure on us for regional integration. In Hector's view, this regional state must pursue three crucial goals. First, it must attempt to achieve a much greater degree of food security than presently exists. Second, it must standardize or harmonize the rules for imports and for the entry of foreign capital into our region. Third, this regional state must seek closer cooperation with Central American states.

Along with this unification of the power and scope of insular states must go a renewing and expanding of their democratic spirit and traditions. In other words, new and expanded spaces must be created, where regional management and labor can meet and talk on equal terms, new and expanded spaces where workers, political parties, and other civic associations can share information, exchange ideas, and coordinate plans and strategies.

In addition to these more direct democratic changes in the nature of the regional state and the sectors of the economy it controls, Hector also argued for expansions in the power and scope of the co-operative sector. These expansions were to counter-balance increases in the power of the central state and thus to keep alive the long-standing traditions—of co-operative practices and also to further empower workers.

However, Hector was fully aware that these changes would not be enough to meet the challenge of globalization. To be effective, they would need the support of a new international mobilization of workers, women and youths around the world all networking and exchanging ideas over email and all the new media (1999: 9). To this new international mobilization, the Caribbean Left must be able to give articulate accounts of its struggles to build socialism on the basis of this three-sector model of political economy.

In this more regional projection of Caribbean socialism, Hector took the time to remind us that the primary normative concern of socialism is still the subordination of economic production and capital accumulation to human development. That, even as we respond to the economic challenges of globalization, we must remember that all the economic development we are pursuing must not be an end in itself, but like works of art should rest gently on the shoulders of our psyche providing both material bases and outlets for its inherent creativity. This engagement with globalization was the last reformulation of Hector's changing socialist vision with which he left us.

CONCLUSION

I wrote this paper with the Antiguan and Barbudan Left in mind, or should I say what is left of our Left. The hope was to rally us so that we can take stock of our long heritage, and in particular the rich body of work that Hector has left us. I have tried my best to outline his ideas in all their complexity as well as the changes that they went through as things changed both at home and abroad. With this legacy that Hector has left us, the Left needs to keep before our society the choice of seeing itself and its economy from both a socialist and a capitalist perspective.

It is now more than ten years since Hector had to retire his very agile pen and the last "Fan the Flame" column was written. As I have tried to indicate, much has happened in our world since 2002. Thus, the major challenge confronting the Antiguan and Barbudan Left is the careful evaluation of this legacy in the light of these continuing changes—particularly neoliberal globalization, the global crisis of socialism, ecological degradation, and increasing social inequality—and what they mean for our future. Even though our socialist project is currently in a state of collapse, the problems that socialism had set out to address are not only still very much with us, but continue to grow more urgent with every passing decade.

The end of this essay is not the place to begin this careful evaluation of Hector's socialist legacy. That should be the topic of another paper all its own. However, in the course of writing this one, I have emphasized the urgent need for us to rethink the economics of our socialist project. Although Caribbean socialism still lives in the shadow of the collapse in Grenada, our politics, as Hector's writings make so clear, has for the most part been deeply democratic. Ideally, the writing of such an evaluative paper or set of papers should follow some intense discussions by members of the Antiguan and Barbudan Left. We need to be clear on what we see as the major changes in the world and our nation since 2002, and what, if any, modifications they may require in Hector's views of socialism. Have we changed? Have the masses of Antiguans and Barbudans changed? What of our co-operative heritage? Is that still alive in us after the urbanization of our social life, and globalization of our economy? Will it emerge in the next popular upsurge as it did in the upsurge of the 1960s? These are some of the questions we need to ask as we reflect on Hector's legacy.

Humanity is still very much in the making, and hence in need of genuine ideals. We have not yet arrived at utopia or the end of history. Or as Hector was wont to say, we have not yet arrived at the rendezvous of victory. The current order of state capitalist convergence between market capitalism and state socialism is a transitional one. Hector looked with confidence toward a period beyond the current dominance of finance with its rolling set of global meltdowns and its increasing separation from the productive bases of real economies. Thus he looked forward to a period in which commodity production would once again determine the flow of financial resources and transactions. The socio-historical forces that brought us our last popular upsurge have not gone into retirement. They are still very much alive and at work. We can feel them at work in the current wave of wildcat strikes in China (over 1,400 in 2014), and in the Solidarity Economy movements in Brazil and South Africa. We also saw these insurrectionary forces on display in the Occupy Wall Street movement, and the popular uprising in Egypt that brought down the Mubarak regime. Therefore new futures beckon us. We must rise to meet them. But we can only do so on new wings made with feathers from legacies such as Tim Hector has left us.

NOTE

* First published as "The Socialist Legacy of Tim Hector," *Antigua and Barbuda Review of Books* 8, no. 1 (Summer): 109–31.

Epilogue

An Interview with Paget Henry (2015)

Editors: How do you understand the relationship between your formative and early work in physics and philosophy, your advanced academic training as an empirical sociologist and political economist, and your more recent engagements with and contributions to Caribbean and Africana philosophy?

Paget Henry: Let me begin by saying thank you for doing this interview and for all of your hard work on the volume in which it will appear. Let me also take this opportunity to thank you, Jane, for all of the wonderful work that you are doing as the president of the Caribbean Philosophical Association (CPA). I feel very honored by this volume and the conference and also a little surprised. This really good work that you, Lewis, Aaron and Neil are doing is certainly making more real my approaching 70th birthday than I had allowed myself to acknowledge. Your first question is really taking me back several decades to the early 1960s when my interest in philosophy first began to emerge.

As you already know, I was born on the Caribbean island of Montserrat and grew up on the neighboring island of Antigua. In 1960, at age 14, I entered the fourth form of the Antigua Grammar School after living for four years on the island of Tortola in the British Virgin Islands. As an even younger boy, I identified very strongly with my body and with nature, and thus enjoyed physical activities such as swimming, bike riding and being outdoors. Reflecting on that early period now, I would describe myself as a budding naturalist. However, regular church attendance was an integral part of our family life. My parents had the life of a Methodist minister all planned out for me. So from about eight to fourteen, this growing Christian identity rather imperceptibly eclipsed my earlier naturalism as the two were constructed within me as irreconcilable opposites.

In my last two years in Tortola, I began the study of physics and chemistry at the Virgin Islands Secondary School with a very good science teacher from Guyana, Mr. Allen. I took to these two subjects immediately. They were certainly engaging something in me, of which I was barely aware. All I knew was that I found them eye-opening, exciting and naturalistic. In my first year at the Antigua Grammar School, this growing interest in science was greatly reinforced by being in the same class with my cousin, Roy Daniel, who was an even better physicist than I. He has been for a long time a professor of physics at the University of the West Indies in Jamaica. Together we started exploring the world of physics and chemistry, with a greater emphasis on the former. We started reading books on physics that were not assigned in our class, and every afternoon we would meet to talk about what we had read about one of the great physicists. We read books about Newton, Einstein, Clerk Maxwell, Max Planck, Niels Bohr, and many others.

Unbeknown to me, all of the specific things that I was learning about atoms, molecules, light, sound, and electro-magnetism in physics and chemistry were forming a coherent picture of the world that was very different from the one my Methodism had given me. Then one afternoon while waiting for Roy to begin our talk, suddenly and quite unexpectedly this subconscious scientific worldview became very conscious, superseding and replacing my Christian worldview. It was instantaneous and definitive. I was a different person from the one that arrived a little earlier at Roy's home on St. Mary's Street in St. Johns, the capital city. I experienced this transformation as the return of my earlier naturalism, but newly empowered by the wings of physics.

When Roy came out and we started our walk, I shared my experience with him. To my surprise and delight, he had earlier gone through a similar transformation but was afraid to share it with me, as I was still fully inscribed in the Christian worldview. We talked extensively about their meaning and also about whether we should tell our parents or our other cousins, brothers and sisters who were not into science. We decided not to tell! However, we did bring them up in classes at school and got into heated debates with both teachers and fellow students.

In the months that followed, I examined carefully the meaning of this experience, its implications for both science and religion, and for my future. This was really the period in which my interest in philosophy was born. I turned to it in my effort to evaluate the competing arguments of science and religion. In short, I rather spontaneously appropriated it as an adjudicator between the two. Much more than Roy, I started reading books on philosophy. The first was A. C. Ewing's *Ethics*, which appeared in a larger series, "Teach Yourself Philosophy." The chapter on Kant was the one that really engaged me. Not long after, I read Bertrand Russell's *Why I am not a Christian?* and Sir James Jeans's *Physics and Philosophy*. These two texts took me into the heart of the issues with which I was grappling at the time.

Although very much on the side of science, I was not completely satisfied with the materialist arguments that were being made by Russell and Jeans. The latter's way of rejecting and removing all of the anthropomorphic projections of the human subject onto nature (Sylvia Wynter's de-goding of the world) was throwing away too much. However, at that time I could not say exactly what I thought should be retained. Reflecting on it now, it was something on the order of: while these projections needed to be withdrawn in order for us to do science, this did not mean that they were useless or without epistemic value. Thus they should be carefully evaluated before we discredit them. This position struck me as being more consistent with Jeans's powerful critique of all attempts at constructing pictorial representations of the world of nature based on the laws and paradigms of physics. These he argued were always limited and partial, and even when put together do not give us a truthful picture of the whole. With the truth of our world beyond the complete grasp of science, how can we be sure about throwing out the mythic and religious projections of the human subject.

After graduating from the Antigua Grammar School in 1964 and not getting into the University College of the West Indies in Jamaica, I left Antigua for the United States. By the time I entered the City University of New York in 1965 with plans for a major in physics, the above issues were still live concerns for me. As a result, I enrolled in several philosophy classes along with my physics courses. Among the former was a class on the philosophy of science with a very different Professor Michael Levin than the one that we have come to know in more recent times. It really was a great course for me, in which my final paper was one on science and religion. The paper allowed me to bring together all that I had been thinking about these issues up to that time, and I enjoyed writing it very much. It was a major factor in Professor Levin's decision to nominate me for the Frederick Sperling Award for the best student in philosophy, even though I was a sociology major.

By the middle of my sophomore year, these intellectual issues on the relationship between science and religion, which had developed while I was in Antigua, began to be eclipsed by a new set of issues: being black in American society. I arrived in the U.S. at the height of the African American civil rights and black power movements. Moving from Newgate Street in St. Johns to 116th Street between Lenox and 5th Avenues was a shocker, to put it mildly. My limited understanding of the condition of people of African descent changed overnight. Being so involved with physics, I was certainly not paying very close attention to the political and racial struggles that were taking place within the emerging nation-state of Antigua and Barbuda. To the extent that I did grasp what was happening, my understanding of the social conditions of people of African descent was framed by the labor-based movement that had become the basis for the struggle for political independence from Britain. My parents were not deeply involved in this movement, so it did not penetrate my everyday life directly.

Living in Harlem and absorbing the sounds of the black struggle, the condition of people of African descent appeared to me in a much starker light than it did when I was in Antigua and Barbuda. The heroin epidemic that was raging at the time, the crime problems, the racial uprisings, the sense of Harlem as a black ghetto, all brought home with a grimmer sense of reality the social condition of people of African descent. This realization made me appreciate more fully the depth and accuracy of the lectures of Mr. George Weston, a very good friend of my parents. Weston had been living in the U.S. for some time and was a vice-president of the New York chapter of Marcus Garvey's UNIA [United Negro Improvement Association]. However, he returned regularly to Antigua and Barbuda and would give public lectures on race relations in the U.S.

Adding to the starkness of my Harlem experience was the fact that in the heart of this black ghetto was the City College, the flagship undergraduate institution of the City University of New York. During the years that I was there, City College was about 95 percent white, and the tuition fee was $5 a term! Students from all of the boroughs of the city were arriving via subway or bus to attend classes at 137th Street and Broadway. Yet, there were so few African American in attendance. Something was radically wrong! Black protests were all around, coming at me from all directions. This was the era of SNCC, CORE, SCLC, the Black Panther Party, and other activist organizations. On the City College campus, we had the Onyx Society and the Caribbean Students Association. Pernell Charles, who would later become the deputy leader of the Jamaica Labour Party, led the latter. In the midst of all this political activity, I realized the extent to which my intellectual endeavors so far had taken the form of a conversation with nature through physics, the reinforced philosophy of naturalism that it had produced, and the tensions between this naturalism and religion.

Adjusting to life in Harlem made necessary the putting aside of this conversation with nature and the opening of another with society through the discipline of sociology. Coming to grips with the conditions of blacks in America and the changes they produced in my relationship to the surrounding social environment called forth this new conversation. The need for it and my desire to be more active in the political movements around me took me over to the sociology department in my junior year. There I was very fortunate in meeting three remarkable professors: Jay Shulman, Frieda Silvert, and Marlis Krueger.

Professor Shulman was a scholar of Karl Marx, and his classes really introduced me to Marx's thought. Professor Silvert introduced me to the work of Max Weber and also to the field of urban sociology. She organized several reading groups, including one on Barrington Moore's book, *The Social Origins of Dictatorship and Democracy*, to which she invited me. These were wonderful learning experiences as I got to exchange ideas with graduate students and other professors. Professor Krueger was from Germany, and she is responsible for my long-standing interest in the work of Jürgen Habermas. She just looked at me one day and said, "You should be reading Habermas. You think like him." This was long before

Habermas was well known in the U.S., and not long after it came out, she presented me with a copy of his *Toward a Rational Society*. In the economics department, I took the introduction to economics with Professor Sirkin, who did everything possible to get me to be an economics major. It was too late. My conversation with society was going to be through sociology.

Coming to grips with the issue of racial oppression was now foremost on my mind. I was reading works by Marcus Garvey, Martin Luther King, Jr., Stokely Carmichael, Malcolm X, Angela Davis and many others, and often thought of my cousin Roy going through his physics books as he was now at the University College of the West Indies in Jamaica. I started comparing the position of blacks in the U.S. with that of blacks in the Caribbean. I did a paper on this for Professor Shulman but was not happy with it. I did not feel as though I had secured a firm enough grasp of the problem—particularly with regard to the case of the U.S. The black labourist lens that I brought with me from the nationalist struggle in Antigua and Barbuda was clouding rather than illuminating the U.S. scene. In 1969, we had the takeover of the South Campus of the college by black students, which resulted in substantial changes in the admissions policies that significantly increased the number of black and Hispanic students attending City College. This was an important political and learning experience for me, as it helped to confirm my inadequate grasp of the complexities of these racial and anticolonial struggles.

Out of this rather inconclusive wrestling with the racialized social environment of New York, the issue of Caribbean economic development gripped me as the issue I should explore. Black economic development became the theme of my senior year. I started graduate school at Cornell University in the fall of 1970. When I arrived on campus, the talk was all about the takeover, with guns, of Willard Straight Hall, which had occurred earlier that spring. Among many of the black students on campus, the Ujamaa socialism of Julius Nyerere was very popular. Also on campus was a very able group of Caribbean students, who would go on to very distinguished careers. Among them were economists Trevor Farrell, Vincent Richards, Allan Williams, and Warren Smith. There was also the linguist, Bernadette Farquhar, and literary scholar Selwyn Cudjoe. Later Cudjoe and I, along with Paul Buhle, would found the *C. L. R. James Journal*, later to be the journal of the CPA.

From my economist friends, I learned so much. I was in a seminar with them on Caribbean economic development that was taught by Professor Tom Davis. In this seminar, we discussed very extensively the work of the rising Caribbean school of dependency economics—particularly the works of Lloyd Best, George Beckford and Norman Girvan. Later, within the context of the Caribbean Students Association, we brought to campus C. L. R. James, Lloyd Best and Walter Rodney. I was now searching very intensely for a position that would bring together some of the key ideas of James and Best, as a theoretical framework for looking at Caribbean economies, and the larger issue of black economic development. With Vincent Richards, I sat in on several sessions of a seminar on workers' self-management that was taught by Professor Jaroslav Vanek. Also very important to my graduate years was meeting and becoming friends with Dominick LaCapra, who was a masterful historian of ideas—particularly of French intellectual history. All of my work on the classical sociologist Emile Durkheim was done with him. Responding to me in a way that was similar to Professor Krueger, Professor LaCapra took it upon himself to introduce me to the work of Jacques Derrida and to invite me to a small seminar with Michel Foucault that he had organized.

However, it was the occasion of having to write a final paper for Professor Davis's seminar that brought me face to face with the paucity of literature on Antigua and Barbuda in the period after the Second World War. I ended up doing my paper on Norman Girvan and Jamaican economic development. Out of that experience came the decision to do my dissertation on economic development in Antigua. This later became my first book, *Peripheral Capitalism and Underdevelopment in Antigua*.

In the sociology department, I worked closely with Robin Williams on issues of race, with Joseph Khal on Latin American development, and with Leonard Reissman on theory, particularly Weber. Reissman was a very good friend of Professor Frieda Silvert, my undergraduate Weber teacher. They were both strong Weberians. Professor Khal was in the conflict tradition of C. Wright Mills, while Professor Williams was very much a Parsonian structural functionalist. There was also Professor Robert McGinnis, with whom I took a methods course, and he was very much the mathematical sociologist in the tradition of James Coleman. As a result, within the department, intense debates raged over these and other theoretical and methodological approaches to doing sociology.

The primary strategy I employed in navigating these stormy waters was to revive my interest in philosophy. I approached that aspect of my graduate training in a way that was similar to how I had earlier addressed the tension of conflicting positions and claims between science and religion. This earlier case of interdisciplinary conflict served as a paradigm for responding to these methodological and theoretical conflicts in the field of sociology. Once again the philosophy of science became a live issue for me, along with the philosophy of history. This use of philosophy within the field of sociology would in turn become an important base for my work in the field of Caribbean philosophy.

Editors: Which figures, texts, concepts, and problems have impacted your thinking most? How would you characterize how they have influenced your thought and practice?

Paget Henry: As I just indicated, while in graduate school, I was searching for a position that brought together the Marxism of C. L. R. James and the political economy of the Caribbean Dependency School. James theorized the inherent creativity of the collective subjectivity of workers, which constituted the intentional foundations of proletarian socialist movements. At the same time he also drew clear lines of distinction between this form of socialism and the Fabian socialism of Arthur Lewis and even more so with the authoritarian socialism of the Soviet Union. However, there was little in James about the day-to-day management of worker controlled socialist economies. There was more on this in the work of the Caribbean Dependency School, particularly the work of Clive Thomas, George Beckford and Norman Girvan.

Thus in reference to your second question, the first set of problems that engaged my thinking, after I started teaching at the State University of New York at Stony Brook in 1976, was this issue of black economic development, particularly in the Caribbean. With George Padmore, I saw the combination of slavery, colonization and racialization that had dominated the lives of people of African descent as the first institutional expressions of modern totalitarianism. Recovering from this extreme form of oppression was not going to be easy, whether one was speaking psychologically, politically or economically. Theorizing accurately the distinct nature of postcolonial economies, the unique challenges they faced, and the impact of race on these challenges was both an important and an urgent problem. As a result, I was in search of a discourse of black political economy that brought together the insurrectionary subjectivity of people of African descent and the management and developmental ideas of dependency economics.

Given the central importance of this problem of black economic development to my thinking at this point in time, the figures that influenced me the most were C. L. R. James, Frantz Fanon, W. E. B. Du Bois, Clive Thomas, Norman Girvan and Samir Amin. As I indicated earlier, James's ideas on the collective or public self of Caribbean people provided the theoretical space for the subjective conditions that were motivating the push for change in the Caribbean region. Who were these people? What were they saying through their insurrectionary demands for political independence and economic development? What were they saying about the subjective impact of their experiences of the period of totalitarian colonialism? These were difficult issues to grasp and even more difficult to theorize and link to streams of everyday thought and experience. It was in this context that James's *The Black Jacobins* became an extremely important text for me. It was the perfect model for learning how to deal with these big historical issues such as slavery, colonialism, racism, and the violence of totalitarian domination.

In addition to thematizing the key subjective aspects of the process of postcolonial transformation, this text also made clear some of the major challenges of economic and political governance that would have to be confronted in the period after independence. In particular, James's book takes up the issue of the nature of the postcolonial state, and the significance of Toussaint's difficult decision to revive the plantation system in Haiti after taking power. James's discussion of this issue was one of the major links that I made between him and the Caribbean Dependency School.

At this point in my development, the Fanonian text that had impacted me most was *The Wretched of the Earth*. First, it contained a still unsurpassed phenomenological description of the revolutionary subjectivity that totalitarian colonialism has called forth out of the colonized, and at the same time the most insightful critique of the limitations and contradictions of that subjectivity and its national consciousness. Second, the theorizing of race in this revolutionary context of postcolonial economic and political transformation made it an extremely valuable contribution to the kind of black political economy for which I was searching. It was after reading this text that I began using the term *racial capitalism* and linking it to a discourse of Black Marxism.

W. E. B. Du Bois's *Black Reconstruction in America* was another important text for me in the late 1970s. I had first encountered this text earlier as a member of the Left Movement in Antigua and Barbuda: The Antigua Caribbean Liberation Movement, better know as the ACLM. Even though I did not understand all of its 700 pages at the time, it made a great impression on me, calling to mind James's *The Black Jacobins*. By the late 1970s, I came to see it as a great contribution to that discourse of a black political economy for which I was searching. Two ideas in particular caught my attention. The first was Du Bois's reading of African Americans joining en masse the Civil War on the side of the Union as a general strike against the plantation system of the American South. Du Bois portrayed this mass movement as insurrectionary and contrasted it with the revolution in Haiti. Although different both were seen as uprisings against similar totalitarian systems of highly racialized domination and economic exploitation. The second idea of Du Bois that caught my attention at this time was his notion of "the dictatorship of labor" as a structure of economic and political governance in the period after the fall of totalitarian internal colonialism. I saw it as an important social formation on the steep road from the totalitarian past that people of African descent were now traveling.

Samir Amin's *Accumulation on a World Scale* was for me the most important systematic work of black political economy to date. This work was followed by his equally influential text, *Unequal Development*. Both of these works incorporated and developed more rigorously ideas from the Latin American Dependency School while linking them to well-known schools of Marxist economics. Most important for me was the concept of peripheral capitalism and the ideas of Raul Prebisch on how the terms of trade affected economic development. From Prebisch and Amin I learned some of the thorny issues involved in the theory and practice of international trade. At the time, following Norman Girvan, I summed these up as the tensions between the comparative advantage and the imperialism of trade. This was the framework within which I began to understand Caribbean trade agreements, the various rounds of GATT negotiations, and later the formation of the WTO.

Clive Thomas's *Dependence and Transformation* was for me the work that addressed most directly the economics of the transition of a peripheral capitalist society to a socialist one within the constraints of the postcolonial period. Thomas's focus in this text was definitely on transformation and all that was involved in making a politico-economic break with the totalitarian colonialism of the past. Like Walter Rodney, Thomas had been to Tanzania and had absorbed important lessons from the Ujamaa socialism of Julius Nyerere. These were all incorporated into a highly original synthesis that effectively integrated ideas from Lloyd Best, George Beckford and other dependency economists as well as a number of Western Marxist economists. Thomas formulated the crucial structural changes by which colonial economies were produced and institutionalized as a dynamic divergence between domestic demand and domestic resource use. Thus for him the primary economic challenge of the postcolonial period was the dismantling of this divergence and the institutionalizing of a dynamic convergence between domestic demand and domestic resource use. This latter goal would require deep structural changes in peripheral economies that for Thomas required not just a nationalist state, but one that was ideologically committed to some form of peasant/proletarian socialism and popularly controlled by a worker/peasant alliance. This formulation of the problems involved in postcolonial economic transformation has stayed with me, and thus is one that I still use.

Together, these key texts by James, Fanon, Du Bois, Amin and Thomas have been the foundation of my work on Caribbean political economy. Thus my first book, *Peripheral Capitalism and Underdevelopment in Antigua*, and an essay like "Towards a Theory of Peripheral Cultural Systems" would have been inconceivable without the contributions of these texts. The unsuccessful attempts to implement the policies of nationalization and de-linking associated with dependency theory and the collapse of socialist projects in the Caribbean and elsewhere have clearly called for significant revisions in these theories. However, their lasting importance for me will become even clearer when I talk more directly about my philosophically oriented work.

So at this point in our conversation, in order for me to complete my response to your complex and many-sided question, I must now address those figures, texts, problems, and concepts that impacted my thinking and writing around the late 1980s. Many factors were operating during this period—the global crisis of socialism, the rise of poststructuralism in the academy, the third world debt crisis and the related policies of "structural adjustment" that were being implemented by the IMF and the World Bank. But the most important of the many new factors of this period was the growing presence of African and African American philosophy. The names of V. Y. Mudimbe, Anthony Appiah, Alexis Kagame, Cornel West, Lucius Outlaw, Bernard Boxill, and my longtime friend Charles Mills kept intruding into my sociological world. Then from John Ladd, a professor of philosophy at Brown, I got word of a young energetic Jamaican graduate student in philosophy at Yale, someone you know very well, Lewis Gordon.

The work of this group of black philosophers captured my attention more than any of the other developments that were shifting the foundations of my academic terrain. I knew I had to find out exactly what was happening here and to get involved in some significant way. It really excited the philosopher in me that had been restricted to adjudicating methodical and theoretical differences in sociology. Being at the time the chair of Africana Studies at Brown, my initial response was to bring this movement in African and African American philosophy to our department and to the Brown campus, by doing a hire in this field. The first move I made in this direction was, with the cooperation of John Ladd, to invite Lewis Gordon to give a talk to both philosophy and Africana Studies, even though he was still in the process of finishing his dissertation. He spoke on Fanon and existentialism, and before the talk was over I knew that this was the hire that I wanted to make in order to bring Africana philosophy to Brown. Actually writing philosophy was definitely not on my mind at the time of making these plans. I saw myself as continuing to work on James, Thomas, Amin, etc., and to deal with the new challenges to Caribbean development in the period after the imploding of the socialist revolution in Grenada.

After much effort, and with the cooperation of President Vartan Gregorian, I succeeded in bringing Lewis Gordon to Brown in Africana Studies and Religious Studies, rather than philosophy. It was the combination of having Lewis in Africana Studies but not being able to get him an appointment in the philosophy department that actually triggered my writing of philosophy. Daily conversations with Lewis really revived many of my old interests in the field of philosophy, which now began to move beyond the limited use I found for them in sociology. This was a breath of fresh air that I welcomed. Lewis and I talked extensively about Fanon, Sartre, Du Bois, Frederick Douglass, Anna Julia Cooper, and about this new field of black existentialism, which he was developing, and its somewhat tense relations with poststructuralism. This was just wonderful. I was taking it all in and was soon going to meetings of the American Philosophical Association with Lewis, where I first met Cornel West, Lucius Outlaw, Bernard Boxill and the other Africana philosophers. Lewis and I organized several talks and seminars on Africana philosophy through which I met other Africana philosophers such as Kwame Gyekye, Teodros Kiros, Nelson Maldonado-Torres, and Kwasi Wiredu.

Not being able to get Lewis an appointment in the philosophy department (Africana Studies was still a program at the time) was the disturbing factor in all of this. Something was rotten in the kingdom of philosophy, and Lewis was the victim of it. I was certain that if he had been a sociologist, I would have been able to get him an appointment in sociology. Once again I felt called into the service of my race. It was time to join this band of courageous brothers and sisters and contribute to the revival of the tradition of Africana philosophy.

Some time after meeting this group of philosophers and publishing some papers in volumes edited by Lewis, it dawned on me that the strongest contribution that I could make to this exciting project of reviving Africana philosophy was to do a book on Afro-Caribbean philosophy. I could feel this work forming in me as a response to this new situation in which I found myself. Thus, by the time that I started seriously working on *Caliban's Reason*, it all came together quite naturally. The forging of a synthesis between my use of philosophy for theoretical, methodological and interdisciplinary purposes and the ideas and challenges arising from the works of this new group of Africana philosophers was the creative foundation and force behind the writing of *Caliban's Reason*. But it would also be fair to say that the writing of this book aided the crystalizing of this philosophical synthesis.

If I had to give this synthesis a name, I would call it historicism/poeticism—a mode of thinking that plays a crucial role in the book. Indeed, one could say that I discovered my own historicism/poeticism in the course of writing this book along with its relationship to figures like James, Fanon, Harris and Wynter. Further, one could also say that writing this book made me more aware of my differences with other groups of Afro-Caribbean philosophers, as my aim was a systematic presentation of Afro-Caribbean philosophy as a whole and not just its historicism/poeticism.

In the course of making this contribution to the larger field of Africana philosophy, the figures and texts that influenced me most were C. L. R. James's *Notes on Dialectics*, Frantz Fanon's *Black Skin, White Masks*, Cornel West's *Prophesy Deliverance!*, Lewis Gordon's *Bad Faith and Anti-Black Racism*, Sri Aurobindo's *The Human Cycle*, the later essays of Sylvia Wynter, and the novels of Wilson Harris. Cornel West's text made it clear to me that the project of a systematic presentation of Afro-Caribbean philosophy was a viable one. After reading West, I knew that I was going to take an ontological approach in my attempt at a systematic presentation of Afro-Caribbean philosophy. James and Wynter opened for me the transcendental terrain of Afro-Caribbean philosophy. In particular, the nature of Afro-Caribbean *a priori* categories, their relations to issues of class and race, and the difficulties involved in changing these categories. Given the ontological focus of my project, I was very aware of the limited use that I was making of this *a priori* terrain of Afro-Caribbean philosophy. Gordon and Fanon revealed with great clarity the existential foundations of anti-black racism. In doing so they also exposed its deep roots in the dynamics of ego formation and also in the inter-subjectivity of self-other and We/They relations. These ideas fitted very nicely with the ontological orientation that was guiding the writing of the text. I saw immediate connections with pre-colonial African theories of self-formation — particularly with the work of Kwame Gyekye and the famous Adinkra signs. These connections resulted in my work on African existentialism.

From Wilson Harris and Sylvia Wynter I came to a much fuller understanding of the poeticist tradition and also a deeper appreciation of how rooted I was in the historicist wing of this larger philosophy. The key trigger was Harris's well-known claim in *History, Myth and Fable in the Caribbean and Guianas* that "a cleavage exists between the historical convention in the Caribbean and Guianas and the arts of the imagination." He also went on to note that he believed "a philosophy of history may well lie buried in the arts of the imagination." What was this philosophy of history? I was determined to find out and to explore this cleavage that could be standing between it and my own historicism. Thus came about my long engagement with Wilson Harris.

I came to Sylvia Wynter through my reading of her breath-taking essays on C. L. R. James. They were highly original, profound, and thus among the best essays on James that I was reading at the time. It was the transcendental orientation of Wynter's essays that caught my philosophical imagination. This was a new departure for us and made me think immediately of the work on *a priori* categories that James had begun in *Notes on Dialectics*. It was Wynter's notion of the auto-poetic instituting of identities, categories of thought and epistemes, along with her concept of the mode of producing the human that linked so powerfully the poetic, the transcendental and the historical. This was definitely a keeper. Further, the very constructive manner in which she presented the concept of the mode of producing the human as a counterpoint to the Marxian notion of the mode of economic production was to my mind absolutely brilliant. These engagements with Wynter and Harris really transformed my historicism into a historicism/poeticism, and also made me realize how much of James's poeticism I had overlooked.

I discovered Indian philosophy while I was an undergraduate at City College with Professor Irani. I was immediately drawn to the works of Sri Aurobindo, Rabindranath Tagore, and Jiddu Krishnamurti. Even though I was drawn to them, I was not able at the time to articulate what exactly was so appealing about them. I was also unable at the time to incorporate them into the exchanges between science and religion that I was grappling with, or into my work on political economy. I realized that they were not rooted in dogma but were experientially based. However, although highly engaging they remained just beyond my capacity for philosophical articulation. By the time I came to write *Caliban's Reason*, I was much more spiritually literate. Thus I was able to make some profound connections between Aurobindo and Wilson Harris. From both I learned how to link discourses of spirituality to my new found historicism/poeticism.

In my view, Aurobindo is one of the greatest philosophers of all time. His vision is comprehensive, and his spirituality is awesome in its depth. For similar reasons, I consider Harris one of the greatest writers of all time. Both of these men are just incredibly gifted at suspending the normal functioning of their everyday egos and at describing the worlds that open up in the aftermath of that suspension. Harris does his descriptions in fiction while Aurobindo does his in philosophy. Both take up in great detail the ethical and self-transformative significance of such experiences of ego transcendence for the persistent human search for both wholeness and the good society. From both I have taken the notion of degrees of spiritual literacy and linked it to pre-colonial African discourses of spirituality, and to the black existentialism of Fanon and Gordon.

These are some of the major figures and texts and the syntheses that I made between them, which have really influenced the course of my philosophical work. After taking so long, I hope that I have answered your question.

Editors: How do you envision the future of the Caribbean? As someone who has devoted forty years to charting the socio-political development of the Caribbean state, what real hopes of transformation do you think currently exist?

Paget Henry: In thinking about the future of the Caribbean, there is no escaping the profound crisis in which the project of nation-building in the region is currently caught. The euphoria of the years following independence has long evaporated as the many difficulties attendant to this national project have become day-to-day realities. Indeed, one suspects that this is one of the reasons why a "large" island like Puerto Rico has been reluctant to claim its political independence. Thus, to answer your question is really to look at the major obstacles blocking the paths to a Caribbean nation-state, and the prospects for strategic shifts in these forces that could make the success of this nationalist project more likely than it appears now. These mountainous forces that must be scaled are basically of two types. First are the local and international centrifugal forces that block regional economic development and also the formation of genuinely regional centers of national power. The second are the centripetal forces that motivate and support the formation of such regional centers of national power and regional economic development. Given the long history of the region, we can divide both of these sets of centrifugal and centripetal forces into historic and more contemporary ones. Let us begin with the historic centrifugal forces.

The first centrifugal force that Caribbean nation-building has to overcome is insularism. The fact that the majority of the territories making up the region are separate islands with, in many cases, hundreds of miles of ocean between them has been a powerful obstacle to the building of a regional nation-state. In spite of being so small, the patriotic attachments to these insular spaces are as strong as in the cases of larger territories, and thus have become major political forces to be reckoned with. These insular attachments have led to intense feelings of suspicion, rivalry, and jealousy that have been major blocks to both economic and political union.

The second historic set of centrifugal forces that we must take note of here is the linguistic divisions that have marked the region following its colonization by Britain, France, Spain, Holland, and the United States. These linguistic divisions have been like so many mountains that we need to but have not been able to climb. They have inhibited regional communication, reinforced cultural and intellectual differences, and thus have made regional cooperation that much more difficult. Without greater degrees of regional cooperation, it becomes extremely difficult for a national imagination that is regional in scope to emerge.

The third historic set of centrifugal forces that Caribbean nation-building has inherited is a very fragmented pattern of decolonization from European and American rule. Although decolonization began with the Haitian Revolution of 1791, there are Caribbean territories that today are still colonies or semi-colonies, even after a large number of them became politically independent between the 1960s and the 1980s. This fragmented pattern of decolonization is in sharp contrast to the unified revolutionary pattern of the original thirteen American colonies. The American Revolution of 1776 was a powerful centripetal force in the making of the federalism that forged the U.S. nation. Such a federal or regionally unifying political center has been absent from the pattern of Caribbean decolonization.

The fourth historic set of centrifugal forces with which Caribbean nation-building has had to do battle is the extroverted nature of the economies of the region. The primary problem associated with extroversion is that individual economies respond much more to the economic and financial currents in their former imperial economies than to similar currents and policy initiative in each other's economies. This pattern follows directly from the primary function of these economies during the colonial period, which was the supplying of agricultural goods to Europe and the U.S., using the labor of a super-exploited black working class, within the framework of an empire-based system of protected markets. Breaking these patterns of extroversion and getting local economies to grow in response to local demand has not been easy for most postcolonial states. In the case of the U.S. colonies, it took the years between the revolution of 1776 and the decades after the end of the Civil War in 1865 to break their inherited patterns of extroversion. Given the factors listed above, it is not surprising that it looks as though it is going to take the Caribbean ex-colonies longer to achieve this turn around than the North American ex-colonies.

Very closely related to this factor of economic extroversion is the lack of control over the ever-changing conditions under which Caribbean economies have gained access to the external markets upon which they are so dependent. This lack of control has been a major source of disruption and instability for Caribbean economies. A more recent example of such externally imposed disruption is the rise of neoliberal globalization and its ending of the empire-based system of protected markets. Many Caribbean and African economies, their governments and their entrepreneurs were neither ready nor prepared for the disruptive impact of this ending of protected markets. Consequently, the period of neoliberal globalization was a very difficult one for both Caribbean and African economies with many experiencing declining growth rates.

These five factors are in my view the key historic centrifugal forces that have overpowered the projects of nation-building in the Caribbean region. They are all of long standing, have deep roots and therefore will not be easy to overcome.

Among the historic centripetal or federal forces that have been pushing the region together, we have three that really stand out. The first of these is pressure to cooperate that has consistently come from the small size of the territories. By most measures, the territories that make up the Caribbean region are indeed very small. Further, within the region there are the micro-states of the Eastern Caribbean such as Grenada, Antigua and Barbuda, Dominica, and St. Lucia, which have come together in the Organization of Eastern Caribbean States (OECS). In a world of nations of the size of the U.S., China, Brazil, India or Russia, even the larger territories of the region seem tiny. This question of size has consistently raised issues about the viability of Caribbean nation-states. Hence, in spite of past failures, such as the 1958–1962 Federation of the English-speaking territories with its federal capital and parliament in Port of Spain, we continue to get the persistent push for forms of regional economic integration, which have now gone from free trade area (CARIFTA) to common market (CARICOM) to single market (CSME). This movement has been an important and persistent centripetal force pushing and pulling the territories of the region together. It has been the primary form of federalism that, since 1962, has been in contrapuntal tension with insularism.

The second set of historic centripetal or federal forces that has fed the projects of a Caribbean nation-state is the persistent sense of a "We," a living Caribbean subjectivity that is indeed regional in scope. It is derived largely from sharing the geography of the region and from inter-regional patterns of migration. This structure of a collective subjectivity that goes beyond and embraces the competing insular subjectivities has been nurtured and given form by the intellectual and cultural traditions of the region. However, it remains contained and badly fractured by the insular and linguistic divisions of the region.

The third of our historic centripetal forces is the sense of embattled solidarity that has been forged in various regional fights against slavery, colonialism, and racialization. As noted earlier, at its height, European colonialism was a totalitarian system of domination that called forth intensive and extensive resistance on the part of those subjected to it. This resistance has been an important source of this sense of a regional "We," and thus a contributor to the centripetal forces operating in the region. However, this solidarity through resistance to totalitarian colonialism has never been synchronized and mobilized into a concentrated and coordinated regional force for national liberation. As a result, it continues to make only brief periodic appearances when something great is achieved by one of us, or something major threatens the region as whole.

Arrayed against these centripetal forces are the more powerful and numerous centrifugal forces discussed above. When both are set in motion, the result has been this history of low levels of national development that we have seen so far in the region.

To bring this analysis up to date, we must now take into account some of the major changes in the values and strengths of these historic local and international forces that have been shaping the prospects for national development in the region. Among the changes in the global environment that I must mention are the following three. First is the decline in power of the international labor and socialist movements after the late 1980s. Second is the symbiotic relationship that has emerged between the U.S. and Chinese economies since the 1990s. Third are the significant changes that are taking place once again in the rules of trade and thus of gaining access to the external markets upon which the extroverted economies of the Caribbean still depend.

With regard to the decline in labor and socialist movements, it is important to recall that the Caribbean independence movements that started in the 1930s were insurrectionary uprisings against the colonial/plantation system, which were empowered and informed by the international labor and socialist movements. The dominant political philosophy that emerged from these movements was in various forms of democratic socialism, whether it was in Puerto Rico, Jamaica, Martinique, Guyana or Antigua or Barbuda. As the cases of Jamaica and Guyana make clear, there was consistent and strong Western opposition to these democratic socialist models of development. During the 1960s and 1970s, these socialist projects were steered in state capitalist directions by foreign capital coming in from the major Western powers. They erupted onto the political stage once again in the 1980s particularly in Jamaica and Grenada, making clear the strength of this socialist current.

However, after the dramatic imploding of the Grenadian Revolution and the electoral defeat of Jamaica's Michael Manley regime in the 1980s, the prospects of reviving and reforming this more indigenous political tradition became considerably more difficult. As these were soon followed by the even more dramatic collapse of authoritarian socialism in the Soviet Union and Eastern Europe, the fate of this tradition only got worse. Further as the strongly anti-labor governments Ronald Reagan and Margaret Thatcher came to power in the U.S. and Britain, the labor governments of the region lost considerable power and were forced to move in the more capital-friendly directions of Prime Minister Tony Blair in Britain and President Bill Clinton in the U.S. All of these external changes have profoundly shifted the orientation, power and influence of Caribbean states, and thus the direction and prospects for nation-building.

The second more contemporary international factor that has significantly changed the direction of nation-building in the region has been the convergence of interests that emerged between U.S. and Chinese economies since the 1990s. This convergence has been so striking that many scholars have referred to it as "Chimerica." This convergence has been more beneficial to China than many expected. China's growth rates in the first decades of this century have broken all records. However, by giving Western capital access to its cheaper labor, this convergence has given Western capital the leverage it needed to disempower trade unions and to weaken their bargaining powers in both the U.S. and the Caribbean. This in turn has led to the rapid industrialization of China but also to the de-industrialization of both the U.S. and Caribbean economies. The collapse of regional manufacturing sectors as a result of the rise of Chimerica has been a major blow to both regional economic development and nation-building.

The third factor that needs a more contemporary updating are the changes in the order of trading represented by new agreements such as the TPP and the TTIP that are currently being negotiated between the U.S. and Europe. What is significant about these agreements is that they are being negotiated outside of the framework of the WTO. I've long suspected that with the collapse of the Doha Round of trade negotiations that the era of the WTO was over. This now appears to be much more the case. Some scholars have begun calling this new era in international trade "global corporatism." If indeed this trend toward global corporatism continues to develop, external access to markets for the region will most likely get more difficult with the associated consequences for national development.

As the impact of the recent shifts in the values and strength of these three international forces are likely to make things more difficult for the region, it would have been nice to have some positive movements in the values and strengths of local centripetal forces to report. Unfortunately, this is not the case. For example, given the rising levels of competition brought on by neoliberal globalization and now by global corporatism, levels of entrepreneurial activity in the region should be rising to meet these new challenges. I cannot say that I have seen a lot of evidence of these needed increases in levels of entrepreneurship.

Given the dramatic increases in social inequality both within and between nations that have resulted from the project of neoliberal globalization, I have long suspected that these are likely to call forth insurrectionary forms of resistance from those middle- and working-class sectors who are feeling the boot of this increasing inequality. However, these movements of resistance such as the protests against the meetings of the WTO, the Solidarity Economy movement in Brazil or the Occupy Wall Street movement in the U.S. have been rather limited in their scope and have not been able to achieve the global reach needed to address this growing problem of social inequality. In the Caribbean, we have not seen a rebirth of the democratic socialist tradition that so effectively addressed the social inequalities of the 1930s and 1940s. Thus, along with increases in levels of entrepreneurship, the present moment also calls for the revival of the democratic socialist Caribbean developmental state. Mired in debt payments and related budgetary crises, there are really no signs of this needed reform and revival.

Third and finally, given the even larger trading blocs that are likely to result from the global corporatist trading regime, it is going to be all the more urgent for Caribbean territories to strengthen existing structures of regional economic integration and inter-regional trading. This will become more necessary as getting into or being able to compete within these larger trading blocs will be more difficult than they are now. Thus along with the already noted needs for reviving the tradition of democratic socialist developmental states and for increasing levels of entrepreneurship, it would have been good if there were significant advances to report on the fuller implementation of the CSME. Unfortunately, once again there is not much evidence that this is taking place. In grasping some of these difficulties in the way of implementation, a helpful reference case would be the European Union. The play of centrifugal and centripetal forces there is quite similar, with the latter forces being stronger than in the case of the Caribbean.

Now that we have updated the values and strengths of the contrapuntal forces, the play between federalism and insularism, affecting nation-building in the Caribbean, we are ready to answer your question more directly. To do this, we must now work out the algebra of these forces, adding up the pluses and the minuses, and see where we stand. First, given the power of insularism and the fragmented pattern of decolonization in the region, it is highly unlikely that we will see in the near future a unified state in the Caribbean such as emerged out of the U.S. colonies. Such a strong federalist center is unlikely to emerge, given the relative weakness of the centripetal forces such as size that we have discussed. Rather, the path of national development in the region will continue to be one of consolidating individual states, while deepening regional economic integration. In other words, it is more likely to resemble the European than the U.S. model.

However, if regional economic integration is to be a growing federalist or centripetal force with future potential, then there must be greater progress on the economic development front. We have already noted the need for a renewal of the democratic socialist developmental state and for higher levels of entrepreneurship. Only a strong combination of these two can break persistent patterns of extroversion, dependence on foreign entrepreneurs, and reverse rising levels of social inequality. These are the conditions that generate and sustain features of neocolonialism and post-colonies.

Increasing existing levels of entrepreneurial activity is going to be a long and difficult adjustment for both regional private and state sectors. Both should work together to confront this challenge, and not cultivate the oppositional relationship that has developed in the case of the U.S. This increase in the entrepreneurial capabilities of Caribbean states must be an integral part of the revival of the democratic socialist tradition of the region. Within the region, socialism has always been as much about production as redistribution. In the years following the collapse of the first socialist experiments, it is all the more important that the two be kept together and not separated. Further, now that we are much more familiar with the production and management problems that arise when markets are even partially suspended, we must be fully aware that with such a revival of the socialist tradition we will be entering unchartered waters. In this algebra of Caribbean nationalism that we are calculating here, it is vital that these centripetal forces of regional economic integration and a developmental state assume more positive values and grow in strength to counter the forces of global corporatism.

Another existing centrifugal force that could shift in a more positive direction is the future of Chimerica. As the cost of labor in China continues to rise and as the Chinese economy continues its shift to a consumer base that is driven primarily by local demand, this turn could ease some of the pressures on Caribbean economies. With the related reductions in labor cost competition, it could become possible once again to think of a more diversified Caribbean economy, which would include an industrial sector. Further, the Chinese state is becoming a major investor and source of aid in the region. The early studies of Chinese state investments in Africa suggest that they have had more positive impacts than both private Chinese and private Western investment. This is a trend that needs to be closely monitored, as a positive turn in the impact of China could significantly affect economic prospects for nation-building in the region.

Finally, although, as you can see, I like to lay things out in ways that allow us to gauge the play of the negative and positive forces, my conception of history remains very Jamesian. For James, there were always those unpredictable moments of spontaneous creativity on the part of the masses that have continued to make history an expression of the freedom of the "We," the collective subjectivity. These are the moments in which something new is brought onto the historical stage and an unforeseen path is charted. In thinking about the future of nation-building in the Caribbean, while it is important to assess the forces that I have outlined above, we most certainly cannot leave out when creative upsurges may take us in a direction not visible in terms of the play of my centripetal and centrifugal forces. The history of the region has been punctuated by such creative eruptions of the Caribbean public self. This public self has many more such eruptions to make, some of which will certainly affect the course of national development in the decades ahead.

After all of these twists and turns, all these pluses and minuses, I sincerely hope that I have answered this and all of your questions to your satisfaction.

Bibliography

SELECTION OF PAGET HENRY'S WRITINGS

1973	"Antigua: A Society in Transition," *Shango* 1, no. 1.
1976a	"A Sociology of the Sociology of Modernization and Development," *Cornell Journal of Social Relations* 2, no. 1 (Spring): 117–21.
1976b	"Reply to Mr. Cox," *Cornell Journal of Social Relations* 2, no. 2 (Fall): 203–6.
1979a	"The Aftermath of the Coup in Grenada," *Blackworld* 8 (October).
1979b	"The Coup in Grenada," *Blackworld* 7 (May).
1980a	"Sartre: A Tribute to an Outstanding Freedom Fighter," *Caribbean Contact* 8 (June).
1980b	"The Reagan Policy and the Caribbean," *Outlet* (July and August).
1981a	"Antigua's Independence: The New Challenge," *Outlet*, Independence Issue (October).
1981b	"The Mass Media and Foreign Domination," *Outlet* (November).
1981c	"State-Class Relations in Antigua," *Bulletin of Eastern Caribbean Affairs* 7 (November/December).
1981d	"The Mass Media and Foreign Domination," *Outlet* 10 (November).
1982a	"Decolonization, Tourism and Class/Race Structure in Antigua," in (ed.), *Contemporary Caribbean: A Sociological Reader*. Maracas, Trinidad: College Press, 243–63.
1982b	"The Antiguan Political System," *Antiguan and Barbuda Forum* 1, no. 1 (September).
1983a	with Carl Stone, eds. 1983. *Newer Caribbean: Decolonization Democracy and Development*. Philadelphia: Institute for the Study of Human Issues.

1983b   "A Setback for Democracy in Grenada," *Newsday* (27 October).

1983c   "Grenada: A Return to the Big Stick," *Village Times* (10 November).

1983d   "Decolonization and Cultural Underdevelopment in the Commonwealth Caribbean," in *Newer Caribbean*, 95–120.

1983e   Review of Novelle Richards, *The Struggle and the Conquest*, Vols. I and II, in *Antigua and Barbuda Forum* 1, no. 2 (Spring): 25–27.

1983f   Review of Ulf Himmelstrand et al., *Beyond Welfare Capitalism*, in *American Journal of Sociology* 88, no. 6 (May): 1299–1301.

1984a   "Slavery: Its Historical and Symbolic Importance," in Ralph Prince (ed.), *Antigua and Barbuda: From Bondage to Freedom, 150th Anniversary of Emancipation*. St. John's, Antigua: National Emancipatory Committee for the Ministry of Economic Development, Tourism, and Energy, 30–33.

1984b   Review of A. J. Payne, *The Politics of the Caribbean Community 1961–79*, in *Studies in Comparative International Development* 19, no. 2 (Summer): 86–89.

1985a   *Peripheral Capitalism and Underdevelopment in Antigua.* New Brunswick, NJ: Transaction Books.

1985b   "En Busca de la Nacionalidad: La Politica Exterior en el Caribe Oriental," in Heraldo Munoz (ed.), *Las Politicas Exteriores Latinoamericanas Frente a la Crisis*. Bueno Aires: Grupo Editor Latinamericano, 125–42.

1985c   "Parties and Elections in Antigua," *Bulletin of Eastern Caribbean Affairs* 10, no. 6 (January/February): 28–33.

1986a   "Democracy and Crisis in the Eastern Caribbean: The Cases of Antigua and Grenada," CISCLA Working Paper #27, Puerto Rico: Inter-American University.

1986b   "Indigenous Religions and the Transformation of Peripheral Societies," in J. Hadden and A. Shupe (eds.), *Prophetic Religions and Politics*. New York: Paragon Press, 123–50.

1986c   "Towards a Theory of Peripheral Cultural Systems," Working Paper #10, Center for Comparative Development, Brown University.

1986d	Review of M. Bloodstrom and B. Hettne, *Development Theory in Transition*, in *Contemporary Sociology* 15, no. 5 (September): 772–73.
1987	Review of E. Huber-Stephens and J. Stephens, *Democratic Socialism in Jamaica*, in *The New West Indian Guide*.
1989	"Marxism and Intellectual Life at Brown," *Imbroglio*.
1990a	"Grenada and the Theory of Peripheral Transformation," *Social and Economic Studies* 39, no. 2 (June): 151–92.
1990b	"Socialism and Cultural Transformation in Grenada," in Jorge Heine (eds.), *A Revolution Aborted*. Pittsburgh: University of Pittsburg Press, 51–82.
1991	"Political Accumulation and Authoritarianism in the Caribbean: The Case of Antigua," *Social and Economic Studies* 40, no. 1: 1–38.
1992a	with Paul Buhle, eds. *C. L. R. James's Caribbean*. Durham: Duke University Press.
1992b	with Paul Buhle, "Caliban as Deconstructionist: C. L. R. James and Post-Colonial Discourse," in *C. L. R. James's Caribbean*, 111–42.
1992c	"C. L. R. James and the Caribbean Economic Tradition," *C. L. R. James's Caribbean*, 145–73.
1992d	"C. L. R. James and the Antiguan Left," in *C. L. R. James's Caribbean*, 225–62.
1993a	"African Philosophy in the Mirror of Logicism: A Review Essay," *C. L. R. James Journal* 4, no. 1 (Winter): 70–78.
1993b	"Afro-Caribbean Philosophy: An Introduction," *C. L. R. James Journal* 4, no. 1 (Winter): 2–11.
1993c	"C. L. R. James, African and Afro-Caribbean Philosophy," *C. L. R. James Journal* 4, no. 1 (Winter): 12–43.
1994	"To Plunge or Not Plunge: NAFTA and the Caribbean," *Third World Affairs* 2 (Spring): 30–35.
1995	with Leara Rhodes, "State and Media in the Caribbean: The Case of Antigua," *Journalism & Mass Communication Quarterly* 72, no. 3 (Autumn).

1995 "Sociology: After the Linguistic and Multicultural Turns," *Sociological Forum* 10, no. 4 (December): 633–52.

Reprinted in Steven Cole (ed.), *What's Wrong with Sociology?* New Brunswick, NJ: Transaction Books, 2001, 319–40.

Reprinted in Bruce Hare (ed.), *2001 Race Odyssey: Sociology and African Americans.* Syracuse, NY: Syracuse University Press, 2002, 77–94.

1996 "Fanon, African and Afro-Caribbean Philosophy," in Lewis R. Gordon, Tracy Sharpley and Renée T. White (eds.), *Fanon: A Critical Reader*, Malden, MA: Blackwell, 220–43.

1997a "Rastafarianism and the Reality of Dread," in Lewis R. Gordon (ed.), *Existence in Black*, New York: Routledge, 157–64.

1997b "Rex Nettleford, African and Afro-Caribbean Philosophy," *C. L. R. James Journal* 5, no. 1: 44–97.

Reprinted in *Caribbean Quarterly* 43, no. 2 (1997): 31–53.

1998a "C. L. R. James as Political Theorist: A Review Essay," *C. L. R. James Journal* 6, no. 1 (Winter 1998): 72–83.

1998b "On Erich Fromm," in Paul Buhle, Mari Jo Buhle, and Dan Georgakas (eds.), *The American Encyclopedia of the American Left*, 2nd ed. New York: Oxford University Press.

1998c "Philosophy and the Caribbean Intellectual Tradition," *Small Axe*, no. 4 (September): 3–28.

1999 "Wilson Harris and Caribbean Philosophical Anthropology," *C. L. R. James Journal* 7, no. 1 (Winter): 104–34.

2000a *Caliban's Reason: Introducing Afro-Caribbean Philosophy.* New York: Routledge.

2000b "Framing the Political: Self and Politics in Wilson Harris," *Journal of Caribbean Literatures* 2, nos. 1, 2 and 3, (Spring): 82–95.

2000c "Myth, Language and Habermasian Rationality: Another Africana Contribution," in Lewis Hahn (ed.), *Perspectives on Habermas.* Peru, IL: Open Court, 89–112.

2001a "Antigua and Barbuda," in M. Ember and C. Ember (eds.), *Countries and Their Cultures*, Vol. 1. New York: Macmillan, 70–76.

2001b   "Commodification and Existence in African American
             Communities," in Robert Birt (ed.), *The Quest for
             Community and Identity: An Africana Philosophical
             Anthology*. Lanham, MD: Rowman & Littlefield,
             185–209.

2001c   "The Culture of Antigua and Barbuda," *The
             Encyclopedia of National Cultures*. New York: Macmillan.

2001d   "On the Revolutionary Pulse of the Caribbean: A
             Review Essay," *C. L. R. James Journal* 8, no. 2 (Winter
             2001): 187–94.

2001e   "Randall Collins, Ideas and Ritual Solidarity,"
             Sociological Forum 16, no. 1: 167–74.

2001f   "Self-Formation and the Call: An Africana Perspective,"
             Listening 36, no. 1 (Winter): 27–45.

2002   "Culture, Politics and Writing in Afro-Caribbean
             Philosophy: A Reply to Critics," *Small Axe* (March):
             179–90.

2002–2003a   "Cultural Dependence in the Age of Informatic
             Capitalism," *Radical Philosophy Review* 5, nos. 1 & 2:
             29–53.

2002–2003b   "Between Naipaul and Aurobindo: Where Is Indo-
             Caribbean Philosophy?" *C. L. R. James Journal* 9, no. 1
             (Winter): 3–36.

2002–2003c   with Jose Itzigsohn, "Special Symposium on
             Development Theory: Introduction," *Radical Philosophy
             Review* 5, nos. 1 & 2 (2002–3): 24–28.

2003a   "Afro-American Philosophy: A Caribbean Perspective,"
             reprint from *Caliban's Reason* in Tommy Lott and John
             Pittman (eds.), *The Blackwell Companion to African-
             American Philosophy*. Malden, MA: Blackwell, 48–66.

2003b   "Ethnicity and Independent Thought: Lloyd Best and
             Indo-Caribbean Philosophy," in Selwyn Ryan (ed.),
             *Independent Thought and Caribbean Freedom: Essay in
             Honor of Lloyd Best*. St. Augustine, Trinidad: SALISES,
             115–44.

2004a   "Between Hume and Cugoano: Race, Ethnicity and
             Philosophical Entrapment," *Journal of Speculative
             Philosophy* 18, no. 2: 129–48.

2004b   "The Caribbean Plantation: Its Contemporary
             Significance," in Bernard Moit (ed.), *Sugar, Slavery, and*

Society: Perspectives on the Caribbean, India, the
Mascarenes, and the United States.* Gainesville: University
of Florida Press, 157–85.

2004c   "Extending and Defending *Caliban's Reason*: Replies to
Critics," *C. L. R. James Journal* 19, no. 1: 150–90.

2004d   "The Future of the Post-colonial Subject: Sylvia Winter
and Wilson Harris," Benedicte Ledent (ed.), *Bridges
Across Chasms: Towards a Transcultural Future in
Caribbean Literature*. Liege, Belgium: Liege Languages
and Literature, 26–38.

2004e   "Whiteness and Africana Phenomenology," in George
Yancy (ed.), *What White Looks Like*. New York:
Routledge, 195–210.

2004f   "Wilson Harris and Caribbean Philosophies of Art:
A Review Essay," *C. L. R. James Journal* 10, no. 1: 213–30.

2004g   Review of Anténor Firmin, *The Equality of the Human
Races*, in *Constellations* 11, no. 2: 305–7.

2005a   "Africana Phenomenology: Its Philosophical
Implications," *C. L. R. James Journal* 11, no. 1: 79–112.

2005b   Review of Bill Schwartz (ed.), *West Indian Intellectuals in
Britain*, in *The New West Indian Guide* 79, nos. 3 and 4:
339–41.

2006a   "Afro-American Studies and the Rise of Afro-American
Philosophy" in Lewis R. Gordon and Jane Anna
Gordon (eds.), *A Companion to African- American Studies*.
Malden, MA: Blackwell, 223–45.

2006b   "Black Heretics, Black Prophets and Double
Consciousness: A Review Essay," *C. L. R. James Journal*
12, no. 1: 177–84.

2006c   "From the Pattern to Being: Howard Thurman and
Africana Phenomenology," *C. L. R. James Journal* 12, no.
1: 61–83.

2006d   "Sylvia Wynter and the Transcendental Spaces of
Caribbean Thought," in B. Anthony Bogues (ed.), *After
Man, Towards the Human: Critical Essays on the Thought of
Sylvia Wynter*. Kingston, Jamaica: Ian Randle, 258–89.

2007a   "Africana Political Philosophy and the Crisis of the
Postcolony," *Socialism and Democracy* 21, no. 3: 36–59.

| 2007b | "C. L. R. James and the Orthodoxies of John McClendon and David Scott: A Review Essay," *C. L. R. James Journal* 13, no. 1: 275–89. |

| 2007c | "Philosophy and Antigua/Barbudan Political Culture," *C. L. R. James Journal* 13, no. 1: 239–64. |

| 2007d | "Ramabai Espinet and Indo-Caribbean Poeticism" in Marina Banchetti and Clevis Headley (eds.), *Shifting the Geography of Reason*. Cambridge Scholars Press, 25–30. |

| 2008a | "Lewis Gordon, Africana Phenomenology and the Crisis of European Man," *C. L. R. James Journal* 14, no. 1: 71–101. |

| 2008b | "Signs, Markets and the Caribbean Left," *International Journal of Humanistic Studies and Literature* 9 (Spring): 107–11. |

| 2008c | "Wilson Harris: Concluding an Envisioning of Infinite Genesis," *C. L. R. James Journal* 14, no. 1: 332–42. |

| 2008d | "Portraits of Agency: A Review of Althea Prince's *Loving this Man*," *Antigua and Barbuda Review of Books* 1, no. 1: 36–42. |

| 2009a | "Antigua and Barbuda: Inching Our Way Toward Economic Autonomy," *Antigua and Barbuda Review of Books* 2, no. 1: 22–34. |

| 2009b | "C. L. R. James and the Creolizing of Rousseau and Marx," *C. L. R. James Journal* 15, no. 1: 179–205. |

| 2010a | *Shouldering Antigua and Barbuda: The Life of V. C. Bird*, 2nd ed. London: Hansib. |

| 2010b | "Caribbean Dependency in the Phase of Informatic Capitalism," in Brian Meeks and Norman Girvan (eds.), *The Thought of New World: The Quest for Decolonisation*. Kingston, Jamaica: Ian Randle, 2010, 172–205. |

| 2011 | "Gender and Africana Phenomenology," *C. L. R. James Journal* 17, no. 1: 153–83. |

| 2013a | Afterword to Aaron Kamugisha (ed.), *Caribbean Political Thought: The Colonial State to Caribbean Internationalisms*. Kingston, Jamaica: Ian Randle. |

| 2013b | Afterword to Aaron Kamugisha (ed.), *Caribbean Political Thought: Theories of the Post-Colonial State*. Kingston, Jamaica: Ian Randle. |

| 2013c | "Intra-subjectivity in the Philosophy of Wilson Harris," *Journal of Postcolonial Writing* 49, no. 2 (May): 209–21. |

2013d   "C. L. R. James, Walter Rodney and the Rebuilding of
                Caribbean Socialism," *C. L. R. James Journal* 19, no. 1 & 2
                (Fall): 458–84.

2014a   "Badminded Nikki: A Review of Joanne Hillhouse's *Oh
                Gad!" Antigua and Barbuda Review of Books.*

2014b   "Black Power in the Political Thought of Antigua and
                Barbuda," in Kate Quinn (ed.), *Black Power in the
                Caribbean.* Gainsville: University of Florida Press.

2015a   *The Art of Mali Olatunji: Painterly Photography from
                Antigua and Barbuda.* London: Hansib.

2015b   "Gordon Lewis and the Writing of Afro-Caribbean
                Political Thought," in Brian Meeks and Jermaine
                McCalpin (eds.), *Freedom, Power and Sovereignty: The
                Thought of Gordon K. Lewis.* Kingston, Jamaica: Ian
                Randle, 14–45.

2015c   "The Socialist Legacy of Tim Hector," *Antigua and
                Barbuda Review of Books* 8, no. 1 (Summer): 109–31.

CITED WORKS BY OTHER AUTHORS

Aganbegyan, Abe. 1988. *The Economic Challenge of Perestroika.* Bloomington: Indiana University Press.

Alcaly, Roger. 2003. *The New Economy.* New York: Farrar Strauss and Giroux.

Alcoff, Linda Martín. 2006. *Visible Identities: Race, Gender, and the Self.* New York: Oxford University Press.

ALP White Paper. 1976. St Johns, Antiguan Labour Party.

Antigua Times. 1971 (18 August).

———. 1973 (No. 38, 16 May).

Ambursely, Fitzroy, and Robin Cohen, eds. 1983. *Crisis in the Caribbean.* New York: Monthly Review Press.

Amin, Samir. 1974. *Accumulation on a World Scale: A Critique of the Theory of Underdevelopment.* New York: Monthly Review Press.

———. 1976. *Unequal Development: An Essay on the Social Formation of Peripheral Capitalism,* trans. Brian Pearce. New York: Monthly Review Press.

———. 2002–2003. "Globalization and Capitalism's Second Belle Epoque." *Radical Philosophy Review* 5, nos. 1–2: 86–95.

Antigua and Barbuda Herald. 1986 (May 23).

Antigua Magnet. 1938 (February 21).

———. 1939a (March 14).

———. 1939b (March 20).

———. 1939c (September 15).

Aurobindo, Sri. 1987. *The Life Divine.* Pondicherry: Sri Aurobindo Ashram.

———. 1993. *Integral Yoga: Sri Aurobindo's Teaching and Method of Practice.* Twin Lakes, WI: Lotus Press.

———. 1999. *The Human Cycle: The Psychology of Social Movement.* Twin Lakes, WI: Lotus Press.

Baran, Paul. 1968. *The Political Economy of Growth.* New York: Monthly Review Press.

Baudrilliard, Jean. 1975. *The Mirror of Production*, trans. Mark Poster. St. Louis: Telos Press.

Beauvoir, Simone de. 2000. *The Ethics of Ambiguity*, trans. Bernard Frechtman. New York: Citadel.

Beckford, George. 1971. *Persistent Poverty*. New York: Oxford University Press.

———. 1972. *Persistent Poverty: Underdevelopment in Plantation Economies of the Third World*. Kingston, Jamaica: University of West Indies Press.

———, ed. 1975. *Caribbean Economy*. Kingston, Jamaica: I.S.E.R.

Beckford, George, et al. 1985. *Pathways to Progress: The People's Socialist Plan*. Morant Bay, Jamaica: Maroon Books.

Benn, Denis. 1987. *The Growth and Development of Political Ideas in the Caribbean, 1774–1983*. Kingston, Jamaica: I.S.E.R.

Bernal, Martin. 1987. *Black Athena: The Afroasiatic Roots of Classical Civilization*. Vol. 1: *The Fabrication of Ancient Greece, 1785–1985*. New Brunswick, NJ: Rutgers University Press.

Best, Lloyd. 1999. "Economic Theory and Economic Policy in the 20th Century West Indies: The Lewis Tradition of Town and Gown." *The Fourth Sir Arthur Lewis Memorial Lecture*. Basseterre, St. Kitts: Eastern Caribbean Central Bank.

Bhabha, Homi. 2004. *The Location of Culture*. New York: Routledge.

Blyden, Edward. 1994. *African Life and Customs*. Baltimore, MD: Black Classics Press.

Bogues, B. Anthony, ed. 2006. *After Man, Towards the Human: Critical Essays on the Thought of Sylvia Wynter*. Kingston, Jamaica: Ian Randle.

Bourdieu, Pierre. 1984. *Distinction: A Social Critique of the Judgement of Taste*, trans. Richard Nice. Cambridge, MA: Harvard University Press.

Brathwaite, Kamau. "Caribbean Man in Space and Time." *Savacou* 11/12 (September 1975): 1–11, 106–8.

Caribbean Contact. 1987. Vol. 14, no. 12 (May).

Caribbean Times. 1987. No. 302 (January 9).

Castoriadis, Cornelius. 2000. *The Imaginary Institution of Society*. Cambridge, MA: MIT Press.

Césaire, Aimé. 1972. *Discourse on Colonialism*, trans. Joan Pinkham. New York: Monthly Review Press.

Cohen, Stephen. 1996. "Geo-economics: Lessons from America's Mistakes," in Martin Carnoy et al. eds. *The New Global Economy in the Information Age*. University Park: Pennsylvania State University Press.

Collins, Randall. 1998. *The Sociology of Philosophies: A Global Theory of Intellectual Change*. Cambridge, MA: Harvard University Press.

Cooper, Anna Julia. 1988. *A Voice From the South*. Oxford: Oxford University Press.

Craig, S., ed. 1981. *Contemporary Caribbean*, Vol. 1. Maracas, Trinidad: College Press.

Cugoano, Quobna Ottobah. 1999. *"Thoughts and Sentiments on the Evil of Slavery" and Other Writings*, ed. with an intro. and notes by Vincent Carretta. New York: Penguin Books.

Danns, G. 1981. *Domination and Power in Guyana*. New Brunswick, NJ: Transaction Books.

Davies, Carole Boyce. 2008. *Left of Karl Marx: The Political Life of Black Communist Claudia Jones*. Durham, NC: Duke University Press.

Davis, Angela Y. 1983. *Women, Race, and Class*. New York: Vintage.

Davis, Gregson. 1997. *Aimé Césaire*. New York: Cambridge University Press.

DeLoughery, Elizabeth. 1998. "Tidalectics: Charting Caribbean 'Peoples or the Sea.'" *Span* 47 (October): 18–38.

Derrida, Jacques. 1976. *Of Grammatology*. Baltimore: Johns Hopkins University Press.

———. 1989. *Edmund Husserl's The Origins of Geometry*. Lincoln: University of Nebraska Press.

Descartes, René. 1960. *Meditations on First Philosophy*, trans. Laurence J. LaFleur. Indianapolis, IN: Bobbs-Merrill.

Du Bois, W. E. B. 1938. *Black Reconstruction in America, 1860–1880*. New York: Harcourt, Brace.

———. 1969. *The Souls of Black Folk*. New York: Fawcett.

———. 1996. *The Philadelphia Negro*. Philadelphia: University of Pennsylvania Press.

———. 1999. *Darkwater*. New York: Dover.

———. 2000. *Dusk of Dawn*. New Brunswick, NJ: Transaction.

Duménil, Gérard, and Dominique Lévy. 2004. *Capital Resurgent: Roots of the Neoliberal Revolution*, translated by Derek Jeffers. Cambridge, MA: Harvard University Press.

Dupuy, Alex. 1989. *Haiti in the World Economy*. Boulder, CO: Westview Press.

Dussel, Enrique. 1996. *The Underside of Modernity: Apel, Ricoeur, Taylor, and the Philosophy of Liberation*, trans. Eduardo Mendieta. Atlantic Highlands, NJ: Humanities Press.

Emmanuel, P. 1979. *General Elections in the Eastern Caribbean: A Handbook*. Cave Hill, Barbados: I.S.E.R.

———. 1983. "Revolutionary Theory and Political Reality in the Eastern Caribbean." *Journal of Interamerican Studies and World Affairs* 25, no. 2 (May): 193–227 (modified version of a paper presented at the Seventh Annual Conference of the Caribbean Studies Association held in Kingston, Jamaica, 25–29 May 1982).

EPICA Task Force. 1983. *Grenada: the Peaceful Revolution*. Washington, DC: EPICA Task Force.

Ewing, A. C. 1953. *Ethics*. London: English Universities Press.

Fagen, Richard R., ed. 1979. *Capitalism and the State in U.S.-Latin American Relations*. Palo Alto, CA: Stanford University Press.

Fanon, Frantz. 1967. *Black Skin, White Masks*, trans. Charles Lamm Markmann. New York: Grove Press.

———. 1968. *The Wretched of the Earth*, trans. Constance Farrington. New York: Grove Press.

Farrell, T. 1976. "Review Article: Dependence and Transformation." *Social and Economic Studies* 25, no. 2: 307–11.

Fedon Publishers. 1982a. *In the Spirit of Butler*. St. Georges, Grenada: Fedon Publishers.

———. 1982b. *To Construct From Morning*. St. Georges, Grenada: Fedon Publishers.

———. 1982c. *Grenada Is Not Alone*. St. Georges, Grenada: Fedon Publishers.

Fox, Annette Baker. 1949. *Freedom and Welfare in the Caribbean: A Colonial Dilemma*. New York: Harcourt Brace.

Gaspar, David Barry. 1985. *Bondmen & Rebels*. Baltimore, MD: Johns Hopkins University Press.

Girvan, N. 1971. *Foreign Capital and Economic Underdevelopment in Jamaica*. Mona, Jamaica: I.S.E.R.

———. 1976. *Corporate Imperialism: Conflict and Expropriation*. New York: Monthly Review Press.

———. 2005. "W. A. Lewis, the Plantation School and Dependency: An Interpretation." *Social and Economic Studies* 54, no. 3: 198–221.

Glissant, Édouard. 1992. *Caribbean Discourse*. Charlottesville: University of Virginia Press.

———. 1997. *Poetics of Relation*. Ann Arbor: University of Michigan Press.

Gooding-Williams, Robert. 1991–1992. "Evading Narrative Myth, Evading Prophetic Pragmatism: Cornel West's *The American Evasion of Philosophy*." *Massachusetts Review* 32, no. 4: 517–42.

Gordon, Jane Anna. 2014. *Creolizing Political Theory: Reading Rousseau through Fanon*. New York: Fordham University Press.

Gordon, Jane Anna, and Neil Roberts, eds. *Creolizing Rousseau*. London: Rowman & Littlefield International.

Gordon, Lewis R. 1995a/1999. *Bad Faith and Antiblack Racism*. Amherst, NY: Humanity/Prometheus Books. Originally published in Atlantic Highlands, NJ, by Humanities International Press.

———. 1995b. *Fanon and the Crisis of European Man: An Essay on Philosophy and the Human Sciences*. New York: Routledge.

———. 2000. *Existentia Africana: Understanding Africana Existential Thought*. New York: Routledge.

———. 2006. *Disciplinary Decadence: Living Thought in Trying Times*. New York: Routledge.

———. 2015. *What Fanon Said: A Philosophical Introduction to His Life and Thought*. New York: Fordham University Press.

Green, Cecilia. 1999. "A Recalcitrant Plantation Colony: Dominica 1880–1946." *New West Indian Guide* 73, nos. 3 and 4: 41–71.

Greene, John Edwards. 1974. *Race vs. Politics in Guyana: Political Cleavages and Political Mobilisation in the 1968 General Election*. Mona, Jamaica: I.S.E.R.

Gyekye, Kwame. 1995. *An Essay on African Philosophical Thought: The Akan Conceptual Scheme*. Revised Edition. Philadelphia: Temple University Press.

———. 1997. *Tradition and Modernity: Philosophical Reflections on the African Experience*. New York: Oxford University Press.

Habermas, Jürgen. 1971. *Knowledge and Human Interests*, trans. Jeremy Shapiro. Boston: Beacon Press.

———. 1975. *Legitimation Crisis*, trans. Thomas McCarthy. Boston: Beacon Press.

———. 1987. *The Theory of Communicative Action*, trans. Thomas McCarthy. Boston: Beacon Press.

———. 1992. *Postmetaphysical Thinking*, trans. William Mark Hohengarten. Cambridge, MA: MIT Press.

Hardt, Michael, and Antonio Negri. 2000. *Empire*. Cambridge, MA: Harvard University Press.

Harris, Wilson. 1967. *Tradition, the Writer and Society*. London: New Beacon Books.

———. 1987. *The Infinite Rehearsal*. London: Faber & Faber.

———. 1995. *History, Myth and Fable in the Caribbean and Guianas*. Tacarigua: Calaloux.

Hector, Tim. 1976. *Independence: Hi/The Old Mess: No!* St. Johns, Antigua: Outlet.

———. 1983. *Antigua for Antiguans, Barbuda for Barbudans*. St. Johns, Antigua: Outlet.

———. 2000. "Review of *Caliban's Reason*." *Outlet* (February 4): 6.

———. N.d. CD: *Leonard Tim Hector's Fan the Flame Articles*. Vol. 1: *2002–1998*. St. Johns, Antigua: Outlet.

Hegel, Georg Wilhelm Friedrich. 1956. *The Philosophy of History*, trans. J. Sibree. New York: Dover.

———. 1967. *The Phenomenology of Mind*, trans. J. B. Baillie. New York: Harper & Row.

———. 1971. *The Early Theological Writings*, trans. T. M. Knox and Richard Kroner. Philadelphia: University of Pennsylvania Press.

The Herald. 1987. Vol. I, no. 58 (January).

Hillhouse, Joanne. 2012. *Oh Gad!* New York: Sirebor Books.

Holmes, Leslie, ed. 1981. *The Withering Away of the State?* Beverly Hills, CA: Sage.

Hurst, Lionel. 2007. *Democracy of Diplomacy*. London: Authorhouse.

Husserl, Edmund. 1970. *The Crisis of European Sciences and Transcendental Phenomenology*. Trans. David Carr. Evanston, IL: Northwestern University Press.

———. 1975. *Ideas: General Introduction to Pure Phenomenology*. Trans. W. R. Boyce Gibson. London: Collier Macmillan Books.

Ince, B., ed. 1979. *Contemporary International Relations of the Caribbean*. St. Augustine, Trinidad: I.I.R.

Jacobs, W. Richard, and Ian Jacobs. 1982. *Grenada: The Route to Revolution*. Havana, Cuba: Casas de las Américas.

Jagan, Cheddi. 1975. *The West on Treat: The Fight for Guyana's Freedom*. Berlin, Germany: Seven Seas Books.

James, C. L. R. 1938/1989. *The Black Jacobins: Toussaint L'Ouverture and the San Domingo Revolution*. New York: Vintage.

———. 1962. *Party Politics in the West Indies*. San Juan, Trinidad: Vedic Enterprises.

———. 1983. *At the Rendezvous of Victory*. London: Allison &. Busby.

——. 1986. *State Capitalism and World Revolution.* Chicago, IL: Charles Kerr.

——. 1992. *The C. L. R. James Reader,* ed. Anna Grimshaw. Oxford: Blackwell.

——. 1993. *World Revolution 1917–1936: The Rise and Fall of the Communist International.* Atlantic Highlands, NJ: Humanities Press.

James, C. L. R., Raya Dunayevskaya, and Grace Lee. 1972. *The Invading Socialist Society.* Detroit, MI: Bewick.

James, C. L. R., Grace C. Lee, and Pierre Chaulieu. 1974 [1958]. *Facing Reality.* Detroit, MI: Bewick.

Jean, Sir James H. 1942. *Physics and Philosophy.* Cambridge: Cambridge University Press.

Jules, D., and D. Rojas, eds. 1982. *Maurice Bishop: Selected Speeches, 1979–1981.* Havana, Cuba: Casas de las Américas.

Kamugisha, Aaron, ed. 2013a. *Caribbean Political Thought: The Colonial State to Caribbean Internationalisms.* Kingston, Jamaica: Ian Randle.

——. 2013b. *Caribbean Political Thought: Theories of the Post-Colonial State.* Kingston, Jamaica: Ian Randle.

Karabell, Zachary. 2009. *Superfusion: How China and America Became One Economy and Why the World's Prosperity Depends on It.* New York: Simon & Schuster.

Keynes, John. 1964. *The General Theory of Employment, Interest and Money.* New York: Harcourt, Brace & World.

Kincaid, Jamaica. 1984. *At the Bottom of the River.* New York: Farrar Strauss Giroux.

——. 1985. *Annie John.* New York: Farrar Strauss Giroux.

——. 1988. *A Small Place.* New York: Farrar Strauss Giroux.

——. 1996. *The Autobiography of My Mother.* New York: Farrar Strauss Giroux.

——. 1990. *Lucy.* New York: Farrar Strauss Giroux.

King, Richard. 1999. *Indian Philosophy: An Introduction to Hindu and Buddhist Thought.* Washington, DC: Georgetown University Press.

Lake, Edgar, 2004. *The Devil's Bridge.* London: Athena Press.

Lamming, George. 1970 /1953. *In the Castle of My Skin.* Reprint. Introduction by Richard Wright. New York: Collier Books.

——. 1984. *The Pleasures of Exile.* London: Allison and Busby.

——. 2004. *The Sovereignty of the Imagination.* Kingston, Jamaica: Arawak.

Lenin, V. 1929. *What Is to Be Done?* New York: International Publishers.

——. 1970. *The State and Revolution.* Peking, China: Foreign Language Press.

Levering-Lewis, David. 1995. *W. E. B. DuBois: A Reader.* New York: Henry Holt.

Levitt, Kari. 2005. *Reclaiming Development.* Kingston, Jamaica: Ian Randle.

Levitt, Kari Polanyi, and Lloyd Best. 1975. "Character of Caribbean Economy," in George L. Beckford (ed.), *Caribbean Economy: Dependence and Backwardness,* 34–60. Mona, Jamaica: I.S.E.R., University of the West Indies.

Lewis, Arthur. 1954. "Economic Development with Unlimited Supplies of Labour." *Manchester School* 22, no. 2: 139–91.

——. 1970. *The Theory of Economic Growth.* New York: Harper & Row.

——. 1977. *Labour in the West Indies.* London: New Beacon Books.

——. 1983. "Socialism and Economic Growth," in Mark Gersovitz (ed.), *Selected Economic Writings of W. Arthur Lewis.* New York: New York University Press.

Lewis, Gordon. 1968. *The Growth of the Modern West Indies.* New York: Monthly Review Press.

Lewis, Rupert. 1998. *Walter Rodney's Intellectual and Political Thought.* Detroit, MI: Wayne State University Press.

Lewis, V., ed. 1976. *Size, Self-determination and International Relations: The Caribbean.* Mona, Jamaica: I.S.E.R.

Lovell, Harold. 1982. "Anthonyson King: Mathematician, Co-op Manager and Liberator." *Outlet* (10 September).

Maldonado-Torres, Nelson. 2008. *Against War: Views from the Underside of Modernity.* Durham, NC: Duke University Press.

Mandle, Jay. 2010. "The Role of Migration in the Caribbean Integration and Development." Paper presented the 11th Annual SALISES Conference, Trinidad (24–26 March).

Marx, Karl. 1967. *Capital*. Vol. I. New York: International Publishers.

Mehta, Brinda. 2000. *Diasporic Dis(locations): Indo-Caribbean Women Writers Negotiate the Kala Pani*. Kingston, Jamaica: University of the West Indies Press.

———. 2009. *Notions of Identity, Diaspora, and Gender in Caribbean Women's Writing*. New York: Palgrave Macmillan.

Michels, Robert. 1968. *Political Parties*. New York: Free Press.

Mills, Charles. 1998. *Blackness Visible*. Ithaca, NY: Cornell University Press.

———. 2001. "Prophetic Pragmatism as Political Philosophy," in George Yancy (ed.), *Cornel West: A Critical Reader*, 192–223. Malden, MA: Blackwell.

Mohanty, J. N. 2000. *Classical Indian Philosophy*. Lanham, MD: Rowman & Littlefield.

Moore, Barrington. 1966. *The Social Origins of Dictatorship and Democracy: Lord and Peasant in the Making of the Modern World*. Boston: Beacon Press.

Moutoussamy, Ernest. 1989. "Indianness in the French West Indies," in Frank Birbalsingh (ed.), *Indenture and Exile: The Indo-Caribbean Experience*, 27–36. Toronto, Canada: Tsar Publishers.

Munroe, T. 1972. *The Politics of Constitutional Decolonization*. Mona, Jamaica: I.S.E.R.

Munroe, T., and R. Lewis, eds. 1971. *Readings in Government and Politics of the West Indies*, Dept. of Governments, UWI, Mona, Jamaica.

Naipaul, V. S. 1964. *An Area of Darkness*. London: Andre Duetsch.

———. 1979. *India: A Wounded Civilization*. London: Penguin Books.

———. 1980. *A House for Mr. Biswas*. London: Penguin Books.

Negri, Antonio. 2003. *Time for Revolution*. New York: Continuum.

Nettl, J. P. 1967. *Political Mobilization*. London: Faber.

Nettleford, Rex. 1993. *Inward Stretch, Outward Reach*. London: Macmillan Press.

Neustadt, R. 1980. *Presidential Power*. New York: Wiley.

Outlet. 1977. Vol. 2, no. 8 (17 March).

Outlet. 1977. Vol. 3, no. 6 (21 July).

Outlet. 1986. Vol. 14, no. 9 (9 May).

Outlet. 1986. Vol. 14, no. 23 (6 June).

Outlet. 1986. Vol. 14, no. 228 (11 July).

Outlet. 2000 (4 February).

Peirce, Charles Sanders. 1931. *Collected Papers*. Cambridge, MA: Harvard University Press.

Perry, Jeffrey B. 2010. *Hubert Harrison: The Voice of Harlem Radicalism, 1883–1918*. New York: Columbia University Press.

Polanyi, Karl. 1966. *Dahomey and the Slave Trade*. Seattle: Washington University Press.

Poster, Mark, ed. 1988. *Jean Baudrillard: Selected Writings*. Palo Alto, CA: Stanford University Press.

Prashad, Vijay. 2000. *The Karma of Brown Folk*. Minneapolis: University of Minnesota Press.

Radhakrishnan, S. 1969. *Eastern Religious and Western Thought*. London: Oxford University Press.

Reid, Richard J. 2002. *Political Power in Pre-Colonial Buganda*. Oxford: James Currey.

Roberts, Neil. 2015. *Freedom as Marronage*. Chicago: University of Chicago Press.

Rodney, Walter. 1983. *How Europe Underdeveloped Africa*. London: Bogle L'Ouverture.

Russell, Bertrand. 1967. *"Why I'm Not a Christian" and Other Essays on Religion and Related Subjects*. New York: Touchstone.

Ryan, S. 1972. *Race and Nationalism in Trinidad and Tobago*. Toronto: University of Toronto Press.

Said, Edward. 1979. *Orientalism*. New York: Vintage Books.

Sartre, Jean-Paul. 1956. *Being and Nothingness: A Phenomenological Essay on Ontology*, trans. Hazel V. Barnes. New York: Philosophical Library.

———. 1968. *Search for a Method*, trans. Hazel Barnes. New York: Vintage.

Satprem. 1993. *Sri Aurobindo or the Adventure of Consciousness*. Mount Vernon, WA: Institute for Evolutionary Research.

Schweitzer, Albert. 1957. *Indian Thought and Its Development*. Boston: Beacon Press.

Seligson, M., and J. Boot, eds. 1978. *Political Participation in Latin America*. New York: Holmes & Meier.

Selvon, Sam. 2000. *A Brighter Sun*. London: Longman.

Shakespeare, William. 1954. *The Tempest*. London: Methuen.

Soyinka, Wole. 1990. *Myth, Literature and the African World*. Cambridge, England: Cambridge University Press.

Spivak, Gayatri. 1999. *A Critique of Postcolonial Reason*. Cambridge, MA: Harvard University Press.

Stone, C. 1974. *Electoral Behaviour and Public Opinion in Jamaica*. Mona, Jamaica: I.S.E.R.

———. 1980. *Clientelism and Democracy in Jamaica*. New Brunswick, NJ: Transaction Books.

Sweezy, P. M. 1978. "The Transition from Feudalism to Capitalism," in R. H. Hilton (ed.), *The Transition From Feudalism to Capitalism*. London: New Left Books.

Thomas, Clive. 1974. *Dependence and Transformation*. New York: Monthly Review Press.

———. 1976. *Dependence and Transformation: The Economics of the Transition to Socialism*. New York: Monthly Review Press.

———. 1984. *The Rise of the Authoritarian State in Peripheral Societies*. New York: Monthly Review Press.

Trouillot, Michel-Rolph. 1988. *Peasants and Capital: Dominica in the World Economy*. Baltimore, MD: Johns Hopkins University Press.

Ulyanovsky, R. 1974. *Socialism and Newly Independent Nations*. Moscow: Progress Publishers.

Vogel, Ezra F. 2011. *Deng Xiaoping and the Transformation of China*. Cambridge, MA: Harvard University Press.

Walcott, Derek. 1993. *The Antilles*. New York: Farrar, Strauss, Giroux.

———. 1995. "A Tribute to C. L. R. James," in Selwyn R. Cudjoe and William E. Cain (eds.), *C. L. R. James: His Intellectual Legacies*. Amherst: University of Massachusetts Press.

Walker, Corey. 2008. *A Noble Fight: African American Freemasonry and the Struggle for Democracy in America*. Urbana-Champaign: University of Illinois Press.

Weber, Max. 1978. *Economy and Society*, Vol. I. Berkeley, University of California Press.

West, Cornel. 1989. *The American Evasion of Philosophy: A Genealogy of Pragmatism*. Madison: University of Wisconsin Press.

Williams, Eric. 1994. *Capitalism & Slavery*. Chapel Hill: University of North Carolina Press.

———. 2004. "The Economic Development of the Caribbean up to the Present," in E. Franklin Frazier and Eric Williams (eds.), *The Economic Future of the Caribbean*. Dover, MA: Majority Press.

Womack, James P., Daniel T. Jones, and Daniel Roos. 1990. *The Machine that Changed the World*. New York: Rawson Associates.

The Worker's Voice. 1949 (June 8).

———. 1971 (31 August).

———. 1986 (5 February).

Wynter, Sylvia. 1984. "The Ceremony Must Be Found: After Humanism." *Boundary 2*, no. 12 (Spring–Autumn): 19–70.

———. 1991. "After the New Class: James, *Les Damnés* and the Autonomy of Human Cognition." Paper presented at Wellesley College (19–21 April).

———. 1992. "Beyond the Categories of the Master Conception: The Counterdoctrine of the Jamesian Poesis," in Paget Henry and Paul Buhle (eds.), *C. L. R. James' Caribbean*, 63–91. Durham: Duke University Press.

———. 1995. "1492: A New World View," in Vera Lawrence Hyatt and Rex Nettleford (eds.), *Race, Discourse, and the Origins of the Americas: A New World View*, 5–57. Washington, DC: Smithsonian Institute Press.

———. 2003. "Unsettling the Coloniality of Being/Power/Truth/Freedom: Towards the Human, After Man, Its Overrepresentation—An Argument." *CR: The New Centennial Review* 3, no. 3 (Fall): 257–337.

Zamir, Shamoon. 1995. *Dark Voices*. Chicago, IL: University of Chicago Press.

Index

About the Editors

Jane Anna Gordon teaches Africana Studies and Political Science at UCONN where she is also Director of Graduate Studies in Political Science. Most recently she is author of *Creolizing Political Theory: Reading Rousseau through Fanon* (2014) and co-editor (with Neil Roberts) of *Creolizing Rousseau* (2015). She is currently completing two monographs, one titled *A Theory of Contemporary Enslavement* and the other titled *When Women Do Political Theory*. She is President of the Caribbean Philosophical Association.

Lewis R. Gordon is Professor of Philosophy and Africana Studies at UCONN-Storrs; European Union Visiting Chair in Philosophy at Université Toulouse Jean Jaurès, France; and Nelson Mandela Visiting Professor of Politics and International Studies at Rhodes University, South Africa. He was co-editor with Paget Henry of the Routledge book series *Africana Thought* and is co-editor of the Rowman & Littlefield International series *Global Critical Caribbean Thought*. His most recent book is *What Fanon Said: A Philosophical Introduction to His Life and Thought*. His website is http://lewisrgordon.com, and he is on Twitter at https://twitter.com/lewgord.

Aaron Kamugisha is Senior Lecturer in Cultural Studies at the University of the West Indies, Cave Hill Campus. His current work is a study of coloniality and freedom in the contemporary Anglophone Caribbean, mediated through the thought of C. L. R. James and Sylvia Wynter. He is the editor of *Caribbean Political Thought: The Colonial State to Caribbean Internationalisms* and *Caribbean Political Thought: Theories of the Post-Colonial State* and *Caribbean Cultural Thought: From Plantation to Diaspora*.

Neil Roberts teaches Africana Studies and Political Science at Williams College. Guest editor of a *Theory & Event* special issue on the Trayvon Martin case, co-editor (with Ben Vinson III) of *CAS Working Papers in Africana Studies* and co-editor (with Jane Gordon) of *Creolizing Rousseau* (2015), Roberts is the recent author of *Freedom as Marronage* (2015). He is currently completing the volume *A Political Companion to Frederick Douglass*.

www.ingramcontent.com/pod-product-compliance
Lightning Source LLC
Chambersburg PA
CBHW050616110726
47899CB00001B/128